MOTHER TERESA OF CALCUTTA

14926

Mother Teresa of Calcutta

A BIOGRAPHY

Edward Le Joly, S. J.

1817

Harper & Row, Publishers, San Francisco

Cambridge, Hagerstown, New York, Philadelphia
London, Mexico City, São Paulo, Singapore, Sydney

Part One was originally published in the United States by Harper & Row, Publishers, Inc. under the title *Servant of Love.* Copyright © 1977 by E. Le Joly. Part Two was originally published in India by St. Paul Publications under the title *Messenger of God's Love.* Copyright © 1983 by Fr. E. Le Joly.

FIRST EDITION

Library of Congress Cataloging in Publication Data

Le Joly, Edward.
    MOTHER TERESA OF CALCUTTA.

    Includes index.
    1. Teresa, Mother.   2. Missionaries of charity—Biography.   I. Title.
BX4406.5.Z8L4   1985   271'.97 [B]   84-48238
ISBN 0-06-065217-9

85   86   87   88   89   HC   10   9   8   7   6   5   4   3   2   1

Contents

PART ONE. WE DO IT FOR JESUS

1. Father, Tell Them   *3*
2. The Call   *7*
3. The Upper Room   *19*
4. Pentecost   *32*
5. Service of Love   *42*
6. Witnesses of Christ to the Nations   *51*
7. In His Footsteps   *67*
8. Sharing His Cross   *82*
9. Training the Sisters   *89*
10. The Brothers   *100*
11. The Helpers   *105*
12. Publicity   *113*
13. Mother Teresa Speaks   *117*
14. The Jubilee   *127*
15. It Was Thirty Years Ago . . .   *136*

PART TWO. MOTHER TERESA: MESSENGER OF GOD'S LOVE

1. Prelude: The Jubilees   *145*
2. A Christocentric Spirituality   *157*
3. Instrumentality   *167*
4. An Evangelical Spirituality   *172*
5. Living the Gospel   *182*
6. Perfection for All   *188*
7. Mary in Their Life   *193*
8. Devotion to the Church   *199*
9. Prayer and Contemplation   *207*
10. Christ in the Poor   *220*
11. Universality   *230*
12. Foundations   *235*
13. Spiritual Affinities   *244*
14. The Fourth Vow   *248*

15. Interlude: With Mother in Rotterdam   256
16. Conscientization   266
17. No Partisanship, No Politics   272
18. Proclaiming the Word of God   280
19. The Awards   287
20. The Media and the Apostolate   298
21. The Energizer   306
22. The God-Seekers   312
23. Joy in Suffering   321
24. The Co-Workers   328
25. Volunteers in Calcutta   336
26. Finale: A Symphony to God's Glory   342

Part One

WE DO IT FOR JESUS

CHAPTER 1

Father, Tell Them

I heard a voice behind me shouting like a trumpet: "Write down all
that you see in a book, and send it to the seven churches."

(REV. 1:10–11)

"I want to see you," said Mother Teresa. "I must talk to you."

She was just back from Mexico where, as a Vatican delegate at the
International Women's Conference, she had spoken on woman's role in
society. She led some eighty American tourists into the courtyard of the
mother house. I was delighted at the prospect of meeting her again.

We entered the courtyard, followed by the tourists. The Indian lady
serving as official guide to the tourists approached Mother Teresa and
asked her, "Would you kindly address them? They would like to hear a
few words about your work." Mother agreed.

First she was made to pay the price of celebrity: as she stood before the
crowd, cameras clicked. After this Mother sat down on the cement floor
of the courtyard. Some tourists followed her example; others stood in a
semicircle. In a corner of the courtyard, sisters were filling buckets of
water from a hand pump. In a classroom, others were studying. From the
chapel came the sound of voices singing psalms to the praise of the Lord.
Mother very simply spoke of the work of the sisters and of the love for
Jesus that prompted them; of the poor who were so patient and kind and
joyful; of crippled children whom she had befriended and knew by name.
She spoke of God and of the happiness of serving him in the poor, with
simplicity, humility, homeliness. This was an echo of the Sermon on the
Mount. The gospel came alive: Blessed are you the poor, and you the
patient, and you, eager to listen to one who speaks of God.

When she was free, Mother Teresa returned to the tiny parlor where
ministers, cardinals, and bishops have sat on simple wooden chairs before
a small table, talking to one of our generation's great spiritual energizers.
On the wall, charts spelled out the aims, activities, and location of the
Missionaries of Charity, the religious congregation she founded.

"How was Mexico, Mother?" I asked.

"Too much politics," she answered. "Disappointing. They did not
mention God."

She added, for fear of being unfair to anyone, "Maybe someone did, but I did not hear the name of God mentioned." No doubt, God's name would have rung a bell in her heart.

"This is rather strange," I said, "considering that many important Moslem ladies were present at the meeting."

"I spoke of the dignity of women," she continued, "of their God-given functions and prerogatives. As mothers, as wives, they are called to be the heart of the home, to make a happy home for their husbands and children. What a noble calling, to be the mothers of the human race. I told them it was their privilege to give generously, as God himself gives to his children."

"Did the president of Mexico call you to the palace?"

"Yes, he wants us to start a house in Mexico itself. At the palace I met the president, his wife, and three of their eight children. I spoke of our work and of the love of Jesus. When I spoke of Jesus, his wife was crying."

"Yes, of course, women are more sensitive to religion than men."

"No, it is not so. The president is deep. He gave me the impression of being very deep. He insisted on our coming without delay. He said he would give us a house and see to the travel expenses of the sisters. I must send him some of my best sisters. I told him that as religious we require the permission of the cardinal to establish a house in his archdiocese. This should not be difficult, since the cardinal had already asked us to come to Mexico.

"I think the civil and religious powers do not collaborate much there. I had an excellent occasion of bringing them together. The president himself contacted the cardinal and gave me his authorization to start a house in Mexico. I hope to return there in October with some sisters and to start work without delay."

Speed is typical of Mother Teresa. At times she opens a house a few weeks after the official request has been made. As superior general, she has to refer to no one, to ask nobody's permission. Later that will change, as the institute continues to increase in numbers.

"From Mexico I went to Lima, Peru, where we have recently opened a house; then to New York, to London, Rome, and back here."

"What was Lima like?"

"Latin America offers tremendous opportunities for religious work. It is mainly religious help that is asked of us there. The people are short of priests and nuns. My sisters must do all that priests normally do, except say mass and hear confessions. In practice they are like deacons. Take the case of marriages: the sisters make all the preparatory arrangements and have the marriages celebrated. In one place they had thirty marriages celebrated together. In another village they regularized the unions of three generations of couples living together: grandparents, parents, and children. A lawyer works with them to arrange for the civil marriages—he gives his time free. When they have received the sacrament of matrimony, the couples are so happy."

"Splendid, Mother. You require more sisters to do God's work over there. I hear you have received a large number of applications from girls wanting to join the institute?"

"Yes, I have received of late fifty applications from girls who wish to join us, from America, Australia, England, Africa. We have some very good postulants in Africa. One Japanese girl has applied, though we have as yet no house in Japan."

"We have three novitiates: in Calcutta, Melbourne, Rome. Altogether at present we have 209 novices. Most of them are in Calcutta."

"Why do they join you, what brings them to you?"

"I have received a sheaf of beautiful letters from candidates from Europe and America. The girls say they want a life of prayer, a life of poverty, humility, in the following of Jesus. Is that not wonderful? And this happens at a time when others complain of a lack of vocations and say that the youth of today are not ready for a life of humility, poverty, and obedience. I find nothing of the sort. Ask them to do something hard for Jesus, and they will come forward.

"We require many more sisters. I have fifty-eight applications for new houses. I cannot take them all. The archbishop of Trinidad asked me for a house. We have recently opened one in Papua. The sisters had to look on the map to find out where that country is. The bishop is extremely poor; he cannot help much. But I thought it was one more reason for us to go to his help."

Fifty-eight houses asked for; as Mother puts seven or eight sisters in each house, that would mean about four hundred and fifty sisters just to start these houses. She has 209 novices in the two years' novitiate, which allows her to dispose of about a hundred sisters a year at present. The congregation is young, and the mortality rate is very low; few die, and not many leave after their first vows. Still, it would require about five years to comply with all the requests; and many more will be coming meanwhile. The backlog of applications will go on increasing, unless the recruitment can be much accelerated, which seems highly probable.

Then I presented my own request:

"Mother, I have to ask you a favor; may I write a book on you and the Missionaries of Charity? Will you allow me to do so? We have worked many years together. I intend to write from the spiritual angle, to show your motivation, the hand of God directing and protecting your congregations."

"Yes, Father, write about us. You have known us well, you have been with us from the beginning. We have the same ideas.

"You must have our constitutions. But mainly you must tell people what brings us here. Tell them," said Mother, and she became eloquent, pleading, passionately involved—"tell them that we are not here for the work, we are here for Jesus. All we do is for him. We are first of all religious; we are not social workers, not teachers, not nurses or doctors, we are religious sisters. We serve Jesus in the poor. We nurse him, feed him, clothe him, visit him, comfort him in the poor, the abandoned, the sick, the orphans, the dying. But all we do, our prayer, our work, our suffering is for Jesus. Our life has no other reason or motivation. This is a point many people do not understand. I serve Jesus twenty-four hours a day, whatever I do is for him. And he gives me strength. I love him in the poor and the poor in him. But always the Lord comes first.

"Whenever visitors come to this house, I take them to the chapel to pray for a while. I tell them, "Let us first greet the master of the house. Jesus is here; it is for him we work, to him we devote ourselves. He gives us the strength to carry on this life and to do so with happiness. Without him we could not do what we do; we certainly could not continue doing it for a whole lifetime. One year, two years, perhaps; but not during a whole life, without thought of reward, without expectation of anything good except to suffer with him who loved us so much that he gave his life for us. Without Jesus our life would be meaningless, incomprehensible; Jesus explains our life."

Mother Teresa took a deep breath, then summed up her briefing with a strong command: "Father, tell them, WE DO IT FOR JESUS."

As I walked home, the thought struck me: she is Paul writing to the Colossians: "There is only Christ: he is everything, and he is in everything" (Col. 1:11). And Mother Teresa's command rang in my ears: "Tell them: we do it for Jesus."

CHAPTER 2

The Call

One day . . . the Holy Spirit said, "I want Barnabas and Saul set apart
for the work to which I have called them."

(ACTS 13:2-3)

FATHER HENRY SPEAKS

Father Julien Henry received me in his small office at St. Teresa's church
presbytery. This room was so crowded with boxes, books, gadgets, and
instruments that there was not even a chair in it and we both had to stand
for one hour. He usually writes at a high desk, standing. I asked him,

"Father Henry, you have known Mother Teresa longer and better than
anyone else. What struck you most in her? What would you say is her
main quality? Why did she succeed to such an extent?"

Father Henry reflected silently, as if lost in prayer. Then he answered
slowly, with deep feeling and emotion:

"What is most extraordinary is the enormous amount of good almighty
God has worked through this humble instrument. God has used this
woman with all her qualities and defects, yes, her great qualities and her
defects, with her weak training, to do his work, because she is completely
subservient to him. She obeys his promptings, his direction, without
questioning. She does not think of herself, she does everything for him.
And she does it with such complete trust in his power that nothing seems
impossible to her. It is all done for God.

"In all her interviews, even with unbelievers, even with non-Christians,
she insists that what she and the sisters do is for God, for our Lord Jesus
Christ. All they do is for Christ; and they find in their love for Jesus, in
prayer, and in adoration of the Blessed Eucharist the strength to serve
the poor.

"She comes from peasant stock and from a community of hill people.
An Albanian from Yugoslavia, she is tough and a revolutionary. If the
structures stand in the way of fulfilling your ideas, change them, destroy
them, ignore them—that is what happened in her case.

"God made use of her spiritual and human qualities and weaknesses
to produce extraordinary fruits. In his hands she has been supple. He
guides her. Her ideas came gradually, her aim became clearer and clearer,

until one day it was concretized in a deep spiritual experience in the train taking her to Darjeeling.

"In those days she was educating Bengali girls at St. Mary's High School, Entally. She was very insistent about their spiritual training, as was also Mother Cenacle, her companion.

"We must remember what had brought Mother Teresa to India. As a schoolgirl, Agnes, as she was then called, was caught in the wave of enthusiasm for the missions and for the expansion of the Kingdom of Christ, a truly spiritual kingdom 'not of this world,' and for the work of spreading the gospel in the missions, an enthusiasm generated by the writings of Pope Pius XI and highlighted by the institution of the Feast of Christ the King."

In the sodality she prayed and meditated on these ideas; she became aflame with the desire of spending herself for the cause of Christ, for the gospel that was to be preached to all people.

"And so," continued Father Henry, "through the paper of the Sodality of Our Lady, Agnes learned about the Indian missions. Some Yugoslav Jesuits who had recently come to Bengal worked in the Ganges Delta, south of Calcutta.

Anthony, while studying theology at St. Mary's College at Kurseong, in the Himalayas, regularly despatched news of the Bengal mission and of the work among the Nepalis of the Darjeeling district. He sent hundreds of letters to friends in Yugoslavia and elsewhere.

"So," continued Father Henry, "Agnes learned of the religious, educational, and charitable work carried on by missionaries in Bengal. She decided to consecrate her life to this apostolate and enquired about the means of going to India. She was advised to seek admission into the congregation of the Loreto nuns who worked in Bengal. Their headquarters were in Dublin. Agnes would have to join them, learn English, and ask to be sent to the missions. She did so."

When she arrived in India in January 1929, she was sent to the novitiate at Darjeeling, in the Himalayas, where the very scenery speaks of God's majesty, power, and beauty.

"At the end of her two years of novitiate, she took her first vows of religion. She was then attached to the high school for Bengali girls run by the Loreto nuns at Entally, on Calcutta's eastern side. There for some twenty years she taught geography and history; later she became head-mistress. She was also put in charge of the Daughters of St. Anne, a diocesan congregation of Indian sisters, who wore a blue sari and taught in the Bengali secondary school.

"The Loreto nuns at Entally occupy a large property purchased with the money bequeathed to them by a wealthy Protestant planter. In this spacious property the sisters run an English high school for over five hundred girls, boarders, including a large number of orphans who pay no fees whatever. In the same property, the Bengali high school houses two to three hundred boarders and some day scholars, mostly from families of modest means.

"The Loreto nuns are well known for their college and six high schools in Calcutta. They are generally esteemed and respected as hard-working religious and as first-rate educators. At Entally, Mother Teresa devoted herself wholeheartedly to the intellectual and spiritual formation of Bengali girls under the direction of Mother Cenacle, a Loreto nun from Mauritius, a saintly person.

"At Entally there was a Sodality of the Blessed Virgin for the girls, where they imbibed the same ideas that had brought Mother Teresa to India."

"You were the spiritual director of that sodality, Father Henry?"

"Yes. Besides the spiritual meetings, there was a study club to which Hindu girls also asked to be admitted. Then we had various activities. Every week a group visited the Nilratan Sarkar Hospital. We rotated the girls so as to have some continuity in the apostolate. We first sent Numbers One, Two, Three; the next week Numbers Two, Three, Four; then Numbers Three, Four, Five and so on. The girls grew enthusiastic about this work, which was mainly religious: consoling the patients, cheering them up, rendering them small services, writing letters for them. Another group went to visit the slums. Behind the wall of the school, there was the slum of Motijhil. The girls went to do service there. Mother herself never went with them.

"Mother saw the dire poverty of many people in and around Calcutta. She felt an inner prompting to do something to relieve the hardships of the very poor, and to lead them to God. Spiritually they were completely neglected—truly sheep without a shepherd. She realized that within the structures of organized education, aimed mainly at the middle classes, in which she worked, it would be impossible to achieve this aim. She had to get out of the system and start something quite different.

"At the same time, some of the girls she was teaching and who visited the poor in the slums and the sick in hospital, expressed to her the desire of becoming nuns so that they could devote themselves fully to the apostolate among the very poor."

Then came God's call. "It was," Mother Teresa told me, "on the tenth of September 1946, in the train that took me to Darjeeling, the hill station in the Himalayas, that I heard the call of God." In quiet, intimate prayer with her Lord, she heard distinctly what she says was for her "a call within a call." "The message," she explains, "was quite clear: I was to leave the convent and help the poor while living among them. It was an order. I knew where I belonged, but I did not know how to get there."

She had already been called by God to the religious life, and there was never any question of abandoning it. God was calling her to another kind of work and service in the religious life.

Mother felt intensely that Jesus wanted her to serve him in the poorest of the poor, the uncared for, the slum dwellers, the abandoned, the homeless. Jesus invited her to serve him and follow him in actual poverty, material poverty, to practice a style of life that would make her similar to the needy in whom he was present, suffered, and loved.

As at the Annunciation Mary Immaculate had answered, "Yes, be it done to me according to your word, according to God's will," so, wholeheartedly, to this call of God she heard in her heart, Mother Mary Teresa answered, "Yes." She did not know how it would be done, but she surrendered to God in unlimited faith.

It was a flash of light on the road to Damascus, a meeting with Jesus, injecting a new spirit and direction to her apostolic life. This light did not blind her—she was prepared for it, accustomed as she was to follow God's inspiration and having reflected as she had on the unfortunate lot of so many who had little chance of knowing God's infinite love for them. Mother accepted. There was no encounter, no struggle, no compulsion: obediently, lovingly, she accepted. Was she not wedded to Jesus, ready to follow him in utter poverty? Did she not always trust him and do his will fully?

The Missionaries of Charity keep this day as "Inspiration Day," for truly it was the start of their institute.

As the apostles had been prepared by Christ for the final call, not only to discipleship, but to be apostles, so, says Father Henry, "Mother Teresa had been prepared."

In the train, the inspiration or call was crystalized, became a clear and definite expression of God's will. This "call within a call" originating from God resembled that of Barnabas and Paul.

"One day," say the Acts, "while they were offering worship to the Lord and keeping a fast, the Holy Spirit said, "I want Barnabas and Saul set apart for the work to which I have called them." So it was that after fasting and prayer they laid their hands on them and sent them off" (Acts 13:-2–3). The Christian community, aware that the call came from the Holy Spirit, sent them off cheerfully, with prayers and their blessing. In these days, more distant from Pentecost, the Holy Spirit's call came to a nun who would have to reveal it to the authorities of the church, the archbishop of Calcutta, and her superiors, and obtain their approval and blessing.

On her return to Calcutta, Mother Teresa made her desires known to some members of her community—who listened to her, as may be expected, with mixed feelings.

"When he had become very old and retired to St. Xavier's College, Archbishop Périer said to me," recalled Father Henry, " 'One day, as I was making the visit of Entally convent, someone told me that a young nun of the community had some queer ideas. Now, whenever anyone tried to put me on my guard in this way, I always asked myself whether the hand of God might not be there, and gave full freedom to the person to explain his or her case. If the religious is humble, obedient, dutiful, the impulse may come from God.' "

The archbishop applied St. Paul's advice to test the various spirits to find out if they come from God. He gave the young nun with strange ideas a sympathetic hearing as she outlined her plan to work among the poorest and most needy. Of course, to realize her plans she would have to leave her religious congregation and start a new one.

After speaking to the archbishop of her plans, she was transferred to Asansol for reasons of health. But the archbishop insisted with her superior that she be brought back to Calcutta, since she had applied to him for permission to leave the convent for a time. Meanwhile, trouble arose in the school, fanned by the political situation of the day. The school authorities could not settle the dispute with the girls. When Mother Teresa returned to Entally, she called the girl leaders together, and within half an hour the trouble was over. They could not resist her appeals to sanity.

The magnetic influence she exerted was to be the trump card that helped her to fulfill her desire to start her new congregation.

Many years later, I asked Mother,
"Did the archbishop ever ask you for a sign from God?"
"No, he did not ask me for a sign."
"Did you give him one?"
"No, I did not give him any."

Had the archbishop done so, he would have set the matter immediately in a spiritual and supernatural context. A superior may do this. A religious who seems specially able to perform a task at home, when he requests to be sent to the missions, may be told by his superior, "Give me a sign that God wants you to go to the missions." The religious then convinces his superior somehow.

But in the case of Mother Teresa things did not go so far. The religious authority tried to discover whether Mother's vocation to a special work was not an illusion, but was true and had chances of success. Some indications convinced the archbishop that the finger of God might be there.

The first difficulty was political, and arose from the atmosphere and the mentality prevailing in the days preceding and following the declaration of the independence of India.

"One day," said Father Henry, "the archbishop asked me,'What would you think of a European woman who dressed in Indian style and went out to work among the very poor in the slums, at the head of a group of Bengali girls? Would she succeed? Would she be accepted?' " The point was, in those days of acute nationalistic feelings, what would be the reaction of the thinking public? This was before India became independent, when under the inspiration of Gandhiji groups of congressmen went out to do social service among the poorer classes.

"I answered the archbishop, 'Undoubtedly this is a gamble; there is a real risk of arousing opposition. But it could be tried, especially if you have the right person. She will have to make herself acceptable to the civic and political leaders. With the poor, the matter presents less difficulty—they will be won over by the charity of the person who bends over their misery, whatever her nationality."

"And so the archbishop agreed to try the gamble and give Mother Teresa a chance."

The second difficulty was that Rome did not favor an unnecessary multiplication of religious institutes of women. There existed already too many small ones. A bishop who applied for the approbation of a new religious institute in his diocese had to show that none of the existing ones could do the particular work for which the new one was established. Now, the Calcutta archdiocese already had a religious congregation, the Daughters of St. Anne, under the jurisdiction of the archbishop. They devoted themselves to the care and education of the poor in the villages and in Calcutta. They dressed in Indian style, slept in a dormitory, ate very simple food, lived in the Indian manner, spoke Bengali, worked among the poor and unsophisticated.

The archbishop would have liked Mother Teresa to first try to work out her plans with their help and collaboration. But Mother quickly found that she could not. The sisters had their tradition, their own activities, their ways of proceeding. She wanted a group that would be highly mobile, that would visit the people, that would work not only among the poor, but among the poorest of the poor. She could not simply follow in others' footsteps. She wanted to start from scratch, train her novices in her own way, make them imbibe her own spirit. The future was to prove her right.

The Daughters of St. Anne lived in the same compound as Mother and worked in the school of St. Mary's where Mother Teresa had been head-mistress. They were understandably worried about their future prospects and asked me, as I was then their spiritual advisor, to speak to them on the consequences of this new religious institute that would compete with them for the few Bengali girls who wished to enter the religious life. I told them that this was a challenge to them. . . .

Indeed, they have multiplied, and their congregation has increased in strength, initiative, the variety of works undertaken, in self-reliance. They now have their own mother general; they run their own schools and orphanages very successfully. Competition has proved to be an excellent stimulus.

It took some time and much discussion and prayer for light before the archbishop was ready to apply to Rome for permission to start in his archdiocese a new religious congregation for women. At least ten novices had to join Mother. Constitutions would have to be drafted and sent to Rome for approval. The first step was to obtain from Rome exclaustration or permission for a religious, bound by perpetual vows, to live for a time outside a convent and to be no longer under religious superiors, but directly under the authority of the bishop.

Mother Teresa's request for exclaustration was duly despatched to Rome, in February 1948. When the permission arrived, Mother prepared to leave.

"Did you have any difficulties with your religious superiors before you left?" I asked her at the time of the Jubilee.

"None whatever." she answered. "They were most understanding and cooperative."

And so Mother Teresa, in response to God's call, on 16 November 1948 walked out of the convent, closed the door behind herself, and found herself on a Calcutta street, alone, in the dark.

God had called her to himself in a very special way. Twenty-seven years later, Mother confided to me,

"To leave Loreto was my greatest sacrifice, the most difficult thing I have ever done. It was much more difficult than to leave my family and country to enter religious life. Loreto meant everything to me.

"In Loreto I had received my spiritual training; I had become a religious there. I had given myself to Jesus in the institute. I liked the work, teaching the girls."

As an adolescent Agnes had been called by God and had turned to him. Following his call, she left her family, her father's house, her culture, her country, all she had been accustomed to see, to hear, and to love, to go to a foreign land. In the first flush of youthful enthusiasm and generosity, it was not too difficult. But the first period of training would exact more self-denial.

Then, gradually God invited her to a more complete donation of herself, a second turning toward him in deeper faith and a more intense yearning to do only what pleases him. This grace must have come after some years of religious life, when she had acquired the habit of doing the difficult thing for God, of choosing to carry the cross with Jesus, of thinking only of the beloved, until she saw the world in God and God in the world. This grace is given or offered to many a person faithful to God's grace and ready for great sacrifices.

One day, she received from God a special invitation. Some chosen souls are granted a great grace, which may be offered once or twice only; if they accept it, they start on the road to holiness.

God bestows this grace on those he finds sufficiently generous, and on whom he has special designs, whom he wishes to entrust with a special mission or task, who have the mettle and the will to accept suffering in his service and for his glory.

Masters of spirituality describe the soul's progress: it turns to God in a more intense, complete, thorough manner, after a heroic self-sur-render, in response to a powerful grace, which invites and strengthens the soul.

Mother went through this spiritual experience.

"It was much more difficult than leaving my family when I entered the convent. Yes, when I left the convent I did not run away from it to obtain more freedom."

She left the security of the convent, its friendliness, its way of life, its spiritual help, in order to throw herself blindly into God's hands, in pure faith, not asking, not knowing, not questioning, but blindly surrendering to God's guidance.

She was on the street, with no shelter, no company, no helper, no money, no employment, no promise, no guarantee, no security.

"My God, you, only you. I trust in your call, your inspiration; you will not let me down." Now she was his.

PATNA

After the break with her past way of life, a period of training afforded a welcome period of transition and reflection. Mother Teresa left Calcutta and proceeded to Patna for a short course in nursing and outdoor dispensary work under the guidance of the Medical Missionary Sisters of Mother Dengel. To be of service to the poor, she had to know, therefore she had to learn.

At Patna, on the bank of the Ganges, the Medical Missionary Sisters run an efficient hospital to which is attached a popular and well-attended outdoor department. The sisters also direct an excellent nurses' training course.

In July 1969, as a patient in the hospital's surgical department, I enquired about the Calcutta student sister. She was still remembered as a keen student who had packed as much knowledge and experience into her three or four months' stay as anyone could acquire in so short a time.

At Patna, Mother Teresa also sustained the first shock and upset to her plans and ideas concerning the way of life she and the girls she expected to join her would embrace. She had intended to live in utter poverty—they would live, dress, and eat like the very poor among whom they would work, in an effort to bring them to God, and whom they would serve as the suffering members of Christ.

Now, Mother Dengel, an Austrian-born woman of unlimited zeal and energy, had obtained from the Holy See the permission for her nuns to practice both surgery and midwifery in hospitals run by them, something new in the Catholic church. Thus, she could understand and sympathize with a nun wishing to start new ways and activities in religious life.

Mother Teresa explained to Mother Dengel and her sisters that she planned to start a congregation whose members would live like the poor in India. The nuns' diet would not even consist of simple rice and legumes, which is modest enough, but would be just "rice and salt," a diet considered to be below the poverty line, the humblest of Bengali diets.

"We shall eat rice and salt," said Mother Teresa, with determination.

"If you make your sisters do that," retorted Mother Dengel, emphatically, "you will commit a serious sin. Within a short time those young girls will fall a prey to tuberculosis and die. How do you want your sisters to work, if their bodies receive no sustenance? The very poor work very little, become sick, and die young. Do you want your nuns to suffer that fate? Or do you wish them to be strong and able to labor for Christ?"

Mother Teresa accepted this expert advice. She could not tempt God, could not ask his divine providence to go continually against the laws of nature he had established, and work a continual miracle for the health of her sisters, when food was available. Humbly she changed her plans. The sisters would receive the sustenance their bodies required, their food would be simple, without luxury; obediently they would eat the portion they were given.

Years later, Mother told me, "The Medical Missionaries of Patna said I was to feed my sisters well; I have followed their advice."

Indeed, years ago several Indian bishops had trouble with poorly fed nuns and seminarians who suffered from tuberculosis and other diseases. The bishops took adequate measures and among the younger generation the trouble is over.

The good Lord was training his loving spouse, correcting here and there, moderating where need be what might have been otherwise excessive zeal. Mother's sisters could not all be expected to receive the same charisms and grace God had granted her with such lavishness.

At Patna Holy Family Hospital, Mother met Jacqueline de Decker, to whom she revealed her plans. This young Belgian woman would have liked to join the future institute. But her physical condition would not allow it. She was later to become one of Mother's "second selves" and to organize the wing of the sick and suffering who would pray and suffer for the success of the institute and its apostolate.

And in this hospital Mother later lost her first religious, who left earth for heaven. One of her novices died there, after taking her religious vows on her death bed, the first fruits the congregation offered to its Lord.

The short stay at Patna was soon over—an interlude in the drama. Like her master coming out of the wilderness after preparing himself for his public life by prayer and fasting, Mother Teresa was ready to begin the task the Father had appointed her to perform for the glory of his Son. She returned to Calcutta, where she found a temporary shelter with the Little Sisters of the Poor.

FIRST BEGINNINGS

"One day in December 1948," said Father Henry, "on her return from Patna, Mother appeared at St. Teresa's presbytery dressed in a white sari with a blue border."

" 'Do you recognize me?' she asked me.

" 'Of course, Mother Teresa.'

" 'Where is Motijhil?'

" 'What? You don't know? Just behind the wall of the school where you were teaching.'

"I asked a woman to show her the way. They went together. Soon I heard that Mother had found a vacant room in the slum.

" 'What rent?' she asked.

" 'Five rupees per month,' said the owner.

" 'I'll take it,' she said.

"The next day," continued Father Henry, "as I was passing through Motijhil, a very poor slum area, where we had some Catholics, I heard a voice repeating the first letters of the Bengali alphabet. I looked inside the room and what do I see? Mother Teresa teaching a few children. No table, no chair, no blackboard, no chalk. With a stick she drew figures on the earth."

After that she went to see the corporation scavengers in their quarters, inquiring about their families, the sick, the children.

At night she stayed at St. Joseph's Home, run by the Little Sisters of the Poor for aged people without means or relatives able to support them. It is one hour's walk from Motijhil.

Jeanne Jugan, the French nun who started the congregation of the Little Sisters of the Poor, had much in common with Mother Teresa. She insisted on absolute poverty—the houses of the institute were to have no foundations, no regular income, not even a bank account. The sisters went out and still go out daily on a begging mission to obtain the support needed for their inmates.

The spirituality of the Little Sisters is centered on humility and charity, a delicate, refined, exquisite, perfect charity. There lived in the house a sister who for forty years remained in charge of the kitchen—a wonderful soul, a true mystic who would tell her confessor, "I love our Lord to the point of madness." To him she had given everything, and our Lord as usual had asked her much.

The sisters looked after some two hundred old people who had no resources. Mother Teresa lived in that holy house for a short time. God, who had called her, would soon show that she was his chosen one.

MOTIJHIL, THE FIRST SMALL SCHOOL

Right at the beginning, when she was still alone, Mother took me round to show me her work, as she would do with many visitors later on.

We went along by the dwellings of the corporation sweepers, crossed some railway lines, walked through a slum area. No one seemed to notice her, no one greeted her or gave any sign of recognition. She was not yet part of their life. We looked inside a mud hut.

"This is our schoolroom," said Mother Teresa.

"How many pupils do you have?"

"Thirty-five," I think she said, "when they are all present. But usually some are sick or absent for some reason or other.

"I teach them the alphabet, and also how to wash and comb their hair. I give them a cake of soap as prize for regularity, attention, and cleanliness."

I thought they would prefer sweets, but made no comment.

"Then they receive milk at midday."

She was taking the wrong person round; as a professor of economics, who knew how to obtain the maximum results from limited resources, I could not be impressed. The whole thing was rather pathetic and inefficient. Here was the headmistress of a fairly good high school trying to teach the alphabet to children who would never become literate, and teaching the use of soap to children who would not be able to afford to buy it.

She was making a desperate effort to uplift the very poor, to give them a sense of respectability and teach them that God loves them. Unless she could gather a team around her, these efforts would produce no fruits. But would anyone join her for this task? Or would she find some other means of helping the sufferers of humanity?

"This is not much," she commented.

But we, who were doing more pleasant work, gave her all encouragement.

These were the pathetic days of the small entries in the diary she then kept. Years later she showed it to me. There were no special secrets, no revelations, just small notes on the people she had met or on some particular happening. Some of them remained embedded in my memory twenty-five years later.

"Met N., who said there was nothing to eat at home. I gave him the fare for my tram, all the money I had, and walked home."

At the time of the jubilee, I reminded Mother of the small notebook and asked if she still had it. She shrugged her shoulders and said, "No, I think I threw it away." The right thing to do.

Meanwhile God was training her—she had to feel utterly useless, inadequate to the task. She had to cling to him, throw herself entirely on him:

"You, Lord, only you, all for you; make use of me.

"You pulled me out of my convent where I was useful. Now guide me, as you wish."

The Lord heard; he took over. He got her a house, he sent her helpers. She was to become the leader of a team that would extend her in time and space, as she extended Christ himself. Her first great task would be to build and train her team.

CHAPTER 3

The Upper Room

"Listen," said Jesus, "as you go into the city you will meet a man carrying a pitcher of water. Follow him into the house he enters and tell the owner of the house, 'The Master asks: Where is the dining room in which I can eat the passover with my disciples?' The man will show you a large upper room furnished with couches. Make the preparations there."

(LUKE 22:10–12)

MICHAEL GOMES SPEAKS

"Brother Michael, tell me all you remember about Mother Teresa during her stay in your house."

I called him *Brother* because for many years we had worked together in the Legion of Mary. We were sitting in one of the rooms occupied by Mother Teresa in his family's three-story house.

"Willingly, Father. But first I must repeat what I said some time ago. The chairman of a group of Co-Workers of the Missionaries of Charity praised me, saying, 'We are happy to have today in our midst the man who did so much for Mother Teresa, by putting her up free of charge in his own house and giving her his time and all possible help.' I answered,

" 'Friends, it is we who have been benefited. If we have given much, we have received much more in return. Mother Teresa's presence in our family house has been a wonderful source of blessing.

" 'Mother,' he continued, 'occupied the second floor. From the ground floor the staircase leads to the top floor directly into the room the sisters used as chapel. The wooden altar and wooden candlesticks and furnishings were made by Father Henry with the help of his boys. Above the altar hung the picture of the Immaculate Heart of Mary given by Father Van Exem, who was then the rector of the church of Our Lady of Dolours. It is now in the chapel of the mother house.

"Archbishop Périer came several times to say mass for the sisters during the first years. Cardinal Spellman also came to see Mother in this house."

"How did it happen that she came to your house?"

"Well, Father, we were four brothers living in this house. At the time of the partition of India, two of my brothers opted for East Pakistan, now Bangladesh. Two of us stayed in Calcutta.

"One day Father Van Exem came to our house and asked me 'Could you find some place for Mother Teresa to stay; a mud house, a hut, something simple, anything, but close by. Can you find something?'

"Then came the voice of a child. My daughter, age eight, said, 'Daddy, the rooms upstairs are empty; there is nobody. Mother could come here.'

" 'No,' said Father Van Exem, 'that is far too good, it is not what she wants. She wants something much more humble.'

"But we insisted, 'Father, send her here. She is a nun, she must be treated well. She does the work of God.' And so in February 1949 Mother came and occupied the second floor."

"Was she alone?"

"No, she came with a woman who served at St. Mary's School, Charur Ma, a widow."

"Mother took my eight-year-old daughter to visit the slums with her. Then she needed medicines. So I went out to beg for medicines with her.

"Once we went to a big shop with a list of medicines she required. The manager was very busy. Mother showed her written list and asked for them all free.

" 'You come to the wrong place, lady,' answered the manager. 'Let me finish my work in peace.'

"Mother and I sat down. She said her rosary. When she had finished, the manager said, 'All right, here are three parcels with the medicines you need. You may have them as a gift from the company.' "

In March 1949, on the Feast of St. Joseph, there was a knock at Mother's door. She opened it and stood motionless, while her heart beat faster, faster, as she looked at the frail figure facing her, and heard her say, "Mother, I have come to join you."

"It will be a hard life; are you prepared for it?"

"I know it will be hard; I am prepared for it." And the girl stepped in.

Mother turned to her Lord, in gratitude: "Dear Jesus, how good you are. So you are sending them! You keep the promise you made me. Lord Jesus, thank you for your goodness."

This first candidate to join Mother Teresa became Sister Agnes, taking Mother's baptismal name.

At her evening prayers Mother Teresa poured out her heart in thanksgiving and expressed her joy and confidence in God, who protected her and blessed her in this manner. Now they would start work.

I did not ask Mother what her reaction had been; I did not need to. I experienced the same feelings when the first of my ex-students told me, "I want to become a Christian." I also asked him, "Do you realize that it will be terribly hard for you? Have you the courage to do it?"

"I have the courage," he answered.

"Dear Lord, thank You," I prayed. "So, in spite of all they told me—that I had false hopes and was wasting my time, that educated people were not ready to embrace Christianity—you have heard my prayers and those of my parents and friends."

Mother never forgot that Sister Agnes had been the first to believe in "the cause" and to trust her inspiration as coming from God. A special relationship was established between the two of them, which everyone respected and understood. They were like Paul and Timothy. Paul had brought Timothy to the faith and appointed him as a church leader. A special friendship would unite them until death; together they would work for the glory of the Lord Jesus, even when separated physically.

Sister Agnes became Mother's second self; for a time she replaced her as mistress of novices; then she was put in charge of the mother house and replaced Mother during her frequent absences when new foundations were being established.

Some weeks later, a second candidate appeared, and then a third. With joy Mother could say and write that their numbers were increasing.

In May 1949 Mother writes to a friend in Europe, "You will be glad to hear that at present I have got three companions—great and zealous workers. We have five different slums where we go for a few hours. What suffering; what want of God. And yet, we are so few to carry our Lord among them. You should see their eager faces, how they brighten up when the sisters come. Dirty and naked though they be, their hearts are full of affection. I trust in your prayers. Ask our Lady also to give more sisters. In Calcutta itself, we could have full work even if we were twenty."

And so they were four. Six months later Mother could report that they were five: a slow increase. As for work, what were even twenty sisters among Calcutta's 6 or 7 million people? Mother did not seem to foresee that one day they would be not twenty, but two hundred, and still unable to cope with the task.

In November 1947 she writes, "Pray much that the little society may grow in sanctity and members if it is the will of God. Yes, there is so much to be done; at present we are five. But, please God, more will join, and then we will be able to make a ring of charity round Calcutta, using our centers in the different slums as points from whence the love of our Lord may freely radiate on the great city of Calcutta."

Here she expresses her aim clearly to a person able to understand and share her life's goal to make Jesus known and loved by the poorest of the poor.

She succeeds in bringing children to church on Sundays; she writes, "You will be glad to know that at Boitakhana we have a Sunday mass for poor slum children. We bring the poor children and their mothers to church. We have up to one hundred twenty mothers and three hundred children. We started last May with twenty-six children only."

Already Mother has obtained the active collaboration of many lay-people whose devotion she praises: "At the dispensary the Catholic doctors and nurses are wonderful. The way they look after the people, you would think they were the princes of the country. Their charity is most wonderful."

Mother adds a charming note: "In the slums you can now hear the children sing. Their little faces smile when the sisters come. And their parents too do not ill treat their children. This is just what I have been longing to see among the poor. Thank God for all."

A year after she had found a haven of peace and love at 14 Creek Lane, Mother could rejoice that the Lord had sent her six disciples. In 1950 she writes to her friend in Europe,

"You will be glad to know that we are now seven, and in a few days we shall be eight. Our little chapel was blessed on the eighteenth of December. The work is slowly forming. Ask our Lord to help me to realize his plan."

Michael Gomes recalls how the group increased and multiplied according to the promise God had made Abraham, the man of faith, whom Mother Teresa had imitated in his trust in God: "The sisters started coming after a few months. First Sister Agnes. She had been in school under Mother, and she believed in her. Mother never forgot it, Sister Agnes imbibed Mother's spirit. Though very simple and humble, she has always been the second in command, replacing Mother whenever she is out of Calcutta.

"Then came Sister Gertrude, then others, Dorothy, Margaret Mary. This one came from Bangladesh; when she heard Mother had started, nothing could stop her. She knew no English at the time. Many years later she returned to Bangladesh as superior of the foundation there. She had to organize relief work. She had been well trained. A consignment of good French blankets arrived for distribution to the poor and the refugees. A minister sent his bearer, a bishop sent his driver for a blanket. Sister sent them back empty-handed, saying, 'They are for the poor; you are not poor people; you are working men with a decent salary.' "

"How many sisters were there when they left?" I asked.

"Thirty or thirty-two."

Mrs. Gomes interposed, "No, they were exactly twenty-eight." She was positive about it. She remembered better.

Michael Gomes continued, "Mother took first one room, then another for the sisters. Then some got ill, they had to be isolated; Mother asked for a room for the sisters who were infectious. As the numbers increased, she took the whole floor, and even the annex."

"Yes, it has always been like that, she takes all she can get."

"At first there were only two bathing rooms on their floor. As the number of sisters started to increase, this created some difficulties, as they had to get ready early. So Father Henry with some of his boys built some bathing rooms on top of the annex.

"By eight A.M. the sisters were all out. They came home for lunch. In the afternoon there was perfect silence in the house. The sisters had classes, studies, and instructions. But after dinner the house was filled with laughter and singing. The sisters ran on the terrace; they played tug-of-war and made the whole house tremble. It was good to hear them laugh. After recreation, it was time for prayer and again there was complete silence. They were truly God's children."

Father Henry recalls that when Mother's first disciples arrived, they expected that the life would be terribly hard and that the food would be insufficient. At their first meal, as Mother put before them a plate well filled with food, they looked at it with astonishment. "Eat it," said Mother, "that is your portion." They were to learn that God wants "obedience rather than victims." They had come here to do not their will according to the flesh, but the will of the one who had called them and would send them out—as Christ, who was sent by the Father, said, "I came to do not my will, but the will of the Father who sent me."

Father Henry adds, "In one of my instructions right at the beginning, I told them, 'Yes, you have plenty to eat now; food is not lacking. But it may happen that one day on coming home from work you find that there is nothing to eat. . . .' Sister Dorothy interrupted me and said, 'That day will never come.' She had already acquired Mother's trust in God's providence, who looks after his own."

The house of the Gomes brothers proved to be truly a replica of the Cenacle—the Upper Room in a disciple's house where Jesus took the Last Supper with his apostles. It was a cenacle hallowed by the presence of the Lord; daily the Last Supper was reenacted in it and the place remained full of his spirit during the rest of the day.

In this cenacle, the sisters were, as Jesus had prayed, closely united and acutely conscious of their oneness in the Lord. There they worshipped, prayed, studied, ate, slept, talked, sang, and relaxed. There they cooked, washed clothes, scrubbed floors, prepared bandages, mended clothes, There, mainly, they learned the principles and the practice of the spiritual life, of life dedicated to God in union with Jesus. As more novices were admitted, the group grew, took shape, gathered strength.

Mother was Christ in their midst, instructing them, demonstrating to them the purpose of the institute. They listened, rapt in admiration, full of the desire of giving themselves completely to Jesus. Then, at the end of a full day's work and prayer, they retired to take their rest. Within a few minutes most of the sisters were fast asleep.

Mother remained working at a small table, writing. She wrote to candidates who wished to join her institute, to inform them that it would be a hard life; she wrote to priests and to helpers in India and abroad. She drafted some articles of the constitutions. For a long time she wrote; then, when the task was ended, she joined her hands and slowly fell on her knees to pray to her Lord.

In this atmosphere, close to the living Presence of Christ in the Eucharist, responsible to God for the disciples he had sent her, she summed up the purpose of her coming here as Jesus in his sacerdotal prayer had summed up the purpose of his coming on earth. With him she consecrated herself to the Father for the full and perfect sacrifice he wanted of her. With total faith in God's help, protection, and goodness, she prayed.

"Father, glorify your Son that your Son may return the glory to you; Father, glorify your Son, let him be glorified through your unworthy instruments, for it is for him, for his glory that we are here, that we work and suffer and pray; all we do is for Jesus; our life has no meaning if it is not all for him. Let us know him, and thus come to possess the eternal life he brought us.

"Eternal life, Father, is to know you, the one true God and Jesus Christ, whom you have sent.

"May we bring this eternal life to the poor, deprived as they are of all comfort, of material possessions; may they come to know you, love you, possess you, share in your life, you who are the God and Father of men and of my Lord Jesus Christ, source of all truth and goodness and happiness.

"May we bring to you those we meet, those for whom we work, those who help us, those who die in our hands, those we receive as Jesus received the children he blessed, the sick he cured, the sufferers he befriended.

"Father, I pray you for these sisters, whom you have chosen to serve you and belong to you; they were yours, and you gave them to me; you want me to lead them to you; you wish them to be an image of your Son, your own perfect image, that men may believe that you have sent him; that seeing their works, men may acknowledge that Christ was sent by you.

"You gave them to me, and I bring them to you.

"You took them away from the world and its spirit, that they may live in the world as the brides of Jesus, neither belonging to the world nor following its corrupt ways.

"Holy Father, I pray for them that they may be dedicated to your holy name, sanctified to you, reserved for your service, immolated to you in sacrifice. To this end I consecrate myself to you, I dedicate myself as your victim with Jesus Christ, the victim of the sacrifice.

"Father so good, I pray not only for these my sisters, but for all those who will come to join them and those who through them will be drawn to you and believe in you.

"Father, grant that my sisters may all be one, as you and Jesus are one; that they may live through your Spirit.

"That the love with which you loved us may be in them and that Jesus may be in them."

Mother Teresa let the Spirit pray in her, and asked him to love her divine spouse Jesus in her.

Slowly her head fell on her hands. She needed some sleep; tomorrow or perhaps already today there was much work to do for Jesus. She lay down and slept, God's angel close to the sisters she was to mold for his service.

They were in the world, but not of the world—they were to keep away from its spirit of greed, pride and sensuality. They wore humble saris of coarse material, like the poor; from their left shoulder hung a small crucifix. The cross was to be in their life, the cross on their arm, the cross in their heart; the cross calling, teaching, a constant reminder of the cross Christ had carried out of love for humanity, out of love for them. They were to be for the whole of their life on earth like Paul "crucified to the world and to whom the world is crucified," brides of Christ, similar to their divine spouse.

Mother trained her young sisters by word and example, as Jesus had done with his apostles at the Last Supper. She told them how they were to treat the poorest of the poor, in whom they were to see Jesus, their Lord and master, the Son of God become man.

The Gospel of John recalls how Jesus taught his disciples humble charity: "As they were at supper, Jesus got up from table, removed his outer garments and, taking a towel, wrapped it round his waist; he then poured water into a basin and began to wash the disciples' feet and to wipe them with the towel he was wearing." (John 13:2–5). Jesus thus assumes the dress and performs the work of a slave. A Jew could not ask a Jewish servant to wash his feet, he could only ask a slave.

After he had washed his disciples' feet, Jesus told them, "Do you understand what I have done to you? You call me master and Lord, and rightly; so I am. If I, your Lord and master, have washed your feet, you should wash each other's feet. I have given you an example so that you may imitate what I have done to you." And Jesus added, "Now that you know this, happiness will be yours if you behave accordingly."

This took place as Jesus was about to institute the Eucharist and give to the world the greatest proof of his love for us. He would not give them spiritual food once only but thousands of times, if they so wished. Similarly he wanted his disciples to perform acts of love and humility not once but many times.

Mother Teresa was teaching her young sisters to wash the bodies of those in need, to clean their sores and bandage their wounds. They were to do this not a few times, but thousands of times. Their service of love was to last not a few days, not even a year or two, but a whole life, as long as the Lord God wanted them to serve him in their sisters and brothers.

The poor would come to them, emaciated, covered with sores and ulcers, suffering from elephantiasis, venereal disease, cancer, leprosy.

"At times," Mother told me, "they arrive in a terrible state, filthy, covered with sores, eaten up by syphilis. We wash them all. Of course when a case is really too bad, I do it myself."

"Of course, Mother."

Every religious superior worthy of the name would do so. But it was good to hear it said in all simplicity. Seeing their mother doing this, the sisters also understood what they would be expected to do later, when they would be in charge of a community in some near or distant land. The sick and the dying would be brought to them. Knowing neither their names, nor their place of origin, nor their antecedents, the sisters were to treat them all in a loving way.

"It is Christ you tend in the poor," explained Mother. "It is his wounds you bathe, his sores you clean, his limbs you bandage. See beyond appearances, hear the words Jesus pronounced long ago; they are still operative today: 'What you do to the least of mine you do it to me.' When you serve the poor, you serve our Lord Jesus Christ."

And in the morning, on the way to the slums, the dispensaries, the homes for the dying, the children's homes, the sisters remembered that it was the Lord they had received in the Eucharist at mass that they were going to attend, nurse, serve lovingly in his suffering brothers and sisters. They would see him with the eyes of faith and perform their task with utter respect for Christ present in the poor.

Was it pleasant? It was not; except perhaps for a few who were granted an extraordinary grace. But they did it with faith; they believed in the words of the Lord: "Now that you know this, happiness will be yours if you behave accordingly."

They performed their various tasks with cheerfulness, as Mother asked them to. On their way home they might experience the joy the Holy Spirit pours into the hearts of those who belong to God and serve him only.

Meanwhile Mother was busy writing the constitutions of the congregation she wished to found; they were to be sent to Rome for approval. The structure of the new institute, its aims and rules had to be determined and approved before the congregation could start to exist. For this difficult work Father Van Exem's help proved invaluable. He helped Mother to present her case, and defended her plans before the archbishop.

At the time of the jubilee, as she remembered the difficult first years, Mother said, "God was good to me, he gave me good priests to help me in my work: Father Henry, Father Van Exem," and she named two others.

Father Celeste Van Exem proved a great help to Mother. He was a Belgian Jesuit who had been prepared to establish contacts with Moslems. He had learned Arabic and lived for some time with the Arab bedouin to imbibe their spirit, assimilate their language and culture, become acquainted with their religious life. He came to know Mother Teresa; he espoused her cause and lent it his support. He greatly helped to frame the constitutions of the Missionaries of Charity. He knew canon law and could foresee what might be introduced into the constitutions and what would not be allowed by Rome.

Although he supported Mother's ideas, he had to oppose certain provisions that could not or would not be accepted by the Roman Congregation for Religious. He spoke for Mother before the archbishop; the weight of his knowledge, experience, and perseverance helped her to such an extent that some sisters called him "the co-founder" or "the cardinal." Priests would say jokingly, "the cardinal protector."

The other priest who helped Mother most was Father Julien Henry. Father Moyersoen, the Jesuit superior in Calcutta, had asked the Belgian Provincial to give him some priests ready to start work in Bengal immediately. Father Julien Henry offered his services. Soon he was in Calcutta, where he worked for many years at St. Teresa's parish. He may be the man who best knows Mother, as her spiritual advisor, and who helped most in the training of her sisters. He is well informed about the wonderful saga of love of God and Christian charity for the most needy enacted by the Missionaries of Charity.

THE CONSTITUTIONS

"Father Henry, who wrote the constitutions?" I asked him.

"That is a good question," he answered. "The first draft of the constitutions was entirely due to Mother Teresa herself. Her spiritual background and aspirations are expressed in the constitutions she gave to the Missionaries of Charity. You find in them her passion for the Kingdom of Christ, for preaching the gospel and making Christ known and loved by all people; also her devotion to the Sacred Heart, to our Lady, to the Blessed Eucharist, and her faithfulness to the church and to the pope.

"Father Van Exem helped her, especially with the juridical and organizational aspects of the constitutions. As a canonist and theologian, he knew what would be acceptable to Rome and what would not. Mother wanted to introduce some measures that were impossible: for example, she did not wish them to own any property, even their own houses. The ownership would have been vested in the church, which was not possible, since the church of Rome or the Vatican is a foreign body in India."

St. Francis of Assisi had wanted something similar. He did not want to own the houses in which the friars would live and work, in order to be perfectly poor. But Rome would not allow it for practical reasons.

There were some points on which Mother and Father Van Exem disagreed. The healthy tensions that ensued between these two strong characters, each wanting to have his or her own way, resulted in a remarkable equilibrium.

The first draft of the constitutions, drawn up by Mother Teresa, was given to Father de Gheldere for eventual correction. He improved the wording here and there, but otherwise made no changes. "The finger of God is here," he said, and respected the work he considered to be inspired by the Holy Spirit.

Christ, who lived in her, must have inspired, guided, and sustained Mother as she wrote the constitutions of the institute that was to work entirely for his glory.

The constitutions were the work of a woman who knows by personal experience "the length and breadth, the height and depth of the love of Christ." That love excels all human understanding, proceeding as it does from the Savior's heart; that love the Spirit of Jesus pours into the hearts of those who eagerly open themselves to receive it.

Mother begins by stating the goal of those who will join the institute, as revealed on the day of her inspiration:

"Our aim is to quench the infinite thirst of Jesus Christ for love by the profession of the evangelical counsels and by wholehearted free service to the poorest of the poor, according to the teaching and life of our Lord in the gospel, revealing in a unique way the kingdom of God.

"Our particular mission is to labor at the salvation and sanctification of the poorest of the poor.

"As Jesus Christ was sent by his Father so he sends us too, filled with his Spirit to preach his gospel of love and compassion to the poorest of the poor all over the world.

"It shall be our utmost endeavor to proclaim Jesus Christ to men of all nations, especially to those who are under our care."

Then Mother states the fundamental duty of the sisters, which flows from God's nature, his purpose in creating, the reason for his calling the sisters to the religious life as expressed in the very name of the congregation:

"We are called the MISSIONARIES OF CHARITY.

" 'God is love.' A Missionary of Charity must be a missionary of love. She must be full of charity in her own soul and spread that same charity to the souls of others, Christians and non-Christians."

Mother's vision encircles the world in a passionate desire to make it answer the love of God and of Jesus Christ. It recalls to mind the great rules of Benedict, Bernard, Francis, Ignatius.

The constitutions charm by the kindness and gentleness, the balance and moderation they display, which do not weaken their passionate outburst of love for God and for his children. Tact and sensitiveness are apparent: the author is a woman.

In October 1950, on the Feast of the Most Holy Rosary, Mother received from Rome permission to start a new congregation of sisters destined to work among the poorest of the poor. Archbishop Périer came to celebrate mass in their little chapel. Father Van Exem, who assisted him, read the bull received from Rome, sanctioning the existence of the Congregation of the Missionaries of Charity, approving and confirming the aim for which they were established. This gave great happiness to Mother and her young team of generous apostles. They sang the praises of the Lord in thanksgiving for his kind protection.

From this moment onward, the recruitment to the congregation never slowed down. Candidates came in increasing numbers, from Bengal and Chota Nagpur, from the East Coast and South India, and also from foreign countries.

SISTER EUGENE SPEAKS

The first candidate from Kerala to join the Missionaries of Charity came by way of Shillong, a hill station in the northeast. In June 1976, I met her at Darjeeling—she was the superior of the house there—and asked her to tell me her recollections of the early days.

"Tell me, sister, what struck you most when you were in the Upper Room right at the beginning?"

"I was Number 21. We all received a number in the order in which we joined. I was only fifteen years old, still at school at Shillong. I had come to work with the sisters during the holidays. But I got to like the work and stayed. At first I had no idea of what the religious life meant; I was serving the poor and found it stimulating. Only when I took my profession did I really realize what it meant to be a religious.

"What struck me most was the spirit of faith, the tremendous faith shown by Mother; we lived in that atmosphere. We depended fully on God for everything. I remember two instances when essential things were missing in the community. There was no food for the evening meal; but Mother said, 'Do not worry, it will come.' And by the evening, someone, unexpectedly, brought what was required.

"During the day I went to work in the dispensaries or the slum schools."

"How many were you when you left Creek Lane?"

"Twenty-six."

"And with Mother that would mean twenty-seven. Were you not twenty-eight?"

"Perhaps. But before we left, we started praying very intently to obtain the Kalighat Home for the Dying and a new house for the novitiate. During about three months, we went in the evenings in procession to Fatima Chapel. Father Henry had erected an open chapel."

"Yes, about two kilometers from St. Teresa's Church, where the church dedicated to our Lady of Fatima stands now."

"Well, Father Henry organized a procession every evening. He accompanied the sisters as we went through the Calcutta streets saying the rosary aloud. Some laypeople came to join us. And from six to about nine, we went on the road from our house to St. Teresa's Church and thence to Fatima Chapel, praying there and again on our way home. We were asking our Lady of Fatima to obtain for us the new house we needed to expand our novitiate, and also the refuge for the dying of Kalighat.

"After a full day of work we were on our feet walking and praying. We truly stormed heaven to obtain these two houses. We forgot that we were tired, so caught were we by enthusiasm for our work. God had to give it; our Lady was to help us obtain it. And God granted our prayer. Kalighat was turned over to us. Immediately we went to work there. As I was not yet a novice, I went every day."

"Did Mother go with you daily?"

"Yes, she came with us and worked with us; but not daily. The sisters took turns; sometimes Sister Dorothy, sometimes Sister Gertrude, and some others. We received much help from Mrs. Chater, a Chinese lady."

"Yes, I knew her well. She was devoted, generous, and a good organizer. Businesslike, efficient, she would certainly fit in with Mother's style of work."

"She took us in her car daily, at the beginning, when we did not know Calcutta well and the trams and buses we would have had to take to reach Kalighat, which was very far from our house. Mrs. Chater took us at eight in the morning and brought us back at three in the afternoon. We ate something there. I fed the patients, sponged them, and so on. Mrs. Chater often sent the food for the inmates. Then her cook came and prepared things on the premises. He was a Moslem; he became so attached to the place that he stayed at night, and after some time worked only there. He died still in harness. He had a deep devotion to our Lady and decorated her altar for her feast days."

"Did you experience any opposition?"

"From where?"

"From people of the locality or other groups?"

I was told by Mother that there had been difficulties at the beginning.

"Mother did not tell us anything. We did our work and then returned to Creek Lane. We continued going there from the new house. We shifted to the new novitiate only after some time. I remained there and became a novice. Kalighat became our first big work."

"It was something quite distinctive. Before that you only had dispensaries and small schools as other religious institutes also have."

"Yes, Kalighat was the result of Mother's faith and the prayers of all."

"Truly it was our Lady's gift to the Missionaries of Charity, that you might devote yourselves there to the glory of Jesus, her Son."

The second floor at 14 Creek Lane was now full. Mother had taken every available room, and also the annex. Applications from candidates came in increasing numbers. The works were developing and becoming more diversified. The Holy Spirit indicated that it was time to give up the friendliness and intimacy of the Upper Room, to "launch into the deep," and to prepare to spread out the apostolic endeavors of the sisters throughout the world.

Mother Teresa could repeat after St. Paul, with full strength, and the senior sisters could gently echo her words, "I have been through my initiation, and now I am ready for anything, anywhere. There is nothing I cannot master with the help of the One who gives me strength" (Phil. 4:12–13).

CHAPTER 4

Pentecost

When Pentecost day came around they heard what sounded like a
powerful wind from heaven, the noise of which filled the entire
house.... They were all filled with the Holy Spirit and began to speak
foreign languages as the Spirit gave them the gift of speech.

(ACTS 2:1–4)

In February 1953 Mother Teresa, her novices and postulants moved to
larger premises, to what is still the mother house of the congregation.
Mother brought with her the picture of the Immaculate Heart of Mary,
which had stood above the altar in their chapel.

The spirit of Pentecost soon invaded the new house. Like the apostles,
the sisters were united in prayer around Mary the mother of Jesus. Full
of confidence, they rejoiced because the Lord is risen, has appeared to
Peter, and has shown himself alive to his disciples. Gloriously risen he
now manifests his power to us.

God our Father, who accepted the sacrifice of Christ, and raised him
from the dead, had also rewarded the sacrifice of Mother Teresa and her
sisters. Their institute and constitutions had been approved by the authorities of the church. In April 1953, at the Cathedral of the Most Holy
Rosary, the first group of sisters took their first vows and Mother Teresa
her final vows in the congregation.

Now the sisters had a house of their own to receive and train postulants
and novices. The new house at 54A Lower Circular Road stood some ten
minutes from the parish church of St. Teresa, where Mother had opened
a dispensary, and twenty minutes from the "Cenacle" in the house of the
Gomes family.

The sisters were able to occupy a three-story house that was part of a
small complex of buildings erected around a courtyard. The sisters
erected a statue of our Lady in a conspicuous place. Since Mother did not
have the money to buy the property, Archbishop Périer advanced her the
sum. By shouldering the risk, he proved his sympathy and effective support for the Missionaries of Charity. The age of large, generous donations had not yet arrived. The sisters lived in the years of pure faith and
uncertainty of the morrow, but Mother says that the thought of having

to repay debts contracted in the name of almighty God never troubled her. It was for his glory and the service of his children.

When the house was bought for her, Mother objected, "What shall we do with such a large house?" But the Lord God soon sent her postulants and novices to fill it.

Vocations came in increasing numbers. It was as at the beginning of the church when the disciples rejoiced, seeing God's power call more and more members to be added to the glory of the Lord.

With more members they could expand and diversify their works of charity: visits to the slums, slum schools, dispensaries, home for the dying, soon a home for abandoned and crippled children, work among tuberculosis patients, work among leprosy patients, training for poor girls, adoption plans for orphaned children.

God's visible protection and the infusion of his Spirit filled them with optimism; they were a dynamic group, contagiously enthusiastic.

As at Pentecost, the Holy Spirit gave them a character of universality, as participants in the universal mission of the Church. Sisters from different parts of India, speaking various languages, came to join their ranks.

Support came from all sides: from the archbishop of Calcutta and many priests; from the chief minister of West Bengal, and later from the prime minister of India; from scores of Indian friends—Christian and non-Christian—from groups of American and British ladies.

Charitable agencies sent supplies of food and medicines; the local and national press praised the work, while international reviews also became interested in the young congregation.

Like the apostles, the sisters are witnesses to Christ's death and Resurrection and to his glorious exaltation in heaven; their lives, their works proclaim him as the Lord, who, after redeeming humanity on the cross and rising up to a glorious life, has sent the Holy Spirit on them. Through his power they perform their service to God and humans (see Acts 2:22 ff). The sisters could also say,

"All of us are witnesses that God raised Jesus to life . . . what you see and hear is the outpouring of that Spirit."

They are witnesses to the nations. Many see it, and, perturbed by this fact, ask us, "How can they go on with this life among the downtrodden?" The answer is

"They do it by the power of Jesus."

Like the first disciples of Jesus, the sisters "remained faithful to the teaching of the apostles, to the brotherhood, to the breaking of bread and to the prayers. They all lived together and owned everything in common. They shared their food gladly and generously; they praised God and were looked up to by everyone" (Acts 2:42–47).

This "brotherhood" or "fellowship" implies a united purpose and also concern for the poorer members, so that everything is pooled in common; which shows perfect charity.

Thus, the young Missionaries of Charity relived the first years of the Christian church, by their faith, by their optimism, their joy, strong in their belief that they belong to Jesus who sends them to bring to all people the good news of God's love and redemption.

The Holy Spirit filled them with charity, an active charity manifesting itself in an unquenchable desire to help their neighbors to God.

The group was animated by a healthy enthusiasm, resulting from the belief that theirs was God's work and from the certainty that the Lord himself had inspired and still animated their young congregation. His protection was evident as they went forth, progressing in numbers.

We see among them the same happiness at the growth of their community that had possessed the members of the early church: "day by day the Lord added to their community." It was his call; he supplied the grace. Mother repeated to them the words of Christ: "I chose you, you did not choose Me." It kept the young novices and soon the young professed in humility: the merit was not theirs, the call came from God. It gave them great confidence, for the Lord who calls also gives the grace necessary to obey his call.

Joy was manifested by their singing of hymns and canticles; by their prayer in common and in private. By their dedication they made of themselves daily to the Lord as they repeated together: "Lord, make me an instrument of your peace. . . ."

"Yes, an instrument: "I wish to be supple, obedient, docile in your hand." Mother put before them the three virtues she wished would characterize them: total surrender, trust, and cheerfulness.

There were other similarities between the young church and the young institute that was now part of the great Catholic church.

At the beginning of the church, a man called Simon Magus was struck by the power the apostles had of giving the Holy Spirit to the believers and by the extraordinary works they did; he asked them to give him that power, for a consideration, which of course the apostles did not do. Peter rebuked him, saying, "May your silver be lost for ever, and you with it, for thinking that money could buy what God gave for nothing." In a similar way, the influence the sisters acquired over people through the good works they performed by the grace of the Holy Spirit, and their example of brotherly love moved some communist workers to approach them and ask them to share with them the secret of their attraction and power.

Mother told me, "Communist workers in Calcutta, especially in the Entally area, want to know the secret of the sisters' influence. Why do poor people listen to the sisters and not to the Communists, who promise them comfort on earth. There is no secret; the sisters preach and practice love."

Some time later Mother told me, "I met in Delhi an official of the Ministry of Relief and Rehabilitation who is very much impressed by our work. He gives us all the help he can. Now he has written to me, asking if I could train some of his officers. He would send a batch of some twenty to be trained by us for three months and would pay all their expenses. He hopes that thus they would imbibe our spirit and follow our methods. Do you think I should accept? And would you give them lectures if they came here? I cannot do the whole work myself."

We discussed the matter. The gentleman seemed to be mistaken about the reason for the sisters' success and influence on the people. He thought they had evolved some new technique and used some method not described in the textbooks of sociology. How could their approach to the people be assimilated and emulated? Other official agencies had also asked her how she succeeded in getting the confidence of the poor; why did people trust her, and what made her sisters devote themselves to such an extent?

"Mother, I would suggest that you inform this gentleman that what activates your sisters is their motivation, which cannot be passed on to professional people who do not believe in Christ. We can at most deal with ten people at a time. Send them by batches of two to accompany your sisters every morning, see how they work, and give them one or two talks in the evening. But they will not relish this program. They cannot imitate your sisters."

I tried to draft a program, and devise a system of motivation that might agree with the beliefs and feelings of the officials. Of course, if they had the spirit of devotedness, if they believed in a humanitarian cause, we could help them in some way. But without a firm belief in God and in humans as God's children in the dignity of every person, the poor, the lepers, the slow-witted, the abandoned, how could they enter into our spirit?

A week later we discussed the matter again. Mother informed the officer in Delhi of the difficulties of the project and what we were prepared to do. Nothing came of the proposal, as we had expected.

A cause of deep frustration and disappointment was the provision of canon law forbidding new institutes to open houses outside the diocese during ten years after their inception. On that point the archbishop was adamant: "Mother, you may not start any house outside the diocese before ten years are completed."

Mother felt an irresistible urge to go forward, to spread, develop, occupy new territory, start new houses, new ventures. Her active temperament was coupled with an unquenched zeal. Needs were great, while time was short; why these delays?

This meant that between forty and fifty years of age, when a person's activity is normally at its peak, while she was burning with the desire to produce, to start new ventures, during those strong creative years, she was to sit still and wait.

She was told to concentrate on training her personnel, especially future superiors. She was to learn later the wisdom of the church's law; ten years to build up a team and fill it with a new spirit, pattern it on the simplicity of the gospel, and to mold women of character, capable of taking charge of new foundations, was not excessive.

Once Mother saw a chance of opening a house outside the diocese of Calcutta. The offer, the call even, came from Father Harrison, who had sent her many candidates from Chota Nagpur. As the parish priest of Mahuadan, he had a house ready for Mother Teresa at Daltonganj in his parish, with a garden, a well, and all that the sisters might need. He invited her to come and work there.

Mother asked Archbishop Périer for permission to accept this offer, but he could not grant this. Father Harrison was disappointed, but both from Mahuadan and from Noatoli, where he was moved, he sent girls to join the Missionaries of Charity in Calcutta; at times he sent as many as ten in one batch. He thus helped to give to the new institute an all-India dimension and the possibility of opening houses in Hindi-speaking areas.

The day the ten years' probation period ended, Mother started houses in the archdioceses of Ranchi and Delhi and the diocese of Jhansi. Nothing would stop her now. Her pent-up energy and zeal poured themselves out with the full power the Spirit gave her.

In all fairness to the delay caused by the church's prescription, it should be said that when in 1976 she was asked, "Mother, what is your greatest difficulty?" she answered, "Superiors, Father. To find suitable superiors and keep them zealous when they are in charge. Once they exercise authority, they may lose the sense of poverty and do things independently." In fact, several of the perpetual professed who left were or had been superiors.

THE NOVITIATE

When I was appointed confessor and spiritual director of the novices and the postulants, Mother asked me, "Please, Father, do not interfere in the running of the house. You know, some fathers want me to change certain things. For instance, they tell me that the sisters should have fans in the common room or in the chapel. I do not want them to have fans. The poor whom they are to serve have no fans. Most of the girls come from village homes where they had no fans. They should not be more comfortable here than at home. The same for the routine of the house. Please do not interfere."

I told her, "Mother, I shall not interfere in material things; I have been appointed spiritual advisor; that is my province; I shall not go beyond that." She trusted me, since she had asked the archbishop to appoint me. We always had the best of relations. I respected her judgment, admired her zeal and spirit of faith, envied her humility and charity.

Mother had much experience of the spiritual life, its problems and requirements. She gave stimulating spiritual conferences to her sisters, speaking four or even five times a day, to different groups.

The novices were "hand tooled," receiving personal attention from Mother. When the number of new foundations started growing she had to leave the mother house more often, and the burden of forming the novices fell on the shoulders of Sister Agnes, the mistress of novices, of Sister Frederick, her assistant, and of other sisters, later put in charge of groups of novices.

When I started, there were about thirty-five novices and postulants. After a year or two there were fifty, later sixty-five, then eighty-five, then the number reached one hundred. It was wonderful to see how the Lord blessed the young institute. Candidates arrived from various parts of India and also from abroad. Twice a year some novices took their vows; they were soon replaced by others. Larger numbers meant more work for the confessor. My weekly task started with a spiritual instruction; then there was a holy hour during which I began hearing confessions and the exercise went on, from three o'clock till five, six, and seven P.M., as the number of novices increased. It even became necessary to devote two afternoons to them to have more time for the spiritual direction of the sisters.

For some months the novitiate was shifted to a house on Park Street. But later the novices returned to the mother house and junior sisters were lodged in the house in Park Street.

For many years I went every week to the mother house. No one ever brought me tea or anything else; there was a glass of water in the sacristy. I felt that was normal; since the sisters did not take any refreshments, why should their confessor have a more comfortable life than theirs? The material side of life, creature comforts, seemed to count for nothing. I had been allowed to join an expedition, difficult and thrilling; hardships were part of the game; real, practical poverty had to be experienced. I felt indeed grateful that the sisters accepted me, who came from a more comfortable house, as a part of the team, and let me live their life for a while.

Now things have changed. The heroic days are over. More consideration is shown for the poor human body, for aging and suffering. After a talk, the sisters may request you to stay for a while and take some refreshments.

When of late, Mother saw me removing my shoes and walking on the cold cement floor, she came to me and insisted,

"Father, please keep your shoes on, otherwise you will catch cold."

"But Mother, you walk barefoot, can I not do it also?"

"We are accustomed, Father, and you are not."

This was like Paul writing to Timothy, the old fighter showing his concern for a fellow worker: "Timothy, take a glass of wine; it will help your weak stomach." To crown heroic detachment and the mortification of all human affections and desires, there is kindness and gentleness.

The novices were very similar to the novices of other religious congregations. They exhibited the same desire for holiness, generosity in making sacrifices, eagerness to progress on the way to perfection. They belonged to the same race as their sisters, friends, and neighbors who joined other institutes, without knowing them very well.

But one sensed—or was it only imagination—a definite spiritual quality, that particular brand of enthusiasm, joy, and submission to the guidance of the Holy Spirit, which are found specially in all new religious ventures relying on deep faith and trust in God.

The community lived in circumstances that brought it close to the original Pentecost. They could see God's hand in their foundation. They needed more faith in God's day-to-day protection than the well-established institutes; they needed more simplicity, the "one step enough for me" process and progress, which brought its own reward: simplicity, trust, joy.

The few novices or sisters with intellectual problems or complicated minds, those worried by the inadequacy of present political and social structures, did not persevere very long in the institute. Partly on this account, and partly for reasons of the material conditions of life, the few foreign candidates and novices presented their confessor with as many problems as all the Indian sisters, who were ten or fifteen times as numerous.

Obviously for a novice from Germany, England, or Malta, climate and living conditions at the mother house were a challenge requiring an unusual dose of courage and self-denial. And so some went home. A fair number remained, went through the training, and became excellent professed nuns. Indian novices hailing from comfortable homes and arriving with university degrees found the way of life no less uncomfortable, but could better foresee what their life would be than those who came to India for the first time.

I did my best to foster, in the generous young recruits to the religious life, love for God and total surrender to his guidance, in a joyful offering of their service. Mother often came to listen to the instructions, sitting on the floor like the novices. When it was time for the sacrament of penance, she took her place among the sisters.

Often Mother would come to the parlor, when confessions and adoration were over, to talk of spiritual matters and apprise me of the progress of the institute and its works. The praise of God was always on her lips;

she never complained of any hardship. We never disagreed or had any argument. She wanted a serious, solid spiritual formation to be given to her sisters, and it was her responsibility to see that they received it.

It was good at times to hear a senior sister remark, "Mother doesn't see; she can't understand. . . ." They were fully obedient to their superior, but showed mature judgment and ability to think for themselves, as also interest in the well-being and progress of the congregation. These sisters had to prepare themselves to shoulder responsibilities and take decisions —even if at times they would be blamed for them. A superior must be able to decide for herself, after due consultation, and cannot be expected to be always right.

They had special problems. Food was one of them, but not in the manner we would have expected.

"At the Holy Family Hospital at Patna," said Mother, "the superior told me, 'You must feed your sisters well. They will have much work, and move among the sick in unhealthy localities; to resist disease they must be well fed.' "

"And so the penance of the sisters is to eat what they are given; they should not deprive themselves of what they need to be good workers. Their penance is not to choose, but to eat their portion and obey."

This posed a problem for the spiritual director. Several times young novices asked, "What must I do? I cannot eat what is put on my plate. I have made frantic efforts to eat it and swallow it. They give me four chappattis, which is too much for me. What should I do?"

The rule was for their good; they required strong nourishment, being out much of the day, visiting homes, nursing the sick, often performing hard work.

Once the sisters discussed together the matter of food. So many people are going hungry; should the sisters not reduce their own consumption? They might perhaps do with only three chappattis per head for one of their meals? The question was considered by those in charge. Mother argued from the standpoint of her sisters' health. Some nuns in other congregations and also in her own suffered from tuberculosis. She did not want this to happen to her sisters if it could be prevented.

A few days later, one of the sisters announced smilingly, "The question of the chappattis has been decided. Instead of four, we are to get five per head and eat them with obedience."

From the start, Mother Teresa received much encouragement from Dr. B. C. Roy, the eminent statesman who for many years presided over the fortunes of West Bengal as its chief minister. A giant of a man, in more senses than one, who seldom appeared at public functions or political rallies, he administered what Nehru once called "the problem state" with remarkable ability, competence, and assiduity.

To meet him, Mother, at the beginning of her career, went at six o'clock in the morning to the free medical consultation he gave every day for an hour at his residence. A medical practitioner of repute who attended on celebrities like Gandhi, Nehru, and the king of Nepal, he kept in touch with the medical art by giving daily free consultations to those who approached him. A few people seized this occasion to present him with their petitions.

The scene is worth seeing. Admitted by his secretary, the patients sit on benches or chairs along the walls of the hall near the entrance. Dr. Roy goes round, looks at a patient's face, eyes, tongue, puts his stethoscope to his chest, feels his stomach, and asks a few questions. He quickly sizes up the situation, and has an extraordinary gift of diagnosis; prescribes, advises, passes on to the next patient. The whole thing is done in public, without wasting a moment. All feel themselves to be members of a great family and trust the famous doctor.

Mother does not come to consult him about her health but to put forward the case of some poor people who need help or redress. Could she obtain a water connection for a slum? Electric light for another? The chief minister signs a memo addressed to the officer in charge. It is as good as an order. "Please inquire into the matter." "Please look into this complaint." After a few such requests, he has noticed the little nun who cares only for others—and they are not people of influence, but always poor.

Soon Dr. Roy tells Mother to call on him at his office. Later he will tell her that she need not make an appointment but just come in while he is at his desk, where he works most of the day. Thus began a real partnership, with the two of them trusting one another, working together for the good of the poor. He a man of immense experience, wielding powers in the whole state; she a fledgling in the work of uplift and organization, but strong with the power of her divine Lord. Dr. Roy was a member of the Brahmo Samaj, a believer in one God, excluding all image worship, deeply respecting Jesus Christ and his teachings.

Soon it was he who urged Mother on.

"Dr. Roy wants me to expand Sishu Bhavan," Mother told me. "He said, 'Bigger, Mother, bigger. We have so much misery here. Our problems are enormous.' "

Another time, she said, "Dr. Roy asked me if we could take charge of the government-run vagrancy homes in Calcutta."

"How many are there?" I asked.

"Four. He told me, 'I trust you. I shall not ask you for any accounts. You will have no financial problem. Just put your nuns in charge of these houses.' But I had to refuse. I do not have enough sisters. I do not want to put too many of them into the same work. There is too much to be done."

It was true at the time. But also I suspect that she did not want to take over other people's work. In this case she would certainly have made enemies among the officials, which she always tried to avoid. "Dr. Roy never gave me money," said Mother, "but his protection, his recommendation to an official department was worth much more than money."

At times they differed, even strongly disagreed. Both of them had too much character to bow down easily. Mother argued for the leper asylum Dr. Roy wanted to remove from Calcutta's neighborhood, since the town was expanding. I think he was right. He saw the good of the local population; Mother fought for the lepers, who were finally moved to some other place. At least she got them a decent home.

Doctor Roy paid Mother this greatest tribute on his eightieth birthday. On that memorable anniversary, he went to work as usual at his office. Reporters called on him and inquired, 'How do you feel on your eightieth birthday, still being chief minister?' He did not answer, "I thought of Mahatma Gandhi, with whom I fought for independence, or of Jawaharlal Nehru, my friend and India's prime minister," or make any other personal recollection. He said simply, "As I climbed the steps leading to my office, I thought of Mother Teresa, who devotes her life to the welfare of the poor." The next day it was front-page news in the papers. No one could any longer ignore the humble nun in a blue-bordered white sari, who saw Christ in the poorest of the poor.

CHAPTER 5

Service of Love

I was hungry and you gave me food; I was thirsty and you gave me drink; I was naked and you clothed me; I was sick or in prison and you visited me. Whenever you did this to the least of my brothers you did it to me.

(MATT. 25:35–40)

"In the choice of the works of the apostolate," said Mother, "there was neither planning nor preconceived ideas. We started work as needs and opportunities arose. God showed what he wanted us to do."

So they began schools for the poorest children of the slums, dispensaries, Sunday schools to teach the children prayer, craft schools that the poor might learn how to earn a living.

The first big work of the Missionaries of Charity was the Kalighat Home for the Dying, begun while they still lived at 14 Creek Lane. Michael Gomes remembers vividly how the search for a place to house the dying destitute started.

"One day, we saw alongside the Campbell Hospital (now the Nilratan Sarkar Hospital) close to our house, a man dying on the roadside. Mother inquired; the hospital authorities could not accommodate him. We went to a chemist to get some medicine for him; when we returned with the medicines, the man was dead on the street. Mother did not hide her feelings. 'They look after a dog or a cat better than a fellow man,' she said. 'They would not allow that to happen to their pets.' She went to the commissioner of police to complain about this state of affairs. That was the origin of the Kalighat Home for the Dying.

"Are you positive on this point? The story as written by journalists is usually that Mother saw a woman on a pavement, full of sores, with maggots in her wounds. She stayed with her the whole night, keeping the rats away from her, and in the morning the woman died in her arms."

"That is not the truth. First, Mother never stayed out at night while she was in our house, not a single night. And Kalighat Home was started from our house. I was with her when the man died on the street, in front of the hospital where he had not been admitted."

Such occurrences were not exceptional; Mother must have seen more than once destitute people lying on the pavements, sick or at death's door. She herself narrated that one day she came across a dying woman on a pavement close to a hospital, who had festering wounds and was lying on a piece of sackcloth. Mother succeeded in getting the woman admitted into a hospital. Something had to be done about it; she moved heaven and earth to this end. It is no exaggeration to say that she moved heaven, since the young Missionaries of Charity went for several weeks to pray at the shrine of our Lady of Fatima. That she moved earth at the same time is evident: she approached the commissioner of police, who was most happy to help her to find a place and remove this blot on Calcutta's reputation. Mother also approached Dr. Ahmed, the health officer of the corporation, for a place to receive the more hopeless cases, the people dying on the street: "Give me at least a room," she pleaded.

Calcutta has excellent doctors and very good hospitals and nursing homes. There are free beds in the hospitals. But the city's population was swollen by an influx of refugees at the time of partition, and of villagers in periods of scarcity. Thus the number of beds to receive the huge number of sick people proves insufficient. Naturally the hospitals prefer to admit patients who have a hope of recovery rather than those dying of old age or malnutrition.

Mother Teresa offered to take care of the homeless destitute, sick, starving, those dying on the streets. She needed a house, but had neither the funds nor credit. An empty wing in a rest house for pilgrims was found; it was attached to the famous temple of the Goddess Kali in South Calcutta. Mother Teresa was allowed to use the building "provisionally." From this day one of the headaches of the police commissioner was removed. The city's social-minded citizens felt relieved. No one could write any more to newspapers lamenting the state of affairs in a city in which some people were allowed to die without a roof, without food, without medical care.

The help of the police also proved useful in another way. Mother knew that to open a house where food and shelter can be had for the asking in Calcutta is to invite an endless rush of candidates. Hence it was decided that only people brought by the police would be admitted.

Mother called the home, or hospital, Nirmal Hriday: the Immaculate Heart of Mary. It can accommodate about sixty men and sixty women inmates in two wards. Over thirty thousand destitute have been admitted. Half of them died in the home, decently, peacefully, prayerfully. The sisters and their co-workers washed them, fed them, consoled them, cheered their spirits, prepared their souls so that, rejoicing in the hope of a happy life in heaven, each one of them might "die with God."

Some opposition was to be expected. The home stood on sacred temple ground. The Kalighat temple, which enjoys tremendous popularity and a considerable income, is served by four hundred priests. Recalling the first days of that new venture, Michael Gomes says, "At first there was opposition. A group of young people said that Mother was coming to convert people to Christianity here in the center of Hinduism.

"A political leader told the young men that he would get her out. He came to see the place. Mother offered to take him round. He answered he could see things by himself and needed nobody to take him round. As he went round, he saw the miserable emaciated bodies, the sunken eyes, the sisters washing the sores, feeding the hungry, distributing medicines, giving injections, all in a gentle, loving manner.

"When he came out he met some of the young men. He told them, 'I promised I would get that woman out of here, and I shall. But, listen to me, I shall not get her out of this place before you get your mothers and sisters to do the work these nuns are doing. In the temple you have a goddess in stone; here you have a living goddess.' That was the end of the opposition organized by this group.

"The sisters went on caring for sick bodies and drooping spirits with a holy unconcern for outside murmurs. They had God's approval, that was enough for them, But their charity could not fail to impress many visitors. It happened one day that a priest of the temple, who suffered from tuberculosis, sought and found a welcoming haven in the sisters' hospital. The service rendered to one of theirs made a deep impression on several of his brethren."

Mother told me at the time, "One morning, as I was washing the patients, a priest of the temple entered the ward. He prostrated himself before me, touched my feet with his hands, which he then laid on his head. Then he stood up and said, 'For thirty years I have served the Goddess Kali in her temple. Now, the Goddess Mother stands before me in human form. It is my privilege today to worship the Mother present to my eyes.' "

Later, Mother said, "The question of the Kalighat Home for the Dying is to come up at a corporation meeting. Some people object to destitute people being brought there to die, on religious grounds; they say it defiles the place."

"Mother, you know how these things are decided. It will be one item on a crowded agenda. The chairman will announce: 'Item No. 67, Mother Teresa runs a home for the dying in a building belonging to the Kalighat temple. Are there any objections? Should she be allowed to continue or asked to vacate the place?' So, Mother, you need an influential counselor to fight your battle and another one to support him. Then you will be allowed to remain until a more suitable place can be found—which means that you stay for good."

And so it was. Some days later Mother was happy to report, "At the corporation meeting, only two members objected on religious grounds. Nobody offered to provide a better place. So the resolution was passed that we are allowed to remain at Kalighat until a suitable place is found to accommodate the dying. My friends told me, 'Do not worry. The objection has been duly registered and put into cold storage.' "

The Calcutta Corporation supported the Kalighat Home for the Dying with a monthly subsidy. One day Mother informed the corporation that she was no more in need of their help, and the subsidy was stopped.

A new house, Prem Dan, was given to the Missionaries of Charity by I.C.I. in 1975. After the inauguration ceremony, I asked Mother, "Will you shift Nirmal Hriday of Kalighat to Prem Dan?" She replied, "I shall never give up Kalighat, unless they eject me forcibly." Soon she had filled the new house with needy people. In Calcutta there was no difficulty in doing this. As for Kalighat's Nirmal Hriday, the Home for the Dying has become a hallowed place. Its very ground has been made holy by the countless acts of love, of devotion, of those who nurse the sick with limitless patience; a place sanctified by the total surrender to God of so many who from there left earth for heaven—a sacred place that all believers enter as respectfully and silently as they enter a temple—because, as Mother put it tersely, "God is here."

Prem Dan is used as a home for those who have a better chance to recover and survive; they can be kept there longer if need be, until they are back on their feet. It serves also for other classes of needy people. Kalighat remains as a home for the dying destitute who have little chance of surviving.

With the inception of the Kalighat Home for the Dying, it was hoped that destitute people would no longer die on the Calcutta pavements. Well, not quite. It was impossible to completely stop this scandal in a city officially numbering one hundred thousand pavement dwellers with no other abode, and unofficially a good few thousands more.

THE CHILDREN'S HOMES

The care of orphans, of abandoned or crippled children, has always been a preferred work of religious institutes. Most Catholic centers in India and other countries have one or more orphanages, and facilities to receive orphans in their boarding schools. Jesus himself gave us the example of love for children, who are naturally trustful, simple, loving: "Jesus then took a little child, set him in front of the Twelve, put His arms around him, and said to them, 'Anyone who welcomes one of these children in My name, welcomes Me; and anyone who welcomes Me welcomes not Me but the one who sent Me' " (Mark 9:36–37). Later, adds St. Mark, "people were bringing little children to Him, for Him to touch them. The disciples turned them away, but when Jesus saw this he was indignant and said to them, 'Let the little children come to Me; do not stop them; for it is to such as these that the kingdom of God belongs. I tell you solemnly, anyone who does not welcome the kingdom of God like a child will never enter it.' Then he put His arms around them, laid His hands on them and gave His blessings" (Mark 10:13–16).

So it is a duty and a source of joy to minister to the children Jesus loves, and to serve our Lord in the person of the child.

"How did the first children's home start, Brother Michael?"

"Well," he answered, "Mother had been looking for some time for a house where she could receive and care for unwanted children. One day as she came home she told me, 'Mrs. X. asked me to pray for her husband that he may stop drinking. He drinks a full bottle of whisky every day, and the market price of imported whisky is ninety rupees per bottle. Well, if Mr. X. can pay ninety rupees per day for his drinks, I can pay five hundred rupees a month for that house on Lower Circular Road that is to let. I shall take it and start a children's home.' "

I remarked to a sister, "I cannot see the logic of arguing from the cost of a bottle of whisky."

"No," she replied, "you men go by logic. We women follow our intuition, and we are more often right than you."

"Here you are correct, sister. Your intuition is based on love, and it is more often right than our dry reasonings."

This was another case requiring trust in God. Was the work really needed for his glory? If so, his providence would see that the means did not fail. He would take care of the work started for him.

And so the house was rented.

There were so many problems, so many needs: unwanted children, unwedded mothers who could not have their babies at home nor take them back there, orphans, crippled children, mentally retarded children to be looked after.

Catholic charity was already active in the field: the Franciscan Missionaries of Mary had a crèche where the police would bring abandoned infants. There were other orphanages. But the needs of Calcutta seemed inexhaustible.

And so Sishu Bhavan, the children's home, was started.

Abandoned infants were brought by the police and by private parties. Some of them were found in dustbins—not many, let us be fair. Some were left at the doors of convents. Others were brought by people who did not want to reveal their names.

One infant was found lying before the altar of the Blessed Sacrament in my own Church of the Sacred Heart, by the sacristan when he opened the church doors in the morning. The child was crying. The sacristan fetched some milk, made the child drink it, and soon the baby fell asleep, happy. The police were informed, and the baby duly taken to Mother Teresa's Sishu Bhavan. He was adopted by a Catholic family and is doing well.

Some infants are sickly or crippled. Some die soon, but many recover, become strong and healthy.

In 1976 a picture of Mother Teresa fondling a smiling child appeared in Calcutta papers. She had just agreed to take charge of 5 babies abandoned by their mothers in the maternity ward of one of Calcutta's main hospitals. Later it was announced that the authorities of the hospital had another 102 babies or infants who had been similarly left behind by their mothers after their delivery. Mother Teresa declared that she would take charge of all the abandoned babies.

After showing such willingness to help the civil and medical authorities to solve their human problems, it is not astonishing that she obtained their full cooperation for schemes to better the lot of the poor. She assumes the duty of charity whether or not she has the means. God will provide, she says.

In most localities where the Missionaries of Charity are established, they receive unwanted or crippled children.

Sishu Bhavan in Calcutta has been for many years the center of varied activities. Apart from receiving abandoned children and cripples, it is a place where some unwedded mothers stay while expecting their children. There also are stored food supplies to be distributed free to the poor. Walking past the house on an afternoon, you may see fifty or eighty women with small children, waiting for the distribution to start. No distribution means for some of them no food for that day.

There are hazards and dangers in the free distribution of food. "Mother has been seen," says Michael Gomes, "pushing back with unexpected physical strength a whole line of women rushing forward to receive rations."

The sisters also have experienced some unpleasant moments when serving the poor. At Sishu Bhavan one day there was no stock to distribute rations to card holders. The agency supplying the sisters for this project had stopped sending food to Calcutta to divert them to another area they considered more urgently in need. The sisters had nothing to give to the crowd standing at the gate. Some people manifested their anger by shouts and even tried to set fire to the house, while they abused the sisters and accused them of robbing their food for their own benefit. But the police and the fire brigade appeared on the scene in a matter of minutes, thus saving the house, the children, and the crippled living there.

The sisters had other moments of danger. Close to Calcutta, two sisters were confronted by a group of lepers, displeased with the arrangements that had been made for them, who locked the sisters inside their van and started pushing it toward a canal. Fortunately another sister called the police, who arrived in time to save the two sisters from an enforced bath or worse. Such things are part of the work of charity.

The sisters narrate their disagreeable adventures during the evening recreation.

Mother defends her policy: "At a meeting in Bangalore, a sister attacked me for distributing food freely to the poor. She said that I spoiled the poor by my acts of charity. I answered her, 'If I spoil the poor, you and the other sisters spoil the rich in your select schools. And almighty God is the first to spoil us. Does he not give freely to all of us? Then why should I not imitate my God and give freely to the poor what I have received freely?' They had nothing to answer." Mother could have quoted St. Paul's words to Timothy: "God who, out of his riches, gives us all we need for our happiness" (Tim. 16:17).

WORK AMONG LEPERS

Mother Teresa was led to start working for the welfare of leprosy patients in an indirect way. It was again the force of circumstances, or to look at it with the eyes of faith, the hand of God working through human instruments, that brought her into that particular field of charitable work.

For many years the Sisters of Charity had run a leper asylum at Gobra, on the outskirts of Calcutta. In this leper asylum lived a hundred and fifty inmates, well cared for by the sisters. It happened that plans for the development of Calcutta covered the area of Gobra. The large compound, including the houses occupied by the lepers, was to be expropriated, to allow the locality to be developed in a planned manner. People would never accept housing close to an area they thought infected by germs of the dreaded disease. And so it was decided to take over the property occupied by the sisters; the lepers would have to find some other shelter.

Mother Teresa, informed of the project, was indignant. What would happen to the poor sufferers? Where would they go? Who would provide them with a suitable place to live? Mother took up their cause and went to plead it before the chief minister. Dr. Roy, her patron, listened to her; but he would not reverse the decision. Calcutta had to expand. The city was bursting at the seams; the housing problem defied solution. Suitable lodgings were to be provided for hundreds of thousands of people. A development project in an area contiguous to the city could not be stopped on account of a hundred and fifty lepers living in a colony with little contact with the outside world. They would be displaced.

At least Mother obtained an agreement that the lepers would not be removed before some alternative accommodation had been found for them. The chief minister offered a place in Bankura District. Mother, not finding the place suitable, complained to him, "You told me you would give the lepers a good place to live in, but the place you offer us lacks a good supply of water, which is essential for leprosy patients."

Thus Mother became active in leper work. She started a Leprosy Collection Day. Collection tins were taken around Calcutta for Mother Teresa's Leprosy Fund, bearing the words "Touch the leper with your kindness." Money poured in from all sources.

"At the time of our Leprosy Day," said the sister in charge of finance, "we just throw the checks into a basket, so numerous are they. One can only admire Calcutta people, so anxious to help the lepers. Leper asylums and villages are needed in India, but they are not enough."

"You missionaries do not seem to understand," a high government official told me several years ago, "that our problems are of a magnitude the developed countries do not suspect, certainly do not experience. Take the case of leprosy; in a leprosarium you can look after two or three hundred patients. But we have two million sufferers from leprosy in this country, out of the world figure of four million. So you do not offer any workable solution to the problem; you do not even scratch the surface. We need an approach to the masses, a method that will reach hundreds of thousands of people."

He was right: and this could now be done. Dr. Hemeryckx, a Belgian who had worked for several years in central Africa, had come to India, and had introduced a method of treating lepers on a mass scale. He favored leaving them at home, from where they could regularly attend mobile clinics. In this manner he reached a considerable number of sufferers; many who were ashamed of showing themselves would come to the clinic. Parents could remain with their children, at least when they were not dangerously contagious.

It may be mentioned that before leaving India Dr. Hemeryckx was received by the then prime minister Nehru, who thanked him for his services and for showing the way to mass treatment of leprosy.

Mother Teresa went to see the center established by Dr. Hemeryckx near Madras. Then she offered to collaborate with government agencies and doctors. And so the sisters started medical assistance to the lepers in a big way. This work became one of their main activities in India.

There would still be a need for some institutions or villages where infectious cases, or lepers with no one to look after them, or unable to take care of themselves, could be received. To this end Shanti Nagar, the "Town of Peace," was founded as a colony and rehabilitation center for lepers in the district of Burdwan.

The same grace that blessed Father Damian, a modern hero of charity, may bless those who today devote their whole life to the apostolate among lepers. Two or three sisters at different times confided to me, "I think I have contracted the disease. What must I do?" They were still young and slightly afraid, though ready to accept; that may have been all God asked from them.

The doctors are rightly cautious, and give the sisters and brothers who work with them strict instructions.

"The doctor forbade me to touch some patients because they are actively contagious. What should I do?" a sister asked.

"Obey the doctor, sister. You should not run any unreasonable risk of contracting the disease. You must take all the precautions ordered by the doctor. Thus you will be able to serve the patients better and for a longer time."

But these devoted brides of Christ know that if the institute assumes this apostolate on a large scale, some sisters may experience what it means to be attacked by leprosy. Thus a religious may be able to give witness to the lepers in an especially convincing manner, by carrying a leper's cross behind the Savior. Nuns of other congregations have suffered and are still suffering from the disease they caught while ministering to leprosy patients. And they bless the Lord for this grace.

Mother Teresa knows that the poor need belief in God more than other people. The poor need hope, they need God. Those who would deprive them of hope, their only solace, commit a crime against humanity. If these others wish to be self-sufficient, not to tend to an infinity of truth, goodness, and beauty, let them be self-sufficient alone—but let them not rob others of their hope.

Mother and her sisters bring the poor hope, eternal hope and belief in God's goodness. The sisters, young and educated, bend over them, wash their sores, smile to them, and cheer them while never uttering a rough word or losing their temper. Why do they treat unknown people as true brothers and sisters? And they do it, not for two or three years, but for a whole lifetime. Simple people are neither fools nor easily fooled; they are not blinded by sophistication; their simple minds discover the truth; those women mirror God's love. Thus through their sufferings they come to God.

CHAPTER 6

Witnesses of Christ to the Nations

You will receive power when the Holy Spirit comes on you, and then you will be my witnesses not only in Jerusalem, but throughout Judaea and Samaria, and indeed to the ends of the earth.

(ACTS 1:8)

Ten years had elapsed since the Congregation of the Missionaries of Charity had been approved by Rome. The sisters had been trained. Together Mother and the sisters had prayed, worked, studied. The Spirit of God had lavished his gifts on them.

Conforming to their Lord Jesus Christ, they lived his life, shared his passion for the salvation of human beings. They had heard from him secret words of friendship, they had learnt his intimate thoughts and desires. Like the apostles they had the promise of Jesus, that he would send them the Holy Spirit, and his command to make him known to the world.

"I shall send you the Spirit of truth; he will be my witness. And you too will be witnesses, because you have been with me from the beginning" (John 15:26–27).

The sisters were ready to go out and bear witness to their Lord. Calcutta was their Jerusalem, the starting point of their apostolate, which had its roots there; but the tree was to spread its branches and bear fruit in many parts of the world.

They had the same purpose as the apostles: to bear witness to the Father's love, who loved us so much that he sent his only begotten Son; to Christ's love for us, who died for our sins, that we might become the Father's children of adoption, in and through him; to the love of the Spirit who pours into our hearts his choice gifts; love for God and for all people.

Their constitutions told them to bring the good news to the poor, to the poorest of the poor. This had been given as a sign of the coming of the Savior; a sign that the kingdom of God had appeared among the people: 'the good news is preached to the poor.'

The third phase of the life of the young congregation was beginning.

Mother did not waste a single day. Some bishops, aware of the sisters' work in Calcutta, wished to obtain their services; they requested Mother Teresa to establish houses in their dioceses.

INDIA

The sisters went first to Ranchi, then to Delhi, then to Jhansi. The Ranchi or Chota Nagpur mission had previously belonged to the Calcutta archdiocese. The church now fully established in the region was the most lively young church in North India. From Ranchi archdiocese, many candidates had joined the Missionaries of Charity. It was only fair that the archdiocese should be rewarded for its generous gift of personnel. At the archbishop's invitation, Mother opened a house in Ranchi.

Next came Delhi. Archbishop Joseph Fernandes had known Mother Teresa during his many years in Calcutta as vicar general and auxiliary bishop. Archbishop Knox, the pro nuncio, was also interested in Mother Teresa's work. Since the number of local Catholics in Delhi was small, to strengthen the Catholic presence in the capital, the policy was to bring religious congregations from other parts of the country, to open schools and institutions that would benefit the people.

Mother found it useful to be close to the center of government, to the ministries, to the offices of agencies providing help for social and charitable work. So she went to Delhi, which was said to be the fastest-growing city in India, receiving as it did one hundred thousand immigrants a year.

Ranchi, Delhi, and Jhansi became for the sisters new fields of apostolate and the sign that the Lord wanted them to spread out through the whole of India. The work pattern for the new houses had been tested in Calcutta. The sisters would bring the dying destitute to a haven of rest; they would take care of orphans, of crippled children. They would teach people to pray to God, organize Sunday schools, prepare children for the reception of the sacraments; they would visit the slums, teach poor girls crafts, and prepare them for marriage and family life.

Mother was only too happy to start work in the capital. She soon received help from many quarters. Mr. Cuttat, the Swiss ambassador to New Delhi, an eminent scholar and devoted Catholic, was instrumental in obtaining his country's financial help for the foundation of a children's home.

Mother, who was generally considered to be a social worker interested mostly in bodies, in health and material well-being, took advantage of this occasion to show the prime minister that her primary concern was the spiritual welfare of the poor. A few days after this memorable occasion, she reported,

"The inauguration of our new children's home in Delhi was attended by Nehru and the Swiss ambassador. When the prime minister arrived, accompanied by Krishna Menon, I said to them, 'Let us first go and salute the master of the house.'

"Then I led them into the chapel where I knelt in prayer. Nehru, standing at the back, made a *pranam* with folded hands. Krishna Menon went up to the altar to read an inscription and asked me its meaning. Then we went to sit on the grounds for the inaugural ceremony. The children garlanded the prime minister and offered him a spiritual bouquet. I explained that it meant that they had offered prayers and small sacrifices to God to obtain his graces for the prime minister. Then I asked, 'Sir, shall I tell you about our work?' Nehru answered me, 'No, Mother, you need not tell me about your work, I know about it. That is why I have come.' "

This simple, absolute word of praise was the finest acknowledgment of the services rendered to the poor of the country by Mother Teresa and the Missionaries of Charity. It came from the man who for seventeen years had spoken the mind of the people of India.

BOMBAY

Mother wished to open a house in Bombay, where she hoped to find good vocations among the large, fervent, well-educated Catholic community. This manufacturing city possessed many mills whose labor force lived in tenements, or *chawls;* there would be plenty of work for the sisters.

Bombay prides itself on being the premier city of India, the main center of the country's trade and banking, the glamor city of cinema; it has a wonderful marine drive, rich villas, and palatial mansions on Cumbala Hill. It is also the Indian town with the largest number of Catholics and the see of the first Indian cardinal. The city has developed a large network of Catholic schools, colleges, social and charitable institutions.

"I have received invitations from several bishops," Mother said, "but no call has come from Bombay, though the cardinal knows what we do."

"Well, Mother," I replied, "you should not wait to be called. The cardinal is an important person, a prince of the church; do not wait till he requests you. Offer him your services, he will accept, you will see."

Two weeks later, Mother was radiant: "Father, I wrote to the cardinal, just two lines to ask him if he would welcome us in his archdiocese. By return post he answered that he would be very pleased for us to work in Bombay."

Soon she was there, and Cardinal Gracias provided a house for the sisters.

"He is very kind," she said. "He told me: I shall give you one of my best priests as a spiritual director for your sisters."

Mother soon returned to Bombay with a batch of sisters, and the work started.

At first the people of Bombay frowned on Mother Teresa. She provoked their displeasure by remarking bluntly at the end of a short visit of inspection of the town: "The slums of Bombay are worse even than the slums of Calcutta." The press was indignant, the people shocked by this quasi-blasphemy. Of course, Calcutta was known as dirty, rowdy, unkempt; but Bombay was the pride of India. How could this nun, after a few days in their city, pass such a sweeping and injurious judgment?

Mother silenced her critics. It did not take her long to size up a slum. She knew the criteria: light, water, garbage disposal, ventilation, air pollution, proximity to the market. In a matter of minutes she saw, weighed, compared, judged.

"The Calcutta slums," she replied, "are mainly single-storied: fresh air enters into the dwellings, there is less congestion, more space for children to move about. Bombay is an island—its *chawls*, built close to the factories on scarce and expensive land, are three- or four-storied; water has to be carried up several narrow flights of steps; ventilation is poor, the children have no open spaces for fresh air and games."

The press soon realized that Mother knew more about poverty than they did. Criticism gave way to respect. Still, the atmosphere would not be as friendly as that of Calcutta, at least for some time.

In November 1963 I was in Bombay to preach retreats to the diocesan clergy at the Bandra Retreat House. One morning, looking at the papers on the newsstands, a title struck my eyes: "Woman Found Dead on Queen's Road." A photo of the corpse, which lay on the road for several hours, was also published. The daily went on to deplore the shame of a city where a person could die on the street and remain there for hours before anyone came to remove the body.

During the retreats I spoke to the priests of apostolic charity and mentioned the wonderful work Mother Teresa's Missionaries of Charity were doing. At least in Calcutta the papers no longer reported cases of neglected destitute dying on the streets. The church of Christ was showing to all what service of the Lord in his brethren meant. The priests were visibly impressed. One of them came to me afterward and said, "I am in charge of a large parish. We have a house that is not used. Perhaps the cardinal might allow me to offer it to Mother Teresa to open a home for the dying."

Two weeks later, Mother said happily, "Thank you, Father, you have helped us to obtain a house in Bombay. A parish priest has offered us a property where we can open a house for the dying." It was quickly established, and became, as in Calcutta, one of the sisters' most characteristic works.

The next year, the Eucharistic Congress took place in Bombay. The president of India, Dr. Radhakrishnan, was there to receive the Holy Father. Pope Paul VI drove in triumph through the Bombay streets in a white Lincoln convertible presented to him by an American benefactor. The popular enthusiasm cannot be described. Not thousands, but truly millions of people lined the 14-mile route from the airport to the congress grounds; never in any country had such a crowd gathered for a reception to a pope or for a eucharistic congress. In this very religious country, people belonging to all religions wanted to have a *darshan*, or spiritual glimpse, of the great holy man of Christendom. They wished to see, listen to, come in contact with the most influential religious leader in the world. Wherever the pope went, a huge mass of humanity surged forward to receive his blessings. Even among the organizers, no one had expected such demonstrations of respect and friendship.

The pope had expressed a wish to visit some of the poorer quarters of Bombay, to meet at least a few slum dwellers. It should not be said that he had come only for the well-to-do, in the land that had produced Mahatma Gandhi, the father of the nation, who traveled third class and journeyed extensively on foot. The pope wished to show his interest in the poor and to approach them in their own houses. But the civil authorities quite rightly would not allow the Holy Father to move among the slum dwellers, followed by hundreds of reporters and photographers, who would have exposed to the eyes of the world the least attractive side of the country's life.

The congress organizers solved the problem by taking the pope to visit some charitable institutions. The pope mixed freely with the children of an orphanage and delighted them by sharing their breakfast of buns and fruit; he showed his appreciation of the devoted work of those running this and similar houses.

Before leaving, the pope donated his white Lincoln convertible car to Mother Teresa to be sold for her works. The occasion was acclaimed in the world press, which displayed photos of the pope and Mother Teresa. Some of Mother's friends decided to raffle the car for her; they sold raffle tickets at 100 rupees each, with the one single prize the car donated by the pope. The sale of the tickets brought about 450 thousand rupees for her charities. A non-Christian was the lucky winner.

VENEZUELA

Mother was visibly thrilled as she said,

"We have been invited by a bishop to go to Venezuela. Is that not wonderful?"

"Splendid, Mother. Where? Caracas?"

"No, not Caracas, a smaller place, not far away. This will be our first foundation in Latin America."

We surveyed the great opportunities offered by the great continent that comprises nearly one-half of the baptized Catholics of the whole world. There the sisters would have real spiritual work, as much as they could cope with, among the millions of baptized Catholics who hardly practiced their religion for lack of priests and nuns to instruct them and nourish their faith.

"Mother, you must make a big effort in that direction. Do accept every offer made by the bishops. Much can still be saved, preserved for Christ, but speed is essential. The church loses adherents in South America every day, due to lack of spiritual care."

Mother agreed: "I shall send my best sisters to start the new house." She hoped to get vocations from the country itself, so that from Venezuela they could move into other South American countries. Soon Mother was on her way to Venezuela. She would see her sisters established, meet the bishop, obtain help and collaboration from authorities and lay friends. In July 1965 the first foundation outside India was started. Mother came back delighted. The people were friendly, the sisters had been well received.

This was only a start. Two more houses were established later in Venezuela. Then one in Lima, Peru. But the spread of the congregation was slower than we had hoped. There was not the same enthusiasm as in India, though ten years later, at the beginning of 1975, she had requests from several bishops and made plans to open houses in Colombia, Bolivia, and Brazil. The bishops were to discover what great help the Missionaries of Charity would bring them for the spiritual uplift of their poor.

Sister Dorothy, who had been superior there and returned to Calcutta, reported, "We were like deacons there. Generally the people are baptized; but many have never seen a priest or a sister, due to the scarcity of priests and nuns in the country. So many people know nothing about Jesus. We had to teach them. We took communion to the sick. Eventually we administered baptism. The poor live in *favelas*. We live in their midst. At first I could not understand them, as they only speak Spanish. But within two months I could manage. I learned the language with the children's help. And some local girls joined us."

"In Latin America," said another sister, "we do much spiritual work. We do all that a priest here does, except hearing confession and consecrating the holy Eucharist. It is really wonderful work."

Still, we had to acknowledge that the Missionaries of Charity had not spread there as fast as in India, as fast as we had hoped. Bishops and priests may not have realized their potentialities for the life of the church. Their spirit and method, their personal, loving approach are well adapted to the needs of the downtrodden and spiritually neglected poor of Latin America.

The sisters do not come with intellectual notions of conscientization, they do not worry about changing structures, or about opposing policies in the church. They go to the poor with the charity of Christ, with open hearts and hands. They speak to the poor a language they can understand. Their action is contagious and challenging—they obtain cooperation with the people among whom they work for their work. They bring a sense of respectability, of decency and self-respect to people who did not know them, did not realize that they count in God's eyes, have value for Christ.

ROME

Mother was radiant as she greeted me: "Father, we have been invited to go to Rome. The pope himself asked us to open a house there."

A rare note of victory rang in her voice. To Rome at the Holy Father's request; what an honor for a young congregation. To Rome, like Peter and Paul. To her strong ecclesial sense, Rome meant much; it was the heart and center of Christianity, the see of the successor of St. Peter, the vicar of Christ on earth.

In a voice more subdued and thoughtful, Mother added, "There is much work to be done, much poverty in Rome's suburbs; many people are in need of the sacraments; many children do not learn their prayers; and there is much anti-God influence and propaganda. But we shall be close to the Holy Father; we shall work in the shadow of St. Peter's."

Mother did not need to reflect on this invitation nor to compare it with other possibilities. This was a sacred duty imposed by the Holy Father, who had befriended the community openly in Bombay. The sisters would get ready as soon as possible, as soon as arrangements could be made.

To Rome the sisters went, thrilled and joyful. They needed to show that they were not afraid of shouldering the cross of Christ. Romans knew more about virtue and vice, through centuries of experience, than any other city existing today.

To Rome had come countless saints—more were buried in Rome than in any other town; in Rome saints were officially proclaimed by the Catholic church. But the Romans do not wait for any official proclamation to establish the fact of holiness. They discovered holiness behind appearances. When Benedict Labre, the Frenchman—who had come to Rome and for years lived in the porches of churches, neither washing much nor changing his clothes, eating whatever people gave him, passing his days in prayer to God—died, immediately the rumor spread through the whole of Rome: " 'Il Santo" is dead.' "

When the sisters were well established and fully at work, Mother spoke with special warmth of her Roman community.

"The sisters are in a slum area; they live among the poor. They go to the market to beg for them. Everywhere they are well received. 'The Indian sisters' as the people call them, even though several of them are European, get chicken every day; at the market, the stall holders give them, free, the less good portions which hotels and restaurants do not want. "The sisters teach the children their prayers and prepare them for the sacraments. They visit the sick and old people in their houses."

Thus the good work of the sisters, backed by the prayers of many Co-Workers and of the Sick and Suffering, produces acts of love for God in Rome. "The good works are links forming a chain of love around the world," as Mother had prophetically written to her Belgian friend during the first days in the Upper Room.

To increase their Roman presence, Mother shifted the novitiate she had established in London to Rome. It was to receive the candidates from Europe and America, and also some from Africa. The postulants remained in London.

AUSTRALIA

In June 1969, after holy Mass, a tall man introduced himself to me and asked, "Could you do me a favor? I would like to meet Mother Teresa." I introduced John McGee to Mother Teresa, who welcomed him.

He opened his briefcase, and pulled out a large bundle of notes, which he pushed across the table, saying,

"Mother, this is to begin with." Mother Teresa took the bundle, made no comment, and started talking of the possibilities of apostolate among the poor in Australia.

Mother had paid her first visit to Australia in April 1969 at the invitation of Bishop Warren of Broken Hill, who wished her to start work among the aboriginals. So Mother and Mr. McGee now made plans for this work. Knowing ministers and officials as he did, he could help to get the required authorization for the sisters to establish themselves in his motherland.

John J. McGee's first visit to Mother laid the foundation for a most fruitful apostolate in Australia. He became a faithful friend of the institute.

In the middle of September 1969, Mother went to Bourke with five sisters to start their first foundation in Australia and to work among the aboriginals.

Mother was invited to Melbourne by Archbishop Knox, who had known her in India. Some objected; in a country as rich as Australia, enjoying an advanced social legislation, surely there would be no work for her. There were no slums, no destitute, no people dying on the streets. Mother retorted, "What, no work for us? And what about the habitual offenders when they come out of prison, what about their wives and children? What about the drug addicts, the alcoholics, are they not God's children in need of guidance and help?"

On 26 April 1970, Mother Teresa and five sisters left Madras by plane for Melbourne. They reached there the next day. Sister Monica was the superior. The very first day, Mother, accompanied by the provincial of the Loreto sisters, found a house and entered it. With the help of co-workers and students, they cleaned the place. They started work immediately.

Sister Monica directed the sisters to go on to the streets and discover the needy people. The sisters came back, saying there were none on the streets. "Then knock at the doors of houses," said the superior. They did so, asking if there were any old person or people in need in the house. At first people found them strange in their Indian dress. Also, they would not believe that they were nuns, wearing those strange habits. But the sisters, by their kindness, gradually won their trust. They prepared the people for the sacraments and for the consecration of the families to the Sacred Heart of Jesus. They were helped and encouraged by some priests, and later by civic leaders who reported cases to them.

Their first big venture was to be a home for the rehabilitation of alcoholics and drug addicts. In 1972 a plot of land was purchased in Greenvale and building started on the convent and the rehabilitation center.

Mother was invited to attend the Eucharistic Congress at Melbourne. There were only three speakers at the main session, and Mother Teresa was one of them. She spoke on her favorite topic: her mission to serve Christ in the poor, to see the suffering Lord in his brethren in pain. Her words and her conviction moved the hearts of her listeners.

The convent was blessed by Cardinal Knox in February 1973.

Before departing in April, Mother Teresa left her sisters with advice they remembered: "I do not want you to perform miracles with unkindness; rather, I prefer you to make mistakes in kindness."

THE MIDDLE EAST

Mother was happy: "Father, we are going to Jordan, in the Middle East; close to the birthplace of our Lord. The sisters will be walking where our Lord walked and preached and worked miracles. Where our Lord died out of love for men. Is it not wonderful?"

Yes, this was truly good news. The Middle East was the cradle of the three great monotheistic religions: Judaism, Christianity, and Islam, the religions followed by more than half the believers of the world. They were born in that rugged country, where one senses God's might and holiness. Abraham, Moses, were men of faith, as Mother was a woman of faith.

Christianity, starting from Jerusalem, had spread over the world in ever widening concentric circles; now it returned to its starting point through these nuns from the East.

In July 1970 the sisters started work in Jordan.

In March 1973 they settled in the Gaza Strip to alleviate the sufferings of the hundreds of thousands of refugees from Palestine. They were thus on both sides of the political frontiers.

Some time later, Mother expressed her happiness at spreading farther into the Middle East:

"We are going to Yemen, Father. We have been invited by the prime minister himself. After six centuries of Christian absence, with no priests in the country, no Mass, no sacraments, there will be Mass again for the sisters. After six hundred years! Is that not wonderful?

"The prime minister promised to do everything for the sisters. He said, they should have no fear. He holds himself personally responsible for their safety. He guarantees that no one will cause them harm. His government will give them every needed help and support. As a sign of goodwill, he presented me with a 'Sword of Honor.' " She laughed: "A sword, to me!"

"Yes, Mother, they are a martial race and good fighters, that is why they present you with a sword of honor."

I thought too late of "the double-edged sword" that is the Word of God. That one the sisters would have to wield—while bringing to all the peace so much esteemed in the East, the peace of Christ.

JORDAN

At the mother house, February 1976.

"Where do you come from, Sister?"

"I arrived from Jordan a few days ago. I am from Kerala, from the diocese of Trichur."

"One of the best in the world for priestly and religious vocations. There is a wonderful spirit in your country. But now tell me about Jordan."

"I was five years in Jordan, Father. I was sent there immediately after my first vows, at the end of the novitiate."

"Did you come into contact with ministers or high officials of the government?"

"No, we met only the poor."

Here all glamor is absent, any feeling of being important and acknowledged as such. There is only the daily, humble, hard work, the contact with the very poor.

"What are your works there, sister? Do you follow the same pattern as in Calcutta?"

"First, we work among the Catholics. Jordan has 8 percent Christians out of which 2 percent are Catholics. We find them, teach the catechism, prepare the children for their first communion. Then we visit the poor families, both Christian and Moslem. We give medicine to the sick. We have a home for the 'unwanted'—old people, mentally retarded, handicapped, abandoned children.

"We also go to the Jordan in a van given us by Caritas, and there we visit the sick."

"What reception do you get?"

"The Moslems are quite friendly. They call us *Hajis,* because we wear white as they do when they go on pilgrimage to Mecca."

"Do the women go to Mecca?"

"Yes, some go on pilgrimage. Of course the Moslems do not know what it is to be a nun; so they do not understand our kind of life. But they respect us."

"At the beginning, how did you solve the language problem?"

"We had to learn Arabic. We were six sisters; there are only five while I am absent. First we had a paid teacher. Then some local sisters in Amman kindly volunteered to teach us."

"Did you find the language difficult?"

"No. It is much easier than some of our Indian languages, say Tamil or Hindi. It has hardly any grammar. We learned enough Arabic to be understood by the people.

"Our house is some distance from the capital. We hope to open a house in Amman itself soon. Then things will be easier; we shall not have to move about as much as we do now.

"You must one day have a Middle East province or region; can you hope to find vocations there?"

"Hardly; unless it be from among the girls we educate."

"Did you receive the spiritual help you required?"

"There are very few Catholic priests in Jordan. In Amman, only two or three ministered to us. We could not find a priest for our annual retreat. Finally, we joined other groups of sisters, and made our retreat with them."

"And books? Do you have the spiritual books you need?"

"No, we are very short of religious books, especially good meditation books. Do send us some."

"Yes, I shall try to help you. As you know, our Catholic charitable agencies provide food for people's bodies, but less sustenance for their souls. That strikes many people in the much more spiritually inclined East."

"Your benefactors should also remember the spiritual needs of the sisters."

YEMEN

At the mother house, February 1976.

Two tertians have just arrived; one is from Kerala, one from Ranchi district. They have been in Yemen more than two years.

"What works do you do there, sister?"

"We have a home for the unwanted, with 120 inmates. We have a handicraft class with a hundred students who learn sewing and various crafts. We have a dispensary.

"You should see the long queue of patients who come, often from far away. There have been up to six hundred in a single day. Now a hospital has been built close by, so we have fewer, but still two or three hundred a day. Sister Gertrude attends to them. They have a tremendous faith in her."

"She was one of the first to join Mother."

"Yes, the second, I think. She came from what is now Bangladesh. She is a doctor. She is very spiritual and has a wonderful way with the people. People come even from the communist part of Yemen to consult her."

"How are the officials? Do they help?"

"The prime minister is very sympathetic. He helps us in all ways. The government officials also. They built our house. They asked us to give them a plan of a Catholic church, as they did not know how it should be built. They wanted to put up a church for our use. But we told them that we would use a room of our house as a chapel. If we used a big building, some might take it as a provocation. Many people are still very anti-Christian.

"The prime minister and the officials send us supplies. Twice a week they send us a pair of goats, so that the children and poor people may have good meat. They help us in every way. We had to open a second house, and they ask for a third."

"Where are you established?"

"In Hodeida."

"Can you go to the communist part of Yemen?"

"People cross from one side to the other without difficulty. But we cannot go to Amman."

"What about the work among the lepers?"

"It is wonderfully successful. At first I was frightened to go to the leper village. Have you seen *Ben Hur*? It was just like that, as in the days of our Lord. We could hardly enter the village, because of the accumulated filth and rubbish blocking the way. We had to wade knee-deep through the filth. Then there were no houses. Only some sort of caverns cut out in the hills, into which people ran when they saw us approach. The women, completely covered by their *burkas*, hid themselves. Children ran for safety. The men were disheveled, the children filthy. We called and waved to them, but they would not come. Slowly Sister Gertrude succeeded in establishing a few contacts. Gradually the people became accustomed to us and showed friendliness.

"For me, to go through the filth to reach the village proved an awful experience. But we had to change the ways of life of these people. With the help of government officials, we cleared the way and removed the rubbish. Houses were built, gardens developed, flowers grown. We taught the women and children cleanliness, introduced some crafts for those able to work, to bring them respectability and make them feel useful."

"Do you manage to prevent the children from contracting the disease?"

"When we arrived, nearly all of them were affected. Now, mainly through cleanliness and by isolating some cases, we hope to be able to protect the children.

"But the village has completely changed. Within two years, from a filthy spot it has become a garden village. The children sing the whole time. It is a real joy to go there. They love us and sing for joy."

We remained silent for a while, thanking the Lord for the wonderful things he had deigned to do through his humble servants.

Seeing the spiritual results of their labors, the sisters felt truly enthusiastic about their vocation. They did not mention the hardships of life, the harsh climate, the difficulty of adapting oneself to a different tradition, culture, language, attitude to life.

They did it all for Jesus.

"Mother mentioned that a number of girls from the country wanted to join you; what do you do about it?"

"Yes. You know, their parents arrange their marriage with boys they have never met. Some of the girls do not like that. Then, after coming in contact with us and seeing our religious life, they want to live like us for God and for their neighbor. Several girls told their parents they would not marry, but would follow our way of life. They would become Christians if they could and enter religious life. But of course we have to be cautious, for there might be a strong reaction from the families, endangering our presence and work. So we let them come during the day and work with us. For the night we send them home. They prove most useful to us, for there is so much to do we could never achieve it alone. We are only five sisters."

"Do you have a priest to minister to you spiritually? I believe there are White Sisters and a couple of White Fathers."

"Yes, the White Sisters reached Yemen a little before us. They have opened a very good hospital. Now there is also a third congregation. Three White Fathers reside in the country; one, who is a doctor, works in the hospital. Now we have mass every day; we did not have mass daily at the beginning."

"Do you hope to return to Yemen at the end of this year of tertianship?"

"Most certainly. I long to be back there and work again among the lepers and hear the children sing and praise God."

INDIA: COIMBATORE

This is a town in South India, which developed in an orderly fashion, where some fifty middle-sized mills, most of them well laid out, give employment to the local people. The place looks prosperous and confident. The bishop says he is invited and welcomed everywhere, at every function organized by different groups. An open society, unbigoted, forward looking. Also, a center of excellent coffee plantations.

The Franciscan Missionaries of Mary, whose host I am, run three well-patronized high schools. Their very well kept orphanage is a model of devoted and efficient medical care. The diocesan congregation of sisters, fully active, also looks after the poor. This town does not seem to be a place where Mother Teresa's sisters are especially needed. Still, the bishop has invited them.

On the road I meet two sisters in blue-bordered saris.

"Father, you do not recognize us?"

"Of course, I do. Can I come to say mass for you?"

"Yes, the day after tomorrow. We shall come to fetch you."

Two sisters arrive at 6 A.M. We walk down the road.

"We shall take a bus. Let us wait here," proposes one of the sisters.

"But there is no bus stop," I object.

"Never mind," she replies. "The drivers all know us and they stop anywhere to take us."

And so it happens. A bus arrives, they wave to the driver. He stops to take us. He does not do this for anyone else on the way.

This makes me reflect: so these recently arrived sisters have already struck the mind of the non-Christian drivers. They are not from the district, do not speak the language fluently, have no big institution; yet already it is accepted: they are for us, they work for us. The sisters have established a personal relationship with these simple folk. They are closer to the people than other religious, who also spend their lives in work of charity.

"It is the same at the market," says the sister. "Everyone knows us and helps us."

We reach their house. In a veranda I see the emaciated faces of four people lying on cots or mats, each covered with a blanket.

"They are close to death," says a sister.

Against the chapel wall stands the crucifix, and the call of Jesus dying is written, "I thirst!" I offer a mass for the sisters and a few children. I also tell them of the work God deigned to do through Mother Teresa, and of his love the sisters must bring to the world.

After mass, a sister tells me: one of the old people has died during the mass.

We say a prayer, asking God to receive his soul in his love.

The sisters then explained how they were gradually settling down, evaluating needs, finding out the possibilities for action. One typical problem: water was not easily available in sufficient quantity. It rains only five or six days a year in the area. For the children and the dispensary, a good supply of fresh, clean water was absolutely needed and had to be found.

On my return to Calcutta, I told Mother that I had been to the new house at Coimbatore, and that this district gave many vocations to the church.

"Yes, Father, that is why we opened a house there," she answered.

Three years later one of the sisters I had met at Coimbatore could report that their hopes were being fulfilled.

Already five novices and ten postulants had come from the district, who would be able later to work in places where there were few or no Catholics.

INDIA: MARIAPOLLI

At the mother house, February 1976

"Mother, you are opening a house at Mariapolli?"

"Yes, Father. It is not a town and there are no slums, but to work in the villages is not against our constitutions."

She sounded apologetic.

"There are so many poor people in the area. We are also established at Takdah, which is not a town, and in Andhra Pradesh in some villages. We shall start with a dispensary; then see what the poor need most."

On the Feast of Our Lady, Mother accompanied the first batch of sisters to Mary's village, Mariapolli in Bengali. Father Gabric had three buildings ready for them in the new mission station he had just started. It was truly pioneering work. For the sisters a chapel, a dispensary, a convent built with bricks were ready. The priest would live in a mud hut, for the present.

There was a nice teak wood *almirah*.

"Will this be for our medicines?" asked the sister in charge.

"No, Sister," replied Father Gabric, "this is for your library of spiritual books, to protect them from the white ants."

Father Gabric, who hails from Yugoslavia, is a priest after Mother's heart. He is the kind of person to whom Mother can refuse nothing; spiritual, austere, dynamic, habitually on the move, always ready to give something, visiting the villages, knowing every one of his parishioners and all the officials of the region. He exhorts his Catholics to pray and fast. He is often seen moving about with his beads in his hand. This helped him when he called on a bishop in Australia.

"I went to visit a bishop in Australia," he recalled, "and as I entered the room he was addressing a clergy meeting. 'Look, Fathers,' he exclaimed, 'here is an old missionary from India who still believes in saying the rosary. See, he prays to our Lady even as he goes about.' After that the bishop was ready to sign any check to pay for my new mission station."

The sisters started by opening a dispensary which proved to be an immediate success. Two hundred patients attended it daily. After a few weeks there were five hundred, and on some days even close to one thousand. People said, "We come for the sisters' prayers more than for medicine."

Expansion goes on with increased momentum, in a cheerful, optimistic manner. The dynamic spirit of Pentecost continues to animate the Missionaries of Charity. New foundations were at first founded three a year, then five a year, and reached the number of twelve a year at the time of the Silver Jubilee.

"I wish to put seven or eight sisters in each house," confided Mother. "This helps to keep up a cheerful spirit. Variety is good; more work can also be taken up."

The new constitutions stipulate that each house should have at least six sisters. In practice the initial number may be reduced to five or even four sisters. Once needs have been estimated, activities can be diversified and expanded.

The geographical diffusion, helped by modern facilities, is probably unparalleled in the history of religious institutes. Starting from Calcutta, as their Jerusalem, the sisters went to five, ten, twenty different countries. They will soon be in fifty countries, and the novices who join now may one day be thrilled to count on the map one hundred countries where their society is at work for the glory of God. They will be happy, but not astonished; expansion is a fact of life for them. Often they have seen on the notice board: "Pray for our sisters who leave tomorrow to open a house in Peru, Tanzania, Trinidad, Papua, Fiji."

A year after the jubilee, even a book of five hundred pages could not describe adequately the genesis, preparation, establishment, and first developments of all the new foundations. The few mentioned here indicate the main areas of development and tell of a few typical foundations in which the sisters work, and show God's hand guiding the foundress and her sisters.

In October 1976 a large map of the world was placed at the foot of the crucifix standing in the staircase of the mother house, showing the various places where the members of the congregation work for the poorest of the poor. Mother's dream has been realized; her sisters form a chain of love for Christ and human beings, truly encircling the world.

CHAPTER 7

In His Footsteps

Take me for your model as I take Christ.
(St. Paul's advice to the Corinthians) (1 COR. 4:14)

FIRST WITNESS

"Sister Dorothy, you were one of the first to join Mother, you have known her well. What would you say is her main virtue? What struck you most in Mother's character?"

She answered unhesitatingly, "Her faith."

"Sister, I would say exactly the same. The rock on which she has built her institute and her whole organization is her faith in God. She is a woman of faith. She deserves the praise Elizabeth, moved by the Holy Spirit, bestowed on the Blessed Virgin Mary: 'Happy are you because you believed.' "

Like Abraham, the man of faith, Mother committed herself fully to God, accepted obedience to his order; sacrificed all she had, her religious congregation, her security, to put herself blindly in God's hands, not knowing what her fate would be. For her obedience in faith, God rewarded her as he promised to reward Abraham, saying, "Because you have done this, I will shower blessings on you, I will make your descendants as many as the stars of heaven and the grains of sand on the seashore" (Gen. 22:17).

Her posterity on earth will be great, her posterity in heaven will be innumerable: the sisters who came to her and all their spiritual children, those they helped "to die with God," the children and adults they taught to know and love God.

Mother's faith and trust in God were never found wanting, being always alive and active.

"I take our Lord at his word," she likes to say.

His word she finds in the gospel, which she respects and obeys as the inspired Word of God. "Our Lord said it" is for her a final argument. Thus she shows her faith in his person, his power, his concern for her. When Jesus said, "It is written," the argument was final; so Mother says, "Jesus said," and holds fast to his word.

SECOND WITNESS

"Father Van Exem, you have helped Mother from the very start; tell me, what struck you most in her?"

"Besides her littleness, her trust in God."

"Yes, the words of the Prophet Isaiah have proved fully true in her case: 'Those who trust in the Lord will renew their strength. They will soar as with eagles' wings' " (Isa. 40:31).

Her spiritual strength has gone on increasing with the years, while her physical forces were renewed in a remarkable manner, notwithstanding a hard life, repeated journeys on foot and by train, lack of sleep, fever, trials, the care of a thousand sisters.

Truly, she can say, "God has never let me down; my trust in him has never been misplaced."

Yes, God knows his own and takes good care of them.

Once as we were talking in the small parlor, I said, "Mother, you remember what our Lord told St. Catherine of Siena: 'Take care of me and I shall take care of you.' Well, you have taken good care of Jesus and he has taken good care of you."

"If it is for God's glory, Father, he will give us the means."

She practices perfectly the advice of Jesus in the Sermon on the Mount: "Do not fret and worry about tomorrow. Your Father knows what you need. If he feeds the sparrows, will he not much more willingly give you good things if you ask him for them?" Mother does not plan ahead; she allows God to guide her and show what he wants her to do.

Her littleness, her sense of nothingness, strikes all who approach her and work with her. Perhaps it can be said that it follows on her faith and trust in God. She echoes the great mystics speaking of God and themselves as "the double abyss": God's abyss of greatness, majesty, and power, the human abyss of littleness, misery, and weakness. By herself she can do nothing, but with him she has power. Power because she is his instrument. Her sense of being God's instrument is extremely acute. Repeatedly she has said quite spontaneously, "I am nothing. He is all. I do nothing of my own. He does it."

One day, in 1975, she took a small pencil, about five centimeters long and, holding it between her thumb and index finger, she said, "See, that is what I am, God's pencil. A tiny bit of pencil with which he writes what he likes."

THIRD WITNESS

"Brother Michael, you have seen Mother at close quarters, tell me what struck you most in her character?"

"Two things I found remarkable in her, first her activity, then her smallness. Her activity is amazing. While others talk, she works. While others put questions, she solves problems. She has a sense of the real, of the urgent. She sees a need and fills it on the spot. An extremely practical person, she can take trouble to get things done.

"Then her littleness. She feels so humble, so insignificant in the hand of God. That is why it does not trouble her to be continually in the news, as she is now. She returns the glory to our Lord. All the good she does she attributes to him."

Her activity, her dynamism are of an exceptional richness and intensity. All her projects started to fill a need she had found. A man dies before a hospital, on the street; she seeks and opens a house for the dying. She sees abandoned children; she starts her Sishu Bhavan. A colony of lepers is expropriated; she goes into leprosy work in a big way. There is a famine somewhere, there are refugees to be looked after; immediately she arrives there with her personnel. She has a scheme, a program; she organizes relief, begs for supplies, distributes help. Whether it be during the Bihar famine, the Bengal famine, the flight of nine or ten million refugees from Bangladesh, or later the earthquake in Guatemala, she is prepared to help. She must open a house in Papua because the people are very poor and the bishop has no money—never mind, she will find the means.

She trains boys of the slums to make very simple pieces of furniture and sell them in the market. The Calcutta streets are littered in places with green coconut shells; she will organize people to gather them and make ropes out of the fibers. She has heard of an organization that rehabilitates lepers, trains them for some useful work; she too will open a house for that purpose.

She works fast; she is ready in a matter of weeks or months, not the years that some other religious societies may take to discuss conditions before opening new houses.

Essentially active by temperament, Mother Teresa cannot understand the long sessions at meetings where nothing or little happens.

"I was at a meeting of superiors general in Europe," she said. "They talked only of changing the structures of society, organizing things in a different way. It all came to nothing; it did not do something for the poor, or preach Christ to those without religion, to those totally ignorant of God. I was happy when it was all over. They had insisted on my going there, but I felt like a fish out of water."

FOURTH WITNESS

Brother Andrew, on his return from Saigon, stopped at Hazaribagh to meet the Australian Jesuits. I asked him,

"Brother Andrew, you have worked several years with Mother Teresa. You were caught by her ideal, and you have successfully established the

Missionary Brothers of Charity. May I ask you what impressed you most in Mother, during your long association with her?"

He remained thoughtful for a while. Then he answered,

"I suppose it is her single-mindedness. She has only one purpose.

"Mother also has a sense of humor; I think people cannot be Catholic if they take themselves too seriously. We must be aware of our inadequacy, our weakness, our nothingness before God.

"Mother works hard," he continued. "She sleeps little. Not more than two or three hours each night. I think she goes on writing letters till one or two in the morning. She always gets up at half past four."

"Thank you, I shall remember that and try to imitate her single-mindedness. Yes, she has one idea, one consuming passion. When we talk it is usually of Jesus and of 'the work'; for her the work is all to the glory of her Lord; she cares for nothing else."

Spiritually Mother Teresa resembles St. Paul. Like Paul she is conscious of having been chosen by God the Father to work for the glory of Christ; to this end she founded her society.

She has St. Paul's passionate love for Christ and the gospel. Like him she is Christ-intoxicated, entirely surrendered to Jesus and completely taken over by him. With St. Paul she can affirm, "Christ lives in me." This presence of Christ acting in their souls has become for them a fact of experience. The truth, believed in faith, that by grace we become partakers of the divinity of Christ, who lives in the soul consecrated to him, has become a matter of experience.

"Christ acts in me; he acts through me; he inspires me, directs me as his instrument. I do nothing," Mother likes to repeat. "He does it all."

When she speaks to non-Christians, *he* means God; when to Catholics, *he* means Jesus, to us she usually says *Jesus*, more intimate, more personal than the word *Christ* and showing her attachment to the person of Jesus. She likes to repeat that all is due to God who acts through her, inspires and sustains her. Thus she accepts no credit for any good effected through her. With St. Paul, she can affirm without boasting, "I live no more of my own life; Christ lives in me." She knows it is not her weak frame, her limited capacity, that turned the little headmistress of an obscure high school into the superior general of a rapidly expanding religious congregation, and a world organizer of charitable works, hailed by the world press, praised by pope and bishops, presidents, and cabinet ministers.

Mother Teresa mirrors St. Paul in her faith, her reliance on God, her burning activity. She shares his zeal, fearlessness, restlessness. Both say, "Preach only Christ and Christ crucified"; both are ready to suffer with him for the progress of the church. Both are urged on by one thought and one passion: "Christ crucified and risen." As St. Paul says, "I rejoice in my suffering," so Mother asserts, "We are happy to do this work."

St. Paul's vision embraced the whole world; he wished to proclaim the gospel as far as possible. Mother from the start wished for a universal society that would work in every country, building a chain of love around the world. She has traveled more extensively than any religious founder ever before. She has opened houses in every continent, and sends her sisters to as many countries as possible.

St. Paul advises, "Treat everyone with equal kindness; never be condescending, but make real friends with the poor" (Rom. 12:16). Mother echoes: "The poor make us the honor of allowing us to serve them." Like St. Paul, Mother is shocked that Christ was not received by his own and is not received in the modern world. "When I see how the poor remain neglected and unrecognized all around us," she says, "I understand the sadness of Christ at not being accepted by his own. Today those who ignore or reject the poor, ignore or reject Christ."

When addressing the rich, Mother follows St. Paul's advice to Timothy: "Tell them that they are to do good, and be rich in good works, to be generous and willing to share—thus they will save up riches for the future if they want to make sure of the only real life" (Tim. 6:18–19). And to the poor she says, "Be satisfied with your condition, seek the better things, those that do not perish, are not eaten by moth or by rust, seek the kingdom of God."

To those completely surrendered to him, Christ sends his Spirit in abundance; and the divine Spirit, says St. Paul, brings them: "love, joy, peace, patience, goodness, trustfulness, gentleness and self-control." (Col. 5:22). What a shower of wonderful gifts the Holy Spirit brings us. Love for God and human beings; true divine love animates those in whom the Spirit of love dwells. From love, joy blossoms as God, perfect bliss, brings joy to the soul in which he lives. Peace and harmony follow—we are united to God and friendly to all people. Joy and peace produce serenity, confidence that all God does is well done and that what he sends is for our greater good; as Mother tells her sisters: "Be happy, God loves you, especially when the work you do for him is hard."

Gentleness should lie in our relations with others, seeing in all of them God's image; kindness to all, treating them as we would Christ.

This requires self-control, since the spirit of Christ is opposed to the spirit of the world. And so St. Paul adds, "You cannot belong to Christ unless you crucify all self-indulgent passions and desires" (Col. 5:24). *Crucify*—a harsh word: nail to the cross your selfishness, your vanity, your sensuality.

I found Mother habitually smiling, kind and increasingly serene, as the years went by. The Spirit at times pours spiritual joy in her soul. She has paid, she still pays the price of the souls she wants to save with Christ. The Spirit pours love, joy, and peace into our hearts proportionately to our emptying ourselves of all self-indulgence, vanity, anger, and ambition, and to our willingness to shoulder the cross of Christ. This is the price we must pay for spiritual happiness.

The Eucharist is the center of the spiritual life of the Missionaries of Charity. The Eucharist as sacrifice, as food, as presence. In the Eucharist the sisters find the strength, the inspiration and consolation that make their life both possible and meaningful.

With Christ they offer themselves as victims of the sacrifice of redemption to glorify God the Father. In Christ, received as a spiritual food, they find the strength to devote themselves unceasingly to all sufferers. To Christ, present in their midst, they come for advice, light, consolation. They keep him company in his dereliction, quench his thirst for love.

The cross of Christ and the words "I thirst" face the sisters as they enter the chapel—Jesus calls them, asks for their love, their service, their attention. They go down on their knees to adore him, and then stay with their Lord, whether they are consoled or not; often they will feel like dry, parched land; they will suffer, as their Lord did at Gethsemane or on Calvary. "I thirst," says Jesus, and they understand his pleading: if they do not allay their beloved Lord's thirst, who will?

He is the master, the Lord, the friend, the bridegroom, the divine spouse to whom every one of them belongs body and soul.

They start the day by coming to the chapel for morning prayers, followed by meditation and Holy Mass. In the afternoon, the sisters remain a whole hour in adoration of the Blessed Sacrament.

"I have no difficulty in believing in the real Presence of our Lord in the Blessed Eucharist," said Mother.

"Neither do most priests have any difficulty in that respect, Mother. What really tests our faith is the slow progress of the faith in Christ, the slow progress of his church, the huge amount of sin and unbelief that remains in the world after nineteen centuries of redemptive grace, of the presence of Christ, of the heroic holiness of countless saints."

Christ affirmed that he was present in the Eucharist when he said, "Take and eat, this is my body that will be given up for you; take and drink of this chalice of my Blood that will be shed for you; do this in memory of me."

The fathers of the church unanimously teach the reality of the presence of Christ. The Council of Trent declares most forcefully, "Christ is present truly, really and substantially in the Eucharist."

"Why then," asked Mother, "do some young priests shake the belief of our people by saying that, after the Mass, there is no real Presence in the tabernacle? What do they teach them in some seminaries, nowadays? A newly ordained priest was sent here to give an instruction to the sisters. I was present. The priest laughed at a number of our traditional beliefs; he said there was no need to genuflect before the Blessed Sacrament when you come to the chapel outside the time of Mass, for the presence of Christ was limited to the time of Mass and Communion. He also attacked the idea of religious obedience and ridiculed our traditional devotions. He spoke in that vein for a whole hour. When he had finished I led him to the door, thanked him, and told him he need not come here any more.

"Then I returned to the hall and told the sisters: 'You have just heard what a young priest without experience said; they are his ideas and those of a small group. Now I shall tell you what is the traditional teaching of the church.' And for one hour I refuted all he had said."

"Mother, you did well. The Second Vatican Council reiterated the Christian belief, both Catholic and Orthodox, that Christ remains present under the Eucharistic Species after the Mass, and that Christians should worship him and visit their Lord present in the Eucharist in our churches and chapels."

Mother firmly believes in the teaching of the church, as entrusted by Jesus Christ to the supreme magisterium: the pope, and the bishops united to him.

She obeys the precept of St. Paul, who said, "You must live your whole life according to the Christ you have received—Jesus the Lord; you must be rooted in him and built on him and held firm by the faith you have been taught, and full of thanksgiving. Make sure that no one traps you and deprives you of your freedom by some second-hand, empty, rational philosophy based on the principles of this world instead of on Christ" (Col. 2:6–8).

Mother strongly believes that the sacraments give us God's grace. They also indicate the proximity of Christ, who today acts in the world. The Gospel of St. John, "the spiritual gospel," advocates worship in spirit and truth, giving little importance to structures and external rites, yet proves to be the most "sacramental" of the four gospels. Similarly, Mother's independent outlook and her dislike for structures do not affect her belief in the efficacy of the sacraments instituted by Christ, nor her desire that as many as possible be helped to receive them.

This conviction fits in perfectly with her strong sense of instrumentality. We are God's instruments of sanctification for our brothers, while the sacraments give grace, instruments used by Christ. She has also a peasant's respect for nature and matter, which makes it easy for her to accept the signs established by Christ as signs of grace that all people can understand.

Mother strongly believes in the need for and efficacy of baptism; Christ told the apostles, "Go and baptize in the name of the Father and of the Son and of the Holy Spirit." For anyone who believes in God and his dispensation, baptism is neither a luxury nor an optional practice.

"Father," she said, "I believe in the need for and efficacy of baptism. Some priests, imbued with modern ideas, tell me I am wrong; I answer them, 'Let's not argue. You will not convince me and I shall not convince you.' So we shall continue to baptize those who want to receive that sacrament.

"Our best helpers," she often says, "are all the baptized poor who died and went straight to Heaven. Our best helpers are the forty thousand inmates of our homes for the dying who 'died with God' after making an act of perfect love for him, surrendering fully to his holy will. They now pray for us and for our work; that is what brings so much grace to our apostolate.

"In Latin America many people have not seen a priest for several years, and so they ask the sisters to baptize their young children; what a cause of happiness for the sisters."

Mother recalls with joy that tens of thousand Catholic children belonging to poor families have been prepared by the sisters for their first confession and first communion. They received their Lord in their simple and pure hearts. Some may not persevere in the practice of the faith, but at least they have received the good Lord in their childhood and that grace will always remain with them.

The new constitutions stipulate, "We take special care of the older children. We do our utmost to find out those who have not received the sacraments and instruct them without delay." Thus they will be prepared to receive the sacraments of penance and the Eucharist; also baptism and confirmation if they have not received them.

Mother and her sisters rejoice in seeing many marriages regularised and celebrated according to the rite of the church. In Latin America especially, the sisters have helped to sanctify thousands of unions of people who had not sought out or perhaps not found a priest to bless their union.

In one simple ceremony, said Mother, thirty marriages were celebrated by a sister. In one case three successive generations received the grace of the sacrament of matrimony together, grandparents, parents, and their children, a young couple.

Mother narrated with real happiness, "In Rome, the sisters are doing a wonderful job. They visit the houses of the poor; they wash and sweep, tidy, mend, and cook for those unable to do so. They found an old man who must have been well off in earlier days. He lived all alone. As he was sick, the sisters did all the work for him. One day he told them, 'Sisters, you have brought God here; now, bring the priest also.' They brought a priest who heard his confession. The old man had not confessed his sins for sixty years. The next day he died in the peace of the Lord."

Mother added, "I told this story in the United States at a meeting they had asked me to address. After the meeting a priest came to me and said, 'I had decided to leave the priesthood and sent my letter of resignation to my Bishop. After hearing what you said, I shall cancel my resignation and remain at the service of souls as a priest of Christ.' "

God's merciful ways proved too beautiful for words; we both kept quiet; this was truly the beginning of the joy of heaven: to behold God's splendor in his own light while bathing in his love. Mother's trust in God's divine providence never falters. Twice or thrice, with fifteen years' interval in between, Mother described her attitude regarding money problems in exactly the same words.

"Money, Father, I never think of it. It always comes. The Lord sends it. We do his work; he provides the means. If he does not give us the means, that shows that he does not want the work. So why worry?"

When Mr. Thomas, the chairman of Hindustan Lever, came to see Mother Teresa, to offer her a property in Bombay, he first asked her, "Mother, how is your work financed?"

She answered him very gently: "Mr. Thomas, who sent you here?"

"I felt an urge inside me. . . ."

"Well, other people like you come to see me and say the same; that is my budget."

It was clear: God sent you, Mr. Thomas, as he sends Mr. X., Mrs. Y., Miss Z., and they provide the material means we need for our work. The grace of God is what moved you. God sees to our needs, as Jesus promised.

Her trust is as complete as ever. But it requires less of a foundation of faith, of belief in the words of Christ, than it did at the beginning. Faith was more needed, faith, namely belief in unseen things, as hope is the expectation of things not yet possessed, was more needed in the first dark years. After twenty-five years of the institute, God's protection and help had become a thing of experience, a fact of life. It astonished no more, since it was always there. But it continued to warm and comfort the heart, while it called for never-ending gratitude. Mother could not possibly budget; that is, put down on paper her receipts and her spending for the year in advance. She could not foresee how many Mr. Thomases would appear during the year. It was God's secret.

The Missionaries of Charity had benefited from the fact that some multinational companies had disposed of their unwanted properties. These had shown the way to other companies. In Calcutta, there was the Prem Dan of I.C.I., in Bombay there was the Asha Dan of Hindustan Lever. Mother called them respectively Gift of Love and Gift of Hope. Another company might provide later a Viswas Dan, a Gift of Faith; then the three theological virtues would be represented. And one could foresee a gift of grace, a gift of joy, a gift of friendship. As needs arose, God would move the donors interiorly. They would be the first beneficiaries of the gifts they made to God, by entrusting them to the sisters.

Mother has sparked many acts of generosity. Various organizations collect for her works. People want to donate.

"Where does Mother Teresa live?" people have asked me several times after church service, or by telephone, or even on the street. "I want to donate some money. How can I meet her?"

Of course, there may be the pleasant feeling of sharing in a noble enterprise, of taking part in a great adventure. One jumps on the band-wagon of a true pioneer of a new era of practical charity. One enters into partnership with "a living saint."

Mother is not affected by this psychology. If it helps the cause of God and the welfare of the poor, good. But she considers before all the spiritual value of the act of giving.

"I hope you are not giving of your surplus," she tells a group of rich businessmen who offer her a purse at the end of an excellent dinner. "You must give what costs you, make a sacrifice, go without something you like, that your gift may have value before God; then you will be truly brothers to the poor who are deprived of even the things they need."

The value of the act before God, not the amount of money given her, that is her main concern. As a girl sodalist, she learned to make sacrifices for the missions, for the cause of Christ; to go without a meal, to do without sweets or a new dress. She had taught her Bengali pupils at St. Mary's High School the same: forgo a picture, an outing, a meal, and give the money to the poor. They did it, trained in self-giving until it hurts, and thus they were prepared to assume the hardships of religious life on a permanent basis, to love without limit the Lord Jesus and to take up the cross with him.

Money did not matter much; still, as good administrators of God's property, as stewards of God's gifts, they had to be faithful. People who sent donations to the Missionaries of Charity knew that everything would be spent on the welfare of the poor.

At times it was the donors who were not sufficiently prudent.

"They steal my checks," Mother complained.

"Yes, such things happen. Foreign checks, sent by post, are stolen and cashed in Hong Kong or in the Middle East. Have you lost many in that way?"

"I have informed my benefactors to send money only through bank drafts. But they do not always take this precaution."

It was found that at least one hundred and fifty thousand rupees had been stolen from her; a man had even opened an account in her name and was signing for her in a bank located in Calcutta. But that fraud was discovered by the Security Department and the racket was stopped.

Money comes in from everywhere. Nineteen thousand pounds after the B.B.C. program in 1975. The different prizes and awards were spent immediately on new foundations.

New foundations were started without debt, were paid for even before they were occupied. Benefactors have shown themselves extremely gen-erous.

"We are opening a house at Nagpur," says Mother. "This is a town of a million inhabitants, with many cotton mills. The children's home and the house for the sisters are paid for by an Australian friend, fifty thousand in his currency. How many rupees does that make?"

"Five hundred and fifty thousand rupees, Mother."

"Well, that is too much; the buildings cost only four hundred and fifty thousand rupees. May we use the rest of the money for another foundation, where the bishop is very poor?"

At times the inviting bishop provides the property and buildings. At times the government makes all the arrangements. In Orissa, India, the chief minister, Mrs. Satpathi, complained "Why do you neglect our state, have you anything against us?" And soon the Missionaries of Charity opened a house there.

Once, on the feast day of St. Teresa of Avila, as I wished Mother a happy feast, she laughed: "I am not the great Teresa, I am the little Thérèse," she said. "She is my patron."

"No," I retorted, "you are not the little Thérèse, who called herself 'the plaything of Jesus, the football of Jesus,' you are not the charming little saint, who never left the four walls of her convent and died courageously at the age of twenty-four. You are Mother Teresa, a follower of the great Saint of Avila, always ready to go out to start new foundations. For your sisters you are Mother; for us priests you are La Madre: a woman with an iron will, dynamic and efficient."

Spiritually, Mother is not a Carmelite. She follows St. Francis, the poor man of Assisi, and also St. Vincent de Paul.

"In the plane from Madras to Calcutta," she recalled, "I spoke of God to my neighbor, a gentleman I had never met. It was just like meditating for the two hours of the journey."

According to Indian spiritual usage, holy people, when traveling, usually keep quiet to apply themselves to the contemplation of the divine Presence. Everyone respects this silence and communion with God. Nor is there a better way to remind ordinary folk of the divine reality to whom we are all going, whom some know to be close to themselves. But for St. Francis, the joy of loving God and being loved by him deserved to be told to the neighboring traveler, who otherwise might remain ignorant of it. So, when you travel, make your choice, edify by your words, or by your silence. But I know what I would recommend to the young nuns who have not yet reached the sphere of perfect detachment from earthly things. To imitate the perfect joy of St. Francis in complete surrender to God and full trust in his divine majesty, such is the program of life Mother proposes to her sisters.

Her spirituality owes much to St. Francis. She emulates him in the cult and practice of evangelical poverty, the love of the cross and the suffering savior, as also in obedience to God's guidance expressed in the Scriptures. Like him she adopts a simple, unsophisticated approach to life and its problems.

Every day the sisters recite St. Francis's prayer, to obtain from God kindness, gentleness, devotion, love, and joy. They pray "Lord, make me an instrument of your peace." The prayer fits in with Mother's idea of instrumentality. We are just "God's pencil" to write in people's hearts what he wants. Like the Lord's Prayer, this prayer has the advantage that it can be said by all believers in God to whatever religion or denomination they belong; they can pray it together, making a ring of love around the world. It provides those who say it with a complete program of life.

The kind of works the sisters perform and their style of life also recall to mind the Daughters of Charity of St. Vincent de Paul and St. Louise de Marillac. Vincent de Paul wished his Daughters to visit the poor in their houses, at a time when most nuns were restricted to their enclosure and worked in their convents. He sent out his Daughters of Charity to nurse the poor and sick at home, carry food to the hungry, take care of orphans. They dressed at first like French peasant women, and lived poorly and austerely.

At times, Mother looked rather sad. Several times she remarked, "Father, we do so little. They praise us for our actions, but what we do is not more than a drop of water in the ocean. It hardly affects the immensity of human suffering."

"You are right, Mother, but we are not divine providence. You do all you can with the means and the personnel at your disposal. God does not ask you to do more."

Indeed, the magnitude of human problems in several Asian countries might discourage, if not appall. The sisters may work in twenty Calcutta slums, but an official estimate speaks of three thousand slums in Calcutta. Then there are at least a hundred thousand pavement dwellers. If the sisters reach one hundred thousand lepers, there are another two million in the country, and also two million blind people; and, according to an official declaration of May 1976, three-quarters of a million regular beggars and vagrants.

Still, the work of the sisters amounts to much. The sisters work, the Co-Workers are active, and a stimulus has been given to the cause of charity all over the world among the millions who read or heard about the Missionaries of Charity. We have all become better for hearing of Mother and her sisters' and brothers' love and devotion.

Again, Mother remarked, "Father, our work among the slum children seems hopeless. When we succeed in educating a child, the child goes to live in better surroundings and the slum people remain without any leader able to uplift them."

On another occasion, Mother said somewhat sadly, "Father, I do not build the church."

"No, Mother, perhaps not, but you are its best advertisement. You show the charity of Christ to all who come into contact with your institutions. And you have brought many children and adults to know Christ and receive the sacraments they otherwise would not have received."

"You see," she said, "we may not preach Christ as we would like to, because we receive help from the government and from various agencies. So our hands are tied. You may preach because you receive no help from anybody. A government official told me, 'Tell the truth, you would like me to become a Christian, you are praying for that?' I answered him, 'When you possess something really good, you wish your friends to share it with you. Now, I think that Christ is the best thing in the world and I would like all to know him and love him as I do. But faith in Christ is a gift of God, who gives it to whom he likes.' The gentleman went away satisfied."

Mother has ever been a woman of action, indefatigable, always practical, concrete, quick to decide and implement her decisions. She brooks no delays, believes in today—yesterday, she says, is past, tomorrow is not under our control, it may never come, we have only today to be up and doing, to work for the glory of God.

She is a dynamo, an energizer, getting everybody to work. While Mother is discussing matters of property with a government official, a sister comes in and interrupts: "An American tourist wants to see you; he is the person who came the other day."

"Tell him to go and work in Kalighat."

"But he says he went there yesterday."

"Yes, he can go again today; the poor are still there."

Another day I tell Mother, "A lady would like to meet you."

"No need. She can go and help. What can she do?"

"Well she runs a restaurant. I suppose she knows about catering."

"We have no need of a caterer. Our meals are simple. Tell her to go and help at the dispensary. How many days a week can she spare?"

"I shall ask her."

Many years ago Mother suggested, "Father, you should write a book of meditations for my nuns."

"No, Mother," I replied, "I cannot do it. I am not good enough."

Some years later, she comes charging in again, "Father, write a book of meditations for the sisters. There are so few books of meditations adapted to the spiritual needs of the sisters."

"Mother, I cannot do it."

Again, a few years later: "Father, what about the book of meditations I asked you to write?"

"All right, Mother, I shall try."

When my publisher a little later made the same request, "No," I said. "I cannot do it."

But a week later I started writing meditations on the Gospel of St. John. Inspiration came, and during a whole year I worked on this book—it was sheer delight. When the book was published, I sent one of the first copies to Mother.

She phoned me up a few days later: "Father, thank you for writing *Remain in My Love.* I use the book every day." I was repaid for all my efforts.

Mother's spiritual outlook has naturally progressed since the inception of her congregation. Those of her generation who have remained in touch with her have noticed how her spirituality evolved during these thirty years, which was to be expected. She progressed in her understanding of the faith, of the ways of God's providence.

In Mother, with the passing of time and prayer, work, self-sacrifice, and a continual outpouring of love, the fruit of the Spirit has ripened and mellowed. In many of us, with age, as our physical arteries become sclerosed, so do our spiritual arteries. But this does not happen to those fully open to God's grace. The sap of divine life renews the arteries, and the fruit of kindness becomes more fragrant and delicious.

Mother's faith and trust increased during the years; they gained in strength, naturalness, spontaneity, surfacing easily in conversation. Ingrained in the soul, they showed the reality of God's protection, his love always present.

At the Kalighat Home for the Dying, as a visitor wondered at the peace reigning in the last resthouse for the poor before their final departure, Mother said simply, "God is here." A concise, terse, perfect summing up of the situation. In earlier years she would have given a more elaborate explanation; now one word suffices: "God" present, active, loving. In all matters, life's pattern appears simpler to her in God's increasingly stronger light.

Mother sees God active in these people as he prepares them for an eternity of happiness with him. The ugliness of poverty and misery recedes into the background, as God's hand comes forward to receive his children whom the sisters help to "die with God."

Serenity increases with age. Looking at the world from a greater height, we discover things those closer to earth cannot behold. We see how events fall in place to fit in God's plan; we realize that God is powerful enough to bring good even out of evil, if we let him do so. All serves to lead us to God, especially our sufferings, if we love him. Suffering unites us to Christ, renders us similar to him, brings merits, obtains grace.

Seen in the light of eternity, poverty, hunger, and sickness shed their ugliness; they are seen as means helping us to reach God. Only sin is to be shunned—a worse evil than all the human suffering not caused by humans. But to lighten the human burden on earth remains a sacred duty —to imitate the compassion of Christ for the multitudes who were as sheep without a shepherd, waiting to be led to good pastures.

Mother now would perhaps no more regret: "We do so little; we do not build the church, our action is like a drop of water in the ocean." She appreciates fully the sisters' call to collaborate with God, to serve him in the poor, in a simple, humble way.

"Father, this is wonderful. . . ." Often she repeats this word of praise of the Lord God who guides her. "Wonderful" is the qualification she uses most frequently when relating some event or mentioning a favor received from God. In the spirit of St. Luke's Gospel, she extols God's goodness, his providence caring for his children, the grace and happiness of knowing and serving Christ.

"They went away praising God" is Luke's usual comment after narrating a miracle of Jesus. The ways of God really are wonderful; all spiritual people discover the divine guidance in the events of their lives.

"How good God is," Mother likes to say. "His guiding hand is here." It is. This renders her habitually optimistic.

Coming daily in contact with physical and mental suffering, with misery, injustice, trampled-down human dignity, she suffers from it, and tries to remedy the situation in a practical manner. But she also sees all the good there is in the world: devotion, service, love, sharing, compassion, mercy, acceptance, gratitude, goodwill.

Camus, author of *The Plague*, though an agnostic, thought that in the world the sum total of goodness exceeds that of evil. He could not give a reason for his belief. But a believer in God's providence and a disciple of Christ our Savior can explain why it is so.

CHAPTER 8

Sharing His Cross

Follow Christ by loving as he loved you, giving himself up in our
place as a fragrant offering and a sacrifice to God.

(EPH. 5:2)

Mother knows suffering. She has shared in the cross of Christ. Like every
loving soul, she would not wish it to be otherwise. "We always find," says
St. Teresa of Avila, who knew by personal experience, "that those who
are closest to Jesus have most to suffer."

Mother puts before her nuns this ideal: to quench the thirst of Jesus
crucified for souls. To do this they should be ready to suffer with Christ
and even wish to be similar to him and to suffer for the redemption of
souls.

"The wounds I bear in my body are those of Christ," writes Paul;
indeed, they are the wounds he suffered because he belonged to Christ.
The sisters, when they enter the chapel for their morning prayers, see the
picture of the crucified Savior, calling to them, "I thirst." They will soon
receive in communion the victim of the sacrifice, who will give them
strength to serve him in the poor and suffering.

With Jesus, they are to bring the world back to God our Father. This
call brings them joy as they ponder Paul's words expressing the mystery
of Christian love: "It makes me happy to suffer for you, as I am suffering
now, and in my own body to do what I can do to make up all that is lacking
from the suffering of Christ for the sake of His body, the Church" (Col.
1:24). In this process of redemption, as in everything connected with our
existence and well-being, God wants our collaboration. We are to be his
active instruments, sharing in his work.

Mother knows suffering. How could she have true compassion without
a sharing of experience, a "symbiosis," between those she cares for and
herself? The sick understand the sick; the bereaved, those who lose a
loved one.

Mother has known fatigue, hard work, tiring walks, long waits; she has
traveled in crowded trams and buses, she has sat up whole nights in cheap
compartments; she has eaten rough food, and squatted on the floor with
the poor in unfurnished dwellings.

"God made me a great gift: good health," Mother told me. She has the hands of a peasant woman: strong, active, energetic, working and praying hands. She looks frail, increasingly so, as the years go by, but she is a bundle of energy. Her power comes from above: Christ is her spiritual powerhouse.

Like Paul, she can be compared to an athlete perpetually in training, wishing to obtain the crown. With him she can say, "I treat my body hard and make it obey me" (1 Cor. 9:27). Up at four-thirty every morning, she soon comes to the chapel for prayer. She goes to sleep late at night or even in the early morning. Sister Fabienne, who lives in the mother house, tells me, "She works habitually till midnight or one in the morning."

I always saw her sitting on the edge of her chair, her back erect, even when dog-tired, even when visibly feverish. When she is sick, it is difficult to get Mother to take some rest, still more so to keep her in bed. At times, Sister Agnes or a doctor has succeeded in forcing her to rest a little.

"I cannot ask Mother to come down today," Sister Agnes said one day. "She is not well. If I told her you were here, she would come down the two floors from her room and then climb up again. People come the whole day to see her. I must keep them away."

"You are right, Sister Agnes. Look after Mother, protect her, give her the short rest she badly needs."

She usually travels by train, in the lower class; she enjoys a free pass on the Indian railways, granted her by the railway minister. To spare her much time and fatigue, Indira Gandhi gave Mother a free pass for the Indian airlines, in 1973. She can thus travel to all the important towns in India by plane.

TRIALS

Mother was deeply affected when some of the sisters she had patiently formed and led to Jesus decided to leave the congregation. Years ago, when she was asked, "Do you lose many sisters?" she replied, "Very few. In fact you could count those who have left on the fingers of a single hand, and you would not even need all the fingers." It is thus no more. With the considerable increase in number of the sisters, it must be expected that more will leave the congregation.

"Do you lose many sisters?" I asked Mother after the jubilee.

"No," she answered, "not many. Last year three left. The superior of one of our houses went away with the parish priest who was the spiritual director of the convent. I went to see the archbishop of the place, who told me he knew this priest had his own ways. I answered him, 'Your Grace, if you knew he was not reliable, why did you put him in charge of our sisters?' "

But, if Adam proved weak, Eve was not altogether blameless. She had been advised not to go alone to the parish house in the evenings. As the superior, she had not listened to her sisters.

A senior sister gave me a more complete picture of the losses the congregation had sustained during the previous year. "Three sisters," she said, "left after their final profession. Nine more sisters left after their first profession." These were free to leave at the expiration of the period for which they had bound themselves by vows. "Danger," added this sister, "comes from priests, drivers, lepers, and co-workers. One sister left to marry a leper she had attended to; another left to marry the driver of the community's van; still another left with a co-worker who had come to help us."

After the jubilee, Mother suffered a hard blow when a sister in London who had been one of the pillars of the congregation expressed the intention of leaving. Mother was so distressed that she took the plane for London when she heard that this sister, a trusted and efficient helper on whom she had much relied, had decided to leave the congregation—perhaps on account of ill health. Mother tried to make her change her mind, but failed. Her magnetic power did not work. There remained only to thank God for the good effected through this sister, and to pray for the spiritual well-being of those who had left the congregation, as the constitutions recommend in Mother's own words: "Pray for all those who have been in the society that God may protect them and keep them in his love."

"We remain very human; we have our ups and downs," Mother confessed several times.

"Yes, Mother, they keep us humble and make us feel the need of God's grace."

Mother feels intense pain and immense sorrow when people who have committed themselves for life prove unfaithful to God's call and to their promise to live with Christ and to die for him.

"How is it," she asked, "that nowadays all over the world so many priests and nuns abandon their calling? Were they not chosen by Christ? Did they not commit themselves to follow him after long and mature reflection? How then can a nun pronounce perpetual vows, and some years later give up the religious life? Are married people not bound to remain faithful to each other until death? Then why should the same rule not apply to priests and nuns?"

Mother suffers for her Lord, who is treated as an unwanted person while his love is despised. Yes, someone will have to offer him reparation for the faithlessness of those he had favored with his call and his love, and who turned away after first following him.

Mother has personally experienced that the Lord purifies us interiorly, in a subtle manner, depriving us of all spiritual consolations. Every loving soul must expect at times to be tried and deprived of all sensible consolation, of every feeling of God's sacred presence, as it is made to pass through the tunnel of the dark night.

In that *noche oscura*, as St. John of the Cross calls it, that Dark Night known by all mystics and by many others, the marriage between God and the soul is being prepared.

Then those who out of a passionate love for God have left everything for him—or perhaps not yet everything, since He asks still more from them—are heard to complain, "I have no faith; I work without faith, without feeling. Do I still believe? I see nothing." They suffer with Christ in the garden, with Christ on the cross, sharing his apparent abandon by his Father, and exclaim, "My God, my God, why have you abandoned me?"

To his chosen disciples Jesus says at some stage of life, "From now on you must keep constantly before your mind: the Son of man is to suffer. . . ." And with him they set their face determinedly toward Jerusalem. Their pace does not slacken, their faith in him does not weaken, as they show him their love by sharing in the great act of redemption.

That grief and pain will also give way to the joy and serenity of the Resurrection. Then perhaps, right at the end, or close to the end of the road, the Lord will make the soul pass through a final purification.

SETBACKS

The Missionaries of Charity have experienced a few failures, which is all to the good. Mother certainly thanks the good Lord for them. Failures render us more similar to our Blessed Lord, who failed with Judas; failed with the rich young man he invited to walk in his footsteps; failed to attract and convert most of the priests and Pharisees of his nation. We should also experience that aspect of our master's life: his disappointment at the treatment meted out to God's prophets and even to his chosen one. Still, the failures of the Missionaries of Charity have been remarkably few.

There was Simla. The sisters opened a house in that hill station. They came from the hot plains. The hills were very cold in the winter; their clothing and style of life were not adapted to cold days and nights. There being few Catholics in the area, the opportunities for spiritual work were slender. The sisters lost heart, found their work useless, and left the place. Yet they remained at Darjeeling, which has a similar cold climate in the winter, and flourished there; they went to Takda, as cold as Darjeeling, and more isolated. Such disappointments may depend on the grit, determination, spirit of penance, enterprise, and enthusiasm of the first group.

Then there was Colombo. When Mother told me that the sisters had been invited to Sri Lanka, I asked her, "Why is it that other foreign religious have been asked to leave, whereas you are invited by the prime minister to open a house?" Mother answered, "Ah, that is because we do what others don't do." But later the Missionaries of Charity were also asked to leave, and they returned to India.

Belfast proved a more humiliating failure. Mother took four sisters there to open a house in 1972. The place offered a challenge: Protestants oppressed the Catholic minority, economically weak. Hatred was preached even from the church pulpits. Some Catholics in desperation retaliated with acts of terrorism. Mother was told, here is a place for you, go and practise Catholic charity in Ulster; try to unite Protestants and Catholics through deeds of charity. Mother took up the challenge, in the spirit of St. Francis going to the Holy Land occupied by the Moslems. Francis did get away with it, but the friars he sent a little later were soon despatched to enjoy the Beatific Vision in heaven. Their time of trial on earth ended with martyrdom.

The Missionaries of Charity did not die martyrs in Ulster, which would have covered them with glory and might have awakened world opinion. The Indian sisters in their saris had to pack and go home; they were not wanted.

What happened at Ranchi sounds less believable. As Mother arrived with some sisters to open a new house, she was met with cries of "Go back, Mother Teresa!"; she found a barricade erected on the road to prevent her going farther. Mother tried to argue, but in vain. The people were determined not to allow her to occupy the land bought for her new foundation. Mother told them "By refusing entrance to the sisters, you refuse entrance to God." But this proved of no avail, and they had to turn back.

This was due to a misunderstanding, but also to a wrong choice of location. When doing good to the poor, we should respect the local people's interest and susceptibilities. Rumor had it that the new foundation was to be a home for lepers. The sisters said it was not. It would be a house for the old and destitute. But the local people, who had built decent houses with their savings, feared that a home for the destitute would diminish the value of their properties and spoil the name of the locality.

A peaceful solution was found; the children's home established in another part of the town was shifted to the new property and the home for the dying destitute was moved to the former children's home.

Mother suffered a personal failure when she tried to settle a quarrel between the laity, some priests, and the hierarchy. At Cuttack, Mother went to speak to the Catholics who opposed the appointment of a bishop; she spoke of the love of God, of faithfulness to mother church, of our duties as Catholics, and of obedience to our Lord, and they said they would stop their protest. The peace lasted a few days. Mother went back to her other duties, and soon the fight broke out again.

All this, and a little more, does not add up to much in the way of failures. Other religious founders have known much greater disappointments than this.

OTHER PROBLEMS

Like St. Paul, Mother experienced some trials on her journeys. One memorable incident happened on a hill road. A terrible landslide had shocked Darjeeling, affecting a whole section of this hill station; the whole of Bhutia Basti had been destroyed, scores of houses had collapsed; some people had died, and others, many of them, had been rendered homeless. It was the beginning of the monsoon, and heavy rains had caused large chunks of earth to run down into the valley.

As soon as she heard of the plight of the people, Mother Teresa was on her way to Darjeeling to organize relief operations.

Then an accident happened. "We were in the jeep," recalled Bishop Eric Benjamin, "the driver, myself, and Mother Teresa, sitting on the front seats, and traveling on the old military road—for the regular road was blocked by several landslides. Suddenly, at a bend of the road, we were met by a lorry, and there was a head-on collision. The driver and myself, seeing the lorry come straight on us, steadied ourselves in order not to fall forward, and we escaped injury. Mother Teresa fell forward, her head went violently against a steel fixture attached to the windshield, and she was badly cut. I noticed that she was bleeding under the sari that covered her head. She said it was nothing. But we returned immediately to Darjeeling, and I took her to the Planters' Hospital, where the doctor attended to her and put in nineteen stitches. Had the wound been a little lower, she would have lost an eye.

"That very evening Indira Gandhi, who was in Darjeeling, hearing of Mother's accident, called on her at the hospital to express her sympathy and to convey her good wishes for a speedy recovery."

A few days later Mother was back in Calcutta. When I met her at the mother house, she still appeared bruised and shaken. She smiled and said only, "I am all right, Father."

The sisters also encountered dangerous animals. Dogs were not always friendly: A sister at Raipur was bitten by an unknown small dog. She did not take the injections against rabies. For several weeks nothing happened to her. Then one day she was attacked by the dreaded disease. When she was brought to a Pasteur Institute and received antirabies injections, it was too late. She died; the Lord rest her soul and reward her for her good works.

At the mother house there was a terrible animal, a barker and a biter, aptly nicknamed by the sisters *Kala Shaitan,* Black Devil. It was as fierce as a dog can be. It disturbed the classes and the study. While I spoke on the Gospel of St. John, the Black Devil barked so loudly from its lair next to the hall that I repeatedly had to interrupt my instruction. One day, as I was leaving, it tried desperately to bite me, but I managed to escape its threatening jaws. A little later, it broke its chain and attacked Sister Camillus, whom it bit in the leg, the arm, and two other places. It had previously bitten Sister Fabienne, who was in charge of the choir, and a sister in charge of novices. Then it bit a little novice in charge of nothing.

I suggested to some professed sisters that the dog might be dispensed with; but they objected that Mother would be very sad; she loved Shaitan, who behaved like an angel toward her.

The sisters also argued that Shaitan was to protect them against thieves. But a novice then told me, "I live in fear and trembling of that dog, because I must cross the courtyard for my work in the evening, when Shaitan is let loose, and I am too small and weak to fight him back."

It seemed to me that Shaitan had no right to disturb the peace and recollection of the novices, so I told this sister, "There is only one way out, we must pray the Lord to deliver us from this Black Devil." Our prayers were heard sooner than we had expected.

A few days later two thieves came at night, and threw poisoned meat to the Black Devil. It ate the meat and became sick. The sisters tried to save the animal, but their efforts failed. Kala Shaitan had to be given an injection by the veterinary a few days later. The novices could now cross the courtyard without fear, even after dark.

CHAPTER 9

Training the Sisters

What do you think is our pride and our joy? You are; and you will
be the crown of which we are proudest in the presence of our Lord
Jesus when he comes; you are our pride and our joy.

(1 THESS. 2:19–20)

Soon after the jubilee, Michael Gomes said, "Mother asked me lately,
'Michael, do you know what is my most important work?' "

" 'I suppose, to work for the poor,' I answered."

" 'No,' she said, 'try again.' "

"I tried to find the answer, and proposed several things. Each time she
said, 'No, that is not the most important thing for me.' Then she said,
'Well, I shall tell you: my most important work is to train my Sisters.' "

"Of course, Brother Michael," I said, "what could she do without the
sisters?"

"And what could they do without Mother?" he retorted.

"True, but she needs a team. She cannot run a single institution without the sisters, who multiply and extend her influence. Mother knows that
the society will live after her only if the sisters are fervent religious; she
has told me so repeatedly."

At first it was her main occupation. Now, due to her society's growth
and expansion, Mother can devote less time to the essential work of
formation, which she must entrust to the sisters she trained.

Mother has to form Christ in the young candidates who come to join
her congregation. Like St. Paul she can say, "My children! I must go
through the pain of giving birth to you all over again, until Christ is
formed in you" (Gal. 4:19).

For two years she watches over each new batch of novices, preparing
them to become the chosen brides of Christ. She introduces them to
spiritual life, abnegation, humility, service, love of God and of their
neighbor, and trains them to find God in prayer.

Mother carefully prepares her young sisters to become worthy of their
bridegroom Jesus, so that their Lord may say when they take their vows
and pledge themselves to live only for him, to serve only him, to love only
him, to follow him even unto death on the cross, in the words of the

bridegroom of the Song of Songs: "You are wholly beautiful, my love, and without a blemish." These words the Catholic tradition applies to our Lady. They are an ideal we can aim at, an ideal put before the young religious.

"If the sisters are not to be faithful," Mother told me, "let the Lord suppress the institute. He can do without it, the church can do without it. They must be faithful to him who has called them, who is the ever faithful one."

"Mother, they will be faithful."

Having spared herself no pains for their training, to each of her sisters Mother can say with rightful pride, "I have betrothed you, a chaste virgin, to Christ."

"Father, I tell them, 'You are the brides of Christ. He deserves all your love. None of you must love Jesus less than a wife loves her husband.'"

"Yes, Mother, Jesus is the perfect bridegroom, always faithful, thoughtful, attentive to their needs, seeing to their spiritual progress. But as a true lover, he is exacting. 'I am a jealous God,' said Yahweh."

"If they start seeking consolation in human things," she added, "if they divide their hearts between God and men, he may let them fall."

Mother teaches her sisters by her example, and her words; she guides them by her letters, and her visits to the various houses.

St. Paul wrote to his disciples at Corinth, "Take me for your model, as I take Christ" (1 Cor. 11:1). Mother can say the same to her sisters in all truth, without ostentation or self-praise. Indeed, the Holy Spirit inspires the founders of approved religious institutes, whose members are expected to live according to the ideal expressed in their constitutions and their founders' lives.

Mother can ask much because she has given much. She does not ask the sisters to do anything she has not done herself. She has washed feet, like Jesus; she has bathed sores and bandaged wounds like the Good Samaritan; she has pressed babies to her heart as Christ did; she has lifted up the cripple. She has visited the slums; she has begged for the hungry and the sick. She has experienced hunger, thirst, tiredness: she has passed sleepless nights; she has had fever but still attended to her duties as superior.

Mother constantly teaches the sisters by her example. She arrived with five sisters in Melbourne in April 1970. The same day, helped by the provincial of the Loreto nuns, she found a house that had been deserted after the death of the previous owner. It had been badly neglected, the roof was leaking, the floor covered with dirt. Mother announced, "Well, we can start cleaning." Immediately the front room was cleaned, prepared for Mass, and the beds were made ready. Since there was room for only five beds, one sister slept under the table. Mother's arm had been fractured, and so the sisters, to make her comfortable, disposed some blankets on one side of her bed that she might rest her arm.

When the night came, the sisters soon fell into a sound sleep. On waking up, they discovered that the blankets had been spread over them to keep them warm during the cold night. Mother had seen to it; she could live in discomfort, like her Lord. No doubt her action impressed the sisters more than any instruction on charity could have done.

At the very beginning, the sisters were hand tooled, a carefully finished product coming from the hand of Mother, who spoke frequently to the several groups of sisters. "I give four of five instructions a day," she could say at the time of the first foundations, "and I meet personally every one of the sisters."

Gradually, as the number of houses increased, she had to rely more on her first companions. They were becoming seasoned and experienced; having imbibed Mother's thoughts, they transmitted her ideals and ideas, even using her favorite expressions. They were rightly exacting; candidates and novices had to be ready for a hard life under strict discipline. As Mother became more and more frequently absent, due to the opening of new houses, the senior sisters shouldered an increasing share of the work of forming the postulants and novices.

From the start several priests also helped. Father Van Exem contributed much to the sisters' training, as the confessor and spiritual director of the community in Calcutta. He helped to mold the character of the sisters in the spirit of the constitutions he explained to them.

Father Julien Henry also helped Mother in the spiritual formation of the novices and professed sisters. He exerted a considerable influence on Mother and on the sisters, stressing the need for prayer, insisting on devotion to the Sacred Heart, the Blessed Eucharist and to our Lady. After twenty-eight years of service to the institute, he still gives an instruction daily to one or another group of the sisters.

"Father Henry," said Mother with an impish smile, "tells them things no one else would dare tell them. He knows all their defects and points them out in his instructions. When novices spot him on the road, if they are not praying the rosary as they are expected to do, they quickly reach for their beads and start praying. But Father Henry has seen their gesture, and in his next instruction he is certain to make them a remark. Nothing escapes him, even though he himself, when alone on the road, usually says his rosary."

When they have left the mother house, Mother continues to teach her sisters through her letters. She directs, reproaches, redresses, advices, suggests. She solves problems, encourages, and stimulates.

"I keep in touch with all the houses and all the sisters," she says. "I visit them as often as I can; of course my visits become less frequent as the number of foundations increases. I also write often to the sisters."

They are always present to her mind. Their problems are hers to solve, their difficulties she must help to settle. She sends them in the name of Christ, whom she represents for them; hence she must know whom to send where, whom to appoint as superior of the local community, what apostolate the sisters should undertake in a particular place. She goes to inspect the site of every new foundation, by herself or with her counselors. Once the sisters are established, she continues to guide them through her letters and visits. She directs, encourages, reminds, corrects, stimulates them in all religious and apostolic matters.

Sister Letitia, who later became the first superior in Papua, when she was in charge of the house at Amravati wrote to Mother that the bishop was giving the house two hundred rupees a month. Mother replied, "Next month return the money to the bishop and tell him you need this contribution no more. You must get the local people to help and support the work."

At times she adds a note of humor to her advice, as when the sisters from Dorunda, Ranchi, wrote to Mother that they could not sleep at night because thieves climbed the pipes along the walls of the house and tried to enter the rooms were they slept.

"I wrote back," chuckled Mother, "since none of you is so pretty that a thief would want to take her away, they can be coming only for money and supplies. Well, allow them to take these things they need, and let the sisters enjoy the sleep of the just. God will look after you."

St. Paul directed that his letters be read publicly to the assembled Christians, and then passed on to other communities. Mother's letters are also read in the community and travel from house to house. Many quotations from these letters have found their way into the second edition of the constitutions, written in 1975.

A Belgian journal asked Father Van Exem to interview Mother. Among other questions asked her was "What would you consider to be most important in the formation of nuns today?"

"What is most important," Mother answered, "is to train the sisters to a deep, personal love for the Blessed Sacrament, so that they may find Jesus in the Eucharist; then they will go out and find Jesus in their neighbor, and they will serve him in the poor."

This stress on the presence of Christ in the Eucharist and in one's neighbor as a key to spiritual training shows how concrete and incarnational her spirituality is: Christ is to be found on earth today, in definite conditions of time and space, in a truly tangible manner. Thus the keynote of the training she imparts to her sisters is Jesus found in the Eucharist, Jesus found in the neighbor.

The Eucharist is the victim of the sacrifice to which the sisters unite themselves, the sustaining food that gives them the strength to carry out their apostolate and the sacred presence of their Lord and Savior, to whom they come to offer consolation and love, and to receive inspiration and comfort.

Mother insists on prayer before the Blessed Sacrament, on faithfulness to the hour of adoration every evening, which the new constitutions prescribe. Mother takes visitors to the chapel and invites them to greet the master of the house. She rejoices when she learns that groups of her Co-Workers organize hours of adoration.

This devotion to the Blessed Eucharist, fully in the tradition of the church, was again recommended by Vatican II.

Popular Indian tradition favors a concrete religion. But the deeper current of Indian spirituality seeks God's presence in the world and especially in the soul. The sisters pass much time away from their houses, since their work is largely outside. They spend much time on the road or traveling. Thus, they must learn to converse constantly with their Lord and to find God present everywhere.

When speaking to the tertians, I insisted on the divine Presence within. Some of the sisters understood this; some did find God present in their soul, and this discovery rendered their prayer personal, intimate, habitual.

The one who loves Jesus will keep the two great commandments: Love for God and for one's neighbor. Thus the sisters by their vocation are called to love, in a thorough and at times a heroic manner. They discover God's presence, wonderful, inspiring, drawing the soul to himself. With utter respect, they serve him in their neighbor, as they tend the wounds of Christ's suffering brothers and sisters.

Then the soul is itself a tabernacle. My Lord dwells always with me, in me. Once as I spoke to Mother of the presence of God in the soul, she said, "The indwelling? Yes, we have too long neglected it."

Like St. Paul, Mother likes to feel close to the one she loves. She sees the Eucharist as a continued Incarnation; she finds Christ in the tabernacle and in his brethren; he is the head, and they and she constitute his body. Christ in the tabernacle and in the suffering poor expects the sisters; they can visit him and attend on him. Devotion to the Blessed Eucharist appeals to affective souls, to those with a vivid imagination, to people who like concrete things and situations. Several sisters report that they find strength to perform the day's work and shoulder its crosses in their prayer before the Blessed Sacrament, telling Jesus in effect, "Lord, take everything, all is for you."

For her sisters, Mother has a high ideal: "Father, I want to give saints to the church."

"Yes, you are right, Mother; to produce saints is the task of the church."

And so she asks much and obtains much. She trains her sisters to perfect obedience.

For Mother obedience means complete disponibility to Christ's service, wherever and in whatever capacity he calls us. Like St. Francis of Assisi, she asks from her religious perfect submission to God's will as known through the order of the superior, in a spirit of love, and prompt execution of that will.

In the summer of 1968 there took place at Darjeeling the blessing and inauguration of a new building at the home for orphaned, crippled, and handicapped children. The bishop blessed the new premises; the governor of West Bengal praised the wonderful work performed by the sisters. The superior, who had brought a difficult task to completion, might have thought of relaxing for a while, but no—Mother Teresa, just back from America and Europe, had news for her:

"Sister, I want you to go to Africa and start a new house there."

"When, Mother?"

"As soon as you can obtain your passport. There is plenty of work for us in Africa."

Indeed after starting a first house in Tanzania, the sister was appointed to establish a second foundation in the same country. This was a true acknowledgment of her pioneering ability.

To another Mother says, "Sister, you leave for South India."

"When, Mother?"

"This evening, sister, by the first train that goes there."

The sisters are usually told of their assignment on the day they take their vows, except for a few who require passports or visas to go to their destination. When Mother is absent, they must wait till she comes back.

"There is no problem of packing for us," said a sister. "Since we have nothing, we are ready in ten minutes."

The sisters' training in poverty proceeds in a rigorous manner. They must not only know and esteem, but also experience practical poverty during their period of probation and during their whole religious life.

Poverty in dress comprises the following:

- A simple and modest white habit, covering them from neck to ankle and wrist
- A white sari with blue border to cover their head and most of their habit
- A crucifix hanging from the left shoulder
- Sandals

They are allowed three habits: one to wear, one to wash, one to dry; and two saris of coarse material, such as the poor would wear, one to wear and one to wash or dry.

The houses must exhibit poverty in style, in furniture; the manner of traveling must be the cheapest available: much is done on foot; when trams, buses, or trains must be used, they choose the cheapest class.

Food should be of the most simple, yet sufficient to keep up the sisters' health so that they can work strenuously for the good of the poor.

The sisters sleep in dormitories, without any privacy, like the poor who live in crowded slums or tenements.

Cleanliness should be observed so as to give an example to the poor, who should be taught to work and not to be lazy.

The reason for the practice of poverty is love. Mother writes, "Our people are poor by force, but our poverty is of our own choice. We want to be poor like Christ who, being rich, chose to be born and live and work among the poor." The constitutions state, "We and our poor will rely entirely on divine Providence. We are not ashamed to beg from door to door as members of Christ, who himself lived on alms during the public life and whom we serve in the sick and the poor." St. Francis of Assisi was not ashamed to beg for the poor and to receive the scraps of food he would share with them. Similarly, the sisters are not to be ashamed to ask for the poor, even if begging represents a form of poverty that has come to be despised in the modern world.

The sisters must learn to ask; they start doing it during their novitiate. Two young novices come to the parish house, all smiles, and ask, "Have you any candle drippings, Father?" Then both novices burst out laughing. They laugh and laugh heartily as only young girls can laugh. Who could refuse them?

"What do you need them for, Sisters?"

"To make a paschal candle."

This is Passion Sunday. The two young novices went out early, gathered the children of a parish for the Sunday mass and catechism class. On their way home they ask from other churches if there are drippings of wax with which they can make a paschal candle.

Another batch of novices went to ask for biscuits from a factory to prepare a treat for the children that they may share in the joy of the Resurrection of the Lord.

Bishops and government officials who invite Mother want her spirit, her approach to the poor and the abandoned, her way of work. Through the sisters she has trained, she can multiply her presence and her influence, her activity and her apostolate; they are the spirit and presence, the influence and work of Christ, living in his humble, docile, indomitable instrument.

Like Paul writing to the Corinthians he had nursed and formed into images of Christ, Mother can tell her sisters, "You are yourselves our letter that anybody can see and read, and it is plain that you are a letter from Christ, drawn up by us" (2 Cor. 3:1–3).

The sisters are to be a small replica of the foundress, modeled on her. In their behavior and their work, all people must see and read what Mother thinks and teaches and does. And because her spirit is truly the

Spirit of Christ living in her, the sisters are a letter from Christ, speaking to the world of his mercy, his goodness, his kindness, his power, his concern for every individual person.

Since Christ lives in them and acts through them, they should not fear to let the world see their good deeds.

"I tell them, Father, not to be ashamed when people praise them for what they do. They must let people see what Christ does through us, His humble instruments. It is all to his glory."

"Yes, Mother; that is what Jesus told us: 'Let your light shine before men that seeing your good works they may glorify your Father who is in heaven' (Matt. 5:16). Christ is the supreme light, 'the light that comes into the world to enlighten all men.' He wishes us to be small lights, reflecting his truth, his splendor and glory."

The Spirit of God grants the sisters various charisms; it is for Mother to discover them, to help to develop them and to allow them to be used to the full.

At the mother house, I often saw a particular sister speak to women and children on religious matters. As I mentioned this to Mother, she answered, "Yes, this sister has a special gift for contacting people and getting them interested in religion. She speaks to them of God with simplicity and conviction. Yet she only studied up to the eighth standard."

"Well, Mother, if she has that God-given charism, use her entirely for that work. It is most important."

"I shall," said Mother.

Mother can ask much from her sisters; but she also knows the limitations of human nature.

"I find it difficult to appoint a good mistress of novices," she told me one day.

"You might try Sister X.; She is a woman of God, given to prayer."

"No, she would be too strict. She exacts much for God and might break some of the young, weaker novices."

In 1975, I asked Mother, "Do you still know all the sisters?"

"I know personally and individually every professed sister of the congregation," she answered. "But not all the novices and postulants."

She judges them quickly. With correct insight, it would seem. Once, to test her knowledge of her sisters, I asked her about a recently professed sister.

"Where is Sister Y. at present?" If she knows the state of sister Y.'s soul, she will comment, I thought.

Mother answered, "At our house at Z." She added, "She is a very spiritual person."

"Yes," I said, "a very spiritual person." We understood one another. She knew that I knew, and I knew that she was aware of the treasure the Lord had given her.

Mother does not want mass production. There are nine separate groups of novices for the two years' novitiate at the mother house, with a sister in charge to guide each group. Mother naturally puts her best sisters to train the young candidates.

The novices do some field work, thus receiving training in the kinds of work they will have to perform later. The first-year novices go out for work on Thursdays and Sundays. The second-year novices go out for work every day except Thursdays.

Three points Mother stresses especially in the training of the sisters are total surrender to God, loving trust, and cheerfulness.

These three virtues must enable them to go through their religious life, coming closer and closer to the Lord Jesus, whom they serve in the poor.

Each renovation of vows is preceded by a triduum of prayer during which the preacher is asked to take one of these subjects each day. Thus the nuns are prepared to give themselves again to God, to renew and perfect their offering to the divine majesty in the spirit of the congregation.

Cheerfulness in the fulfilment of the most unattractive task is a characteristic of the institute. Mother teaches, and her words are inscribed in the constitutions: "Never let anything so fill you with pain or sorrow as to make you forget the joy of the risen Christ." This is written at the top of the chapter on bearing the cross of Christ, which is the proof of the greatness of his love and of ours in return for his.

Mother's faith has carried her through all the trials of the beginning of the institute. Faith in the power of the risen Christ and of the Holy Spirit he sent us will see the sisters through all the difficulties of their life of service to the poorest of the poor.

Twice a year, on a feast day of our Lady, takes place the ceremony of the vows. Those who have just finished their novitiate or are still juniors take temporary vows for a period of one year; those who end their tertianship, after six years of temporary vows, take their final profession, binding themselves for life to serve Christ in the Congregation. On these days Mother brings to Jesus the best offering she can make, the young religious she has carefully trained. For the sisters, these are solemn occasions.

In December 1975, in crowded St. Mary's Church, twelve sisters were ranged in a single row before the altar; the archbishop was going to concelebrate with twenty priests the holy Mass during which the sisters would offer themselves forever to Christ.

They were living the words of Hosea: "I will betroth you to myself for ever, with integrity and justice, with tenderness and love; I will betroth you to myself with faithfulness and you will come to know Yahweh, your God" (Hosea 2:21–22).

It was their great day, long expected, long desired, long prepared. The day of their exchange of gifts with their bridegroom, Christ. They were coming forth in total surrender, joyful trust, perfect love.

The King who had called them to leave their families and every human attachment to serve him, had told them, "Set me as a seal on your heart, as a seal on your arm" (Song of Songs 8:6).

A seal to attest its owner's will—the seal that will guide and inspire her for ever, since "Love is strong as death."

After the gospel and the homily, the deacon calls those to be professed, each one by her name: "Sister Mary Edward."

"Lord, you have called me," answers the bride, acknowledging that her vocation is from God, not from human beings.

The celebrant asks, "My dear Sister, what do you ask of God and his church?"

"I ask that I may follow Christ my spouse and persevere in this religious community until death."

The celebrant explains that this religious profession aims at the holiness of the nun who promises to follow Christ and work for the good of souls. By baptism they have already been consecrated to Christ; now they wish to be more closely united to him so that all they do and say, think and desire, may be only for his glory.

"Dear Sister, are you resolved to unite yourself more closely to Christ by the bond of perpetual profession?"

"I am so resolved."

"Are you resolved with the help of God's grace to follow the life of perfect chastity, obedience, and poverty that Christ our Lord and his Virgin Mother chose for themselves and to persevere in it for ever?"

"I am so resolved."

"Are you resolved, by the grace of the Holy Spirit, to spend your life in wholehearted free service to God's poor?"

"I am so resolved."

"Are you resolved to strive constantly for perfect love of God and your neighbor by zealously following the gospel and the rule of this religious community?"

"I am so resolved."

The whole congregation then prays that they may be faithful to God's calling and to their vows.

The sister reads the formula of the vows, in which she says, "I, Sister Mary Edward, vow for life chastity, poverty, obedience, and wholehearted free service to the poorest of the poor according to the constitutions of the Missionaries of Charity. I give myself with my whole heart to this religious community so that by the grace of the Holy Spirit and the help of the Blessed Virgin Mary I may seek to practice perfect charity in the service of God and the church."

The person who receives the vows then tells the sister,

"By the authority entrusted to me, I accept your vows in the name of the church for the community of the Missionaries of Charity. I commend you earnestly to God that you may fulfil your dedication, which is united to his Eucharistic Sacrifice."

The newly professed goes to the altar, places on it the document of her profession, which she has just read, and leaves it there to be united to the offering of the Body and Blood of Christ. She is to be a victim and a witness of God's love.

The celebrant proceeds to offer the Holy Sacrifice. At the time of communion, the words of Paul to the Galatians, expressing his proud profession of faith, are sung: "I am nailed with Christ on the Cross; I live, not by my own life, but Christ Lives in me!" (Gal. 2:19–20).

They belong entirely to Christ, they are ready to be sent out to any part of the world to do his work. They will go and integrate themselves into a community of the Missionaries of Charity, which, as their constitutions direct, should—by its fervor and active devotedness—radiate peace, joy, and love.

CHAPTER 10

The Brothers

After this the Lord appointed seventy-two others and sent them out
ahead of him, in pairs, to all the towns and places he himself was to
visit.

(LUKE 10:1)

"Behind Bishop's College in Ahiripukur Second Lane," Mother said one
day, "the sisters have discovered a group of Catholics who do not seem
to be known by the parish. Nobody goes to church, and the children have
not made their first communion. Several unions are irregular. The sisters
would like to regularize a few marriages. The same happens in other slum
areas; we discover people who were not married in the church and yet live
together. The sisters try to obtain the information and documents required to regularize the situation of these people. When dispensations
are required, parish priests do not always prove very helpful. I need one
or two sympathetic priests to work with the sisters; they would visit the
slums and cooperate with them. Then we could do more spiritual good."

I quite understood their predicament. The prescriptions of canon law
had to be followed. Some matrimonial situations were intricate. As happens in every large city, people came to Calcutta in search of a job, leaving
a wife or husband at home, and then settled down with another person
to cook and keep house for them. Children were born out of wedlock. We
all tried to help these innocent children. Mother said she needed sympathetic priests to help her sisters, visit families with them, and settle cases.
She seemed to throw out an invitation.

But I told her I was not her man, as I had a full-time job as professor
of economics. Mother foresaw many difficulties in the way of a man
visiting the slums when the menfolk were out at work, and only the
women and children were at home. That would hardly be tolerated. The
man would be suspected and unwelcome.

One or two priests did try the experiment of slum work with the sisters.
But Mother had larger plans. She was considering a new foundation: a
congregation of brothers, similar to that of her sisters, trained in the same
spirit, working together with them.

The beginnings of the Missionary Brothers of Charity proved more
laborious and less successful than that of the sisters. But Mother's perse-

verance prevailed. The church does not favor, even does not allow a woman to be the head of a religious congregation of men. So Mother Teresa had to find a suitable priest or brother to direct the new institute and launch it into being. Divine Providence sent her the required person, a Jesuit, author of several books and booklets presenting the Catholic faith to non-Christians, and destined to work at the Catholic Enquiry Centre of Poona and the Institute for Home Studies. He was Father Ian Travers-Ball, an Australian Jesuit, then in his tertianship.

The tertianship brings to an end and crowns the long religious, philosophical, and theological training of a Jesuit, with ten or at least several months of prayer, study, reflection, and experiments conducive to spiritual development and to discovering the will of God for his religious. Father Travers-Ball made it with zest and zeal. He felt the call of God to work with Mother Teresa, in the same spirit, to work among the poorest of the poor in the slums, among the most needy and abandoned. He received all encouragement from his religious superiors and from his brother Jesuits. All rejoiced at seeing one of their own help to develop the family of the Missionaires of Charity by opening its male branch.

Mother Teresa was delighted, as she saw God truly bless her work. She could not expect better than a fully trained religious priest, young and dynamic, experienced in the religious life.

Some years later the congregation of brothers had grown, and I had a chance to learn more of their work.

In September 1975, I chanced to meet Brother Andrew, the bearded superior general of the Missionary Brothers of Charity, who had just arrived in India from Saigon.

"I was not exactly expelled from Vietnam," he said, "but the Communists took away the three houses we had and occupied them. With no possibility of work, of starting anything, and no place wherein to reside, I took the plane for Bangkok and India."

He had previously sent home to the United States four American brothers and also a brother from the Netherlands; the Americans would have been in danger at the time the Communist troops entered Saigon.

Three Indian brothers had already returned to India from Cambodia. One American postulant refused to leave when the Khmer Rouge entered the city where he was working. The last that was seen of him—and that was five months before we spoke—was that he was marched away by soldiers from the Cathedral Square.

"I am going to write a book on Mother Teresa and the Missionaries of Charity," I told Brother Andrew.

"Yes," he answered, "by all means do it. Tell them that we are very ordinary people, that God does everything. You must 'demythologize' what has been written about us, and what many people think of us."

He hesitated before pronouncing the word *demythologize;* as a theologian, he knew its ugly undertones. He was aware of the harm some religious theories had done to the faith of many, by tearing off and discarding all the miraculous elements in the gospels. But he used the word, and repeated it without any sign of regret.

"You must demythologize what has been written about us and our work. No doubt much good has been done to a large number of readers by what has appeared. But we have to spend at least six months trying to correct the wrong ideas of the candidates who come to join our congregation after reading some of the things published about us.

"You must say that we are very ordinary people, all of us. We have our defects, our foibles, our shortcomings, the sisters as well as the brothers, even Mother Teresa. She and I do disagree, and at times we quarrel. We are instruments inadequate to the task. But the marvellous thing is that God uses us for his work and has produced through the institute a tremendous amount of good."

Brother Andrew spoke in the true Christian spirit, as Scripture says, "To you, Lord, not to us, to you be the glory" (Ps. 115:1). And when we labor for him in that spirit, the Lord does work marvels through his grace.

Brother Andrew stressed the point, as he must have done often when speaking to his young brothers: the glamor of being in the public eye is dangerous and may do us harm. He had just experienced true poverty and had been forced into complete detachment: of his three years of exertions in Cambodia and Vietnam to establish his congregation, what remained? Of the brothers' work, of their efforts to help people, what were the results? Nothing visible—only a few acts of love of God made in faith, which had value for eternity.

Then we spoke of the very beginnings of the Missionary Brothers of Charity. I asked him, "What influence did Mother exercise on you and your decision? Did she ask you to join her?"

"No, the decision was entirely my own. It just happened. It took very little time. It was during my tertianship at Sitagarha, near Hazaribagh. I had always been interested in the poor and wondered what I could do for them. During my tertianship, I was sent as an experiment to work with the brothers residing at Sishu Bhavan for a few weeks. When I returned to Sitagarha, I spoke to Father Schillebeeckx, our instructor. I told him I wanted to join the brothers. He immediately agreed. The Calcutta Jesuit provincial approved the plan. Permission was asked from Rome to allow me temporary exclaustration. Within weeks this permission was granted, and I left immediately for Calcutta to join the brothers. All the Jesuits were most encouraging and cooperative."

"Was the brothers' congregation already established then?"

"No. There were a few candidates: but Rome did not approve the foundation, though the approbation was requested by Archbishop Albert D'Souza and by Mother. Rome answered, 'First get more candidates, then we shall approve you.' This was a vicious circle; no approbation meant few candidates, since priests would not send us candidates as long as we were not a recognized institute, but recognition by Rome depended on larger numbers. We explained the matter, and finally Rome granted us recognition."

"Who was in charge when you joined?"

"When I joined them, the few candidates were being trained by Mother and Father Julien Henry. I am afraid they did not relish being under a woman superior."

"Neither does Rome allow congregations of priests and brothers to be ruled by women."

"Soon we got a house in Kidderpore, and we started on our own."

"Did Mother have much influence on the training of the Brothers?"

"Well, we disagreed on some points. We had some arguments."

He hid his face behind his hands, and added, "There is a letter not to be published as long as one of us is alive."

Out of discretion I did not enquire further about the cause of their disagreement. Had not St. Paul quarreled with John Mark, who refused to follow him? When later Barnabas proposed that they take Mark with them, Paul refused and "after a violent quarrel they parted company, and Barnabas sailed off with John Mark" (Acts 15:39). This quarrel puts in the shade the disagreement between Mother and Brother Andrew.

Of course the brotherhood was first Mother's brain child, the product of her efforts, her prayers, and her financial backing. For many years the brothers would be known by the public as Mother Teresa's Brothers. Indeed, they are the Missionary Brothers of Charity, having the same name as the sisters.

"How many brothers do you have at present?" I asked.

"The brothers number about one hundred and fifty. We have already opened fourteen houses, in Calcutta, Titaghur, Noorpur, Midnapore, Bokaro, etc. They started in Los Angeles, where two of the four American brothers speak Spanish. The cardinal gave them a house that serves as a novitiate.

"In India vocations have come mainly from Chota Nagpur and Kerala; a few came from Bengal, Tamil Nadu, Bombay, and other regions. Some candidates joined us from the United States and other Western countries."

"It will be more difficult to recruit and train the brothers than the sisters," I commented.

"I am glad you recognize the fact," said Brother Andrew.

The life of the brothers is not easy; it asks for much self-denial and a deep spirit of prayer.

The percentage of brothers dropping out during their training is much higher than that of the sisters. As Brother Ferdinand stated, "We were thirteen in my year of novitiate in 1967; at the end of two years' training seven remained to take their vows. In 1975, for our final profession, we were only four to bind ourselves for life to the institute.

"What are your main works, Brother Andrew?" I asked.

"We try not to go where the sisters are working. But we collaborate with them wherever it is useful. We share the work with them at the Kalighat Home for the Dying. We look after the men, while they take the women's ward. The brothers also take care of some destitute sick who are not too ill or weak, in one of our houses. We look after orphaned, abandoned, and crippled boys. Many of the brothers work among lepers. In villages and small towns, the lepers are much neglected. The brothers have assumed this apostolate in earnest; they render very valuable service in this field."

"Yes, you have here a rich field of apostolic service, calling for genuine Christian self-denial, devotion, and true love."

The brothers took charge of the Titaghur hospital for lepers after the sisters had experienced some difficulties in dealing with the men. This specialization should attract to the brothers good vocations and rich blessings from heaven. Indeed, several brothers, including Brother Sebastian, the master of novices, who is a priest, felt attracted by this apostolate and applied to join the Missionary Brothers of Charity.

While Brother Andrew, the superior general, was away in Vietnam, Brother Ferdinand was chosen to be his vicar in India, and he still occupies this post. This allows Brother Andrew to travel about more freely and organize new foundations abroad. He does not intend to bring to India candidates and novices from Western countries to train them in the Indian manner. He thinks that living conditions are too different, whereas Mother at first brought to Calcutta all her foreign candidates. She started novitiates in Melbourne and Rome only when she found it difficult or impossible to obtain visas for her foreign candidates.

Girls may be more resilient and adaptable than boys. Still, Brother Andrew may be right in adapting the brothers' training and lifestyle to local conditions. His Jesuit formation prepared him to follow the example of St. Ignatius, a founder of genius, who told his religious to adopt the language, culture, and style of life of the people to whom they ministered. The brothers have no distinctive habit; they dress simply and wear a cross pinned to their shirt or coat as a sign of their religious consecration.

The society counts five priests among its members. Some joined it as priests. As a rule no candidate is admitted specially for the priesthood; it is left to the society to decide who will be sent to study for the priesthood. It does help the brothers to have priests among their own members, since this allows them to open houses in mission areas without priests or church.

The Missionary Brothers of Charity, who share Mother Teresa's universal outlook and concern for the souls of poor and suffering children and adults, at present look eastward and plan to open houses in Taiwan, Hong Kong, South Korea. They will expand as much as their resources in personnel allow. In this they depend on God's providence; but prospects for recruitment seem fairly good. The future progress of the congregation will depend mostly on the solidity and depth of the spiritual formation of the young brothers.

CHAPTER 11

The Helpers

You are God's chosen race, his saints; he loves you, and you should
be clothed in sincere compassion, in kindness and humility, gentleness and patience.

(COL. 3:12)

"I have three second selves," said Mother.

Indeed, she has her own, inalienable self, then she considers as her
second self in the congregation Sister Agnes, who replaces her when she
is out of Calcutta. She has of course, her spiritual self, her innermost self,
the Lord Jesus living in her by his grace. Completely surrendered to
Jesus, she allows him to take over her direction and act through her.

"I have three second selves directing groups of helpers, who work on
behalf of our institute. These form three branches: the Co-Workers or
coadjutors, the Sick and Suffering, and the Contemplatives.

"The Co-workers are directed by Mrs. Ann Blaikie in England. They
are forty thousand laypeople. Fourteen thousand in England, six thousand in the United States, some in Belgium, France, Australia, and so on.
They meet regularly; they pray for us; they also prepare bandages and
clothes, and other things we need for the dispensaries, for poor children.
What matters is that they work for God. In several places they have
started organizing holy hours for our work; they have meditation,
prayer."

The material aspect had little importance for Mother; it was only a way
of showing one's love for God in action. That they prayed for her work
delighted Mother's heart. For this woman of God, money counted little
and material services were unimportant, if they did not proceed from love
of God.

For a while we remained silent, thanking the Lord for this auspicious
development.

"Then," Mother continued, "there are the Sick and Suffering, seven
hundred of them, I think, organized by Miss Jacqueline de Decker, my
second self. She worked for some time in India. Now she is in Belgium.
She underwent seventeen operations. Some time ago she wrote to me,

" 'You are going to receive a great favor from our Lord, because of late
my pains have increased.' She offers her sufferings for the work of the

Missionaries of Charity. Miss de Decker has organized several hundred sick people who also offer their pains for the success of the sisters' work."

"My third second self," said Mother, "is a French priest, Father Georges Gorrée, who organizes the wing of the contemplatives who support the Missionaries of Charity by their prayers and penances."

"Have you houses in France?"

"No," she said sadly. "We have not been asked."

"I quite understand. The present French attitude, mainly among priests and religious, may be too sophisticated for your simple approach to religious and charitable work. But some bishop will probably call you before long."

"Do write to my three second selves," concluded Mother, "they will provide you with information for your book on our institute."

THE SICK AND SUFFERING

The Sick and Suffering was the first link to be organized and connected with the Missionaries of Charity. The idea and initiative came from Mother herself and in the first years of the institute. She felt acutely that prayer and sacrifices were needed to obtain graces for the apostolate of the sisters. She felt like St. Paul, writing, "I beg you, brothers, by our Lord Jesus Christ and the love of the Spirit, to help me through my dangers by praying to God for me" (Rom. 15:30) and repeatedly asking for prayers in his letters to his new converts.

Mother had met Jacqueline de Decker at the Patna Holy Family Hospital where she stayed after leaving her Loreto convent. Miss de Decker wished to work with Mother and join her religious institute, but her ill health would not permit it and she was forced to return to Belgium after a stay of two years in India.

Miss de Decker kindly sent me copies of letters Mother wrote to her during the heroic first years, the years of blind faith and trust in God. These hitherto unpublished letters, written with complete openness to a kindred soul, reveal Mother Teresa's ideals, aims, and feelings at the start of her new vocation as no other document does. The letters were written in the Upper Room, in the spirit of the Cenacle. For the history of the beginnings of the Missionaries of Charity, they provide an invaluable source of information.

Mother asks the support of Miss de Decker's prayers and suffering. Very early she wished to organize a "wing" of sick and suffering people to help her fledgling institute.

In October 1952 Mother Teresa wrote from the Upper Room at 14 Creek Lane to Jacqueline de Decker,

"Today I am going to tell you something which I am sure will make you very happy. . . . Why not become spiritually bound to our Society? While we work in the slums, etc., you share in the merit, the prayers and the work with your sufferings and prayers. The work is tremendous and I need workers, it is true, but I need souls like yours to pray and suffer for the work. Would you like to become my sister"—Mother had first written *child* but crossed out the word and wrote above it *sister*—"and become a Missionary of Charity, in Belgium in body, but in soul in India, in the world, where there are souls longing for our Lord; but for want of someone to pay the debt for them, they cannot move toward him. You will be a true Missionary of Charity and you will pay their debt, while the sisters —your sisters—help them to come to God, in body." Here Mother echoes the words of St. Paul: "I fulfil in my body what is lacking in the sufferings of Christ for his body, the church" (Col. 1:24).

Mother continues: "Pray over this and let me know what is your desire. I need many people like you—who would join the society like this—for I want to have (1) a glorious society in heaven, (2) the suffering society on earth—the spiritual children, and (3) the militant society; the sisters on the battlefield.

"I am sure you would be very happy to see the sisters—fighting the devil in the field of souls. They count nothing as too hard when there is a question of souls."

Then Mother adds a remark that will comfort all those who suffer with peace and joy: "Our Lord must love you much to give you so great a part in his suffering. You are the happy one, for you are his chosen one. Be brave and cheerful and offer much for me—that I may bring many souls to God. Once you come in touch with souls, the thirst grows daily." Mother again stresses that what moves her to action is the welfare of souls she wants to help to know, love, and serve God.

In January 1953 Mother writes and explains further the function of the Sick and Suffering: "I am happy you are willing to join the suffering members of the Missionaries of Charity; you and all the sick and suffering will share in all our prayers and works and whatever we do for souls, and you do the same with us your prayers and sufferings.

"You see, the aim of the society is to satiate the thirst of Jesus on the cross for the love of souls, by working for the salvation and sanctification of the poor in the slums. Who could do better than you and the others who suffer like you. Your suffering and prayers will be the chalice in which we the working members will pour the love of souls we gather around. Therefore you are just as important and necessary as we are for the fulfilment of our aim—to satiate the thirst of Jesus we must be a chalice, and you and the others, men, women, children, old and young, poor and rich are welcome to make the chalice." Mother does not discriminate among people; all are invited to help, to contribute whatever they can in the matter of love for Christ.

But there must be unity of purpose among all the members, who should be animated by a common spirit. Mother specifies that they should show forth the three characteristic virtues of the Missionaries of Charity:

"One thing we must have in common is the spirit of our society: total surrender to God, loving trust, and perfect cheerfulness.

"Everyone and anyone who wishes to become a Missionary of Charity is welcome, but I want especially the paralyzed, the crippled, the incurables to join, for they will bring many souls to the feet of Jesus." Again Mother stresses that her aim is to lead souls to Jesus; to achieve this end prayer, work, suffering offered to God are needed. Thus started the link of the Sick and Suffering that was to help the work of the Missionaries of Charity.

In March 1955 Mother writes to the Sick and Suffering, "Every day we offer you or rather offer each other to Christ for souls. We, the Missionaries of Charity, how grateful we must be—you suffer and we work. We finish in each other what is wanting in Christ." Here Mother again refers to the Paulinian idea of our collaboration with Christ in his passion for the good of souls.

She adds, "What a beautiful vocation is ours: to be carriers of Christ's love in the slums. . . . We stand together holding the same chalice and so with the adoring angels satiate Christ's thirst for souls.

"My very dear children, let us love Jesus with our whole heart and soul. Let us bring him many souls." Mother indicates again her main purpose, namely to bring souls to Christ who thirsts for them, who offered himself as a sacrificial victim to reconcile them to his Father.

She ends with her usual advice: "Keep smiling. Smile at Jesus in your suffering—for to be a real M.C. you must be a cheerful victim." She echoes the words of St. Paul: "God likes a cheerful giver" and "I rejoice in my sufferings."

Mother ends with words reminiscent of the Last Supper. "How happy I am to have you all. You belong to me as much as every sister belongs to me here." The Father to whom the Sick and Suffering belong has entrusted them to Mother that she may offer them to Christ for whose glory they were created and now labor. "Often when the work is very hard, I think of each one of you, and tell God, 'Look at my suffering children and for their love bless this work,' and it works immediately. So you see you are our treasure house."

In another letter Mother explains what is for her "the way of love": "Very often I come to you in my thoughts and offer your great sufferings when my own are small or nothing. When it is very hard for you, just hide yourself in the Sacred Heart, and there my heart with you will find all the strength and love that he chooses for you.

"What a beautiful vocation is yours: a Missionary of Charity—a carrier of God's love; we carry on our body and soul the love of an infinite, thirsty God; and we—you and I and all our dear sisters and the Sick and Suffering will satiate that burning thirst—you with your untold suffering, we with hard labor; but are we not all the same—one 'As you Father in me and I in you,' said Jesus. You have learned much, you have tasted the chalice of his agony . . . and what will be your reward? More and more suffering and a deeper likeness to him on the cross. When you pray, ask Jesus to draw me closer to himself on the cross that there we may be one."

Mother shares St. Francis's idea of the "perfect joy" on earth: the soul reaches this fullness of joy when she accepts to suffer for Christ, and even asks to be united to his Passion, so that the master and his loving disciple may be more perfectly similar.

Mother feels specially attached to her Sick and Suffering brothers and sisters, similar as they are to Christ their head, who suffered for the redemption of humanity. She considers their help to her work invaluable.

THE CO-WORKERS

"The organization of the Co-Workers," writes Mrs. Ann Blaikie, "started in a haphazard way when I approached a friend in 1954 to find out if she knew whether Mother Teresa could be approached, as I thought that among our European friends we could collect enough toys for her annual Christmas party, about which we had read in the Calcutta press. (I was living in Calcutta at the time.) Without delay we met Mother Teresa and proposed our plan. She was delighted, and asked us whether we could raise enough money for her to buy dresses or shirts and shoes for her Christian children at Christmas. This we were able to do. After Christmas, Mother came and saw us and asked if we were able to raise sufficient money for the Muslim children's annual festival! After this, of course, we realized that she would be asking us for the Hindu children's party, and so we were, as they say, 'hooked.'

"We called our small group of women the Marian Society, as it had been started in the Marian Year, and we did, of course, also work for many of the Catholic missions. Soon we spread out and were joined by Indian women and other non-Europeans.

"Mother Teresa then asked us to take over the money raising for her leprosy work, and this we also did. Then gradually groups of women formed small working parties to roll bandages and to make paper bags for the lepers' pills.

"In 1960 several of us who had belonged to the original group left India and returned to England. The good Lord saw to it that we settled within ten miles of each other, and it was only a week after my arrival in England that I was caught up again in the work of Mother Teresa by John Southworth, the chairman of a leprosy relief charity. He had been sending money to Mother Teresa, and she told him to contact me as I could give him first hand information on the work. About six months later, Mother Teresa passed through London and appeared on television, and from that small beginning the English branch of the Co-Workers was born. John Southworth was its chairperson, I was its vice-chairperson, and our other ex-India friends in Surrey, formed the committee.

"We based our work on prayer and on giving our members an opportunity for service; people knitted or rolled bandages, collected old clothes and either sent them to India, or sold them and sent the money. But always we emphasized that it was the love that was put into the doing that was important rather than the amount of money raised.

"Some four or five years later Mother Teresa saw the poverty in London and asked her Co-Workers to help those in need in their own neighborhoods; this is the development that is spreading through the country. Co-Workers now work in geriatric hospitals, with the mentally handicapped, with lonely old people and with others.

"Our prayer life, too, has developed, and hours of prayer among the Co-Workers are now held in very many towns and villages. The one in this village is held in the home of a Co-Worker who is a link with the Sick and Suffering. She is an arthritic in a wheelchair, and her husband is an epileptic. We meet with them once a month and pray with them, and meditate on the prayer of the Co-Workers. Day and weekend retreats are also held around the country. All our prayer activities are on an ecumenical basis, as Co-Workers are of all denominations and religions.

"Similar work is being carried on in other countries where there are branches of Co-Workers. Some countries started when nationals returned to their countries and formed groups. Others started spontaneously, as for example, in Ireland.

"Some have started because a sister from the country joined the order, and her friends supported her, and still others have been moved by the publicity about Mother and the Missionaries of Charity to write in and ask what they could do to help. Then after a year or so they have become branches of the International Association. We have Co-Workers also where there is no official association, and these we keep in touch with through our International Newsletters. We have Co-Workers in Poland and Hungary, and as far as Japan and with the Eskimos in the Arctic Circle."

Thus the Co-Workers have penetrated where the sisters have not yet entered.

"Our Co-Workers' way of life," Mrs. Blaikie explained, "is a way of love, seeing Christ in everyone and ministering to Christ in that person. The Missionaries of Charity take a fourth vow, that of wholehearted free service to Christ in his most distressing disguise, and it is this which we as Co-Workers must carry on in our lives. Mother Teresa bases the life of the Co-Workers on prayer. The daily prayer of the Co-Workers is the daily prayer of the brothers and sisters. Our meetings start with the prayer and then two or three minutes of meditation. She also asks her Co-Workers to join together for an hour of prayer once a month.

"The Co-Worker then goes to show his love for his family, for those in his street and in his neighborhood, in his country, and in the whole world, seeking out the lonely, the handicapped, the sick and the old, the bereaved and the abandoned, bringing the love of Christ to them."

On 26 March 1969, the International Association of Co-Workers of Mother Teresa was affiliated to the congregation of the Missionaries of Charity, and their constitutions were blessed by Pope Paul VI.

THE LINK WITH THE CONTEMPLATIVES

Father Gorrée writes from France, "In September 1974, as she traveled through France, Mother Teresa expressed her wish that all the houses of her Missionaries of Charity be adopted spiritually by one or several convents of contemplative nuns. Mother asked me to organize this spiritual twinning on an international level."

Father Gorrée willingly accepted responsibility for this "linking up" of active sisters and contemplative nuns in various countries. He approached a large number of contemplative congregations and found a ready response among many of them. Soon he could contact the houses of the Missionaries of Charity and inform them that "contemplative nuns have agreed to offer to God the Father their prayers and sacrifices in union with those of his Son Jesus Christ, to obtain the graces that will render their apostolate fruitful."

The twin communities were asked to send news of their respective work, apostolate, and spiritual experience to one another, so that by knowing each other better they might both be stimulated to serve God more generously.

The result has been remarkable. Within a year, close to four hundred monasteries in Belgium, Canada, France, Germany, Italy, Luxemburg, England, and some other countries had with joy and enthusiasm agreed to be linked spiritually to a house of the Missionaries of Charity. An exchange of news and letters started; prayers, sacrifices, and work were offered reciprocally for one another.

What struck the organizer of this spiritual twinning most is the joy that it caused among the sisters of both communities. This feeling for Co-Workers we have never seen nor spoken to is a manifestation of the charity the Holy Spirit pours into our souls.

The Spirit Christ sent us brings joy in abundance. This is the joy Christ promised his disciples at the Last Supper, when he said, "Remain in my Love . . . so that my joy may be in you and your joy may be complete" (John 15:9–11). This is the joy of the Risen Christ, the joy of the messianic era that has begun, the joy that the spirit of love, the spirit of holiness pours into the souls of the disciples inasmuch as they are surrendered to Christ who lives in them.

The Contemplatives are on the mountain with Christ alone in prayer to his Father, sometimes in the morning, sometimes in the evening, at times even the whole night. They are reserved entirely for the service of

God, interceding for the needs of the church and the sanctification of human beings, while the Missionaries of Charity, in the field, work for the salvation and sanctification of the very poor, those cherished children of God.

Thus Christian charity stretches out over the oceans, beyond all barriers, all frontiers of language, culture, nationality. United two by two, each team a link of a strong chain encircling the world to the praise and honor of the infinite God.

CHAPTER 12

Publicity

Mother Teresa's success owes much to her remarkable ability to obtain collaboration from every side. She enlisted the help of the pope, of prime ministers, chief ministers, presidents of various states, and a considerable number of laypeople.

She also used all the modern means of mass communication. The media made her known and thus rendered her work possible. They made her first a state, then a national, and finally a world figure. Without the help of the press, radio, and television, her activities would have developed only slowly and would probably have remained confined to India.

The *Statesman,* a leading Calcutta daily, was the first to throw a spotlight on her by mentioning her in its columns. The *Amrita Bazar Patrika,* another leading daily, followed suit. English and American dailies spread her fame abroad; *Time* mentioned her several times and carried her photo.

In 1975, the *Illustrated Weekly,* the weekly magazine most widely read by the middle and upper classes in India, displayed Mother Teresa's picture on the cover. In the main story the editor, Kushwant Singh, praised the work of the Missionaries of Charity. Some months later, in August, Mother told me, "Mr. Kushwant Singh's article has changed the people's attitude toward us. I notice the difference: there are no more misgivings or frowns when we are mentioned. All show sympathy and appreciation for our work. This is really marvelous."

Mother added, "Kushwant Singh wrote to me—he wished to make me meet other newspaper editors when I go to Bombay, so that I may talk to them of the poor and of their responsibilities to the weaker members of society. He ends with the words, 'God bless you,' " she added with a chuckle, " 'though I think he is not a believer.' "

"I gave a B.B.C. interview," recalled Mother. "Malcolm Muggeridge had asked me to appear on one of his programs. That was the first time I appeared on television. They received me at the studio and led me into a small room with a table and two chairs. I sat on one of the chairs and started saying my rosary. After some time, Mr. Muggeridge arrived, sat down in front of me, and started asking me questions. He had a paper with a list of questions before him. He read two of them, which I answered; then I went on talking about what I wanted to say."

Naturally, his prepared questions dealt with her and the history of her work. As usual, Mother did not want to speak of herself, but of God. It was all God's work. He did it, not she. Malcolm Muggeridge, a good journalist and interviewer, was conquered by the personality, the dynamism, the energy, the faith of the woman sitting before him. Still, it was unusual to see a Catholic nun in religious habit lead an experienced writer and producer to the subject she wanted to develop. She would make the public hear about God, his love and power. They would be told of the love of Christ, which alone motivated these sisters to devote their whole lives to the service of their Lord in his suffering brothers and sisters.

"While I spoke," continued Mother, "they were taking pictures of me. But I did not care; I just went on talking, looking straight in front of me, without moving my head."

She was a good subject for the cameraman, who must have shifted his camera from her wrinkled face to her sandaled feet, the white sari with a blue border covering her head and forehead right down to her eyebrows, her right hand holding her prayer beads, the cross in evidence on her left shoulder; then back to the expressive mouth, the straight-looking eyes of a woman with a single purpose and an iron will. She spoke simply, without show; a deep conviction rang in her voice as she appealed to the viewers to understand and love those around them who feel lonely or unwanted or who lack proper care. She made no mention of money, issued no call for help in favor of her institutions. She stressed that even in well-to-do countries boasting an elaborate social welfare service, there were legions of people who looked in vain for love in their own homes, who craved recognition or attention. Further, true love should also embrace those people who belonged to other countries, races and cultures.

Many viewers of the television interview were impressed. Donations for Mother's works poured in.

Malcolm Muggeridge was perhaps the person most impressed. Promoter and organizer of the drama, he had taken an active part in it. He brought a camera crew to Calcutta to make a film depicting the daily life and work of Mother and her sisters. He stayed three days at the mother house, enjoying the freedom of the place. The crew filmed the mass and the sisters at prayer, the dormitories, the classrooms, the sisters taking their meal, the clothes drying, the sisters filling water buckets and carrying them up the stairs.

He visited the dispensaries, the Kalighat Home for the Dying, the children's home, the leprosy clinics.

He made Mother talk—she spoke of God's action and goodness, and of the sisters who worked as his instruments.

Muggeridge interviewed the sisters. The faith of the nuns struck him, and their devotion deeply moved him.

But for the sisters it is a hard life of faith, the uneventful repetition of the same humble task day after day. Mother sees the beauty of their life, not with human eyes, but with the vision of faith God gives her. She has nearly reached perfect Christian joy and serenity, since, as she says, "We do it for Jesus," it is all beautiful. And when she tells us in the Home for the Dying, "God is here," her intuition sees him present, as simply and obviously as she does the destitute.

But the sisters, the Sick and Suffering, the Co-Workers, and all of us, her friends, we have still to discover God's presence the hard way and work in pure faith as we carry the cross after Christ. Mother knows it well when she speaks to her sisters. Her great duty is to train them to constant self-denial, humility, service of the poor, love of God. Close to the great crucifix alongside the staircase of the mother house, I read the words, "The miracle is not that we do this work, but that we are happy to do it." This conviction Mother drills into the minds of the young novices. "Be happy to do this work for God," this disposition, which is neither natural nor easy, requires God's grace and help.

Mother Teresa was the first living Catholic nun privileged to appear on the cover of *Time,* in 1975. The caption was "Living Saints," and the subtitle called them "Messengers of Love and Hope." The cover bore her portrait. The artist made the portrait on the basis of photos taken at the mother house. Mother Teresa confessed that during this ordeal she asked the Lord to deliver a soul from purgatory for every picture taken. On the cover she certainly looked like a sufferer and not at all as we are accustomed to see her, smiling, kind, serene in the certitude that the world moves constantly, if slowly, toward God. She seemed to bear the suffering of the world. It is one aspect of her personality: she knows suffering; but her faith makes her see the love of God calling people to himself. She brings joy wherever she goes and wants her Missionaries of Charity to do the same. The leading article depicted her correctly, as it stressed that her charity was fostered and sustained by an intense spiritual life.

The various awards and distinctions Mother Teresa has received also helped to make her work and that of her sisters more universally known, appreciated, and supported.

In September 1962 Mother received the Padmashree Award from the president of India. Although this is not the highest Indian honor, it was a remarkable sign of appreciation shown for Mother's work.

This was the first time Mother was singled out in this way, and the honor caused some difficulties. Archbishop Dyer asked whether he should let Mother Teresa go to Delhi to receive her Padmashree, as some priests feared she might feel some vanity at being thus noticed.

But others, who knew Mother well answered, "Your Grace, have no fear, Mother does not know what vanity is. Just tell her that by honoring her the president means to honor all the religious who devote themselves to the service of the poor."

On her side Mother was reluctant to be thus honored and she asked the archbishop, "I suppose I should not go to Delhi?" He answered her, "You must go, Mother."

The Indian honor was followed by an international recognition: the Magsaysay Award was given Mother by the president of the Philippines, who invited her to dine with him and his wife. This award helped her to establish a home at Agra and contributed to the knowledge of her as a well-known international symbol of Christian charity.

In 1971, there was a flood of prizes: the Pope John XXIII Peace Prize, given to Mother by Pope Paul VI; the Good Samaritan Award in Boston; the John F. Kennedy International Award; a doctorate of humane letters in Washington.

In 1973 Mother went to England to receive the Templeton Award; the substantial sum of money it carries was immediately spent by her on a foundation for lepers. The award was given her at a ceremony presided over by Prince Philip. At lunch she was seated next to Prince Philip: a slight nun in a coarse cotton sari next to the tall and smart prince consort. Both had at least one thing in common: like Mother, the prince knows his own mind and speaks it publicly.

"Prince Philip was charming," said Mother some days later. "He had kind words to say about our institute. During the meal he inquired about our work, and I told him what we do and why we do it. They served only one course; I suppose it was out of consideration for me, and my work among the poor." This was a thoughtful and tactful gesture in the best British tradition.

Here stood, in this modern world of comfort and luxury, a living replica of John the Baptist. Her cheap dress, her sandaled feet, her hands fingering the rosary, her direct speech, her single-mindedness reminded all of the kingdom of God she was announcing. She stood as an index finger raised up high, pointing to heaven. Her smallness and humility raised her above the powerful of the world, whom she lifted up spiritually. Her very example made them cut down their pleasures and comfort, that they might share their wealth with the poor. In the breast of many arose a clearer consciousness of the needs of their fellows, as Mother reminded them of the words of Christ that were the cause of her service to the poor: "What you have done to the least of my brethren, you did it unto me."

CHAPTER 13

Mother Teresa Speaks

On the fifteenth of October, eight days after the Missionaries of Charity had celebrated their Silver Jubilee, I had an hour-long talk with Mother, a very personal, spiritual, intimate talk. She was perfectly relaxed, serene. It is extraordinary how quickly she had recovered after the heavy exertions of the jubilee, when she looked pathetically tired and physically exhausted. Now she was fresh and smiling as she spoke.

She was to deliver a speech at the U.N.O. Temple of Religions on October 24. She wanted to describe the essential characters of the Christian religion. Her speech was to begin: "God is love." Love in himself, a wonderful process of life, of giving and receiving, of sharing the divine essence. God creates us out of love; the Father sends his Son to save the world out of love, "God so loved the world that He gave His only Son that the world might live" (John 3:16).

The Son gives his life and dies for us out of love for humanity. The Spirit Jesus sends us is the spirit of love, the bond of love between the Father and the Son; he comes to unite us to Jesus and to one another in love. Then, Christ commands us to love one another; and our service to our fellows, who are first the brothers and sisters of Jesus, is a service of love. We serve Christ especially in the needy and the poor, but also in all people, out of love for him. That love will be all the more perfect if we allow the Lord to live in us and love in us with the perfection of his love.

Mother could close her eyes or look straight before her at nothing or nobody in particular, let the Lord speak and explain this Catholic vision of brotherly love, and the great need we all have of it today. That was what the public expected from her. But we agreed that the theological foundation of her vision of love had to be clearly expressed.

Mother took notes, adding to her outline. Then she closed her file.

"When are you leaving?" I asked her.

"Tomorrow I leave for Rome, where a jubilee mass is to be celebrated by a cardinal."

"Will you go to see the Holy Father?"

"If he calls for me; otherwise I shall not go. After that I fly to New York. I shall stay with the sisters in our house in Harlem.

"There are times," she said suddenly, "when I feel absolutely empty; an empty shell; a thing without consistence, with nothing in me to support me; I feel so lonely and miserable."

"Yes, and still you go on working for God's glory. It is as St. Paul said, 'By myself I can do nothing; but I can do all things through him who strengthens me.' "

I said this to console her. But I thought of St. John of the Cross, and understood what she meant. At times God tries us; at times he gives us a share in the dereliction of Christ at Gethsemane. God seems absent; he withdraws from the soul all consolations and all feeling of his Presence. We must plod on in sheer faith; a faith no more felt, dumb, cold, and lifeless.

"Yes, Mother, whoever loves God must pass through the dark tunnel —sometimes more than once; perhaps often and for a long time."

The fact is well known; the details, the frequency, and intensity of the trial vary according to God's plan.

We remained silent for a while, before the mystery of God's work in souls.

Then I asked her,

"When I speak to the tertians, Mother, on what point do you want me to insist especially?"

"Insist on prayer," she said. "In prayer they must find God, find strength to live their vocation, and be faithful to it."

"Yes, in all your chapels on the wall is inscribed the call of our Lord, 'I Thirst.' "

In Yemen "I THIRST" in English and Arabic. In Gaza "I THIRST" in English and Hebrew. In Rome "I THIRST" in English and Italian.

"In every house of ours, you enter the chapel and you see 'I THIRST!' The call of Jesus. We exist to console Jesus, to quench his thirst for love. It is our function, our aim.

"I pray to our Lord that if the sisters are not to be faithful to their vocation, he may let the institute die. God can do without us. The church would go on existing without us. If the sisters are not faithful to their religious calling, our Lord may suppress our congregation."

"They will be faithful, Mother, I assure you. Our Lord will keep them close to his heart; he will not let them go astray. Your prayers and your blessings will help them."

"Yes, the Sacred Heart. In Latin America, we consecrate families to the Sacred Heart of Jesus. The Sisters prepare groups of forty or fifty families, regularize marriages, prepare the children for their first communion. Then, when all are ready, they solemnly enthrone a picture of the Sacred Heart in the house. Is that not wonderful! Our Lord comes to reign over those families, to sanctify them. He brings love in their midst. But first, they must be religiously married, otherwise there is no enthronement. The family must be established on a firm basis to receive God's blessing."

"Latin America, what a field for your apostolate—such poverty, misery, ignorance, but also such goodwill, and desire for spiritual values. Mother, do all in your power to spread there. I wish the bishops would call you more earnestly. Your sisters have the right approach to many of those who live in material and spiritual need in Latin America. Will you open a house in Mexico, now?"

"No, later. Things are not ready as yet."

"I shall come back via Africa. We have already nineteen African novices and postulants. Excellent vocations. They are keen to devote their lives to our Lord."

"You should open a novitiate there and train your African sisters in their own environment, culture, and tradition. Later you can bring some of them here that they may have the genuine spirit of your society."

"We have already two African novices in India. Three are in Rome, and the postulants remain in Africa. Traveling is expensive; it costs much to bring them by air from another continent."

"Have you any financial problems?"

"Money? I never give it a thought. It always comes. We do all our work for our Lord; he must look after us. If he wants something to be done, he must give us the means. If he does not provide us with the means, then it shows that he does not want that particular work. I forget about it."

To the same question put to her some fifteen years earlier, she had given exactly the same answer. So that was truly a part of her attitude in life, her trust in God, her assurance that he looked after this small society. She took our Lord at his word in this matter of material means. Thus a great source of worry and anxiety was removed from her mind, allowing her perfect freedom of thought and action. Having put her full trust in God, she abandoned herself to his holy guidance in all she did, thought, said, and taught.

"Mother, do you still personally know all the sisters and novices?"

"Not the novices. But I know all the professed sisters.

"I write to them all. Last year 153 took their vows. I wrote a personal letter to each one of them, giving them advice on spiritual matters. They also write to me."

"So, that is what you do in the evenings! You must write a huge number of letters."

She smiled.

I thought of the 153 fish caught in the apostles' nets after the Resurrection of our Lord, as recorded by St. John: "Simon Peter went abroad and dragged the net to the shore, full of big fish, one hundred and fifty-three of them; and in spite of there being so many the net was not broken" (John 21:11). This was of course an image of Peter's future work, which was to bring men into the kingdom of God, as followers of Christ. Mother would also catch both women and men and bring them into the kingdom of God.

JANUARY 1976

Mother was back from America, Europe, Africa.

"Each time I go to Europe and America," she said, "I am struck by the unhappiness of so many people living in those rich countries: so many broken homes, children not looked after by their parents. Their first duty is to work among their own people, bring together separated couples, build good homes where the children may receive their parents' love.

"They have material wealth; they lack spiritual values.

"Then there are the mentally handicapped. Have you met Jean Vanier? You must meet him. A fine man. He established *l'Arche,* a home for mentally retarded people. We must work with him, start a home for these people in Calcutta."

"His organization is completely different from yours, he works with volunteers, free to come and go when they wish."

"I met some of them, and this is what I understood. But their aim and spirit resemble ours: both manifestations of Christian charity."

"Did you meet them in Canada?"

"Yes, earlier they invited me to Toronto, and I spoke to them there. I came back via Africa to visit our house in Ethiopia and the two houses in Tanzania. Africa is a land of promise. There is much poverty there, but also a large field of apostolate. We have excellent prospects. We are going to open a novitiate in Africa, at Tabora. Some twenty African girls want to join us. Four are on their way, to join the novitiate here. After a year I shall send them back with four Indian sisters and start a house of formation there. They are very keen to work with us.

"In London seven postulants have joined. One Belgian girl has joined; she is the first from that country. Others are from the United Kingdom, France, the United States. In Melbourne, we have three Chinese novices, and already some candidates from Papua. In Yemen, thirty Moslem girls have refused to marry, and want to work with our sisters. As Moslems of course, otherwise it would not be tolerated."

"Where are you opening new houses?"

"I am going to the Philippines to open a house in Manila. The archbishop is very keen on our settling there."

"You will have plenty of spiritual work in the Philippines. The people are in the majority Catholic, but the number of priests is very small. There are more than five thousand Catholics to each priest."

"Why is that?" she asked.

"Well, there is a scarcity of vocations, as in South America. People are baptized but many do not attend mass or receive the sacraments. Perhaps your sisters will be able to improve matters, at least in a small manner."

"We have also been invited to South Korea."

"Go to Korea, Mother. Go by all means. The church is growing fast in that country and has a tremendous future. But we must not delay."

She did not know this. I wondered how then she could decide where to open new houses to the best advantage. Was she sure of the guidance of the Holy Spirit in every case? She did ask advice from some priests. She had her counselors, but mistakes had been made in the choice of locations.

"Why do you do so much for Darjeeling diocese, a relatively small diocese, as far as population and the number of Catholics are concerned, with a high ratio of priests and nuns to the population?"

"We are going to open a new house in the diocese, at Gangtok, the capital of Sikkim. The bishop is very keen on our going there. The church is not represented in this small town."

"I know many people are well disposed toward the Catholic church, and some are asking for instruction. I said mass in the palace of the Chogyal of Sikkim some years ago. But we have no church there as yet. Tell me, have you a soft corner in your heart for Darjeeling? Is it because you made your novitiate there or because you got your inspiration in the train on the way to that hill station?"

"No," she said, brushing away the idea with a gesture of her hand.

"Then has the bishop mesmerized you?"

She laughed. "Go to see Takdah," she said, "a new house has been given to us there."

That was a cogent argument. When a property suitable for her work is presented to her, then Mother is inclined to accept the gift. She sees the hand of God in the offering of the property for the sisters' work.

"Mother, what do you consider most important in the training of your sisters?"

"Silence. Interior and exterior silence. Silence is essential in a religious house. The silence of humility, of charity, the silence of the eyes, of the ears, of the tongue. There is no life of prayer without silence."

"Yes, Mother, we need silence to find God, and hear him speak to the soul."

"Silence," she said, "and then kindness, charity; silence leads to charity, charity to humility. Charity among themselves, accepting one another when they are different; charity for union in a community. Charity leads to humility. We must be humble.

"It strikes me how God is humble. He humbled himself; he who possessed the fullness of the Godhead took the form of a servant. Even today God shows his humility by making use of instruments as deficient as we are, weak, imperfect, inadequate instruments.

"Then, there must be joy in the heart, the joy of serving God, the joy of doing his work. That is not incompatible with humility."

"Indeed, in her Magnificat, Mary exclaimed that she rejoiced 'because he who is mighty has done great things to me!' (Lk. 1:49)."

"Yes, I tell the sisters not to fear to do good before the eyes of people. Our Lord said, 'Let your light shine before men, that seeing your good deeds they may praise your Father in heaven!' (Matt. 5:16). So, let people see your good deeds: it is Christ who does them through you."

"Father, when they praise us for what we are doing, I do not mind it at all; rather, I rejoice because it all leads to the glory of God."

"You have just returned from Kerala, Mother. Did you visit all your houses?"

Mother did not answer for a moment. She frowned slightly. I thought I sensed some diffidence or disappointment in her voice, as she answered:

"We have five houses there. People used to look down on the sisters because we work for the poor. Now we start to be accepted."

"You are getting plenty of vocations from that state."

"Yes. But I want to keep a good mixture. Many novices come from Bihar and Orissa. Vocations also come from Tamil Nadu. We were invited to go to a place where there are eleven hundred temples. A real citadel of Hinduism, very orthodox, with no Christian influence. The archbishop was very happy when he heard it and he requested me to accept.

"I have to go to Santiniketan to receive a degree. I don't know why universities and colleges are conferring titles on me. I never know whether I should accept or not; it means nothing to me. But it gives me a chance to speak of Christ to people who otherwise may not hear of him."

In fact, universities or institutions, especially perhaps the less known ones, sometimes make use of the world-famous Mother Teresa to get into the news. At the start Mother may have been helped by this publicity; but not any more.

"I have also been asked to speak at the Philadelphia Eucharistic Congress in July."

"That is a reward for your deep devotion to the Blessed Eucharist. You already spoke at the Eucharistic Congress in Melbourne."

"Yes, but this time it will be more complicated. This is an eight-day affair, and they want me to speak every day on all kinds of subjects."

"Well, the Lord will come to your help as usual."

"Here is Sister Dorothy, who is leaving for Australia to take over the office of regional superior."

I felt very unworthy to give a blessing to these two women, whose prayers I needed more than they needed mine, but they trusted in the priestly power conferred by Christ. Still, I suggested that we first pray together. We fell on our knees and I prayed aloud, "Lord bless the

Missionaries of Charity at work in Australia, make them holy, send them chosen candidates, bless those to whom they minister, and bless us all." Then I blessed Sister Dorothy, and Mother Teresa kneeling by her side.

FEBRUARY 1976

"I have just come from a meeting of the Calcutta Co-Workers," said Mother. I told them, "Holiness is not a luxury—you are all invited to it." I said this to Hindus, Moslems, Jains, Parsees, Christians.

"They seemed pleased to hear it. I developed the theme in this way. Holiness is to love God and love people. It is therefore not a luxury reserved for a favored few. All are invited to be holy. I told them also that the sisters need their prayers to be able to do their work; that the poor need their help, their understanding, their love. We all have much to give, to share, to contribute wherever we find ourselves to be living. Holiness starts in the home, by loving God and those around us for his sake."

"Yes, Mother, you spoke rightly; holiness is not a luxury reserved for a few chosen ones. Still, in practice, real holiness is fairly rare."

I groped for the text of St. Peter that so well applies to the sisters Mother must train and to all the Co-Workers she inspires and encourages on the way to holiness: "Be holy in all you do, since it is the Holy One who has called you, and Scripture says: "Be holy because I am holy." These are the words of God, since he is holy, he wishes those who belong to him to be like him" (1 Pet. 1:15).

Mother still felt the pain caused by one of the sisters who had left the institute.

"Happily the cross is still there in your life, otherwise Jesus might not recognize you," I said.

"Yes, we follow Christ, we hear his words 'I thirst.' So many people still misunderstand us; they take us for what we are not, for social workers."

"You are certainly not at fault when this happens; you tell them clearly enough that you are first religious women consecrated to the service of God."

FEBRUARY 1976

Bishop James Toppo of Jalpaiguri was in the parlor with us.

"We are preparing new foundations," said Mother. "We are opening a house at Jalpaiguri, where his lordship has a property ready for us. I am just back from Gangtok, the capital of Sikkim. We intend to open a house there shortly. And yesterday three sisters left for Mexico."

"As a result of your meeting with the president last year?"

"Yes. They have a house ready for us. Later on I shall send a few more sisters. Some sisters are also going to . . . what is the name of that country that was recently badly shaken by an earthquake?"

"Guatemala," I volunteered. "The people are practically all Catholics, but there are few priests in the country."

I was happy to hear that the sisters were broadening their bases in Latin America. And their experience and efficiency in organizing relief in areas afflicted by natural calamities would serve them well.

"Then," Mother went on, "we are starting in Manila. Already several girls from the Philippines have asked to join us."

"Wonderful. You really have the Lord's blessing. I hope you will soon have a network of houses there. The Philippines suffer from a great scarcity of priests."

"Why is that?"

"It is due to political and other reasons. The people have a solid Catholic tradition and a deep devotion to our Lord and to his Blessed Mother. You can build on that foundation. You should get many good vocations from that country."

MARCH 1976

As I enter the parlor, Mother is talking to an elderly gentleman.

"Father, meet Dr. Gupta."

As we exchange greetings, Dr. Gupta tells me that his son was my student in the economics honors class. So we are no strangers.

"Carry on, Mother. I do not want to interrupt your conversation with Dr. Gupta."

"Sit down, Father."

"Mother," says Dr. Gupta, "I own a property that I would like to donate to you for your work. I cannot put up a large building, but I shall get some friends to contribute to the expenses. The property is situated on a road near DumDum."

"Wonderful, Dr. Gupta. We have a house at DumDum. The sisters could go and work in your property. We might establish there an Asha Niketan—a House of Hope—for mentally retarded people."

I give Dr. Gupta my address and invite him to call; then I take leave, as it is time for my talk to the tertians.

Two days later Dr. Gupta comes to see me.

"How did you come into contact with Mother, Doctor?"

"Well, it happened like this. A young woman belonging to a respectable family was brought to me for delivery. Since she was not married, the family would not accept the child. Her parents asked me to find a suitable place for the baby. I had heard of Mother; so I called at her convent. She was absent, but the sister in charge was very kind. She immediately said that this was their work; they would take the child any day I chose to bring him. They would look after the baby and eventually get him adopted. This act of kindness struck me much. Since then I try to help the sisters in whatever way I can."

This was wonderful. Good people were coming spontaneously to offer their help, to share their property with the poor.

MARCH 1976

"More and more often," says Mother, "I am asked to speak in public. This is an ordeal for me; I wish I did not have to do it."

"How do you manage to speak, Mother?"

"I close my eyes and I do this," she answered, making with her right thumb a small cross on her lips. "Then I let him speak. I follow his inspiration."

"Do you look at your audience?"

"No. I look straight in front of me, above their heads. I look at no one. I deliver my message."

She remembers what Christ promised: "When you stand before kings and judges, do not worry about what you are to say" (Matt. 10:19).

Still, when she has been warned that she will have to address a gathering, it would be tempting God to go completely unprepared—that would not be trust but presumption. Her listeners today are not judges and enemies, but friends and sympathizers, who appreciate this opportunity to hear the Word of God. Mother always speaks of God and Christ.

She goes forth in the power of the Lord, as the young David faced Goliath, without embarrassing himself in armor not made for him; he took his sling and five pebbles. God guided his arm and gave him strength. Mother does the same; her words, like pebbles, strike people's minds and shake them out of their ignorance and complacency. They do not kill; they vivify, awaken, stimulate good impulses and generous actions. She can say, like Paul to the Corinthians, that she does not appeal to human wisdom, but only to knowledge of Christ Jesus. "As for me, when I came to you, brothers, it was not with any show of oratory or philosophy, but simply to tell you the testimony of God. The only knowledge I claimed to have was about Jesus, and only about him as the crucified Christ" (1 Cor. 2:1–2).

As Paul confesses, "Far from relying on any power of my own, I came to you in great fear and trembling" (1 Cor. 2:3–5), so does Mother, who finds public speaking a most painful and trying exercise; yet for God's honor, she agrees to do it. Like Paul, she strikes the minds of her audience because she is filled with Christ.

She talks in a homely, simple, but forceful way. Her speech elevates, yet remains always practical and adapted to the audience.

After my instruction to the tertians, Mother said,

"We shall take you home, Father. The van is going to the station with the sisters who take the night train for Kalimpong. We are opening a house there.''

The sisters sang a hymn in honor of those leaving for Kalimpong. Then the latter went into the van waiting outside, full of luggage; somehow they all managed to squeeze in. I sat next to the driver; Mother sat just behind me.

"We always sing when sisters leave," she said.

As the van started Mother led the prayers for a safe journey, and we all answered. The last invocation was, as usual, "Immaculate Heart of Mary, cause of our joy, pray for us." Mary brings joy to the world in the person of Jesus, her child. And now serving Christ in the poorest of the poor, the sisters put the accent on "joy."

We made for the station. On the way Mother spoke of the new foundations she was preparing.

"God," she said, 'is good to the institute. The sisters are invited in many places; we cannot accept all the requests. More sisters are needed. We must pray for vocations."

When we reached Sealdah Station, the sisters unloaded the mattresses, blankets, buckets, bags of food, and all that they were taking with them for the poor.

"We carry all our goods ourselves," said Mother, laughing. "They call us the 'coolie sisters,' because we always do without porters.

"I shall go up to Kalimpong in a few days, when the sisters have settled down and I can see better what their needs are. They will have discovered what kind of work is more urgent."

Thus Mother goes from one foundation to another, spreading her work of love always farther into new cities and new countries.

But even in its vast extension this work remains centered on the human person, as Mother shows her concern for the spiritual and material welfare of the individual.

Every human being counts for her; she sees not crowds but faces revealing human souls to her.

CHAPTER 14

The Jubilee

First I thank my God through Jesus Christ for all of you and for the
way in which your faith is spoken of all over the world.

(ROM. 1:8)

On a Sunday in October 1976 at the Cathedral of the Most Holy Rosary,
the archbishop concelebrated mass with a large number of priests in
thanksgiving to God for the blessings he had bestowed on Mother Teresa
and her Missionaries of Charity and through them on such large numbers
of Christians and non-Christians.

Members of many religious institutes united their prayers to those of
the sisters; children and adults, instructed by the sisters, benefactors,
helpers, all thanked God for the congregation and the good it had
effected.

On Monday, Mother Teresa and one of her sisters came to the Sacred
Heart Church, to invite Monsignor Barber and myself to concelebrate the
mass of the next day, a mass to mark the Silver Jubilee of the Missionaries
of Charity, a great day of joy and thanksgiving. As she sat upright in her
chair, as usual, I noticed how tired she looked. Yet she talked cheerfully
with us for an hour and a half.

"I am so grateful to you and to your father," Mother told Monsignor
Barber. 'Your father was the first to help me when I left Loreto and
started this work."

"You must be very tired, Mother?"

"Yes, but it was all wonderful. People prayed for us and with us;
thanked God for what he had done through the Missionaries of Charity.
These last days, we went every day to pray in some temple or church.
The archbishop gave us permission to do so. We prayed with the Jews,
the Armenians, the Anglicans, the Jains, the Sikhs, the Buddhists, the
Hindus. It was extraordinary. All hearts united in prayer to the one true
God, thanking him for the great things he has done through his ser-
vants."

"Yes, this is the spirit of the Magnificat in which Mary exclaimed, 'My
soul praises the Lord and my spirit rejoices in God my Savior: because
he has done great things to me and holy is his name" (Lk. 1:46–49).

"Yes. We did nothing; he did everything. All glory must be returned to him.

"Today we were with the Jains in one of their temples. There were four Jain priests who wore no clothes. They sat behind a table."

"You have been so long in India and you do not know the habits of the Jain priests of the Digambara sect?"

"No. While they were reading from their Scriptures and praying to God, a woman clad in white, a nun, I think, was pulling out some of her hair. In a spirit of penance, I suppose. I tried also to pull out some hairs from my head. It is painful, you know."

We all laughed. Mother's head is usually so well covered by the border of her sari that I have never seen her hair.

After some more reminiscences, she spoke of the work. Truly she was indefatigable.

In October, on the feast of the Most Holy Rosary, on which the congregation of the Missionaries of Charity had been approved by Rome twenty-five years earlier, a simple, intimate ceremony took place at the mother house. All over the world, in some eighty houses of the congregation, in every continent, in Rome, Harlem, Tabora, Melbourne, London, Lima, Mauritius, Yemen, Jordan, Calcutta, Bombay, Madras, Delhi, Ranchi, among other places too numerous to name, prayers ascended to God in thanksgiving. The Sick and Suffering, the nuns in cloistered monasteries, the Co-Workers of many countries, joyfully sang their gratitude to God and asked him to bless abundantly the Missionaries of Charity during the next twenty-five years.

At six A.M., as I approached the mother house, I looked up; there were no clothes hanging to dry on the roof, as there usually were. On the street a milk distributor went on his rounds. People slept peacefully on the pavements. Before the house a discreet police service indicated that the governor of West Bengal was coming to assist at the mass at this early hour.

Some twenty priests prepared to concelebrate the thanksgiving mass with the archbishop of Calcutta. Father Van Exem was present; Father Henry did not come—he was praying in the church of St. Teresa, not far away. Father Gorrée had arrived from France for the occasion.

The small chapel was filled to capacity. As the priests entered the chapel for mass, they could see the crucifix hanging from the wall, and the inscription next to it, "I THIRST."

There were pews for the special guests. Mother and the sisters knelt or sat on mats.

Archbishop Picachy expressed the gratitude of all present for twenty-five years of grace. He expressed the wish that the sisters be holy and fully dedicated to the service of Christ their Lord.

As the mass proceeded, words and songs of praise of God and gratitude were on all lips while peace, joy, serenity filled all hearts. The promise Jesus expressed in the Upper Room—"I have told you this so that my joy may be in you and your joy be complete" (John: 15:11)—was realized. The Holy Spirit had come at Pentecost to fill the minds and hearts of all present, bringing his gifts: love for God and humans, joy in the service of Jesus and his brethren.

The universality of the society was manifest: sisters coming from the six continents were present, eager to return to their posts for work.

In the afternoon, Mother went to Creek Lane, where she had received such heart-warming hospitality from Michael Gomes and his family, and climbed the stairs leading to her Upper Room. Mother brought the picture of our Lady that had adorned the altar during the years of pure faith. She wished to thank their first helpers and hosts. She stayed ten minutes and left.

The next day, Mother was off to Cuttack, in Orissa, to start a new house there. It was again work as usual, and expansion throughout the world continued.

The jubilee provided a fit occasion to sum up the results of twenty-five years of work under the direction of the Holy Spirit, of twenty-five years of extraordinary graces and blessings.

In India the Missionaries of Charity have been an unqualified success. The results have been beyond all expectations. Mother Teresa is the best known and most loved, most widely respected disciple of Christ in the country. She personifies selfless love and service. Before Mother and her sisters appeared, the Catholic church was mainly known as an educational organization; Mother has made the church known as a charitable organization and as a force for social progress. It still requires a contemplative leader, inspired by the Spirit, to establish the church before the public as a spiritual and mystical force, leading to the knowledge and experience of God.

During the years, Mother Teresa's fame in India has grown steadily. She has always professed to be first a religious, completely devoted to God's service, receiving her inspiration and strength from God. She has proved to be a model of Christian charity, selfless, caring for all, devoted, asking for and ready to accept the collaboration of others whatever their beliefs.

She has been noted for her quick decision, prompt action, and forceful implementation; and for her readiness to start difficult tasks even without the necessary means, in the certitude that God will provide them when the work is for his glory.

The sisters, trained by her, imitate her simple, efficient, practical style; they constitute a highly mobile force always ready to render service in time of emergency or calamity.

Mother has worked in the Gandhian tradition—living simply, poor and frugal in her ways, keeping out of politics, working for the destitute, teaching self-help, making use of local resources. Joining prayer to work, she proved always ready to assume the most unpleasant tasks.

In Latin America, a continent in many respects similar to India, a few outposts have been established. The congregation started with great hopes, which have not yet materialized. Valuable spiritual help has been given; but this is still very little compared to the needs and possibilities of this vast area.

The institute has half a dozen houses and plans to open a few more. But it has not yet taken roots there.

Latin America, with close on half the Catholic population of the world, suffers from a great scarcity of priests and nuns. Its peoples are hungry for religious teaching, leadership and manifestations. In most Latin American countries there is much poverty, a great inequality in the distribution of wealth, large families, numerous slums and terrible poverty in the cities. But there is also a deep Christian tradition on which to build. There are many people who are responsive to the right approach, devoted to *La Madre de Dios* and Jesus crucified.

In such circumstances the Missionaries of Charity could have been expected to succeed as well, or nearly as well as in India. Yet the response has been weak. Calls from bishops came slowly, and are not the numerous, earnest appeals we expected.

When reminded of this, Mother, always optimistic, answered,

"We have two novices. Some girls are applying to join us."

"Yes, Mother, but what is that among three hundred million people of Catholic tradition and belief, with enormous needs?

"You have struck no roots as yet. You have three houses in Venezuela, all right; one in Peru, one in Colombia, one or two elsewhere. But how does that compare with the multitudes, the needs, the possibilities?"

By the end of 1974 the Co-Workers were organized in only one country, Venezuela.

"Why did you fail to effect a real start there, as you did in India?"

The Holy Father himself asked Mother Teresa, in a private audience, to make a big effort to multiply her activities in Latin America. Why did the sisters not succeed better?

A reason may be the present efforts of some young priests to unite Jesus and Marx; the stress put on economic well-being and social justice rather than on faith in Christ and in the sacramental life; the bent toward political action and revolution, sometimes through violent means; the capitalistic structures that are considered the root of the evil, rather than the sin, pride, greed, and sensuality that create them; the move toward communism.

The Missionaries of Charity are outside politics and care not at all for these preoccupations. When in the United States Mother Teresa was asked, "Do you and your sisters go in for politics?" she answered, "We have no time for them."

This attitude in many countries is an advantage: the sisters are suspected by none; they are concerned only with spiritual and charitable work. The sisters' outlook is pragmatic; they are saying, in effect: "We do the work appointed to us; others may discuss and prepare blueprints for the society of the future."

But perhaps people expect from the sisters a greater degree of adaptation to their life, culture, language. Can the Indian sisters in Indian saris catch the imagination of simple folk elsewhere? Should the effort to become adapted to local conditions and the mentality of the people Mother made so successfully in India, not be repeated in Latin America? Various countries have distinctive cultural features that affect their religious life and style.

The adoption of English as their common language has given the Missionaries of Charity a certain universality: it has helped them to spread smoothly in all the countries where English is the language of the people or at least of the educated class. But in non-English speaking countries progress was modest. Should English remain the society's usual language in Spanish- or French-speaking countries?

"A bishop asked me," said one of the sisters who came back from Venezuela, "Why do you not adopt Spanish as your community language?"

In Africa, a good start has been effected. Prospects are bright, possibilities of work enormous, while many vocations can be expected from the English-speaking countries of Africa.

The numerical increase of the Missionaries of Charity, though very remarkable, should not be considered exceptional. On the day of the jubilee, the sisters numbered 1,133, including more than two hundred novices.

The progress of the Franciscan Missionaries of Mary, whose mother house is at Ootacamund in South India and whose story resembles that of the Missionaries of Charity, was still more spectacular. When they celebrated their silver jubilee, the institute, founded in 1877 by Mother Mary of the Passion, numbered about three thousand members.

Both congregations wish to offer signal service to God. The Franciscan Missionaries of Mary add to the religious vows of poverty, chastity, and obedience a promise to offer themselves as victims of love to Christ. The Missionaries of Charity take a fourth vow, to dedicate themselves to the service of the poorest of the poor.

St. Paul wished to go to the ends of the world—at least, to one end. He planned to visit Spain, considered as it was one extremity of the inhabited world by the ancient Greeks and Latins. He may not have succeeded in reaching Spain, though he saw many countries and preached the faith in more places than anyone in his time.

Mother Teresa was more fortunate; with the same desire, to spread the message of Christ, his work, his influence, as far as possible, she went to the extremities of the world. How otherwise would one explain her keenness and happiness to open a house in Papua, to go to places as widely apart as Fiji, Mauritius, New York?

Still, like Paul she would have to suffer some setbacks. Even after a spectacular development, half the world remained beyond her reach. She had not penetrated behind the iron and bamboo curtains. The Chinese communist world and the Soviet communist world, close to one-half of the earth's population, were out of bounds.

China, with her eight hundred million people, all God's children, looked like a dream country. Would she ever enter that Promised Land? Would the people in power really object to the Missionaries of Charity, unassuming, unsophisticated, unattached to any political system or ideology? The sisters were certainly no spies, no revolutionaries, nor did they forward the interest of any foreign country.

Two Chinese sisters had joined in Calcutta, three more elsewhere. Houses were opened in Taiwan, Macao, Hong Kong, perhaps as stepping stones; one day the sisters might cross into the mainland of the Celestial Land.

To China, yes, some day, they will go. Francis Xavier died facing the mainland, on Sancian Island, from where his body was brought back to Goa. The sisters might go one step further: reach the mainland and enter it.

Would the second quarter of a century not see the Missionaries of Charity expand toward the East? Mother had gone east from her native land. Her sisters had gone mainly west, when they left India.

Now, with a footing in the Philippines, the sisters can spread eastwards. The Philippines offer a solid Catholic basis and a promise of many vocations. From there they will be able to go to Taiwan, Hong Kong, Indonesia, Japan, South Korea, and even China, in God's own time.

The most admirable result of Mother and her sisters' apostolic activity is the tremendous number of acts of love for God and the neighbor they have caused to be produced. Acts of love originating from poor and rich, young and old. Acts of love—many of them of heroic quality, coming from the dying destitute whose last words had been "My God, I love you," or "Thank you, Sister."

The acts of love and devotion of children all over the world who went without a meal, an ice cream, or a picture to help some poor brother or sister in some unknown town or village.

The acts of love of viewers of a television program, of listeners at a meeting, of readers of newspapers and magazines, showed and told the beautiful example of a lifelong commitment to the service of Jesus in the poor, and responding to it.

The acts of love of co-workers, sufferers, helpers, many of them performed in a humble and unobtrusive way.

Countless acts of love of God, forming an uninterrupted chain and encircling the world, as Mother had envisioned in an early letter, when her whole community could still fit within a single room. But could even she foresee the wonders God would work through his weak instruments?

THE FUTURE

"After Mother Teresa, what next?" Many asked the question after the glorious days of the Silver Jubilee.

Mother seems to be so indispensable; the whole edifice she has built up appears to rest on her shoulders. She is Atlas carrying the world. The public and the officials know of her above all. Nearly everyone speaks of "the sisters of Mother Teresa," while acknowledging her unique charism. This God-given charism is granted to an individual, not to a group. She believed, remained faithful, divested herself of all human self-love to belong to God, entirely; in her Christ lives and acts in a special manner.

What will happen after her? Charisms are not inherited; God dwells in the individual soul; mystical graces are personal. Then, in the world we know, hero worship is directed to a person, though influence may belong to a group. After Mother Teresa, what will happen to her institute?

"If the society is God's work, it will endure," said Mother. "But if the sisters are not to be faithful, if they are not to work for God's glory, then God may as well suppress the society," she added with determination.

Mother does not wish to see her own particular work extended and continued, but the name of the Lord proclaimed and glorified. This concern should obtain the graces necessary for her society to continue after her.

Mother said, "If the society is God's work." Is it presumptuous to affirm that the society *is* God's work? The institute has been officially approved by the church; it has been blessed and commended repeatedly by the Holy Father, and by many cardinals and bishops; it is daily praised by the voice of the people, which is certainly in this case the voice of God.

People of all nationalities, social classes, and religions are united in admiration for the works of charity performed by the sisters.

"After Mother Teresa, what next?" ask many of her friends and collaborators. "Will all this good work come to a standstill? Will the sisters be able to carry on their apostolate without her leadership, guidance, and support?"

To dispel all lingering doubts concerning this matter, I went to the Darjeeling Children's Home, run by the Missionaries of Charity. It dominates the town, standing on a hill, two thousand meters above sea level.

As I climbed up, I waved my hand to children playing on the roof. One of them ran down to open the door for me, then went to call a sister.

"This building is new," said the sister who took us round. "Two years ago we had here a shed that was destroyed by a violent storm. So we rebuilt this part of the building. The people helped us; the district magistrate also."

We went through the different rooms, which housed about a hundred inmates.

"All these children suffer from malnutrition. We feed them, give them vitamins and injections to make them strong. Many have wounds.

"This girl is sixteen years old; when she arrived she had a large sore on her leg. Now the wound is closed and healing. It was due to malnutrition. This girl has a stunted arm; this one is mentally retarded.

"We have ten orphan boys I sent as boarders to the Pedong High School; we must pay eighty rupees per month for each boy. We have also twenty orphan girls studying at the Bethany and St. Teresa's Convent Schools close by; these come home for the night.

"Here is an old lady who is close to death."

The woman, who was not a Christian, recognized me as a priest and asked for a blessing. I blessed her. The other ten or twelve inmates also asked for a blessing. We said a short prayer together, and I blessed them.

"One person died the other day," said Sister. "Come this side; there are more children. Some are total orphans, others have one parent living. Either the father is at work and cannot look after the small children or the mother is too poor to feed them. One woman has four children here; a widow, working for a very small salary; she could not keep her four children. They all suffered from tuberculosis and malnutrition. Now they are picking up. This boy here seems to have no intelligence; he does not react to anything you say. We are trying to find out if he really is mentally deficient. With better food he may improve.

"Many of these cases come from the villages. We have a van and go down to the valley for dispensary work once a week. We brought here some of the more needy children."

As we reach the chapel, Sister tells me,

"You know this place, you gave us some instructions two years ago."

"Yes, I remember the chapel. Let us say a prayer for these good people and for the sisters who look after them."

The chapel is the source of strength and the oasis of consolation in the midst of all this misery, and among the poor of the Lord.

The visitor who stays one hour in the home, smiles at the children, says a kind word, pats a cheek, gives a blessing, finds this pleasant. But for the sisters it is the same hard task from morning till evening, and sometimes at night, caring for sick children and the dying destitute, not for one or two years, but for their whole lives, with never a break.

The only spot of beauty and intimacy in the house is the chapel. It is as beautiful as they can make it; for the Lord dwells there. I see two vases holding lovely white lilies, lilies for Jesus present in the tabernacle, present in these suffering brothers and sisters. Against the wall stands a large crucifix; above it are written the words of Christ: "I thirst." The sisters are daily reminded of the call of Jesus that brought them here.

As we leave the chapel, I put to the sister the question for which I had come to see her: "Sister, does Mother Teresa come here often?"

"No, she has not come to Darjeeling for a long time."

"Does she write to you often?"

"No, she is too busy. She writes very seldom."

"Do you receive any supplies from Calcutta?"

"We receive some supplies from Catholic Relief Services, as other charitable institutions do. Once a year I go to Calcutta to get a supply of medicines."

"Do you ask the bishop for any help?"

"No, we do not ask the bishop for any financial help. He sends a priest from bishop's house to say mass for us daily."

"Of course, he must look after your spiritual welfare. And did you contract any debt on account of this new building?"

"No, we have no debt. We manage things by ourselves."

"I see that you do it very well." I took her leave and came back singing on the road. I had the answer to the question so many people were asking: "After Mother Teresa, what next?" The answer was simple: "After Mother Teresa, the Missionaries of Charity." This house of the sisters and many others like it were being run quite smoothly without Mother's intervention or help. The foundress had succeeded in her main task. The well-trained sisters could stand on their own feet and take over.

There remained to answer the question: "After Mother Teresa, who? Who will take the reins and guide the society in its progress?" The answer lay in the constitutions that specified how the society was to be governed.

Father Van Exem and Mother had created the pattern of government in conformity with church rules for religious congregations.

In 1975 the General Congregation of the institute had appointed Mother as superior general for six years. All the ballot papers, except one, bore Mother Teresa's name as their choice to direct the institute for the next six years.

Father Van Exem, the presiding officer, destroyed the only differing ballot paper, so that only he knows for whom Mother voted.

When Mother Teresa becomes unable or unwilling to carry on as superior general, the sisters will elect a new superior according to the rules laid down in their constitutions. This superior will not inherit the personal charisms of the foundress; but she will receive from God the graces necessary to carry out her duties of superior general of the Missionaries of Charity.

CHAPTER 15

It Was Thirty Years Ago . . .

SEPTEMBER 1976

"How was the Eucharistic Congress in Philadelphia, Mother?"

"Very fine."

"Did you have to speak many times?"

"Yes, they wanted me to speak everywhere. I went about with eight policemen around me the whole time. The people would have crushed me. . . . I am so small. It was my worst penance to be thus guarded all the time."

"Was there much pomp? Or did you feel in a real religious atmosphere?"

"There was no show of pomp, no display. It was simpler than the congress at Melbourne. The great procession with four hundred thousand participants was very religious. Cardinal Knox knelt on a priedieu behind the monstrance of the Blessed Eucharist, carried on a float. The American people are very pious. There were groups of other, what do you call them?"

"Denominations, they say nowadays."

"Yes, denominations, present at some of the functions. We washed each other's feet, exchanged the kiss of peace, broke bread and ate it together, but then when it came to the Eucharistic sacrifice, they fell back. This was very painful. At mass they would not join us. When there was communion to the Body and Blood of Christ, they were not with us. That was painful."

"Yes, the Eucharist is the sign and touchstone of unity. We are truly one around the altar where the Lord becomes sacramentally present. We must pray for unity, complete unity that we may truly form one body of Christ."

"Your general made a beautiful speech at the congress. I must quote it when I meet some of your Jesuits," she chuckled, "I must tell them to live more poorly and go to the poor."

Soon she was back to her great preoccupation:

"We must work for souls; it is really souls that matter. I feel so happy when I can do good to souls."

She had written this in her intimate letters to Jacqueline de Decker, thirty years earlier. Her hunger for souls had not abated; it had grown with the passing of the years.

"I think the sisters also feel happy when they can do good to the souls. After all that is why we started looking after the dying, that we might help them think of God at their last moments and make an act of love of God before dying; we want them to die with God.

"I think the sisters also see the souls behind the bodies and rejoice when they can do spiritual good."

She said "I think" with imperfect conviction.

"The work does not distract me from God," she continued.

"I went to Mexico. We have opened a house there. When the sisters go round, the poor do not ask them for clothes, do not ask them for food, they ask them,

" 'Teach us the Word of God.' "

"So the people ask to hear the Word of God. . . ."

"No, they don't ask to *hear*, they ask the sisters to *teach* them the Word of God.

"The president himself made arrangements for our house there, not the government. Everything is well arranged.

"Mexico is a huge city. On the outskirts where they gather all the garbage brought by the conservancy department, some five hundred families live on the picking and sorting of refuse, as many people do here. I told the president to leave them to that work, that is what they can do. Make the surroundings better, and improve the houses, and let them go on with that work. Already the sisters have started instructing the children for their first communion.

"We shall buy five hundred New Testaments and distribute them to these families. The whole Bible is too expensive. Also it is too difficult for them. Is this not wonderful that the people are hungry for the Word of God? Of course, in Mexico Catholics have been persecuted; this may be the result. Even now priests and nuns are not allowed to wear clerical or religious dress. Our sisters go about in their habit—nobody knows what the sari is. But they wear their cross."

"But, Mother, it is such a pity. In many places God's children are hungry for spiritual food, and no one is found to give it to them."

"Things are better in Mexico than in South America."

"You are not doing too well there?"

"We have only two vocations. Lima, Peru, seems more promising than Venezuela. The poor hanker for spiritual things. Why must so many priests and nuns busy themselves with politics when their primary work is to teach the faith? Everywhere people tell us: 'Speak to us of Jesus.' "

"Did you not start a new congregation? The news came out in the papers."

"Yes, the Sisters of the Word. They are a contemplative branch. They have three hours of prayer at home and one hour in the church. Then daily two hours to go out and speak of Jesus. Not public speaking in the squares or street corners, just to speak of Jesus to people who want to listen. People are eager to listen to those who speak of our Lord. I wish I could retire there among the sisters and just live a contemplative life, just be with Jesus."

"Not yet, Mother; you have still much work to do. Why did you start that branch in the United States and not here?"

"Because they are ready for it. Sister Nirmala is in charge. She will do very well. She has already seven candidates."

"Is the aim to receive nuns who left their convent and wish to come back?"

"There may be some such cases, of people who wish to do penance and to join the institute."

"I suppose the congregation will develop under the inspiration of the Holy Spirit."

"Yes, and speaking of inspiration, today is Inspiration Day, the tenth of September. It was thirty years ago, in the train taking me to Darjeeling that I heard his call."

"The call to serve Jesus in the poorest of the poor. And you obeyed his call. When did you come to this house?"

"I do not recollect."

"Was it in February 1954?"

"Yes, about that time."

"Did you go to pray to the Fatima Shrine to obtain the house?"

"Yes, I went at times with the sisters, praying on the way. They had first told me about another house, which was to cost us eighty-five thousand rupees. As I did not have the money, I decided to offer the sum in Memorares to our Lady. So we all started saying Memorares. Every sister one thousand Memorares. I said the prayer thousands of times. But we did not get the house. Instead a person told me, 'There is a gentleman who has a suitable house; I shall take you to him.' He did so, introduced me, and then left. The proprietor was astonished. 'I don't know that person, neither did I tell anyone that I wanted to sell the house. But I was contemplating doing so.' The house came to one hundred and twenty-five thousand rupees. Monsignor Barber paid it out of the diocesan funds."

"And you paid them back slowly."

"Yes, I paid back two or three hundreds at a time. I did not pay our Lady again in Memorares, I had paid her once."

"And now it has become too small. You should look for another house for another novitiate. The place is too crowded."

"No," she said.

"But then you will have to refuse candidates, since the numbers are always increasing and you really cannot accommodate more in this house."

"Why not? The sisters can sleep on the floor; the poor do it."

"They require more space; you cannot train them properly in this manner."

"I shall remove the postulants who are here and send them to Park Street. And the candidates can be first received in various houses to see our kind of work and life."

"That will lighten the burden on this house. Even so, you may have to open another novitiate in India."

"No. They must all come to Calcutta."

She thought that only in the historical mother house would they imbibe the real spirit of the congregation.

"You should open a novitiate in the Philippines," I suggested. "Transfer there the one from Melbourne. And from the Philippines you can spread toward the Far East; Hong Kong, if you find a property; Taiwan, Indonesia, Korea, Japan."

"There is plenty of scope there. And one day, China."

"Yes, the Philippines would be better than Australia. We have only two girls from that country, and do not expect to recruit many."

"In the Philippines you will have plenty of candidates. For the training of the sisters in poverty and in work for the very poor, Australia is not the place—the country is too rich."

"You should see our work among the aboriginals; they are terribly backward; it is incredible the way they live."

"But the style of life will be more similar in the Philippines to what the novices meet in the East and Far East, except perhaps in Japan, which has become a rich country. But of course you require the goodwill and support of the bishops of the Philippines."

"Yes, in the course of time we can open a novitiate in the Philippines, and of course one in Africa."

"And how was Rome, Mother?"

"Wonderful. I saw the Holy Father, in private."

"I had told you he would call for you."

"There was nobody else. I talked to him as I talk now to you, just facing him and quite simply."

"Did he inquire about your work?"

"He knows about it already. I spoke of the new congregation, the Sisters of the Word. He sent a blessing to all the Missionaries of Charity, to all the Co-Workers; he gave a special blessing for the Sisters of the Word."

"You had a meeting of the Co-Workers in Germany?"

"Yes, it was wonderful. There are eighty thousand Co-Workers now, twelve thousand in the United States."

"Did you meet Jacqueline de Decker? Was she able to travel to Germany?"

"Yes, she runs the Sick and Suffering. Only the national vice-chairpeople came to Germany. They had to pay their own passages. The organization did not pay for them. I had told them to save the money during the year, that it be not a burden on their family budget. The Germans were marvelous; no one had to go to a hotel; they were all received in families. When we met they insisted on prayer; prayer meetings every week, or every second or third or fourth week.

"I told them to practice charity first in the home, then among neighbors, then in their locality, in their country and finally in the world. But first have a home where there is love and understanding. Love between the members of the family will bring happiness."

The Angelus bell rang in the convent. We said the Angelus. Mother then said,

"In many places the poor are happy to hear the Angelus bell. In New York the poor complained to the sisters, 'Why is it that we don't hear the Angelus now? We were happy to pray to our Lady when we heard the bell rung, the announcement of the good news of the coming of the Savior.' The sisters asked the priest, who said he had no time to ring the bell three times a day, and the parish could not afford to pay a person to come and ring it. So the sisters took up the duty. "We shall come and ring, Father," they said. And now the poor of that very difficult locality are happy that they can again pray the Angelus.

"The poor are hungry for God; they want to hear about our Lord. They do not worry so much about material things; they want to hear that they have a Father in heaven who loves them."

"About the book, I must ask you, nothing personal, that is, no personality, no personal credit. He did it all. It is all his work."

"Yes, you do not want any praise; all praise is reserved for God. But you may say with our Lady in her Magnificat, 'He has done great things to me and holy is his Name.' What the Virgin Mary said you may say also."

She was right; she had no merit in the whole thing except that of having allowed God to work through her. Humility is truth, said St. Teresa of Avila. All good comes from God. But looking back to the moment of her call on the road to Damascus—rather, to Darjeeling—she could say with St. Paul, "I have kept the faith God had reposed in me, I remained ever faithful to him" (2 Tim. 4:7). Then he did great things through his humble handmaid.

"We are not channels," I added, "we are instruments. Channels give nothing of their own, they just let the water run through them. In our action we are instruments in God's hand."

"Yes," she said. "I like the comparison. I feel like a pencil in God's hand."

She looked for a stub of pencil on the table, but there was none. She made a gesture with her fingers; "God writes through us, and however imperfect instruments we may be, he writes beautifully.

"In God," she continued, "I find two things admirable: his goodness and his humility. His love and his humility are striking. God is truly humble; he comes down and uses instruments as weak and imperfect as we are. He deigns to work through us. Is that not marvelous?"

"Yes, it all starts with the idea of the Incarnation. The Son of God assumes our human condition; he walks among us and works with us; he even agrees to die on a cross to atone for our sins."

I knew well that Mother did not want any praise. I had recorded as objectively as possible what I had seen and heard and felt during these years with her and her sisters. I took my clue from St. John writing to the second- or third-generation Christians: "What we have seen and heard and touched of the Word of Life, that we make known to you, that you also may share in our fellowship" (1 Jn. 1:1–3); yes, share our experience, and rejoice at the coming of the Lord, at his manifestation to humanity, at the wonderful works he performed and still performs for our spiritual good, to save us and sanctify us.

I had an obligation to my readers who wanted to know how this page of church history had been written, how this spiritual saga, this wonderful story had started and developed under the guidance of the Holy Spirit. A senior sister had suggested, "Father, please write especially about the beginnings. Say how the Missionaries of Charity started, give us a book that may inspire the younger members, the future novices who have not known the first years."

"Yes, Sister, the years of pure faith, the heroic years. Those who will join you later on have the right to know how the congregation started. There are two trunks full of documents still with Father Van Exem. They may perhaps be opened at the next jubilee. They will reveal details of juridicial proceedings, correspondence dealing with the establishment, the constitutions, the rules of the Missionaries of Charity. That is for the historians who will sift the material, when all those connected with the foundation are gone to their reward."

I had written at Mother Teresa's request to tell those who wanted to hear the simple and beautiful truth about the origins and the purpose of the Missionaries of Charity. I tried to write soberly, critically, constructively. As the spiritual director and confessor of the mother house for many years, I had felt that the Spirit of God guided the young congregation. I had spoken with Mother on spiritual matters; we had discussed various aspects of the work and new foundations.

And now, to crown it all, the Lord had been good to me. In ninety minutes, on the thirtieth anniversary of the day of inspiration when Jesus had called Mother Teresa to be more closely united to his divine Majesty, we had gone over the different phases of the institute, and summed up one by one the chapters of this book. Mother had followed the lead and confirmed what was written. She had always remained single-minded in pursuing her aim; neither the substance nor the emphasis had changed over these thirty years. God had been good to her; he had been good to me.

The bell went for the community supper. I got up and took Mother's leave. She accompanied me to the door; we both folded our hands in parting in the Indian manner. Then she bent down low, very low, out of respect for the priestly character of the man who makes Christ present on the altar. Mother Teresa is a woman of faith.

"Be careful," she said gently, as she opened the door leading to the narrow lane and remembered that I am half-blind. "There are two steps."

Part Two

MOTHER TERESA:
MESSENGER OF GOD'S LOVE

CHAPTER 1

Prelude: The Jubilees

Then Jesus said to his host, "When you give a lunch or a dinner, do not ask your friends, brothers, relations or rich neighbors, for fear they repay your courtesy by inviting you in return. No; when you have a party, invite the poor, the crippled, the lame, the blind; that they cannot pay you back means that you are fortunate, because repayment will be made to you when the virtuous rise again."

(LUKE 14:12–14)

Mother was preparing for a great day, the jubilee of her first big work, the one perhaps closest to her heart, that had started her on the road to fame and success, the Kalighat Home for the Dying, prototype of many such homes the sisters run in different parts of the world. This work had been most dear to her; for weeks and months she had bent with respect and love over the emaciated bodies of men and women picked up from the streets in miserable condition. She had returned to them some sense of respectability, given them hope in an afterlife that would wipe away the tears from their eyes, drive away the hunger from their bellies, the feeling of loneliness from their hearts. In the realm of charity, she had pioneered something unique in today's world, comforting the suffering Christ in the most needy of his brothers and sisters having reached death's door.

On Friday, 28 October 1977, three days before the great event, Mother confided, "For five days, I had high fever and was confined to bed. Still, I came down to the refectory wrapped in a blanket, and we had a meeting to finalize the arrangements."

"It was a very bad attack of flu," said her counselors. "We tried to keep Mother in bed, but we could not. She insisted on working."

It was to be expected that again she would be asked to pay the price for a great favor God would grant her. Before the jubilee of the congregation, had she not said, "I suffered from a cold more severe than any I had since my childhood"?

Her fever did abate, and Mother came to the Sacred Heart presbytery to invite the priests to attend the ceremony. "We chose to celebrate this jubilee on the first of November," she explained, "because it is for Christians the Feast of all Saints, of all those who died with the love of God and whose souls enjoy the bliss of heaven. And I believe that all our people who have died so beautifully in the Kalighat Nirmal Hriday, offering willingly their lives to God, enjoy now the happiness of the vision of God.

"So we shall remember all of them on the first of November and also show our gratitude to all the kind helpers who have made it possible to run the home during these twenty-five years."

JUBILEE OF THE HOME FOR THE DYING

The Nirmal Hriday—or Immaculate Heart—Home at Kalighat had been opened on 22 August 1952, when the first inmates were received and the house was blessed. On the jubilee day, Cardinal Picachy was in Rome. The pro nuncio, Archbishop Storero, presided over the concelebrated mass, for which a small platform and an altar had been erected in a corner of the men's ward.

The government film division had sent a team to record the event. With their powerful lamps, they gloriously lit up the religious ceremony. The pro nuncio and a few priests celebrated the Eucharistic Sacrifice. The pro nuncio preached a homily in English, and bishop-elect Linus Gomes spoke in Bengali, recalling the early days of the Kalighat Home and expressing the gratitude of all for this wonderful work of charity.

Some may have noticed that the little cross Mother wore on her left shoulder was not facing the outside world. The figure of Christ was turned inside, toward his faithful bride. Jesus must have been saying to her deep down in her soul, "I thank you for what you did for me all these years."

After the mass, a man approached Mother. "He is a priest from the temple," she said. He greeted her with folded hands and bowed deeply before her. But he did not take the dust off her feet, as had done that other priest, perhaps his father or uncle or relative, who twenty-five years earlier had confessed to her, "During thirty years I have worshipped the Goddess Kali in stone, but today the Goddess Mother stands before me, alive."

Things had changed; people more than ever wanted to see her and received her blessing; but she had become a great organizer, a world figure, with a large crowd around her.

Indeed, the Home for the Dying had become holy. It was a shrine people of different faiths entered with respect, where they spoke in hushed voices, conscious that they should not disturb the awesome silence of approaching death. It seemed so easy to die here, the natural thing to do. One lingered for a while, got detached from the things of earth, and waited for God's call. Of the thirty-six thousand destitute people who had entered this home, sixteen thousand had, as Mother always put it, "died with God."

Perhaps it was for this reason Mother did not want the patients to be raised on beds. They remained close to the ground from where most of them had been picked up, not knowing what a bed was, close to the earth to which their bodies might soon return. They just waited a few hours or days in this antechamber of heaven, getting ready to go to God.

But today they were preparing for a feast. Elegant women left their cars, carrying themselves parcels of foodstuffs, pots of curds covered with silver paper, obviously coming from the more expensive candy shops. The women entered the home and went to get things ready in the small kitchen attached to the wards.

Mother had asked them to come in person, bring the food they had prepared at home, and distribute it themselves to the poor patients. And this they did with delightful, well-bred simplicity. They would not have taken better care of the smart guests their husbands were accustomed to bring home.

A woman came from the women's ward into the men's ward, where we all stood, and approached me. For more than twenty years she had been helped by our parish. On our books she was known as Miss P., though she had been married twice and received a widow's pension. By her peers she was called "Ginger" on account of her hair, which had been reddish. She suffered from acute elephantiasis, and her feet and legs were so swollen and covered with sores that she had to walk barefoot, not being able to wear any kind of sandals. Today she sported a clean dress, and her legs and feet had been carefully washed and attended to.

"Father, it's the first of the month," she said, "have you got my pension?" I pulled out the amount and handed it to her. She smiled. "That will allow you some little extras to improve the usual diet," I said. "But you won't need anything today. Look at all the good things the ladies have brought for you." She was not yet dying; a few days later, she left the home and was back on her rounds, collecting alms. She might return later to this haven of peace.

A woman approached Mother to offer her a hundred-rupee note. Mother did not take it. "I don't have a bag," she said gently. "Give it to one of the sisters." The idea of the day was not to receive cash donations, but to obtain from the women personal service for the poor. "I want the rich people to do the work themselves," explained Mother. "Each woman was asked to prepare and bring food for ten people. All in the same manner; no competition, no jealousy. All were to produce the same fare, and all the poor were to receive the same, namely rice, chicken curry, potatoes, curds, bananas, oranges."

Mother soon left the company of the pro nuncio, the priests, the smart women, to move among the poor. Again she was her old natural self, and at her best. She saw to every detail, showed interest in each individual, noticed every need, helped to make everyone as comfortable as possible. She arranged pillows and blankets, helped some to sit up, saw to it that no one was forgotten in the distribution of food.

To an old man too weak to eat rice and curry, she brought a banana and peeled it for him. When she found that he could not swallow even small pieces of banana, she asked for an orange and pressed its segments to his lips. At the end of the meal, when bags of nuts were distributed to each of the patients, she told them to keep the nuts for later on. "They might suffer from indigestion if they ate any more; their stomachs are no more accustomed to such a large quantity of food," she explained.

As twenty-five years earlier, Mother was again the person in charge of the ward.

As other guests did, I approached with a well-filled plate a man who was lying flat on his couch, seeming unable even to move his arms. But in his eyes I read an appeal.

"Will you eat?"

"Yes."

"What is your name?"

"Dhinenraj."

"How old are you?"

"I don't know."

"How long have you been here?"

"Four days."

"From where did you come?"

"I was on the street."

"What is your sickness?"

"My stomach is completely flat, quite empty."

So it is malnutrition and starvation, I thought, and set down to remedy this state of affairs.

The man ate eagerly, relishing every spoonful. He opened a huge mouth and was happy to have it filled. "You have not had a meal like this since your youth or maybe your marriage feast," I encouraged him. He smiled, then went back to serious business. There was still some hope of recovery for him, since he was under the good care of the sisters.

When the man had finished his plate of food, he relaxed and like a baby prepared to go to sleep. Mother Teresa was next to us. "This is the only one of all those who cannot sit up who ate this whole plate of rice and chicken," she commented approvingly. Nothing had escaped her. "The ladies have done a wonderful job," she added. "And among them I saw only three Catholics." She had succeeded in getting women from all religions to come and perform this service of charity.

It was glorious to help the poor, all God's children. But we did it once in a while and in very attractive conditions. For the Missionaries of Charity, sisters or brothers, it was their daily bread; they had to perform this work daily, for months or years. Even in scorching heat, even when their backs ached from bending constantly to wash the poor, feed them, give them to drink. They required truly what Napoleon called "the two o'clock in the morning courage," when no one sees you, encourages you, approves of what you do, and all is darkness around you and sometimes in your very soul.

They required faith, a strong faith. Mother had trained her sisters for this work, given them the motivation, and often they would reread the passage of their constitutions that said, "Our homes for the dying are treasure houses for the opportunities they afford us to reach souls. Death —sacred to all men—is the final stage of complete development on this earth. Having lived well, we wish for ourselves and for all men to die beautifully and so enter into the eternal life of full development in God. We train ourselves to be extremely kind and gentle in touch of hand, tone of voice and in our smile, so as to make the mercy of God very real and to induce the dying person to turn to God with filial confidence" (second edition of the constitutions).

Asked what was their most difficult work, a sister answered, "To look after the dying. They arrive in a hopeless state, have to be washed, cleaned, clothed; many can hardly speak. Half of them die after two or three days. If they improve they are transfered somewhere else. No personal contact can be established and developed. And the process starts again daily. This work is physically exhausting and mentally unrewarding. It requires pure faith that we do it for the love of God."

Perhaps that is why Mother felt so attracted to it. It brought you no human consolation, or hardly any. But she would always repeat the consoling testimony of the man who said, "I have lived as an animal; now I am going to die like an angel with this devotion around me." Then at times their last word was "Thank you"; it left a lasting impression on the soul. The main consolation was that they would all die peacefully, surrendering themselves to God, looking forward to the happiness of heaven.

Several people had mentioned that photos taken in this Home for the Dying in half-darkness had come out quite clearly. Why should it not be so? Miracles of charity were daily performed here. This was a place hallowed, sanctified by the deaths of thousands of people who had "gone to God," showing the real benefit to humanity of this small home. And there were another thirty-two similar homes in various parts of the world.

JUBILEE OF THE CHILDREN'S HOME

The next day, Wednesday the second of November, Mother's kind greeting was "Thank you for coming yesterday." Then she pointed to two charts pinned to the wall: "See, tomorrow the poor children will be fed and entertained: 5,300 of them. And the day after it will be the parents' turn to be fed and entertained, nearly twenty thousand people—exactly 19,998."

Several columns on the chart for the children's feast showed the organizing groups, the number of children received, the means of transportation, the places of recreation, the sisters in charge of groups who were to gather the children, and where they had to take them. There were eleven groups. Two thousand children were assigned to the Tollygunge Golf Club, while 500 would be entertained at Loreto College by and at the expenses of the Loreto College students and staff.

The same arrangements were made for the groups of parents, who would receive one ticket for husband and wife. The number of invitees was truly enormous. Who had ever fed and entertained during a whole afternoon twenty thousand poor people in Calcutta—or, for that matter, in any big city?

Mother's ever-active mind, seeking to bring love to the world, had discovered a new means of doing so. What no one had dared to try, or even thought possible, Mother had realized. Of course, she would say that God had touched the hearts of the rich and inspired them to take active interest in the poor, his children, and their brothers and sisters. This service of love would not be for the less fortunate people of their own companies or organizations, but for people completely unknown to them.

Mother wanted No. 1, No. 2, and No. 3 of the large multinational companies, together with their wives, to come and serve the poor, themselves. Several days in advance, Catholic secretaries had been asked by their non-Christian bosses: "By the way, Carol, Mother Teresa has asked me and my wife to go and feed her kids; what are we expected to do? You, as a Catholic, must know those things." And Carol, Lily, and Mary Ann had explained how things would take place.

On the appointed day, all did as Mother had bid them do.

On Saturday the fifth of November, Mother commented, "Was it not marvelous how people became involved in this work of charity? A lady told me that the whole town is talking about what was done for the poor. We received help from every quarter. When some friends said they would entertain two thousand children on the lawns of the Tollygunge Golf Club, which is outside the town, I was wondering how we would take the children there. It was much too far for the children to walk it. So I called on Mr. Jyoti Basu, the chief minister, and told him my difficulty. He put at our disposal ten trams and seven buses. He said he would pay for them. We could have ten trams for the whole afternoon; they would take the children there and wait till the function was over. Most of the children had never traveled by tram. On the way, they chatted and laughed and sang."

"Did you go to all the places where the children were being entertained?" I asked Mother.

"Yes, I went to the eleven centers, in schools and colleges, at the zoo, at the golf club. I had to thank personally the people who had helped to organize the feast."

"Who had the first idea of getting the top people in the firms involved, Mother?"

"Well, when we celebrated the Silver Jubilee of our congregation in 1975, it was all prayer. We went to pray with Hindus, Jains, Buddhists, Zoroastrians, Jews, Anglicans, Protestants, in fact with people of all denominations and religions, in eighteen different places. The jubilee celebration was limited to prayer, to thanking God for all he had done for us and through the Missionaries of Charity, with the help of so many friends. This time, we were to concentrate on the service of love, on practical devotion. We would get the top people in firms and important members of society to come themselves and serve the poor. Not just send money or gifts, but come in person, see the poor, befriend them, come in contact with them, learn their condition; then they would serve them with their own hands. And they responded magnificently.

"The poor were astonished and deeply moved when seeing such well-dressed and educated people come down to serve them. At Kalighat, I saw the Maharani of X. down on her knees, feeding the patients, and her elegant daughter doing the same. Such an example goes a long way.

"On the second day when we feasted the children, the directors of some big companies were present with their wives, distributing food to slum children and to their parents. Some of the children were so poor that the sisters had to make clothes for them, that they might be decently dressed. We did not take the Sunday school children, because they are better off and well dressed; they will have a treat at Christmas."

Mother, while mixing with the children, had noticed their spontaneous reactions. "At Tollygunge, what astonished the children most," she said, "was the luscious, thick, green grass of the beautiful lawns. The kids were patting it with their hands and asking me what made the blades grow so strong. What was there below? They had never seen such grass. As I moved through the groups, I saw many children who did not eat more than one sweet out of the packet distributed to them, in which there were cakes, buns, sweets, fruits, and I asked them why. They answered me that they had brothers and sisters at home and that they would share with them. Poor children have that beautiful idea of sharing whatever they receive, perhaps more than the children of the rich.

"On the next day, we fed nearly twenty thousand poor people. I thought of the gospel advice of our Lord, 'When you give a feast do not invite the rich but the poor, the lame, the blind; go round the lanes and by-lanes and bring them together and feed them; then your reward will be great, for they cannot repay you nor invite you in return' " (Luke 14:12–14).

"Yes, that advice that seems so difficult to put into practice was truly the order of the day; it found its realization in a most perfect manner. It was not only a distribution of food by servants or officials or caterers, but the organizers, the donors paid with their own persons, distributing gifts to the poor, the blind, the lame, the uncared-for in a personal way."

"Did you go round the firms, Mother, to obtain their collaboration?"

"The sisters did everything," she answered. "But I also went out with them to invite the top bosses to collaborate in this scheme. All agreed most willingly."

Thus, moved by the love of God, Mother had managed to bridge for a while the gulfs of inequality, of castes and creeds, of respectability. To the pride, satisfaction, and happiness of all concerned, she had brought the more favored members of society to serve the poor and be among them and with them, just brothers and sisters, as they were together the children of God our Father.

CONSOLIDATION OR EXPANSION

The jubilee celebrations had evoked admiration and gratitude to God for the wonderful work done through the power of his grace. But now many friends felt that the time had come to move cautiously from the stage of expansion to the stage of consolidation. Energies should wisely be concentrated on the training of personnel and the strengthening of existing foundations. They should review the progress made, study the needs, work to deepen the spiritual lfie of the younger members of the congregation. Mother and the sisters had the choice between expansion and consolidation of this God-inspired work.

Later, as we reviewed together the progress achieved, I asked, "Mother, will you stop expanding for a time to concentrate your energies on consolidation of your positions?"

Without hesitation, she replied, "We go on developing, expanding, opening new houses. We are asked to open new foundations in many places in India and abroad. We are invited to go to many countries: the people want us. We cannot stop. My main difficulty is to find suitable superiors. But God will provide. We cannot stop moving."

"Yes, Mother, you have a strong wind blowing in your sails. The Holy Spirit urges you on—make full use of his grace. Go on expanding to God's glory."

THE JUBILEE OF JESUS

Mother Teresa kept quiet for a while. She must have felt our spirits were in communion, for now she opened her heart. Gently, a little shyly, she revealed her secret intention, the motive she had not mentioned before, the reason for her fantastic, humanly speaking excessively ambitious project of new foundations.

"This year we are opening twenty-five new houses. This is the Silver Jubilee of Jesus. We have had the jubilee of our congregation, the jubilee of the Home for the Dying, the jubilee of the Children's Home, the jubilee of our first vows, now we have the Jubilee of Jesus. We are feasting our Blessed Lord. We shall open this year twenty-five houses, that means twenty-five chapels with tabernacles where Jesus will be. In every one of our houses, the first thing we bring is a tabernacle, a chalice, and a ciborium for holy Mass. Each time we open a new house, Jesus becomes present in that house, that locality.

"The other day at Surat, as we opened the new house, only one room was ready, the chapel; the tabernacle was there. I took the mayor inside and showed him the chapel with the presence of Jesus. That was Foundation Number 17. So this year we feast Jesus. This is his own jubilee. In his honor, to his glory, we establish twenty-five new houses."

This decision sprung from pure love, a fresh and delicate, thoughtful and inventive love for Jesus, who had called her to serve him in the poorest of the poor. He had during twenty-five years showered his graces and blessings on the young, expanding congregation. How could the Missionaries of Charity express their gratitude to their Lord? Mother Teresa found the answer: nothing could please the divine bridegroom more than twenty-five tabernacles, where daily his young brides would appear before him, prostrate themselves in adoration, and sing his praises. They would pour out their hearts to the spouse to whom they were wedded, who humbly, lovingly awaited his brides in the sacrament of the Eucharist.

The plan revealed the delicate freshness of love of a young bride. How could the Lord refuse this gift? The scheme had to succeed. Prudence according to the norms of the world had been set aside; trust in God took its place. Some would criticize, find the proposition irresponsible. No doubt it was difficult to carry out. Some less important works might be put aside or have to wait. Resources in personnel would be stretched to the limit; the energies of many would be taxed.

As Blaise Pascal said, "The heart has its reasons which reason does not know." An intuition of love had prompted this decision: this year will be the Jubilee of Jesus, and we shall establish twenty-five new houses in his honor. It had to succeed, it was succeeding through God's grace.

In this young congregation the main difficulty lay in finding able pioneers and superiors. Mother needed sisters capable of going to new places, to foreign countries, among peoples whose cultures, ways of life, languages they did not know. They would have to start from scratch, establish contacts, find friends, supporters, discover needs, approach the poor. The first group of recruits had been trained by Mother. They were hand tooled, imbued with her spirit, flushed with zeal. But they all occupied posts of responsibility. Less experienced sisters had now to be called in to start new foundations.

Mother continued to open new houses, and toward the end of the year her charming plan was nearing completion. "I went to Beirut," she said one day, "they want us to open a house there. They insist very much. I was shocked at the sight of the town. Destruction everywhere. Terrible destruction. Ruins. Misery. Poor people suffering. We are going to open there our twenty-fifth house of the Jubilee of Jesus."

A few days before Christmas, as we reviewed together the year's work we were happy to say, "And so, Mother, you end gloriously the Jubilee Year of Jesus. Your twenty-fifth house has been opened just in time. With God's grace you fulfilled your dream, or was it a promise to Jesus?"

Instead of answering, she reminisced on the beginnings. "Today is exactly thirty years ago that I went to the slums for the first time: 21 December 1948," she said and remained silent for a long time. There she had been alone. . . .

No, she was not alone—she has never been alone. Though none but herself knew who it was who accompanied her, silently, discreetly, invisible to people's eyes. Now, digging in her own experience, she could speak to her sisters of "aloneness with God," as one who had visited the country she described.

The twenty-five houses of the Jubilee Year of Jesus had been opened in time, to the praise and glory of the Lord. Now, some thought, Mother and her sisters could relax happy, and take a little rest. But "Love is a fire no flood can quench, no torrents drown" (Song of Songs, 8:7). At the beginning of the following year, Mother announced, "This year will be the Golden Jubilee of Jesus. The Silver Jubilee of Jesus is over; now, in order to make a total of fifty tabernacles where our Lord will dwell, we must open another twenty-five houses, establish twenty-five tabernacles."

And again it was done. Twenty-five new houses were opened in India and a dozen other countries. The sisters were all learning geography, discovering new lands, new towns. Some started learning new languages.

As the year ended, the Golden Jubilee of Jesus was completed. But the habit had been acquired. Immediately plans were made for a second Golden Jubilee of Jesus. Again twenty-five houses in a year and twenty-five more houses the next year were opened, to make up the golden number. This required a hundred new professed sisters, four to a house; they had more than that number. The recruitment went on regularly: candidates to the congregation came in increasing numbers every year.

In September 1981, Mother could say, "Only two more houses to be opened this year, to complete this Golden Jubilee of Jesus. We have opened two new houses in Washington, D.C.—one for the active branch, one for the contemplative branch. Also a house in Tokyo and one in East Berlin. We now have 210 houses." There was sound of pride in her voice, only gratitude to God, the giver of all good things. Her trust in the Lord had been amply rewarded.

FROM SEED TO TREE

The congregation of the Missionaries of Charity, started thirty years earlier, deserved to be studied more closely to bring out its characteristic

Mother Teresa at prayers. *(Rosario Canzi, Reggio Calabria, Italy)*

Mother Teresa with one of the first groups of Sisters.
(from Le Joly)

Perpetual vows at Saint Mary's Church, Calcutta.
(Chitrabani, 76 RA Kidwai Rd., Calcutta)

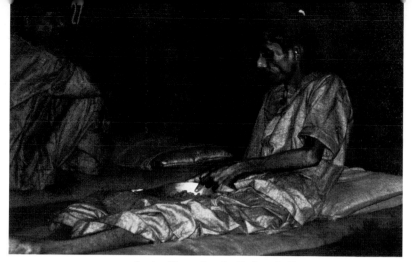

In the Home for the Dying, India.
(Michael J. Christenson)

Treating a leper on the roadside
from the back of a mobile clinic.
(Servants of Love by Le Joly)

Mother Teresa with one of her children.
(Servants of Love by Le Joly)

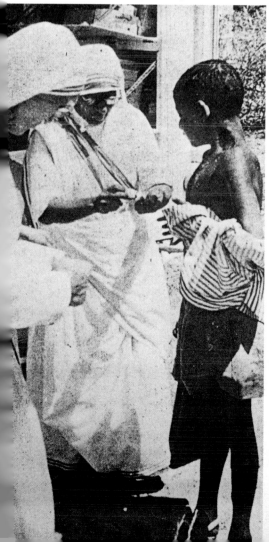

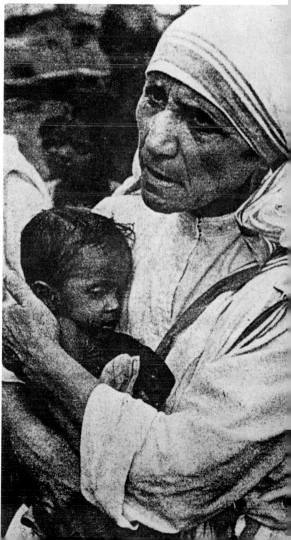

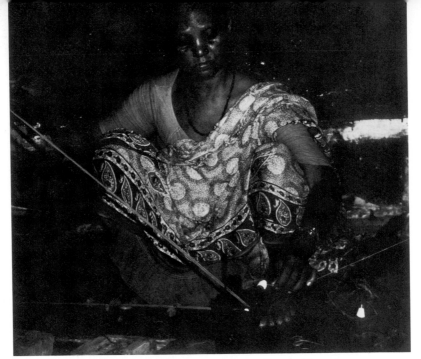

At the Gandhiji Prem Nivas Leprosy Centre, Titacarh.
(Michael J. Christenson)

Reading messages of welcome in Liverpool.
(Catholic Pictorial)

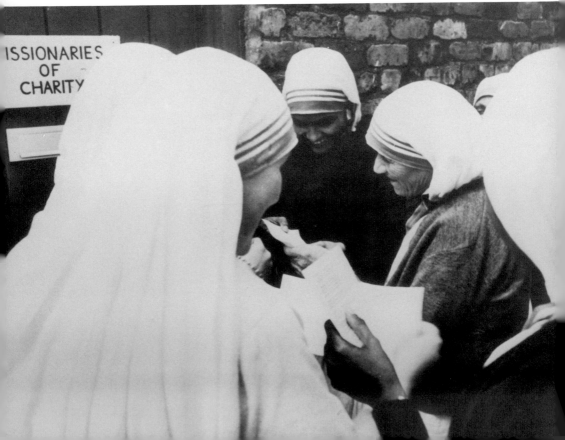

Being greeted by Tom Sweeney,
A Sick & Suffering Co-Worker.
(Catholic Pictorial)

Mother Teresa, on the occasion
of receiving her doctorate from
Cambridge University, with
Ann Blaikie. *(International
Link, Cambridge Evening News)*

Mother Teresa with Indira Gandhi after
receiving the Jawaharlal Nehru Award for
International Understanding. *(Capitol News Photo)*

The Queen presented the insignia of honorary member of the Order of Merit
to Mother Teresa, who is only the 5th non-Briton to receive
the award which is personally bestowed by the Queen. *(RDR Publications, Inc.)*

Mother Teresa with Pope John Paul II.
(from Le Joly)

The Sisters who made their formal religious profession are received at the Motherhouse and garlanded, as is the custom for Indian brides. *(Chitribani)*

traits. What had caused this astonishing success could now be brought to light, studied, appreciated.

Indeed, the congregation seems to reenact the parable of the grain of mustard seed Jesus told his hearers. "The kingdom of heaven, he said, is like a grain of mustard seed, that a man has taken and sowed in his ground; of all seeds, none is so little but when it grows up it is greater than any garden herb; it grows into a tree, so that all the birds come and settle in its branches" (Matt. 13:31–32).

THE GRAIN

A chart hanging on a wall of the parlour of the mother house says,

> Agnes Bojaxhiu
> Daughter of Nicholas and Rosa
> Younger sister to Agatha and Lazarus
> Born on August 26, 1910 at Skoplje
> Baptized on August 27, 1910

The family belonged to the Albanian minority living in South Yugoslavia. She was educated in Croatian at the state high school. She did not live in Albania.

Brother Janez Udovc, aged eighty-three years, remembers, "As the sacristan of the only Catholic church of the town, I knew all the Catholic families. Agnes's family was very religious. She herself had a very fine voice; she was really our prima donna, the soprano soloist of the parish choir. She also directed the choir in the absence of the choirmaster."

"Agnes belonged to the Sodality of Our Lady. They circulated some news items sent by Yugoslav Jesuit missionaries in Bengal. Agnes felt the desire to go and work for Christ in Bengal. She was advised to join the Loreto nuns who were running schools in Bengal. So on September 26, 1928, she left her home for good and went to Rathfarnham, Ireland, to become a postulant of the Institute of the Blessed Virgin Mary. On 29 November 1928, she sailed out for India and reached Calcutta on 6 January 1929."

"Myself, I volunteered for India and my provincial sent me. I came in December 1929. I reached Darjeeling, where Agnes was a novice. Her parents had entrusted to me a parcel for her, which I gave her on arrival. Later, Agnes, after taking her vows of religion, was posted at St. Mary's High School at Entally, Calcutta."

Sister Teresa, as she was now called, continued to teach in that school until Jesus called her to start a new institute for work among the poorest of the poor. The Lord's call took place on 10 September 1947, in the train taking her to Darjeeling to make her yearly retreat.

By calling Teresa a second time to leave everything for his sake, even her religious congregation, though not to give up her vows, Jesus asked from his bride a new total sacrifice. She was to leave the security and friendly support of her community, of her convent and the religious institute she loved, to whom she owed everything in the religious life, and launch into the unknown.

The grain was to germinate first in the Upper Room of the house of Michael Gomes, then two years later, in the mother house at 54 A Lower Circular Road. It developed, gained in strength, grew into a tree, threw out many branches. New foundations were made in scores of countries.

THE TREE

The birds of the skies of God come to settle onto its branches. Thousands of poor people, of orphaned children, of shelterless people, come to take refuge on its branches or under its foliage. Millions of the poor have been helped, consoled, brought back to life, or simply helped to die gracefully in God's love.

The tree has many activities, all directed to the well-being spiritual and material of the very poor. The sisters are truly "messengers of God's love" to the poorest of the poor. A chart in the parlor of the mother house enumerates their activities:

Apostolic: Catechetical centers, Sunday schools, Catholic action groups, family visiting, prison visiting

Educational: Primary slum schools, sewing classes, commercial classes, handicraft classes

Medical: Dispensaries, leprosy clinics, rehabilitation centers for leprosy patients, homes for abandoned children

Social: Family planning clinics, work among alcoholics, mentally retarded

The grain of mustard seed has truly become a large tree to the glory of God, who caused it to be born, to die in the earth, and provided the increment in a wonderful manner.

It may be worthwhile to study Mother Teresa's spirituality, consider her influence in today's world and wonder what will remain after of this beautiful symphony she wrote and directed to God's glory.

CHAPTER 2

A Christocentric Spirituality

I am the Alpha and the Omega,
the First and the Last,
the Beginning and the End.
(REV. 22:13)

The spirituality of the Missionaries of Charity as developed by Mother Teresa is essentially christocentric.

1. *In its origin and inception:* the call of Jesus to serve him in the poor, the road to Darjeeling event, yearly commemorated on its anniversary, the tenth of September as Inspiration Day. The society recognizes that its existence is the result of that call Jesus made to Mother to serve him in the poorest of the poor.
2. *In its purpose and aim,* which is to quench the thirst of Jesus for the love of human beings.
3. *In its exemplar or model:* the Christ of the gospel, his life and teaching. The congregation endeavors to live the gospel as thoroughly, as perfectly, as can be done today.
4. *In its motive force,* found in Christ in the Eucharist and Christ in the poor.

Christ is the cause, the mainstay, and the end of the sisters' vocation, of their religious life and apostolic work.

THE CALL

The call of St. Paul and that of Mother Teresa exhibit striking similarities. The road to Damascus event and the road to Darjeeling event each changed the direction of a life already dedicated to the honor and service of God.

In both cases, Jesus calls, commands, directs, informs. To Paul, Jesus indicates that the zealot of Yahweh's cult persecutes him in his followers: "I am Jesus, whom Saul persecutes" (Acts 9:5). To Mother Teresa, Jesus her bridegroom, to whom she is wedded for life, commands, "Serve me in my poorest brethren." Jesus assumes what is done to his own, as done to himself.

In both cases the Lord gives an order. To Paul, he says "Go." Mother on her part acknowledges, "It was an order." The Lord commands.

They are both to be Christ's instrument for the spread of the good news. The Lord tells Ananias, "This man is my chosen instrument to bring my name before pagans and before pagan kings and before the people of Israel" (Acts 9:15). Paul's mission is to be universal.

Mother has all along been deeply conscious of being the instrument of Jesus. Her purpose of procuring the glory of Jesus, which is limited in immediate scope to the spiritually and materially most needy, indirectly affects all sections of humanity. She has appeared and delivered her message before more kings, presidents, and ministers and before larger audiences than any other religious founder.

What Paul and Mother are to do immediately, how they are to carry out their mission, neither of them knows. Paul is at first blinded and has to be led by the hand. Soon he is entrusted to Ananias and is baptized. Then the Spirit guides him. Mother similarly confesses, "I knew where I had to go; but I did not know how to get there." She was not aware of how she was to fulfil God's will; hence she required perfect trust and abandon to the divine guidance.

Both these "chosen vessels of clay" will have to share in the Passion of Christ for the redemption of the world. "I myself will show him how much he himself must suffer for my name," said the Lord to Ananias (Acts 9:16). Through Paul's letters, we know how he had to suffer. He spoke eloquently of his floggings, stoning, shipwrecks, two nights and a day at sea, persecutions, dangers from every side, false brethren, disappointments from his helpers, and continual anxieties for the good of the churches he had established and nurtured.

After Paul's example and wonderful teaching, inspired by the Holy Spirit, all religious souls know that the following of Christ implies to enter into the paschal mystery, sharing in the Passion and Death of Jesus, before experiencing the joy of the Resurrection. But only with discretion and deep respect for God's action in souls can we speak of the share of a living person in the sufferings of Christ.

Mother has written more than once to people especially tried by God, "Jesus must love you much, since he gives you such a large share in his sufferings." Life has not been a bed of roses for one who rises daily at 4 A.M. to make the stations of the cross, work and pray the whole day, and retire to sleep at 1 A.M. She has to shoulder the burden of many new foundations every year, travel extensively, appear hundreds of times before different audiences every year.

For both Paul and Mother, it was fitting, it was prophetic that God's call should be made and heard on the road, which both would use to such an extent for the glory of Jesus who had called them to the apostolate. They both felt that their mission was universal: the world awaits the good news of the coming of Christ, we must travel as far as we can, spreading the gospel of Jesus in every land.

TO QUENCH THE THIRST OF JESUS FOR SOULS

When she came to Cambridge for the convocation at which she was to receive an honorary doctorate in divinity from Prince Philip, the chancellor of the university, Mother went to the convent around midday. People came to meet her there, including members of the press. A reporter asked her, "What made you start your work, what inspired you and kept you going during so many years?"

Mother answered, "Jesus."

The reporter looked disappointed; he must have expected long explanations, but was told only one word. For Mother one word sufficed to sum up her whole life, to explain her faith, enterprise, courage, love, devotion, efficiency, single-mindedness: Jesus. Everything was due to him, every effort and sacrifice made for him. Mother expressed it again forcefully when she said, "Father, tell them: we do it for Jesus." The sentence has become her motto, her watchword, the explanation she gives of the activity and the success of the sisters, "We do it for Jesus," everything, all the time.

JESUS IS THEIR MODEL

Jesus is the exemplar or model the Missionaries of Charity are to follow: like Christ they bring hope, light, joy.

They have heard the astonishing words the Lord pronounced in the synagogue at Nazareth, after he had read the prophetic passage of Isaiah (61:1–2): "The Spirit of the Lord has been given to me, for he has anointed me. He has sent me to bring the good news to the poor, to proclaim liberty to captives, to give new sight to the blind, to set the downtrodden free, to proclaim the Lord's year of grace. Then Jesus said, 'Today these words are being fulfilled in your hearing' " (Luke 4:18–19, 21).

Following in the footsteps of Jesus, the Missionaries of Charity bring the good news of God's love to humans; like Jesus they go about doing good; like Jesus, they seek those in need; they bring help to the blind, the lame, the lepers; they provide food to the hungry and consolation to the abandoned.

In her spiritual teaching Mother likes to stress the humility of Jesus, who not only gives but comes to ask, to ask so that he may give us. The gentle, kind, thoughtful Lord stops at the well of Jacob to ask a person, to ask a sinner, "Give me to drink." And to dispel the woman's astonishment, Jesus adds immediately, "If you knew who is the one who asks you, you would have asked him and he would have given you living water"

(John 4,10). Jesus stoops to ask. In truth, he was physically thirsty, tired of walking, preaching the good news, seeking souls. But he was still more thirsty for our love, asking us, "Give me to drink." Yes, unworthy as you are, give me to drink and I shall fill you with the water of life and love, and energy.

Christ in the garden asks us, "Wait here and watch with me a while." Watch—he asks for help, for comfort, for sharing in his agony, and finds himself disappointed by his very apostles. "You could not watch with me even one hour?" (Matt. 26:36,40).

Christ stoops to ask on the cross, issuing a call, a challenge, a request, "I thirst."

And again today he tells us, "I stand at the door knocking; if anyone will open to me, I shall come in and share his meal" (Rev. 3:20). Lord, you ask in order to give yourself. Then we shall share with you and all we have, all we are and that will be perfect love.

Christ is the perfect example of love the sisters must seek to imitate. "Love one another," Mother pleads, "as Jesus loved us, who gave his life for us, when we were sinners. He gave his life, nothing less. So we should give what costs, costs much."

CHRIST IS THE MOTIVE FORCE OF THEIR LIFE

"We could not do without him," states Mother.

He inspires and sustains by his grace their detachment, their poverty, their trust, their cheerfulness, their service of the poor. Mother's confidence in Jesus knows no limit. To his presence in her and her sisters she attributes their strength and the remarkable fruits of their apostolate. She says, "We are able to go through the most terrible places fearlessly, because Jesus in us will never deceive us; Jesus in us is our love, our strength, our joy and our compassion."

Mother opposes and reacts against the rather common modern tendency to anthropocentrism, naturalism, materialistic humanism, secular conception of humanity and the universe. Those who hold such ideas succeed in eliminating God from their world vision, doing away at the same time with grace and faith and the supernatural. They center all charitable and social activity on the service of the human being, a being whose origin and destination they ignore.

Mother's conception of humanity is rooted in the gospel, which teaches us the primacy of God, extols the beauty of God's plan for humanity, proclaims the dignity to each and every human person. The two greatest commandments are those of love: love of God and love of the neighbor. The second commandment issues from the first. It has its root in the love of God, God seen in the neighbors whoever, wherever, whatever they be.

Mother stresses that lifelong devoted service of the poor requires a strong motivation, found only in faith. "Without faith no love; without love no service of the poor, the abandoned, the sick, the cripple, the dying. You can do our work two years or three years without religious motivation, but not a whole lifetime. If you do not believe it, try to do it. . . ."

The work of the Missionaries of Charity is not centered on the poor as it has so often been represented in the press. "Mother Teresa saw the misery and poverty on Calcutta roads and her heart went out to the poor sufferers; she felt she had to do something about it." No, this is not the correct story, not the right interpretation of this extraordinary activity, this wonderful work of charity, that has gone on for thirty-five years and will go on much longer. The truth is that Mother heard the appeal of Jesus deep down in her soul. The Lord called her to serve him in the poorest of the poor, and she answered, "Here I am, the handmaid of the Lord, prepared to quench your thirst for love, my Jesus, your thirst as you suffer in the poor, your brethren."

"You cannot love two people perfectly," says Mother, "but you can love all people perfectly, if you love the one Jesus in them all. This means that one should center mind and heart, life and activity on Jesus, see him in every human sufferer.

Mother views all her work as centered on God, depending on him. "We are to be God's associates, doing his work, working with him, for him." Having given themselves up to Jesus for life, without any restriction, the sisters belong to him and belong to those in whom he lives. Mother wants the sisters to devote themselves fully to those who represent Christ for them. She tells them, "Let the sisters and the people eat you up."

Again Mother tells her sisters, "Just as the seed is meant to be a tree, we are meant to grow into Jesus." The brides are to be molded into the image of the divine bridegroom, until as Paul says, "Christ is formed in them," so that they may be able to say in truth, "I live no more I, of my own life, but Christ lives in me" (Gal. 2:19–20).

RELIGIOUS FIRST

The words "for Jesus" explain everything, are the main motivation of their life, which is wholly consecrated to him; whatever they do is for him. Mother repeatedly starts her talks to various audiences in different countries by making her position and that of her sisters clear. She says, "We are not social workers, we are not nurses, we are not teachers, we are religious."

Mother insists on a point of cardinal importance: "I do not see the poor first, but Jesus, Jesus suffering in the poor, Jesus who said, 'I was hungry and you gave me to eat, I was thirsty, I was naked, I was lonely, I was without shelter, I was abandoned by all. . . . Whatever you did to the least of mine, you did it unto Me.' " (Mt. 25:35–40)

When after taking their vows, they receive their assignments, some young sisters do feel at times disappointed. "I was assigned to paperwork, to write letters and do the typing," or "I am put in charge of stores, to receive parcels and consignments, to sort them out and distribute the things to various houses." Yes, this is all part of the game for a religious who carries out the orders of superiors. A religious belongs to a team; every post must be filled; the whole team works for the poor, serves Christ in the poor. And "holiness," stresses Mother, "consists in doing God's will with a smile."

"One of our brothers came to me in distress," narrated Mother, and said to me, 'My vocation is to work for the lepers.' He added, 'I want to spend my whole life, my everything in this vocation.' Then I said to him, 'You are making a mistake, Brother; your vocation is to belong to Jesus. He has chosen you for himself, and the work you do is only a means to express your love for him in action. Therefore it does not matter what work you are doing; the main thing is that you belong to him, that you are his, and that he gives you the means to do this for him." Mother concluded, "For all of us religious, it does not matter what we do or where we are, as long as we remember that we belong to him, that we are his, that he can do with us what he wants."

ALL FOR JESUS

In a talk to the brothers in Calcutta, Mother said, "What you do, Brothers, as religious, is (1) from Jesus, (2) by Jesus, (3) for Jesus."

We are reminded of Paul writing to the Romans in his beautiful praise of God's wisdom and goodness, "How rich are the depths of God. . . . All that exists comes from him, all is by him and for him. To him be glory forever" (Rom. 11:33–36).

Paul insists explicitly on the trinitarian character. He is conscious of the action of the Father, on account of his Jewish background and also because here he addresses the Jews. Whereas Mother called by Christ to serve him in the poor insists more on the Son of God become man. But the habit of bringing back everything that we do, everything that exists and happens to God, Mother shares with the apostle. Her vocation comes from Jesus, what she does is through his power, all is for his glory. In her life and that of her nuns, the Lord Jesus becomes the all in all, being its cause, its motive force, its end. All is done for the glory of Jesus who returns the glory to his Father and ours.

Mother expresses it like this: "What we do is for Jesus, with Jesus, to Jesus. *For Jesus:* ours is a life all directed to Jesus, to his service; we live only for him, to serve him and love him, to make him known and loved; *With Jesus:* he gives us the strength, the comfort, the happiness of working for him; he is our companion on the road, leading us and instructing us; with Jesus, on the road to Emmaus, only we have recognized him. *To Jesus:*

we serve him in the neighbor, see him in the poor, nurse him in the sick; we comfort him in his afflicted brothers and sisters.

JESUS IN THE EUCHARIST

In the Eucharist, called by Newman, "the gift of God's very self," Mother sees the acme of humility on the part of Jesus, who becomes truly a thing, a food, so small, so silent, seemingly so powerless, since "where the priest puts him, there he stays."

Mother sees a challenge in the Eucharistic Presence of Jesus "who makes himself the hungry one," who comes to ask for our love and service. Christ in the Eucharist challenges, calls, invites. Some souls see it as an invitation of Jesus to stay with him in deep contemplation, in union, fulfilling his request at the garden, "Stay awake and pray, pray with me, join me in prayer, share my anguish and suffering." Some are called to be victims with their Lord, offered as the victim of the sacrifice on the altar, and they respond, "Lord, take me if you will."

Mother sees still another aspect of the Eucharist—she has developed the theme hundreds of times: "How great is the love Jesus shows us in the Eucharist. He makes himself the Bread of Life to satifsy our hunger for love and then he makes himself the hungry one so that we can satisfy his love for us.

And here she sees the "humility of God" who comes as a beggar to ask, who waits for men, makes himself so small, stays so quiet that even children are not afraid; the simple, the uneducated, the barefooted, poorly clad people can all approach him. And the loving soul, hearing the call to love in return, comes to love the eucharistic Lord and goes into the world to serve him lovingly "in his distressing disguise," in the poorest of the poor.

Not only people are hungry for love, but God is hungry for our love. This unfathomable mystery is for Mother a reality she perceives, a call to action she hears.

In the Eucharist Jesus gives us also an example of perfect love; not only is his self-gift total, but he makes it to unworthy people.

Mother underlines strongly a meaning of the Eucharist that she feels very deeply: "The love of Christ comes to us as a challenge, as a call, telling us, 'I thirst even today in my brethren, and I gave you an example that you might imitate what I did for you.' "

The Eucharist leads us to God and invites us to lead others to God, others hungry for him. The bread of life is the bread of action.

Mother says, "The meaning of this Eucharist is understanding love. Christ understood. He understood that we have a terrible hunger for God. He understood that we have been created to be loved, and so he made himself a bread of life and he said, 'Unless you eat my flesh and drink my blood, you cannot live, you cannot love, you cannot serve.' You must eat this bread and the goodness of the love of Christ to share his understanding love. He also wants to give us the chance to put our love for him in a living action. He makes himself the hungry one, not only for bread, but for love. He makes himself the naked one, not only for a piece of cloth but for that understanding love, that dignity, human dignity. He makes himself the homeless one, not only for the piece of a small room, but for that deep sincere love for the other, and this is the Eucharist. This is Jesus, the living bread that he has come to break with you and me."

In the Eucharist Christ teaches us, inspires us, stimulates us. He shows us what he wants us to be and gives us the grace to be just that. Mother sums up what the Gospel of John tells us of Jesus, in her characteristic terse, concise, vigorous manner, when she says, "Jesus is pleased to come to us "as the truth to be told, as the light to be lighted, as the love to be loved, as the way to be walked, as the joy to be given, as the peace to be spread, as the sacrifice to be offered."

Gerard Manley Hopkins, the Jesuit priest and poet, expressed in unforgettable words the wonderful intimacy and unity of Christ and the Christian, when he said of the true Christian that "He acts before God what before God he is—Christ."

JESUS IN THE POOR

"In Christ," says Karl Rahner, "the love of God and the neighbor acquires in the person of the one God-man an 'object' of the highest unity, and as a consequence love for man attains its supreme dignity" (*Encyclopedia of Theology: The Concise Sacramentum Mundi*. New York: Crossroad, 1975).

Since Christ has dignified and sanctified humanity by entering into it and redeeming it, all people whoever they be, is an actual or potential sharer in the life of Christ.

And finding Jesus in humanity, in whom he truly lives by grace, we can give to the infinite God a service of love he accepts willingly. Thus we always have the highest motivation for loving our neighbor, however unworthy he may seem at first sight. The one to whom the honor is rendered, for whom the service is performed, is no one else than the infinite Son of God the Father, come into the flesh to sanctify the world and lead it to his Father.

Mother is acutely aware that when she goes to serve the poor, it is to Jesus she betakes herself. One day, in a reflective mood, she asked, "Do you think the sisters see Jesus in the poor as I do?" The answer she received was, "Mother, we see Jesus in the poor according to the intensity of our faith and the grace God gives us."

Certainly the Missionaries of Charity receive a special grace, a charisma linked to their fourth vow of lifelong free service of the very poor. It obtains for them from God the grace to perform their duty in a spirit of faith. The vow binds them to do for God and his glory actions more difficult, less pleasant to nature, and therefore more perfect. God, who inspires the sisters with the desire to take this vow and accepts their commitment, will also help them to carry it out in a spirit of faith. Hence they will normally be helped to see Jesus in the poor they serve.

THE NAME OF JESUS

Mother and her sisters like to say "Jesus" rather than Christ or our Lord. They use habitually the personal, intimate, holy name: "Jesus wants you, Jesus calls you, Jesus loves you, serve Jesus, find Jesus in the poor, all we do is for Jesus."

This way of speaking puts them in a relation of intimate friendship with the Lord whom they serve, to whom they have consecrated their whole lives. Jesus is the name chosen by God the Father for his Son, the name revealed by the angel, the name by which his Mother called her divine Son. This name we cannot pronounce with faith unless the Spirit of God moves us. This name has power; it puts devils and evil spirits to flight; this name brings us salvation.

The name Christ expresses the function of the Savior; the name Jesus his person. Christ sounds more official; Jesus more intimate, affectionate, full of trust in him who said, "I call you no more servants, but friends, beloved" (John 15:15). Jesus revealed to his own his intimate thoughts that they might share them.

Jesus is the Bridegroom's name. That the sisters use it commonly in India to address one to whom they are mystically wedded for life, is all the more striking that Hindu wives never pronounce the name of their husbands. They are strictly forbidden to utter it, on religious and social grounds, because the name is said to hold power, the person's power, which no wife may arrogate to herself or try to steal. If the wife is forbidden to utter the name of the husband whom she must obey, the devotee is advised to repeat thousands of times the name of his favorite deity.

For the Christian, the divine Name has power, gives strength, and expresses love. The prayer of the Name is common in India. Many Christians practice it several hours a day, as has been the habit also of the monks of Mount Athos for centuries. This easy, simple, affective, unitive manner of praying may lead to contemplation the soul that has made it a habit to call on the Name of the beloved often during the day and night.

Mother has the love of St. Bernard and St. Bernardine of Siena for the name of Jesus. She shares the love of the great Abbot of Clairvaux for Jesus and Mary. She speaks continually of Jesus; his name is music to her ear, honey to her tongue, a presence always living in her heart. She must speak of him, sing his praises. She is not happy if time goes by without the name of her beloved being mentioned.

Mother's spirituality is incarnational, stressing the human aspect of the presence of the Son of God in the world. When saying, "God so loved the world that he sent his only Son," she usually adds "Jesus." "He gave us his only Son, Jesus." To Jesus she can cling. He is the spouse to whom she has consecrated her entire being, who lives in the Eucharistic Bread, who suffers in the poor and lonely, who has drawn her to himself.

CHAPTER 3

Instrumentality

We are ambassadors for Christ: it is as though God were appealing
through us.

(2 COR. 5:20)

Once they have accepted complete evangelical poverty in the following
of Christ, the religious imitate him, live of his spirit, continue his action,
extend his presence. Their model is found in the book of glory of the
Gospel of John, beginning with the washing of the feet and the command of Christ, "Do to one another as I have done to you" (John 13:15).
The Gospel then develops the teaching on love for one another in an
unparalleled manner, extension, and depth, the teaching of Christ
on the unity of his followers and their oneness in him, on his peace,
which we can receive only from him that we may share it with others all
over the world.

In his Sacerdotal Prayer, Jesus intimated to us the true purpose of
God's creative action, when he prayed, "Father, glorify your Son that
your Son may return the glory to you" (John 17:1). Jesus thus reveals to
us that the end of the world is the glory of the Son, which glory he will
return to his Father. This is the very purpose and end of the Missionaries
of Charity, established, as state their constitutions, for "the salvation and
sanctification of the poorest of the poor," those that might be easily
forgotten, neglected or overlooked.

The sisters' life is all devoted to the glory of the Lord, and their work
is to be accomplished with Jesus by his power. This union with Christ in
the work of spreading his grace leads to the extremely rich notion of
instrumentality, which Mother has developed considerably and continually insists on.

As the humanity of Christ was the instrument of his divinity, so his
members are the instruments of God to fulfil his purpose, as he said, "I
am the Vine, and you are branches" (John 15:5).

Spiritual people work with God, under God, for God, and know it. The
better they realize their position of dependence, the more God will make
use of them to sanctify the world. Only God gives grace, only he produces
spiritual results; if people were to attribute the good results of their

action to themselves alone, they would be lying; God cannot help them do this.

So the humbler the instrument and the stronger their consciousness that all the good comes from God, the more the Lord of all things will make use of them for the realization of his plan.

"I am God's pencil," Mother likes to say, as sitting in the small parlor, she toys with a stub of pencil, always at hand to write quick memos: "I am God's pencil, I am his instrument."

Once she added, speaking of the Primary Agent making use of his loving spouse, "He does it; I do not do it. I am more certain of this than of my own life." A greater certitude than this no one can have while in this mortal frame.

Some chosen people are aware of the presence of God in their soul. There would be many more, if they knew and sought, and desired and asked to have the experience of his presence in the soul, God at times grants to those who love him. "You are the temples of the Holy Spirit," said St. Paul. Thus Christians can turn their minds to the Lord living in themselves, adore him and even consult him. More explicitly Paul says, "I live no more I, of my own life, Christ lives in me" (Gal. 2:20).

In the same vein, Mother can say, "Jesus living in me does it. He acts in me." More cannot be explained. He not only lives in me and inspires me or suggests to me a course of action, but even I feel that he does it in and through me.

Indeed for anyone who, as the gospel says, has eyes to see with and ears to hear with, it is evident that God's instrument does not have the gifts, the resources, the ability, the intellectual eminence, nor the training and preparation that might explain the extraordinary success and the world-wide influence of her work.

The foundress never attended university courses, did not sit at the feet of gifted masters, did not learn public speaking nor the art of communication. Her only preparation for a worldwide apostolate consisted in directing a high school of some three hundred girls. Suddenly, as she reaches the age of forty, the Lord takes hold of her and gives to her life a new direction, raising her to a new function and status. Under his guidance she becomes in a matter of years a leader, an energizer, an extremely efficient organizer, and a world figure and apostle.

She stands before kings and presidents who listen to her. She addresses huge crowds, moving them to tears by her simple words, conscientizes them, rouses many to action. She has become a leading figure. Hers is a household name, a symbol of devoted love in a world of specialists, of highly trained people, of statespeople, politicians, economists, artists, mass media workers.

Clearly it is God's doing, God's chosen work.

Mother Teresa, as she had just returned from Rome after the first private audience granted her by Pope John Paul II, said, "When taking leave, I told the Holy Father, 'Pray that we may not spoil God's work,' and he answered me, 'and you pray that the pope may do no harm to the church.'

Previously, Mother had remarked, "I marvel at God the Father's humility who deigns to use instruments as weak and imperfect as we are to do his work."

"Yes, Mother, you may look at it that way, but there is the other aspect also; God's power shines more forcefully when he uses instruments humanly speaking inadequate, unqualified, unprepared for his work."

For an important and difficult task people would select only the best, most intelligent, strong, competent people as their agents. But with God the credit cannot go to human beings but to the Infinite who said, "My name is Yahweh, I will not yeild my glory to another." Indeed it would amount to a lie. He is the God who alone IS—the creator of all that exists, the Providence leading all people to their end, the giver of grace. So he uses instruments so inadequate that all can see the work is God's. It must be added that the Almighty, who is bound by no law but his own will, at times makes use of a genius to perform his work, as he did with Paul, Origen, Augustine, Aquinas. But all of them knew that the grace, the light, the vision came from the Lord.

Speaking often in public, addressing large audiences on various topics, with hardly any preparation, answering scores of interviewers, Mother never made a slip, a mistake of any importance. She never had to correct what she had said in her talks to bishops, priests, doctors, nurses, political leaders, university people, religious groups of various denominations. Always she expressed the approved doctrine of the church, had the exact answer on questions of morality, natural law, revealed truth.

In fine, the result of her work cannot be explained naturally: there is no proportion between the personality and talents of the foundress and the results of her activity. *Digitus Dei est hic*—the finger of God is here, patent for all those who have eyes to see with to see.

As God's instrument, the foundress sees her Lord as the Principal Agent, who entrusts the work to her. The plan is his, the realization his, the responsibility his, and the fruit comes entirely from him. She can repeat after the apostle, "Paul planted, Apollos watered, God gave the increment" (1 Cor. 3:6). Paul that is Mother Teresa, Apollos represents the sisters who follow in her footsteps and continue her work, while God makes them produce spiritual fruit, his own gift, to the glory of his Son Jesus.

This deep consciousness of God's overwhelming and everpresent activity in the spiritual order generates in the soul:

1. *Humility.* The attitude of John the Baptist, confident and happy, professing, "Jesus must increase, I must diminish" (John 3:30). If it is all God's doing, why should I glory as if it was mine?

2. *Confidence.* Mother says, "Since it is God's work we are doing, he will give us the means to carry it out. If he wants the work done, he must give us the means; by ourselves we are nothing, we have nothing." If at times we feel tempted to object, "Lord, I cannot do it," deep down in our soul we may hear a gentle voice telling us, "I will do it for you."

3. *A relaxed attitude,* devoid of all human anxiety. As Mother says, "If God wants it the thing will be done; if we do not have the means, then God does not want it done; why worry?"

Again Mother tells the sisters, "God has not called us to be successful, but to be faithful." When a house must be closed, this causes no heartbreak; the personnel are shifted to another one or open a new one. "People do not want us in one place," she says, "or we are not allowed to perform the work for which we are established, we go to another." Colombo, Belfast were closed down. The sisters went to other countries clamoring for them; they obeyed the Gospel injunction, "If anyone does not welcome you, walk out of the house or town" (Matt. 10:13).

4. *Optimism,* the Pauline optimism that is a truly Christian attitude and virtue. Christ defeated the combined forces of sin, evil, the worldly spirit, achieving victory over them by dying and rising again. Christ in heaven reigns gloriously. The world moves toward its end, which is the glory of God. As Paul said, "All things are for you, the elect; you are for Christ; Christ is for God" (1 Cor. 3:22–23).

5. The joy of sharing with God as we contribute to his work. The joy of working for God in the Father's field. True, we shall not reap what we have not sown, and then "The sower and the reaper will rejoice together" (John 4:36).

To show how we are God's instruments used by him, Mother develops fully the Gospel simile of the vine and the branches. Jesus said, "I am the Vine, and you are the branches. I sent you that you may produce much fruit and that your fruit may remain" (John 15:5,16). And Mother stresses that "the fruit is on the branches, nowhere else." The branches, namely we who belong to Jesus, are to bear fruit. We may not sit down idle, we are to be up and doing, or there will be no fruit to the glory of God. The branches that bear fruit in Christ, the Father will prune so that they may bear better fruit still (John 15:2).

The sisters must go out to bear fruit. They are sent out by Christ to do his work and do it with him. Their task is to bring souls to the Lord who thirsts for our love.

This is admirably expressed in the prayer composed by the very sensitive and saintly Cardinal Newman, which Mother loves to say,

Dear Jesus, help me to spread thy fragrance everywhere I go; flood my soul with thy spirit and life; penetrate and possess my whole being so utterly that all my life may only be a radiance of thine; shine through me and be so in me that every soul I come in contact with may feel thy presence in my soul. Let them look up and see no longer me, but only Jesus. Stay with me and then I shall begin to shine as thou shinest, so to shine as to be a light to others. The light, O Jesus, will be all from thee; none of it will be mine. It will be thou shining on others through me. Let me thus praise thee in the way thou dost love best by shining on those around me. Let me preach thee, without preaching, not by words but by my example, by the catching force, the sympathetic influence of what I do, the evident fulness of the love my heart bears to thee. Amen.

This presence of Jesus in the Missionaries of Charity that does all the work of grace through them, gives great confidence. "I can do all things in him who strengthens me," affirmed St. Paul (Phil. 4:13). The same can be said today. To be conscious of our weakness begets humility; humility begets confidence in God; confidence in God begets cheerfulness in working wholeheartedly for his glory.

And so Mother says,

"We will allow Jesus in the Light of Charity, in the Truth of Humility, in the Life of Sanctity, to shine in us and through us, and thus bring a multitude of our Poor to God, to the glory of the Church and the greater glory of God."

To do everything "to the greater glory of God" is the Ignatian ideal and motto. The same words from the ultimate conclusion of the present edition of the constitutions of the Missionaries of Charity, stressing the sisters' intimate union with and their incorporation into Jesus Christ, the Son of God the Father (No. 225).

CHAPTER 4

An Evangelical Spirituality

"What is the basis of your spirituality, Sister?"

"The gospel; especially the Gospel of Matthew. The words of Christ: 'What you have done to the least of mine, you did it unto me.' These words have been dinned into our ears, they have become part of our mental makeup, they are our motive force." She had come to Mother when already not quite young, having experience of life and service to the poor as a nurse in an Asian country. She had been conquered by this lived gospel.

The gospel Mother puts before her sisters is the pure, unadulterated gospel. The gospel as the Holy Spirit has brought it down to the church of today, applied to our times, to our needs, to our circumstances. No frills, no embellishments, no suppressions either. The gospel of Jesus, the gospel Paul preached from the time of his work among the Corinthians.

The gospel bereft of the spectacular elements. Even Jesus had complained, "This generation wants miracles; they will be given only the sign of the prophet Jonah" (Matt. 12:39)—namely, the proof the Savior gives of his love in his Passion, Death, and Resurrection. The sisters also prove their love by their daily service to the poor.

"The Jews demand miracles, the Greeks look for wisdom," had asserted Paul, "and here we are preaching the cross of Christ, madness to the pagans, to the Jews an obstacle they cannot surmount" (1 Cor. 1:22–23). Miracles are for unbelievers; the sisters believe. There are no instances of multiplication of loaves, of the barns or bins being refilled automatically, of food being multiplied as it is distributed. And it is better so. It is poverty, real, actual poverty. When there was no more bulgur, they stopped the distribution of rations to the people gathered at the door.

The miracle is that God provides through the generosity of people who always come forward to give. The dying, the babies, the orphans have never gone hungry. Trust in God is always rewarded. Half-hidden miracles take place in answer to prayer, which only the discerning eye can identify: God with us, God for us, God active in the world, answering our prayers.

The gospel comes alive in all its charming, endearing simplicity; in its totality also, unalloyed, unqualified, unaltered. There are no "buts," no "ifs," no "of course, today things are different, we have to adapt the teaching of Jesus to changed circumstances." No; the word of the gospel; exacting and comforting in its straightforwardness, following the advice "let your speech be yes for yes and no for no" (Matt. 5:37).

"I take Jesus at his word, and he never let me down," says Mother. She is right to do honor to her Lord by trusting him without limit. "Jesus said it," and she acts accordingly.

Thus from the start she expressed the spirit of her congregation in three characteristic virtues: (1) total surrender, (2) loving trust, and (3) cheerfulness.

Total surrender to the Father's will as Jesus surrendered himself to do his Father's will in all things, including the death on the cross. It means to be available to the church for any work entrusted to them in accordance with their constitutions.

Loving trust, in the spirit of the gospel, relying on God for all things needed, bathing in his love, awaiting from him the fulfilment of his promises, trusting in his Providence, who looks after the poor. "We attempt all things, doubting nothing, for with God all things are possible. We will allow the good God to make plans for the future, for yesterday has gone, tomorrow has not yet come and we have only TODAY to make him known, loved and served" (Constitutions, 4, 22).

They obey the gospel's injunction, "Do not fret and worry about tomorrow; tomorrow will take care of itself. Sufficient for the day is the evil thereof" (Matt. 6:34). They heed the warning: "Do it today, because tomorrow you may not be there."

One day Mother said, "I pasted the message Pope Paul VI addressed to our society on the back of a picture, the picture I like best. You may have it to copy the message, but return the picture to me." The picture reproduces a sculpture of two strong hands joined at the tip of the fingers and pointing downwards. Linked to one of the hands and resting against it is the figure of a small child. Mother felt just like the child, made by God, depending on him, resting trustfully in his embrace.

Blessed Julian of Norwich had seen in her "Shewings" the whole world as a small hazelnut resting in the palm of her hand, and had been told, "This is the whole world, all that exists, all that has been created." It was not more before God than a nut in a human hand. And seeing that it was so small, when she asked how it subsisted, she was told, "Out of love. Because God loves it."

The picture that delighted Mother said the same: "You subsist, you act through God's power, because he loves you."

EVANGELICAL POVERTY

Mother chose a very strict kind of poverty for her congregation, in imitation of Jesus, born in a stable, dying on a cross. "Though he was rich, he chose to be poor." During his public ministry, he lived on the alms people offered for the sustenance of the little company of his disciples.

The Missionaries of Charity own nothing, live on what they receive, are ready to beg in case of need, for their poor and for their own food. Their poverty unites them to Jesus, poor by choice; it makes them more similar to their master.

Their real, effective poverty unites them also to the poor, for whom they must work. It helps them to understand their difficulties and privations, to sympathize with them and be one with them.

At times the sisters are to feel the pinch, the lack of even necessary things. Their houses will have no television, no radio, no record players, no cameras.

Their style of life spells poverty: their dress consists of a habit, a girdle, a sari of cheap cotton material, and sandals. They have two saris only, one to wear, one to wash or dry. Like the poor, they wash their clothes with their own hands.

They sleep in dormitories, because the poor have no privacy. They eat simple food, which should be wholesome and sufficient, so that they can do their work for the benefit of the poor. In hot countries they are not allowed fans in their living quarters; yet they may have some in their homes for babies, but only for the comfort of the little ones God loves. The very poor have no fans even under the scorching summer sun; but then they live much in the open, and can profit more of the breeze than the sisters do.

In their Calcutta houses, the sisters do not have running water at every floor. Like the poor they carry buckets of water to wash themselves and clean the premises. In the courtyard of the motherhouse, a hand pump provides the water needed by the more than three hundred religious living there.

Every evening, the sisters fill their buckets and pass them from hand to hand, along a chain they form up the staircase. Visitors seeing them for the first time at this exercise in perfect silence, imagine they are fighting a fire on the upper floor. Later the spiritual meaning of this kind of drill may dawn on them. Mother wants the sisters to be similar to the poor, who must carry buckets and pails of water from street hydrants or community wells.

But the mystical meaning comes to the mind: Jesus at the well of Jacob, asking the Samaritan woman, "Give me to drink" (John 4:7); "Sister, my bride, give me to drink," and the promise made in return, "Ask me and I will give you living water." Indeed they will draw water joyfully from the sources of the Lord.

Like the poor, the sisters are told to travel mostly on foot or by the cheapest way, as by tram or bus, whenever possible. Father Julien Henry narrated with a chuckle that in February 1978 Mother went to the Calcutta docks to take delivery of a truckload of bales of goods donated by friends for the poor, "She drove back through the streets of Calcutta, sitting on top, as the local workmen do." This was no mean feat for a lady in her late sixties. Wrapped in her white sari, uncomfortably perched atop bales of goods, praying to her Lord Jesus Christ, she formed a truly Franciscan picture.

"What do you insist on most when you visit your houses, Mother?"

"I insist mainly on poverty," she answered. "I check whether poverty is kept according to the spirit and word of our constitutions. Especially as regards the superiors of the houses. They can so easily become lax in the matter of poverty."

When starting new houses in rich countries, though the sisters are settled among the poorer sections of the population, and are to work among the very poor, Mother insists on poverty. Opening a house in the United States, she said, "I give you my sisters; take care of them and help them to keep their poverty, because our poverty is our dowry. Do not let my sisters lose their love for poverty."

The Missionaries of Charity live a truly poor life, in the spirit of the gospel and in imitation of St. Francis of Assisi. This forces them to trust fully in God and to rely completely on his divine Providence for their own needs and those of their apostolate. But their attachment to poverty does not have the poetical charm that fitted in with the lovely landscape of Umbria, and the chivalrous spirit of an age that delighted in the story of Francis wedded to his Lady Poverty. As he sang her praises, he felt perfectly free, being encumbered with no possession of his own, while he owned the whole world as the son of the Great King.

Francis could imagine himself as a knight, pledging his troth and consecrating his life to Lady Poverty—an image unsuited to a young nun, pledged to Christ, her only bridegroom. She will espouse poverty in and through him, choosing to be poor with her Lord, who willed to be poor.

The poetry woven as a silk dress around the image of poverty, conceived as a radiant lady may appeal to people who possess and wish to divest themselves of fetters in order to enjoy greater freedom of spirit. But in the Calcutta slums where poverty is seen gnawing at our brother's entrails, where it means naked children with bloated stomachs and thin limbs, the idea of a beautiful, spiritualized Lady Poverty perforce cannot blossom. There remains room only for compassion and an inner urge to get up and do something to help those who suffer hunger.

When they opened a house in the depressed area of Tondo in Manila, someone offered Mother a car for the sisters' use. Mother refused it. "We do not need a car yet," she said. "Later on, perhaps. We shall see when it is needed for the work."

Nothing for comfort. Nothing that is not actually necessary. They do not store nor put aside for the future; that would be to show a lack of trust in God. It would be against their spirit of evangelical poverty. God gave the manna in the desert day by day; and on the eve of the sabbath for two days, since work was not allowed on the day of the Lord. Now also, we pray, "Give us today our daily bread," and so we show our reliance on God's providence.

EVANGELICAL OBEDIENCE

Religious bind themselves by vow to obey, in imitation of Jesus who came into the world to do not his own will, but his Father's will. Their vow implies a total surrender, knowingly and voluntarily, of all self-determination by the human person. Obedience makes the religious available, puts them at the disposal of their superiors for any task within the ambit of their institute's constitutions.

"At the end of their novitiate, when the sisters take their vows and are sent to different houses, do you ask them where they would like to go, Mother?" asked a journalist. "They do not go where they like to go, but they go where they are sent," she replied.

They are sent, as the Son was sent by the Father. The apostles were sent by Christ. Missionaries are sent by the church, in the name of God.

With Mother the practice is thus: after their first or final vows, the newly professed (or the perpetually professed, as the case may be) are told to what house they have been assigned, in what town or district, and they leave for their destination the same day or the next day. Of course, those assigned to another country must get their passport ready. They know in advance that they will go abroad, but may not know to what country or what house they are sent. A consular visa may be obtained by a superior.

The sisters take it cheerfully; they are in God's hands and in Mother's. They try to emulate the obedience and the faith Jesus admired when the centurion replied to him, "I tell a man, 'Go,' and he goes; another, 'Come here,' and he comes; to my servant, 'Do this,' and he does it" (Matt. 8:9). When God commands, there can be no mistake in obeying. The human person giving the order may make a mistake, act on a wrong judgment; but the person who obeys never makes a mistake in obeying.

But the Catholic church stresses that the religious who obeys remains a person with God-given intelligence and free will, who should be spiritually mature and discerning. Thus, in the spirit of the Second Vatican Council, the recent constitutions foresee that "dialogue" may take place between the inferior and the superior, with the proviso that the superior should always have the last, undisputed word.

JOY

Joy is a characteristic mark of the kingdom of God, starting with the coming of Jesus Christ, who brings joy into the world. At Bethlehem the angel announces to the shepherds a great joy for the whole people. Christ proclaims in the Sermon on the Mount, "Happy are you . . ." (Matt. 5:2–12). At the Last Supper, Jesus's bequest to his intimate is "that my joy may be in you and your joy may be complete" (John 15:11). The risen Christ shares his peace and his joy with his disciples "who were happy to see the Lord." At Pentecost, the Holy Spirit brings "a plenitude of joys," as a choice gift of the Spirit, who is divine fulfilment, happiness, supreme bliss. And St. Paul time and again advises joy. The first generations of Christians were conspicuous by their love and their happiness. St. Athanasius says of them, "The saints rejoiced all their lives long, like men at a feast" (Easter Letter 14:1).

Each time we witness a return to the original spirit of the gospel, to pure, unadulterated, courageous following of Jesus in poverty, humility, simplicity, and trust, happiness and the joy of the children of God are seen to come to life again. Such was the case with Francis of Assisi and his followers, exuding happiness, shining examples of joy, laughter, and good cheer.

Again today, the Missionaries of Charity exemplify cheerfulness and happiness. That was Mother's stroke of genius: to go back to the simplicity of the gospel and inherit the happiness of the children of God. Mother writes for a calendar for the year 1981, featuring her and the Missionaries of Charity: "Let us all keep the joy of loving God in our hearts, and share this joy of loving one another as he loves each one of us. God bless you."

Mother sings a hymn to joy: "Joy is prayer, joy is strength, joy is love, joy is a net of love by which you can catch souls. God loves a cheerful giver. The best way to show our gratitude to God and the people is to accept everything with joy. Never let anything so fill you with sorrow as to make you forget the joy of the risen Christ. We all long for heaven where God is, but we have it in our power to be in heaven with him right now—to be happy with him at this very moment. But being happy with him now means loving as he loves, helping as he helps, giving as he gives, serving as he serves, rescuing as he rescues, being with him 24 hours a day, and touching him in his distressing disguise in the poor and suffering.

"A joyful heart is the normal result of a heart burning with love. It is the gift of the Spirit, a share in the joy of Jesus, living in the soul."

The sisters are told, "What will strike people and invite some to embrace the religious life 'is the witness of our own lives, the spirit in which we react to our divine calling, the completeness of our dedication, the generosity and cheerfulness of our service to God, the love we have for one another, and the apostolic zeal with which we witness to Christ's love for the poorest of the poor.' "

Actions impress more than words. "What you are makes so much noise I cannot hear what you say," as Walt Whitman forcibly put it. Some girls decided to join the Missionaries of Charity when they saw their happiness and cheerfulness in God's service. A young woman says,

"I came to Calcutta as a tourist to work for Mother Teresa's poor for a few months. When I saw the happiness and joy of the sisters doing this work, I felt attracted to this kind of life. In my country I had never thought of becoming a nun. Those I had met looked gloomy: they were plagued with problems, worries, anxieties. They thought something had gone wrong with the world, and they were not able to correct it.

"But there the sisters have no problems, no anxieties. They allow God to lead them. This gives them happiness and joy. So I wrote to my parents to inform that I had decided to join the Missionaries of Charity. Now I am a postulant."

Mother tells her young religious in training, "Smiling novices, I can hear the music of your laughter of joy. Learn, my children, to be holy, for true holiness consists in doing God's will with a smile." And the constitutions stipulate, "A spirit of joy should permeate the daily life of the novitiate and the novices should be encouraged to regard the communicating of this joy as a necessary part of their apostolate" (No. 203).

Pope Paul VI in a written message for the sisters, which he gave to Mother during a private audience, ends by saying, "Yes, to belong to Christ Jesus is a great gift of God's love. And may the world always see this love in your SMILE."

Sharing in the cross of the Lord gives us the right to share also in the joy of the resurrection. And so the joy of the risen Christ forms the other half of the diptych depicting the redeeming Jesus, which stands on the high altar of Mother's mind. It portrays in vivid colors the love of the Son who died for our sins, and the love of the Father, who, having sent us his Son Jesus, raised him from the dead and gave him "a glory such as belongs to the only-begotten Son." The risen Christ remains with us in the Blessed Sacrament, the suffering Christ will be with us in the poor till the end of the world.

A choice inspiration of the Holy Spirit prompted the insertion of this joy, this cheerfulness as a characteristic of the Institute. Whatever sorrow, suffering, sadness the sisters have experienced or witnessed during the day, they should go to sleep sharing the joy of the risen Christ.

Mother says, "A joyful sister is like the sunshine of God's love, the hope of eternal happiness, the flame of burning love."

LOVE

"Wrap all those qualities in love," says St. Paul. Then they will be perfect and have values before God, who is love and does everything out of love.

The Missionaries of Charity, like all Christians, have the highest motivation for their love, which is to be inspired by and in imitation of the trinitarian love. The Father in his love begets his Son, giving him all his perfection, all he has. Then "God so loved the world that he gave his only Son" (John 3:16). The Father gave us the best he had, what he cherished most. He could tell us, "This is my Son, the Beloved; to him listen."

Speaking of his Father's love for him, Jesus could say, "As the Father has loved me, so I have loved you; remain in my love" (John 15:9). Quoting these words, Mother adds, "Jesus has asked us to love one another again and again, as the Father has loved him. And how did the Father love him? By asking him to sacrifice himself, through giving him to die for us."

Theologically and spiritually there is no higher motive, no more perfect example of love than the Father's love for his Son, "as the Father loved me." Jesus was speaking of pruning those who belong to him that they may bear much fruit—fruit to the Father's glory. The Father has loved his Son come to live among us and willed him to have the supreme glory of loving people as they had never been loved, and of showing his love for his Father by his supreme sacrifice.

1. The Father's love for his Son has been most exacting, since it includes the redemption of the world through the cross. But then the Father raised his Son from the dead and gave him a glorious life and made him sit at his right hand and as the supreme Lord and King of all the redeemed, in incomparable glory. Without the death on the cross, there would have been no resurrection and conferring on us a new life, a share in the divine life.

Similarly, Jesus wants us to show our love for him through the sacrifice of all our human affections and attachments. Mother Teresa wants the same for her religious; she wants not an easy love, but a hard, generous, all-embracing, even heroic love.

2. The Son's love: "There is no greater love than to give one's life for those one loves" (John 15:13). St. Paul insists still more, when he says, "To give one's life for persons unworthy as we were, when Christ died; sinners, enemies of God, before we became justified by Christ's death and resurrection."

The Son loved us in the same manner as the Father loved him. And his love serves as model to ours. Even before non-Christian audiences, Mother is heard saying, "We must love one another as Christ loved us, who gave his life for us and gave it the hard way." And speaking to her sisters, she insists, "Love is proved by deeds; the more they cost us, the greater the proof of our love." And she will repeat what Jesus said, "Unless the grain falls in the earth and dies, it produces no fruit. But if it dies it will bear abundant fruit." We are all invited to draw the conclusion for ourselves.

3. The Holy Spirit's love: he fills us with love, as he deigns to come and dwell in these "vessels of clay," these unworthy shacks we are, which he transforms into temples of the Godhead. The Spirit brings his

gifts in abundance, freely, for no reward, because love is sharing, giving, and supremely self-gift. So the Spirit gives himself without limit to people unworthy of his gift, and with himself brings them the power to love.

Mother insists on love, saying, "What counts is not how much you give, but how much love you put in the giving." And again, "Give what costs you; that has value before God; it proves your love for him."

Mother wishes her sisters to realize and live that wonderful experience the Little Flower describes in her autobiography, one of the most moving pages of Christian literature. Thérèse narrates how she wished to do something really great for God, show her Lord her love in a conspicuous manner, surrender herself to him completely. She saw that the martyrs were truly the disciples of Jesus who had given all they had and life itself in a heroic manner; they had accepted and endured sufferings, torments, and death for their faith in Jesus.

But in Little Thérèse's circumstances martyrdom seemed to be ruled out. Then how could she prove her love to her Lord? Opening the Scriptures in search of an answer, her eyes fell on the passage of St. Paul's Letter to the Corinthians, in which he states that there are various gifts from heaven. He compares the church to a body in which various organs have different functions. Yet all depend on one another for their harmonious action and development. Similarly, all Christians are not called to be apostles, prophets, teachers, to speak in diverse languages or interpret those sayings, not to heal or serve the needy.

Then the apostle comforts and inspires all his readers by saying, "Now, I will show you an excellent way," a much better way than all those callings or gifts, and it is this: Love is the only thing really worthwhile. It must inspire all we do. Love is divine, love is eternal, love will never perish. And Thérèse reflects: is it not marvelous that it requires no great intellect, no special physical strength, no extraordinary feats? Love can penetrate, inspire, sustain, transform all that we do, clothing it with light, beauty, splendor. After reading St. Paul, Thérèse exclaims,

Dear Jesus, my only Beloved, now I have found, I know what I shall do. I shall take refuge in the heart of Mother Church; I have found my place, my function in the body, my niche in the Church of Christ will be in the Heart.

Is the heart not the most important organ of the body? If it does not pump blood, all the other organs will stop working. They all require energy to function. Similarly, if in the mystical body of Christ which is the Church, the heart does not send love, the apostles will not go out to preach the Gospel, the prophets will stay silent at home, the teachers will not teach, no one will do his appointed work.

So St. Thérèse has found her true vocation, her priceless calling: **"I will be love."** With joy she exclaims it: "In the heart of Mother Church I will be love and thus inspire all others and share in their work."

Mother Teresa can exhort her daughters to imitate this example.

Speaking before a large audience, she could tell her entranced listeners, "That is what we are, the Missionaries of Charity, that is our calling and our function in the world, each one of us must be able to say: I will be love."

And this love brings forth joy, the happiness of making others, of seeing others happy. For "as the Lord Jesus said, 'It is more blessed to give than to receive'" (Acts 20:35).

CHAPTER 5

Living the Gospel

No religious institute today follows more closely, more literally the gospel as expounded by Jesus. None is more faithful to his teaching on trust, on poverty, on love of those in need.

The gospel comes alive today, delightfully fresh and endearing, as it has done only seldom in past years. Yes, of course, it came alive in a remarkable way with Francis, the Poverello of Assisi, his brethren, and the multitude of his followers.

Again we see the advice of John the Baptist being put into practice: "If you have two coats, give one to the person who has none." And like the forerunner of Jesus, the Missionaries of Charity come to prepare us for the kingdom of God and invite us to enter it.

The lifestyle of the sisters imitates the apostles' simplicity, poverty, and dependence on what people offer them. They obey the command of Jesus: "As you go, proclaim that the kingdom of God is close at hand" (Matt. 10:7). The kingdom is certainly not far away for the dying people the sisters help to die in God's love.

Again, as Jesus had ordered his own, "You received without charge, give without charge," the sisters bind themselves by vow to offer "free —absolutely free—wholehearted service to the poorest of the poor."

When they travel or move from one of their houses to another, they take only the very minimum for their needs. They follow the advice of Jesus to his disciples, as they went on an apostolic tour, "Provide yourselves with no gold or silver, not even with a few coppers for your purses, with no haversack for the journey, or spare tunic, or footwear or a staff, for the workman deserves his hire" (Matt. 10:9–10).

Jesus showed a special love for children brought to him by their parents that he might bless them. When the disciples, seeing their master tired, tried to send away the children, Jesus rebuked them saying, "Let the little children come to me; do not stop them; the kingdom of God belongs to such as these." And the Lord added the warning, "I tell you solemnly, anyone who does not welcome the kingdom of God like a little child, will never enter it" (Mark 10:13–16).

Mother one day commented, "I really understood the words of the gospel saying that we must become as children if we wish to enter the kingdom of heaven, when I saw the Holy Father, Pope John Paul II, in all simplicity talking and laughing and singing with us, the sisters, and myself. We had assisted in his private chapel at his mass, and had gone with him to his private study. It was charming and delightful."

Again the gospel tells us that when Jesus came to a town or village, they brought him all their sick. Without warning, without explanation, simply trusting in his kindness and healing power, they brought him a multitude of sick people. Today the sisters in India see hundreds of sick people flock to their dispensaries in towns and villages.

"Every Saturday," related a sister, "we go to a village, some twenty novices and myself. We put out our dispensary tables and medicines and attend to six or seven hundred people. We start at 8 A.M., drive for an hour, work the whole day without a break and return home." From another house, the sisters go every Wednesday to a distant village. They open their dispensary on a market place and attend to twelve or thirteen hundred people, mainly women and children. Wherever the sisters establish a foundation, the multitudes come to them for help and free service.

Normally the sisters leave the house and go to their work two by two. When someone queried, "Why two by two?" Mother answered, "Because two heads have more wisdom than one, and four hands can do more work than two." To this commonsense answer, the inquirer might have replied, "Then, why not three by three? They would have still more wisdom and power for action." Of course, for the sake of efficiency one must stop somewhere, at an ideal number of heads and hands. But a truer reason is stated in their constitutions, namely "Because the Gospel tells us that Jesus sent his apostles and disciples on their apostolic missions two by two. So we go out according to the Gospel pattern, as ordained by Jesus." Two for company, for help, for edification, for support, for recreation, for protection.

SIMPLICITY MAY BE EMBARRASSING

At the end of 1977, as twenty-nine sisters were preparing for their final vows, sixteen of them were told to apply for their passports and prepare to go for service in foreign countries. This meant a heavy burden on the finances of the congregation. But the Co-Workers all over the world had always helped to pay the traveling expenses of the sisters.

"The international air companies have started giving us free passages," said Mother. "We were already helped by the Indian companies, and now the international companies also join in the help. We have been given six free passages on an international flight, and I sent six sisters with 1,000 pounds of luggage."

"What, 1,000 pounds of luggage for six people?"

"Yes. The employees at first looked scared. They had never seen such a thing. The usual allowance is 50 pounds. But then, the pass did not specify any maximum; it said merely 'six sisters and their luggage.' So we sent blankets, medicines, food, all things needed to start work among the poor."

Mother herself, with her sense of humor, enjoyed the joke; it was all for the good cause of charity. The sisters later laughed heartily as they narrated the story:

"Imagine the face of the employees when the sisters checked in, carrying themselves loads of luggage. The whole lot had to go through; there was no stopping them. That is the advantage of total poverty and complete dependence on God: you do not have to pay."

No. Only the big men from the oil-rich countries would travel with great loads of accompanied luggage, in beautiful trunks and suitcases. But now you had those nuns in the cheapest of dresses, sporting neither a watch nor socks, with nothing in their pockets, bringing bundles, bags of burlap and cardboard boxes replete with life-saving, life-preserving things for the poor of God.

THE WIDOW'S MITE

The gospel truly comes alive today under our very eyes, as some of its typical scenes are reenacted. At the civic reception given her by the West Bengal government, Mother recalled how she had been moved by the gesture of a poor beggar. On some festive occasion, people were bringing her offerings for the poor; they were mostly well-to-do donors, when a beggar approached her saying, "I want to give you something also." He presented her a ten-paise coin, the equivalent of a cent or a penny. "This is all I have received today," he said, "please accept it."

"The gift of this poor man," said Mother, "caused me more happiness than the large sums others had given. Because he had given all he had, while the others had given of their surplus."

This was an echo of the remark Jesus made when watching visitors drop large alms into the temple offering box. He noticed a widow deposit two small coins, all she had, and praised her. "Those others," said the Lord, "gave out of their surplus, but the poor widow offered to God out of her necessary" (Mark 12:44).

The parable of the good Samaritan has inspired many generations of religious souls (Luke 10:25–37). Mother from the start of her second call acted the parable, when she saw on a footpath a poor woman full of wounds, whom no passer-by seemed to notice. She stayed with her, comforting her, then took her to a hospital.

The sisters daily repeat her action, as they obey their master's command "Go and do likewise." One instance in a hundred: in Calcutta, in March 1981, an Indian and an Australian tertian walk down a busy street.

On a footpath they notice a man in rags lying on the ground. They look at him with their expert eyes, the eyes of Christ's love, and notice his parlous condition. They enter a house, ask for leave to use the phone, and call for an ambulance. When the ambulance arrives, they lift up the man and take him to the Home for the Dying, where he had only a few hours to live and prepare for death.

Many volunteer helpers come from distant countries to help in the work of love. They spend their holidays working at a children's home, at a home for the dying, at the I.C.I. Gift of Love Home, at the Kennedy Home at DumDum, caring for people unknown, of different religions, nationalities, languages, cultures.

They wash, disinfect, bandage wounds, feed patients, put them to rest, arrange pillows, cut hair, pare nails, befriend, console, encourage people finding themselves abandoned, suffering, wounded, alone on the road of life. The volunteers do all this, because the Lord after narrating how the good Samaritan had helped his brother Jew in his distress, said, "Go and do likewise."

These are wonderful acts of charity, performed in silence, as a matter of course, simply offered to God. But people usually feel better, already rewarded, having learned and having received more than they have given. And so, what they have done, they wish to do again.

Mother Teresa as a true realist approves of this course of action; but she also warns the visitor, the volunteer, the Co-Worker that "Love begins at home. So now, go back to your own family, to your home, your neighborhood and town, and love one another there. Love starts at home and lasts at home, and there is constantly scope for it there: the home is each one's first field of loving, devotion and service. Begin to speak to people who talk your own language and share your culture, but to whom you never addressed a word previously.

"Indeed, we are not to be often traveling to Jericho. Our main job is in the holy city of our birth, our own Jerusalem, where the temple of the true God stands. There we are called to serve him in our brethren, in our house, and in the next-door neighbors."

Talking to Westerners, to people living in comfort, Mother asks, "Do you know the members of your family, of your locality? Do you care for them, do you try to make them happy? First do that and then you may think of the poor of India and of other areas."

The parables are shown in action not on a screen or stage, but in real life, for the benefit of human beings. In the parable of the great dinner and the invitees who would not come, the host told his servants, "Go out quickly into the streets and alleys of the town and bring in the poor, the crippled, the blind and the lame." And again when the servants have done that, and there is still room in the banquet hall, the master orders, "Go to the open roads and the hedgerows and force people to come in to make sure my house is full" (Luke 14:16–24). Thus the sisters go out into the streets, the lanes and by-lanes, and on to the country roads, the highways and the backwater areas, to invite and gather and bring home to God those who cannot walk, who feel shy, who lack clothes or energy to carry on the painful pilgrimage of life.

IN SEARCH OF SOULS

Jesus called himself the Good Shepherd and depicted himself in search of the lost sheep, the wayward sheep, the weaklings too anemic or frail to follow with the rest. The Missionaries of Charity are also to go out and seek what seemed lost, what had strayed, what had lost the sense of life. They certainly will not deserve the reproach God made through the Prophet Ezekiel (34:4) to the shepherds of Israel, "You did not bring back the wayward, you did not go to seek the lost ones."

To discover those more in need, the sisters must seek—go out as Jesus did, as the apostles did, looking for people in need of spiritual or material help, in need of friendship, of support and guidance. The same applies to the contemplative wing, whose members go out daily to offer purely spiritual help to those more in need of it. The sisters go out to give to those, to expect them, because hope was a dead thing for them.

Speaking at the Eucharistic Congress of Philadelphia, Mother described in vivid terms this seeking aspect of their apostolate: "Lately at the invitation of the President of Mexico, we opened a house in Mexico and our sisters, as it is the custom in our society, they go round and round and round and look for everybody, see everybody, and walk and walk till both their legs ache terribly, to see which is the worse place, where is the greatest need to begin with. In Mexico this was difficult, because the poverty of the people was very great wherever they visited."

Striking words, words that penetrate deep into the heart, as they depict the labors of the young sisters seeking the most needy, those in whom the smarting Jesus suffers most.

THE GOSPEL TODAY

By walking faithfully in the footsteps of Christ, the Missionaries of Charity bring to the world youthful enthusiasm and joy. They actuate what the Second Vatican Council says, "By the power of the gospel, the Holy Spirit allows the church to keep the freshness of youth, and leads her to perfect union with her spouse." That refreshing freshness affects all those who do not ask, to discover some who perhaps did not dare who have the good fortune of coming into contact with Mother Teresa and her sisters.

This young institute brings us some of the original flavor and perfume of the gospel. It reminds us of the simplicity, the humility, the gentleness and kindness of the Lord Jesus in Galilee and Judea, which the world may have lost for a while and now rediscovers. It ushers in an era of trust, good humor, laughter, devoid of anxiety, of complications, of prophecies of Doomsday. It speaks of love for the good God and for everyone around us.

Again, as at Pentecost, the Spirit shows his power and showers his gifts on those ready to receive them. "Allotting his gifts as he wills, he also distributes special graces among the faithful of every rank. By these gifts he makes them fit and ready to undertake various tasks and offices for the renewal and building up of the Church, as it is written 'The manifestation of the Spirit is given to everyone for profit' (Constitution on the Church, 4, 12)."

The Missionaries of Charity, guided by the Spirit, contribute to renew the church, as she needs to be renewed in every century, to rejuvenate what might otherwise become sclerotic or unadapted to other times, to keep the church young and worthy of her divine spouse, who never becomes old. They help to build the Body of Christ, the church, and lead it to its full stature.

The Spirit is at work. As Mother never tires of pointing out we are only instruments in the hand of God, so all the glory must go to the Lord. He makes use of his religious to bring spiritual life and strength to a world spiritually anemic, to spread joy in a world of disappointed, prematurely old young people. The joy Jesus promised to give us through the Holy Spirit.

The Holy Spirit in every age enlightens souls through the words of Scripture. The spirituality of the Missionaries of Charity based on the gospel, and their influence in the world contribute to strengthen the spiritual renewal of the church.

CHAPTER 6

Perfection for All

You must therefore be perfect as your heavenly Father is perfect.
(MATT. 5:48)

Like Jesus, Mother Teresa preaches perfection to all:

- To her sisters, since they walk in the way of perfection of their own free will. 'I will give saints to the Church, says Mother and she means it.
- To the dying at Kalighat and in her other homes, as she leads them to a holy death in complete surrender to God.
- To bishops and priests to whom she says, "How holy you must be, who touch the Body of Jesus in the Eucharist. How holy must be your consecrated hands, your lips pronouncing the sacred words, your whole body, your heart in which Jesus dwells."
- To rich people who bring her offerings, to business and professional people.

To all Mother preaches perfection, saying, "Holiness is not for the few only. All are invited to it."

To be holy is the only thing that matters, for time and eternity. When friends asked her what she considered most important for her Co-Workers, she answered, "That they be holy." They should aim at perfection in the world, in their families, their avocations.

The Congregation of the Missionaries of Charity was founded by Mother for "the salvation and sanctification of the poorest of the poor." The aim has never changed. In the early days Mother wrote to a friend, "How good it is to bring the poor closer to God." She wrote this from the Upper Room, where a niece of Michael Gomes discovered her sitting on a wooden box, while another wooden box served as a desk for her correspondence. Her aim was to bring the poor to God. In the process she has helped to bring also the not-so-poor, the well-to-do, and the rich and powerful closer to God, whether as friends, helpers, sympathizers, readers, and viewers of the wonderful story God writes through her as his docile instrument.

PERFECTION

Mother's great aim has become human perfection, every human being's.

It started with the spiritual perfection of the poor among whom she worked; the very poor in the slums, the poor of the Sunday school at Boitakhana. "How good it is to bring children closer to God," she writes.

Then she applied herself wholeheartedly to direct to perfection the young ladies who joined her to follow Christ in poverty and serve him in the most needy of his brethren.

Gradually the circle of her influence became enlarged and Mother preached perfection to all those who helped her in some way, then to those whom she met, to whom she addressed her appeals for love of the neighbor, every neighbor, especially those more in need.

And then her concern for human perfection swept over the whole world. With confidence in God who sustained her, she pleaded for love and understanding among people of different races, religions, social conditions.

To a journalist asking her at some airport, "Have you a message for the American people?" she answered, without hesitation, "Yes, they should pray more." She did not say "give more" as many might have expected, not even "love one another more," but "pray more," aim at greater perfection. By turning to God in prayer, we obtain a deeper faith, a stronger charity, we move toward excellence in all.

Mother can take endless trouble to help a person toward perfection. She likes to recall, as she did at Cambridge, that one day she found a poor woman dying on a heap of rubbish, who said she had been left there by her own son. As Mother picked her up and carried her to a suitable place, the woman lamented not on her physical condition and dying state, but cried out her heart because "my son has done that to me, my son. . . ." That was the worse of the ordeal: her son, to whom she had given life, on whom she had lavished her care and affection, had thrown her away on the street, on a heap of refuse, because she could no more work and had become a burden he refused to shoulder.

"It took me a long time to make her forgive her son," recalls Mother Teresa. "The woman could not get herself to forgive him for that indignity." And Mother, who wanted her to die like a saint, to end her life by an act of heroic forgiveness, pleaded with her, "You must forgive your son. He is your own flesh and blood. In a moment of madness, when he was no more himself, he did a thing he regrets, he will surely regret. Be a mother to him, forgive him. You ask God to forgive you your sins, you must also forgive your son his sin. If you do so, God will love you for your generosity, reward you for ever in heaven."

For a long time, Mother pleaded. "But at the end," she says, "the woman was won over, grace working in her soul, and she said feebly, 'I forgive him, my God, I forgive him.' " Then she died, in the arms of Mother Teresa, her angel offering her sacrifice to God, as she prayed, "Dear God, receive this woman in your peace and your love. Dear God, thank you for this grace."

That Mother should devote so much time and energy to bring an unknown person, close to death, to make a heroic act of which only great souls are capable, shows her esteem and respect for moral values that lead us to God.

TO SEMINARIANS

In August 1980 Mother was invited to address the students preparing for the priesthood at the Morning Star College, Barrackpore. She had brought cards with the prayer for peace of St. Francis of Assisi, which she had distributed. She started by asking all present to join with her in reciting the prayer. She also ended her talk with Newman's prayer, "Radiating Christ."

In the course of her address, Mother Teresa told the seminarians:

It gives me great joy to speak to you, Fathers and Brothers, who are called to be holy as our Blessed Lord is holy. Do you know what laypeople expect from you? What we nuns expect from you? That you break to us the bread of life—the bread of the Word of God and the bread of the Eucharist.

I need holy priests, priests learned in sound spiritual doctrine to guide my sisters on the paths to God.

You are the men of God, the men of prayer; prayer must be your daily bread. If you don't want to pray, go home.

Mother knows the dangers of activism, of giving too much time to the work and keeping too little time for the spiritual life, for direct contact with God. Indeed, the work never seems finished: we must be able to interrupt it to appear before God, seeking light, strength, perseverance, goodness, self-denial, love.

Mother continued,

The work of the priest in society is to give to the people the Word of God and the sacraments; that is what he alone can do, his particular charism, what he has been chosen for by God. As priests, you should be able to speak from the fullness of your heart. What counts is how much love there is in the giving, and not how much we give. . . .

How sacred your hands must be, for you offer the Body and Blood of Christ for others. Every action of yours must be holy, your speech, your thoughts, your whole person. You must allow Jesus to grow in you by his love. Let Jesus use you without consulting you. You bring Jesus to so many hearts, how close you must be to Jesus. Through your love of Christ, you must reach the unhappy ones, the lepers, the dying, the sick, the hungry, the alcoholic, the orphans.

Remember that the poor are hungry for God, especially the youth. The rich are not happy; I give them a chance to serve the poor.

Mother knows there is plenty of goodwill, of latent desire to serve; it needs to be organized, given an outlet; this she provides.

TO VARIOUS PEOPLE

To foster a family life centered on God, the sisters promote the consecration of Catholic homes to the Sacred Heart of Jesus. It happened that some sisters reported to Mother that non-Catholic people witnesses to this ceremony had remarked, "Why is there not something similar for us? We also wish our homes to be sanctified and our families specially consecrated to God, that we may live under his protection."

Mother then proposed, "We should have an act of consecration of the family to God adapted to the beliefs of non-Christians. Write something for them."

And so a prayer of "consecration of the family to God who is love," patterned on the Lord's Prayer, acceptable to all believers in God, was composed. The consecration could be made on a special feast day and repeated every year. It would remaind all the members of the family of their determination to live in conformity with the divine law. It would also incline all hearts to remain united in common harmony and love.

To individual friends and helpers, Mother does at times give some practical tips to holiness. For instance, a woman told Mother that she bought a new sari every month for five hundred rupees. Mother advised her, "Buy one for four hundred and give a hundred rupees to the poor; you will perform a good action." The woman did so. The next month Mother told her to buy a three-hundred-rupee sari and to give two hundred rupees a month to the poor. Again the woman did so. Mother then told her to buy a two-hundred-rupee sari every month so that she could save three hundred for the poor. Again, the woman followed the advice. Then Mother told her to buy a one-hundred-rupee sari and give the four hundred rupees saved to the poor. Again the woman did so. Then Mother said, "Now, stop, that is enough. Buy a nice sari for a hundred rupees every month and give the balance to the poor and you will have a treasure in heaven. You are the wife of a man in high office, you must be well dressed to honor your husband."

ENTHUSIASM

"Religions," said Cournot, the French mathematician-philosopher, "spread through heredity and enthusiasm. Either one is born in a religion or one is caught by it." Enthusiasm helps to explain the mass movements of conversions, the only way a religion can get a footing in a new area or social group.

A lifelong vocation or dedication also presupposes an enthusiastic reception of a divine call. There can be no long-lived service of Christ in difficult circumstances without enthusiasm. "Without faith and religious fervor, you could not do for a whole lifetime what we are doing," says Mother. "Two or three years, perhaps; a whole life, certainly not; that would be impossible."

Enthusiasm is of its very nature contagious; it spreads like a forest fire. The example and joy of the Missionaries of Charity, their happiness in their work and vocation, generate enthusiasm. Vistas of a better world are opened, a world more sympathetic and loving; this love ignores boundaries and frontiers, and in an exhilarating experience unites men and women from near and far.

It is natural that many want to share in this great enterprise, to jump on the bandwagon, to be with it, even to be in it. "I must do something, I cannot miss this opportunity," say many visitors to Calcutta. Mother Teresa's main houses are indicated on the maps of the city distributed to visitors to Calcutta. Tourist buses for foreign visitors may include a visit to the mother house or the home for children in their sightseeing tours. At the Kalighat Home for the Dying, visitors move about quietly, religiously, in a prayerful mood, whatever their religious affiliation or nonaffiliation. Often, someone spontaneously goes round with a hat or a bag taking a collection, which nets a tidy sum. To the sister in charge they say, "Sister your work is wonderful. We want to do something to help you."

At times one sees the tourist bus stop at the motherhouse. Forty men and women come in, look around the small patio, see the grotto of the Virgin Mary. The lady in charge of the group of tourists approaches Mother and tells her, "They would like to hear a few words from you." Mother goes out to meet them, smiles, welcomes all, and speaks simple words of love they will treasure: "Love the poor, as Jesus loved us who gave his life for us; but first of all, love the members of your own family; love starts at home; care for one another. One day, I met a boy on the street and asked him, 'Why don't you go home?' He said, 'My mother threw me out because I have long hair.' Where was her love for her child? The next day the boy was on drugs. Love your children, love your partner."

Mother ends with a call to prayer: "Let us pray to our common Father, as we say together the Lord's Prayer." They pray with conviction, with a newly discovered feeling of unity, of the goodness of human beings, of the greatness and holiness of God. They had come to the motherhouse to have a glimpse; they have seen, felt, breathed the air, and take back something of the spirit with them.

CHAPTER 7

_____

Mary in Their Life

I am the handmaid of the Lord.
(LUKE 1:38)

"Immaculate Heart of Mary, cause of our Joy, bless your own Missionaries of Charity." Such is the invocation Mother composed for her sisters, which they repeat daily many times.

Mary is the patroness of the society; the feast is celebrated on August 22 under the title of Immaculate Heart of Mary, cause of our Joy, queen of the world. On that day the sisters renew their vows and their consecration to our Lady.

DEVOTION

The devotion to our Lady and the deep filial trust and affection they have in and for Mary does not at all replace the devotion still more intense and complete they have for Jesus. It is no substitute, nor competing devotion. On the contrary, it strengthens the complete surrender to Christ and the imitation of his life and holiness. Mary is the first link between heaven and earth. The Son of God became man in and through Mary, his Mother. He gave his Mother to his disciples on the cross, in the person of the beloved disciple, St. John. By so doing, Christ established one more link with his faithful followers: they have the same mother as he has. We can say with him as he said, "Mary is my Mother."

It is certain that none ever did love, nor will ever love Jesus as deeply, as thoroughly, as heroically as Mother Mary did. Thus she is a model for all who wish to love Jesus. Her love was strong, personal, intimate, understanding, generous to the limit of human powers. So Mary will teach us better than anyone on earth how to love Jesus.

But then, to learn to love Mary, the sisters are advised to turn to Jesus and ask him to deepen their love for his Mother, a thing that can only be most pleasing to him as a loving Son. They will ask the beloved Lord that "They may love his Mother as he did, be a cause of joy to her as he was, keep close to her as he kept, be ready to share everything with her as he did, even his cross, as she stood on Calvary offering him to God the Father for the redemption of the world."

The emblem of the Missionaries of Charity, which graces all their official stationery and that of the Co-Workers all over the world, shows a rosary encircling the globe, bringing the cross to rest on India, a symbol of the kingdom of Christ brought forth through prayer and the intercession of our Lady. It is the chain of love uniting all those who follow in the footsteps of Mother Teresa, join in her apostolic effort, her mission of love. The beads are the links between God and humanity.

St. Paul, who writes even before the gospels as we have them now were composed, before the cult of Mary had developed in the church, mentions her unique importance in the plan of salvation of the Father. He writes to the Galatians (4:4), "When the time had fully come, God sent forth his Son, born of a woman, born under the law."

In Mary and through Mary, the Son of God entered into our human history. That Jesus is born of a woman guarantees his humanity, shows that he is really a man. The Father by sending us his Son makes to humanity the best gift, the greatest honor possible, through the incarnation of his Word born of the Virgin Mary.

Devotion to Mary is a pillar of the spirituality of Mother Teresa and her sisters. They see her as inseparable from Christ, which is sound theology. Mary plays an essential part in the redemption of the world. She is the "Yes" of humanity to God's plan. The Father asks her if she will agree to be the mother of his only-begotten Son, who will become man? She says, "Yes, I will."

Mary is the woman of faith: she surrenders to God, ready to carry out his orders to help him realize his plan of salvation. The Father will save the world through the death and resurrection of Jesus, our Redeemer. Mary is associated with this action.

IMITATION

Mary is the perfect model of the virtues the sisters are expected to practice to be faithful to their calling.

If they are to be contemplatives in action, Mary is their model: remaining in the world, she saw the presence and the action of God in everything, "pondering in her heart" what had been done to her by the Lord God, meditating on the presence of Jesus. She is an example of total surrender to God, as the handmaid of the Lord, of "profound reverence in the adoration and deep recollection in the contemplation of God," the sisters are invited to imbibe (No. 20).

Mary gives us a perfect example of the humility, kindness, thoughtfulness, compassion, and love the sisters are told to imitate in their dealings with one another and with the poor people to whom they devote themselves.

Mary shows concern for the hosts at Cana, who might be humbled and pained on account of the lack of wine for their guests. She puts their need before her Son and asks him to do something to relieve this humiliation. And she brings him to manifest his power, to give a sign that will make all present reflect "who is this man who can do such things, who has power over the elements."

Mary is an example of service even before being asked, going spontaneously to help her cousin Elizabeth when she learns that her cousin is with child. The sisters will also have to go out spontaneously, before being called, to render service to those in need.

Mary brings Jesus with her to those ignorant of him. The sisters are to bring Jesus to lanes and by-lanes, suburbs and slums, to places where he is not present, not known. By their presence, their example, their devotion, their cheerfulness in service, they will manifest him, and bring joy into the life of those who did not know it.

Mary, *"umile ed alta piu che creatura"* in the words of Dante, the most humble and yet the most graced of all God's creatures, is a perfect model of love for Jesus and for the neighbor. A perfect instance of womanhood, the only person to be graced with both perfect chastity, reserved to God, and with motherhood.

"I think our mother church has raised womanhood to something beautiful for God by making our Lady the mother of the church." Speaking to women at the Philadelphia Eucharistic Congress, Mother speaks of the glory of Christian womanhood, of the wonderful vocation of women who imitate Mary in the home and in the world. In passionate accents, with burning words, she pours out her soul in thanksgiving to God and in praise of Mary, whom she sees as the forerunner of the Eucharist in the church.

Indeed, Mother likes to link her devotion to the Eucharist, so central in her spirituality, with devotion to Mother Mary, who she sees as the one who can truly say of the body of Jesus that it is her own body and who becomes the first altar on which the body of Christ is offered. Mother tells her eager listeners: "God loved the world so much that he gave his only son" (John 3:16) and I think that was the first Eucharist, the giving of the son whom God gave to our Lady, and our Lady was the first altar, and she was the one who can in all sincerity say, "this is my body." For she gave her body, her strength, her whole being in making the body of Christ. In her the power of the Holy Spirit dwelled and the Word was made flesh, and she in turn in surrendering herself in total surrender to the living God, when this coming of Christ was announced to her through the angel, asked only one question. She had offered her virginity, her chastity, her purity to God and had to keep her promise; but when the angel explained how it would be, she answered with the beautiful words: "I am the handmaid of the Lord, let it be done unto me according to your word" (Luke 1:38).

It should be noted that the term "the first Eucharist" cannot be taken in a literal, strict sense, as anticipating the Last Supper or equal to our eucharistic celebration, neither does Mother intend it to. It expresses an analogy. Mary, speaking in her own name, can say in some way that the body of Jesus is her body, as it issues from her body, is produced by her own lifeblood. Whereas the priest celebrating the eucharistic sacrifice repeats the words of Christ. Speaking in Christ's name, he repeats the words of the Savior at the Last Supper: "This is my body"; that is, the body of Christ and not the priest's own body.

Once we possess in ourselves the presence of Christ, we are urged by an interior grace to share this good news of God's love, this blessing with others, as Mary did. "Our Lady," continued Mother, "the most beautiful of all women, the greatest, the humblest, the most pure, the most holy, the moment she felt she was full of grace, full of Jesus, went in haste, and here she is a model for all women by sharing immediately what she had received. This is, so to say, like the breaking of the Eucharist; and we know what happened to St. John the Baptist: he leaped with joy at the presence of Christ."

Devotion to an imitation of Mary introduces a welcome trinitarian dimension into the spirituality of the Missionaries of Charity. Mother stresses that like Mary they are to be "the handmaid of the Lord"; that is, the dutiful and obedient daughters of God the Father, who elects them to be all directed to his Son. They are at his beck and call, ready to do his will, as the Lord Jesus himself was. They feel and act as the daughters of the Father.

Like Mary they allow the Holy Spirit to rest in their soul and bring into them the presence of Jesus. For the spirit of God who overshadowed Mary to make her fruitful of a Son who was to be named Jesus, the Spirit by whose power the bread and wine are changed at the Eucharistic Sacrifice into the Body and Blood of Christ, the Spirit who makes the Christian at baptism and confirmation into another Christ, the same Spirit makes the church and the nun to be the spouses of Jesus, consecrated to their Lord and master, the divine bridegroom.

And to the Son of God the nun vows her life, her troth, her service, for better for worse, in sickness and in health, for as long as he will decide, in life and in death.

Mary is a beautiful example of our personal relations with the three divine Persons. Like the poet Dante in the *Divine Comedy,* yearning for a glimpse of the divine Essence, for some understanding of the personal relationships of the Father, the Son and the Holy Spirit, we come to the feet of our Lady and beseech her with St. Bernard in endearing terms to grant us a glimpse of the divine Beauty. Looking up to her as she raises her eyes to God, we may be privileged to see in her eyes a reflection, pale perhaps, but exact, of the vision that gives perfect happiness to the elect of God. And if we look into the heart of Mary we shall find perfect love for Jesus, the Father's and Mary's Son, a love inspiring and stimulating.

In November 1980, when the great work of their general chapter framing the new constitutions had been concluded, Mother summed up its spirit: "As the fruit of our general chapter, we decided to insist on two things: right intention and humility, in imitation of our Lady doing everything for Jesus. If we are humble and do everything for Jesus, all will go well."

TRUST

Expressing her gratitude to Mary for her continued protection, Mother says, "The society is due to her, and it is through her intercession that we obtained everything."

Indeed, from the start there were constant prayers to the Mother of God. The picture of the Immaculate Heart of Mary was above the altar in the small chapel of the Upper Room. It now hangs in the mother house. The sisters accompanied Father Julien Henry on his praying processions to the shrine of our Lady of Fatima. Mother asked her sisters and friends to say hundreds of "Memorare" to obtain the house she needed to start a bigger novitiate; it has since become the motherhouse.

In every one of their chapels, as also at the entrance of every house, in the courtyard or portico, there is a grotto or a statue of Mary to welcome all. Mary leads to Jesus, obtains from Jesus, shows how we should behave to please Jesus.

Mother knows that God delights in granting favors through the intercession of Mary. It is to his honor that we make our requests through her. And truly Mother can recall instances when favors quite unexpected were obtained through prayer to Mary.

In September 1980 Mother reported, "Of late I passed through East Berlin, where we have opened our first foundation under Communist rule. I came from the West with one sister I wished to remain there for work. But she had no visa. So she was allowed in East Berlin only for one day. She was to leave before the evening. They are very strict on that point. You cannot stay for the night there without a regular visa. For me, there was no difficulty, as I have a diplomatic passport; but the Indian sister could not remain beyond the evening. We had applied for a visa, but it did not come. So we started praying to our Lady. Together with the other sisters of the house we said nine 'Memorare.' As we finished, a phone call came and a voice told us, 'There is no hope of getting the visa for that sister; she must leave today.'

"Anyway we did not take no for a final answer. Later we again started praying together nine 'Memorare,' down on our knees, and we offered them in thanksgiving for the favor. Just after the eighth Memorare, the phone rang and a voice said, 'The visa has been obtained; the sister may stay.' She was granted a visa for six months, just like the other sisters. So the next day I left her there and continued on my journey."

If this is not the faith that moves mountains, where will it be found?

What pertains to his glory, God gives, and gives it especially through Mother Mary.

INTIMACY

Mother's strong devotion to Mary can be tender, intimate, simple, as she herself at times reveals.

"The other day I went to see Archbishop Fulton Sheen," said Mother. "He was in hospital and no visitors were allowed. Strictly no visitors. I wanted to see him; but the nurse would not allow me to do so. I insisted and finally she gave in, but said I must not make him talk. I went in the room; he looked very low. I told him, 'You have done much for Jesus,' and gave him a little statue of our Lady I carried in my pocket. He took the statue and kissed it.'

"You know, I always carry a tiny statue of our Lady in my pocket. At times, I give it away to some person for a very special reason. Then I get another one. The day I gave this one to Fulton Sheen, someone gave me another one, a very pretty one, in the afternoon.

"Our Lady is my companion on my tours. I call her my companion since the following fact happened. I had asked the father at Berhampur, after bringing my sisters there, to give me a big statue of the Miraculous Virgin with arms extended downward and palms open, sending graces to the world. He did so, packed it well in a large case, and I took it to the station. I had a railway pass for 'Mother Teresa and a companion.' They wanted me to pay for the freight of the case and the statue; but I refused. 'I have a pass for myself and a companion,' I said. 'Here is my companion. It is the statue of Mother Mary, and she travels with me as a companion.' They let me take her without paying extra for the freight of the box. Since then, I say that our Lady is my traveling companion. I am never alone."

CHAPTER 8

Devotion to the Church

Jesus said, "Teach them to observe all the commandments I gave
you. And know that I am with you always, yes, to the end of time."
(MATT. 28:20)

Mother loves the church, respects the church, obeys the church. For her,
the church continues Christ, extends the Incarnation, performs the actions of Christ.

Mother Teresa's ecclesiology follows the teaching of the Second Vatican Council, which sees the church as the sacrament of reconciliation with
God, bringing to humanity the peace of God. The church is the sacrament
of unity, the sacrament of God's love, dispensing to people his compassion, his forgiveness.

The church is sent to the whole world, a beacon of light to the nations;
she is directed to all peoples, all languages, all cultures, all races, to unite
all by a bond of love. She is sent to bring to men the peace and love of
God, especially to the more needy and deprived, spiritually and materially. This constitutes also the aim and the life work of the Missionaries
of Charity, carriers of God's love to the poorest of the poor.

Christ is continued in history in the church he founded, with whom and
in whom he chose to remain. The saints have all shown a deep attachment
to the church of Christ. Mother follows in their footsteps. She respects
and obeys those who speak with the authority given them by Christ who
said, "Whoever hears you, hears me."

St. Ignatius of Loyola in his great respect for the church included "rules
to feel with the church" in his Spiritual Exercises, which formed the usual
basis of the sisters' retreat. A true Catholic wants to think with the church,
feel with her, follow her guidance, given by the magisterium; that is, the
pope and the bishops united to him.

In doctrine Mother is conservative, traditionalist in the good sense of
the word. She moves in the stream of the Bible, the fathers, the tradition
handed over by generations of the united faithful, the people of God with
their divinely appointed shepherds.

In the apostolate, in their style of life, in their chosen works, Mother
and her sisters are forward-looking, revolutionary, plowing a new furrow.

Sure of herself and of her divine inspiration. Mother never looked back. She put her sisters on the roads and highways, sent them to doubtful and dangerous surroundings, two by two, in search of souls. This brought her the admiration of the world and the blessings of the church authorities.

WITH POPE PAUL VI

Pope Paul VI threw the spotlight on Mother Teresa and her work for the very poor. At the end of his visit to Bombay for the Eucharistic Congress of 1964, he donated the white Lincoln in which he had driven through the Bombay streets to the Missionaries of Charity. The car was raffled off and a large sum was given to the service of the poor.

Pope Paul constantly showed his interest in the progress of the society. He advised Mother on its government and also made some remarks that showed that he was well briefed on what was going on.

"The Holy Father wanted us to open a house in Rome," said Mother. She was delighted with the prospect of being in the Holy City and lost no time in complying with the request. Again Pope Paul VI asked Mother to make a big effort in Latin America. Mother was in full agreement. She sent some of her best nuns to start the work there. The initial progress was rather slow; but gradually the momentum increased, as bishops of several countries asked for the sisters. The future looks bright and the society should develop well in Latin America, once a novitiate has been started in the region.

Paul VI called on Mother to speak on matters of the Christian family and ethics. He sent her to various meetings and functions to uphold Christian principles. He trusted her and she showed herself obedient to the Vicar of Christ, who was truly for her as for St. Catherine of Siena "the sweet Christ on earth."

When the pope died, the Missionaries of Charity lost a guide, a protector, and a friendly advisor.

"How did you receive the news of the death of Pope Paul VI, Mother? He always showed himself so favorable to your congregation."

"He had much to suffer," Mother answered. "First mentally; he suffered from the opposition to some of his decisions. Then the unfaithfulness of many consecrated souls was very painful to him."

"Yes, so many priests and nuns left their calling in the wake of the changes brought about by Vatican II. Who could have expected such a thing? But the pope also made it easier for them to settle their cases and continue receiving the sacraments."

"All those consecrated souls who abandoned the service of Jesus," said Mother. "Pope Paul called this his crucifixion. He also suffered much physically. He had arthritis; it was very painful. When he climbed steps they helped him, supporting his arms. But when he said mass, he genuflected fully, touching the ground with his knee, and nobody held him.

Once somebody asked him if he had much pain; he answered, 'I just live my mass.' Isn't that beautiful? 'I just live my mass.' We who are not priests cannot also say the same thing that we live our mass, during the day, in our suffering?"

"Of course, Mother. All Christians share to some extent in the priesthood of Christ through baptism and confirmation. All offer the mass with the priest, and all who receive the Eucharist receive the victim of Calvary who unites them to his state of victimhood. They become little victims with Jesus."

Mother continued, "Pope Paul suffered much anguish on account of the case of Archbishop Lefebvre. I wrote to Lefebvre five times urging him to come back."

"Did you receive any answer?"

"No. But I shall write again."

WITH POPE JOHN PAUL II

"Did you meet the new pope before his election, Mother? Do you know him?"

"No," she answered, "I never met him."

But soon thereafter Mother was in Rome. John Paul II immediately recognized in her a sister soul. As she returned to Calcutta, Mother was asked, "You were in Rome lately? We saw the report of your meeting with the Holy Father at the general audience of Wednesday. Your photo as you kissed the pope's hand appeared in the papers."

"Yes, I met the Holy Father; he kissed my head, right on the top—here." She showed the place.

So, as Mother bowed, holding the pope's proffered right hand in both her hands, and kissed his ring with deep emotion, in an act of faith, devotion, and total commitment to the Vicar of Christ on earth, we understand that the pontiff was himself deeply moved. In an unprecedented gesture, he bent toward her, took her small head into his hands and kissed the top of her head, covered by her religious habit.

At that very same spot, sixty-eight years earlier, the priest baptizing Agnes at Skoplje had anointed her with the holy chrism. This made her share in the priesthood, kingship, and prophetic mission of Jesus, the Son of God made man, who himself had been anointed priest, prophet, and king of the human race by the Holy Spirit.

Mother had been faithful to her mission. The pope's kiss was a sign of acknowledgment and gratitude, while it communicated to her an increased share of God's peace, approval, and love.

"The Holy Father said he wished to see me again," she continued. "Then I asked him whether I should go to Poland where I have been invited by a group of Catholic youths. And he answered, 'Go to Poland.'"

"Mother, it would be splendid if you could open a house in that wonderful Christian country, perhaps the most Christian in the world."

"We have not been invited as yet. But we are invited to go to East Germany and Cuba."

Pope John Paul II did call Mother again—several times. The world's two best known Catholic personalities are perfectly attuned. They share the same ideas, ideals, beliefs, concerns. They can be called kindred souls, with the same love for Jesus, for the church, the same zeal for souls.

They have the same evangelical simplicity, trust in God, joy. The same idea of the sacredness of religious life, of the importance of prayer and contemplation for the apostle.

Later, Mother could report, "When I explained to him the plan of the Co-Worker priests, the Holy Father asked me, 'May I be the first to give my name?' "

"Well, Mother, with such exalted patronage, you should have no difficulty of getting your plan approved and of spreading the idea all over the world."

The Holy Father also entrusted to Mother various functions. She served under him as a public relations officer of the church.

"I am going to Australia," Mother said in September 1981. "This time it is out of obedience."

"What, on orders from the Holy See?"

"Yes." Having been absent previously for several months, she had hoped to have some time to devote to the training and guidance of her sisters. But now she had to go to Australia for meetings, talks, interviews. Then back home via Papua New Guinea, and the Philippines, visiting her houses on the way.

In the summer of 1982 Mother was sent to Beirut to see things for herself and report to the Holy Father.

A SACRAMENTAL SPIRITUALITY

The sacraments are the actions of Christ. They bring us Christ and unite us to Christ, especially the Eucharist, the source and center of the other sacraments, in which Christ is truly present. The sacraments are the great source of grace for Christians, to whom they bring grace much more than proportionately to their efforts, provided they be well disposed.

For the Missionaries of Charity, the Eucharist constitutes the center of their worship. They have, whenever possible, daily mass and communion. They devote daily one hour to adoration, in the active branch, and two hours in the contemplative branch. The adoration was introduced when the society was already well established.

"The general chapter approved of the hour of adoration unanimously and made it compulsory for all our houses," Mother said with visible satisfaction in November 1980.

To make her eucharistic Lord worshipped and loved is one of Mother's great aims. The sisters are to labor to that end. She herself does not miss any opportunity of bringing people to honor Jesus in the Blessed Sacrament. "When I visited a Catholic head of state," she recalled, "I told him, 'If you will have daily adoration of the Blessed Sacrament in your chapel, I will give you a monstrance for that purpose. We have two monstrances in our house. I shall send you one.' He agreed; so I sent him a monstrance through a bishop."

Children especially must be brought to Jesus, prepared to receive him in the Eucharist. Mother knows he loves children. He blessed them, he welcomed them even when he was very tired and the apostles wanted to drive them away. To gather poor children and bring them to Sunday Mass was Mother's first work—when she was still alone. She trained her first helpers to do the same.

The yearly consolidated report of the congregation gives pride of place to preparation for the reception of the sacraments. It lists: so many thousands instructed and prepared for first communion, for confirmation; also the number of adults prepared for baptism, of couples whose marriages were regularized, of dying people prepared for the sacrament of reconciliation and holy viaticum.

The sisters have prepared hundreds of thousands of children for communion and taken them to Sunday Mass regularly. This has been a cause of deep joy for the sisters and for Mother. Had they done nothing else, they would have rendered great honor to God and service to his people.

"I know," Mother said, "that many of these children will later drop out and discontinue to practice their religion. But they will have received their Lord in their youth, in their pure hearts."

"Yes, Mother, they will have been sanctified by this intimate contact with Jesus; something of it will always remain."

When the first reports arrived from the new foundations in Latin America, Mother was delighted. She could say, "Hundreds of marriages were settled by the sisters and blessed by the priest. The couples started to live together. The sisters discovered these irregular unions, prepared the couples for the sacrament of marriage, and brought a priest to bless the couples. Then they consecrated the families to the Sacred Heart of Jesus and the Immaculate Heart of Mary. Thus they established truly Christian homes."

ECUMENICAL AND UNIVERSAL SPIRIT

Already well before the Second Vatican Council, Mother was convinced that their duty was to bring the message of God's love to all people. The sisters would work for all, irrespective of nationality, caste, creed, religion. They would also call upon and accept the collaboration of people of goodwill, with no distinction of belief and affiliation. Indeed, the Co-Workers may well be the first religious association approved by the Holy

See, which is open to all Christians, to non-Christians and to unbelievers. Mother finds a basis of unity of heart and action, a link to join together people wishing to help others in an unselfish manner, in whoever wishes to give free service to those in need, simply because it is good to give, to serve, to spend oneself in order to make others happy. She senses that such a desire, such a determination, can come only from the creator of the human race, who has put in all of us seeds of truth and goodness.

In the ecumenical field Mother knows what unites; she also knows what separates and divides Christians belonging to various denominations.

The most powerful means of bringing unity among all Christians lies in common, silent prayer, seeking God, opening our minds and our hearts to his influence, being ready to receive his grace. "When I was in Taize, in France," said Mother, "Brother Roger, the prior of the monastery, took me to the church where a mixed congregation was gathered. I merely told them, 'Let us unite in silent prayer for an hour.'" Those present may have expected a rousing talk on unity; Mother only told them to listen to God.

Mother's greatest desire, namely that her Lord be universally known and loved, is expressed in her direction to her sisters, "Pray and work daily that all may become followers of Christ."

As the Father sent his Son and his Spirit to the world to bring us true knowledge of God and a share in his life, his love, his happiness, so the Missionaries of Charity are to go throughout the world to bring the good news to the poor.

Missionary activity belongs to the church's very nature and constitutes her most pressing duty. The Missionaries of Charity share in her concern for the spiritual good of all humankind. They aim at bringing to all the light and love of God, and "in some way at making the Lord present to all peoples by their prayer, penance, word, and action" (Constitutions No. 84).

In this activity, as "members of the diocesan family" they follow the instructions of the bishops, the spiritual guides of the people of God, of which they are part (Constitutions No. 85).

To the end that all may tend to God and realize their spiritual potentialities, the sisters are told to teach and encourage people to pray, whether they be Christians or non-Christians. It is their privilege to collaborate with the grace of God and help all to reach as high spiritually as the Spirit invites them to go.

In India and many other Eastern countries where the people are generally religious-minded, there is little difficulty in getting people to pray. The simple people, especially, turn to God in their needs. If he does not hear them, who will? Unless he helps them, they feel they have no chance of succeeding in their endeavors. And so, with non-Christians we pray to the one true God, creator, law-giver, providence, and reward; we pray to him who is truth, goodness, and bliss.

In our search for God's will, in our desire for perfect union with him, in our gratitude for his fatherly gifts and protection, in our surrender to him, we can all be united, as we bathe in the light and love of the Godhead.

In one notable instance, Mother organized common group prayer with non-Catholics and non-Christians. On the occasion of the Silver Jubilee of her institute, she planned to have services of thanksgiving to God with various religious bodies and denominations. The fact was widely publicized in some European magazines, approved of, and extolled.

Every day during about a fortnight, Mother and some of her sisters took part in prayer services in churches, synagogues, and temples, with Jews, Armenians, Zoroastrians, Buddhists, Jains, Hindus, Sikhs, Anglicans, Methodists, Baptists, and some other religious groups. They read from their own Scriptures and from the Bible. They praised the work of charity and thanked God for inspiring and sustaining it. The ceremonies were deeply moving; hearts felt united, if beliefs differed. Still, the group taking part in these common prayer meetings represented less than 10 percent of the population of Calcutta, a city of seven million people. The great majority of non-Christians did not participate in the movement. The orthodox or traditional Hindus, by far the largest group, did not organize any meeting. None of their great religious leaders, the Sankaracharyas or heads of important temples or monasteries, were present.

Nor did the Moslems join in prayer with the sisters. Some had hoped that Mother, at least, would be allowed to address their congregation gathered for prayer in the big public park, as their feast fell on the feast of the Holy Rosary, the very day of the foundation of the Missionaries of Charity's congregation. But Mother could only exchange greetings with some of the Moslem leaders, thus joining in their thanksgiving to God and their holy joy.

This kind of more spectacular prayer meetings has not been repeated. But prayers for all, led by Mother at civic and other meetings, at foundation days, when laying first stones or cutting ribbons to inaugurate new premises take place as a matter of course. "Let us pray to our common Father," and all feel one in the family of humanity under God's paternity.

At meetings of Co-Workers, of helpers, of volunteers, prayer is recommended, whatever be the religion of those present.

In the work of love for the poor and needy, distinctions between Christians and non-Christians, even between believers and nonbelievers are overlooked and forgotten. Only love remains, the bond of divine love uniting all in a common endeavor.

As Pope St. Clement I, writing to the Corinthians, beautifully says,

Love binds us fast to God.
There are no limits to love's endurance, no end to its patience.
Love is without servility, as it is without arrogance.

Love knows no divisions, promotes no discord; all the works of love are done in perfect fellowship.

No divisions, no "you" and "I," as opposed, but only "we," as united under God who loves us all, and loves all through us. Here the Missionaries of Charity score: doing the work of devotion through love, they turn a blind eye and a deaf ear to differences of caste and creed, of race and color. They work for all and with all who wish to join them in serving the poor.

The holy Catholic church holds pride of place in Mother Teresa and her sisters' love, devotion, and service, being truly for them:

the glory of the Wisdom of the Father,
the Body of Christ,
the Temple of the Spirit.

CHAPTER 9

Prayer and Contemplation

Jesus said, "When you pray, go to your private room and, when you
have shut your door, pray to your Father who is in that secret place."

(MATT. 6:6)

"Love to pray," Mother Teresa tells the Co-Workers. "Take the trouble
to pray. Prayer opens your heart until it is big enough to hold and keep
God. We must know Jesus in prayer before we can see him in the broken
bodies of the poor. Ask and seek, and your heart will grow big enough
to receive him and keep him as your own. Then we can bring more of
Jesus, more of the love of Jesus to the people we meet." And again she
insists, "Love to pray—feel often during the day the need for prayer and
take the trouble to pray. Prayer enlarges the heart until it is capable of
containing God's gift to himself."

Prayer is "a hot line of communication with God" available in any
emergency; dying child, important decision to be taken, preparing to
address a large meeting. Prayer works the miracle, here and everywhere; the prayer of faith, humble, persevering, trustful prayer. Again
the gospel is proved right: "Ask and you shall receive; will your Father
not give you his Holy Spirit if you ask him for good things?" (Luke
11:13). What the Missionaries of Charity ask for is the glory of Jesus
and the good of souls.

Mother insists on continuous prayer, a spirit of prayer, a habit of
prayer. We should find God in our soul, in the Eucharist, in the neighbor.
We should be conscious of God's sacred presence, of his action in the
world, of his love poured on us at all times. We should be aware that he
does the work, that we are his instruments; this constitutes a dignity, an
honor unparalleled, a privilege to be esteemed and accepted as a form
of life.

For Mother as for St. Augustine, prayer is "the breathing of the soul,"
as natural, effortless, sustaining, as the breathing of the lungs for the
body. It makes the soul dwell in the pure air of God's love. "Jesus has
drawn us to be souls of prayer," Mother tells her sisters. Prayer inspires
and penetrates their day's work and gives it its true meaning. It is the
"pray always," of Jesus, repeated by Paul, the constant prayer of the

mediator directing the whole creation to his Father. It reminds us that the world is a sacred gift of God to lead us to him, speaks to us of his goodness, makes us crave his presence.

"What impressed us most during our stay in Calcutta as we went daily to work with the sisters," recalled some volunteers, "was first the joy of the sisters, that constant cheerfulness with which they carried out their avocation; secondly, their spirit of prayer. In the car or ambulance we start with a prayer. When we reach our destination, the home for the dying or the dispensary at the railway station, a sister leads all in prayer and starts a hymn. We all pray together as we start our work. The sick people, the dying, the patients are consoled, strengthened, edified. They listen respectfully or even join in the prayer."

The sisters' life of prayer finds a stimulus, a support, and an urgent call in their daily contact with human suffering and misery. It may be helped by the two original activities of the Missionaries of Charity, which remain their two basic works, bringing them face to face with two great mysteries: the mystery of death and the mystery of life.

When they work in the Home of the Pure Heart of Mary at Kalighat, the first of their homes for the dying, or in one of the scores of similar ones they have established in various parts of the world, the sisters come in daily contact with the mystery of death. These are places where silence reigns, broken at times by a scream of pain, a call for help, a gasping for breath, or a death rattle. From time to time a body is removed, not to be brought back. This is an antechamber of heaven.

The mystery of death is overpowering, overwhelming, awe-inspiring. A man or a woman dies alone, utterly powerless to change the course of events. "Naked I came from my mother's womb, naked I return to the earth," said Job (12:21).

And yet, for the witness of the weekly or daily instance of a death, the thing appears so simple: a person returns to God. To help the dying do just that, Mother started the home; to that end the sisters labor and suffer and pray that the dying may turn to God with their whole heart. And they do.

Mother can affirm, "The thousands of our poor who have died in our home, have died with God." And one notes that visitors enter the house with some sort of awe, go round silently or speak in a hushed voice. They feel close to the silence of eternity, when all movement, all change stop, to leave one face to face with "the One who is, Who was, and Who will be," the God who made us out of sheer love.

The other mystery the sisters confront daily is the mystery of life, the struggle to exist. They live with it in the children's home, where so often life hangs by a thin thread. The sisters spend themselves during whole days, trying to strengthen the slight hold on life of the newborn infants, discarded as unwanted property, and yet to our eyes so precious, yes, infinitely precious. They labor to give the little ones a chance to live, to come to the knowledge of God and of themselves, to open their eyes on the wide world.

"I could not sleep last night," confided a sister. "An infant was struggling against death. I stayed with him, praying, fighting with all my energies, and he is still alive. Will he live? It is in God's hands."

PRAYER EXPRESSES UNIVERSAL LOVE

Prayer possesses the unique distinction of being a universal act of charity. It unites the one who prays to all living beings, wishing them well, doing them real good. This is our only way to express effectively our universal love, the only way to do good to all humanity.

As we pray for all men, we can do good to people living thousands of kilometers away, from Kalamazoo to Kamtchatka, people, whose names, languages, cultures, occupations we ignore, whom we shall never see. We appear before God, our common Father, who knows them and their needs, and loves them; we pray with them, for them.

The constitutions of the Missionaries of Charity (No. 104) express this universal love and concern for all people when stipulating, "We pray with those who do not pray, who do not know, who do not dare, who do not want to pray." Yes, even in the matter of prayer, they show their concern for the most needy, the most afflicted. In truth we can pray for the latter and even in their name, since we are all one in Christ, who prayed for all people, and continues to offer to his Father for all people, for whom he intercedes.

Mother considers prayer as a source of power always on tap, never dry, never exhausted, available at a moment's notice. She herself devotes all her free time to prayer. "At Dar-es-Salam," recalls Mrs. Chaya Ghosal, "we regularly attended Sunday Mass at the same church as the president of Tanzania, Mr. Julius Nyerere. One Sunday we saw Mother Teresa in church. She stayed for the four masses that morning. Mother had then no house in the town; she had just returned from Tabora, where she had visited her sisters. As she had nothing special to do in the town but wait for the plane to take her back to India, she remained the whole morning praying in the church. In the afternoon she came to the convent and spoke to the sisters and to us of her trip and her apostolate."

As Mother says, "The mouth speaks from the abundance of the heart; God speaks in the silence of the heart."

PRAYER NEEDED FOR DEVOTED SERVICE

On her return from Oslo, Mother was given a civic reception by the West Bengal government. Mr. Jyoti Basu, the chief minister, presided over it. Television crews from India, France, Japan, were at work; dozens of photographers took pictures while Mother smiled to all.

In the open air, sitting and mostly standing, were three thousand people.

When Mother's turn came to reply to the address of the chief minister, she started by saying a prayer. Then she explained the rationale of their work: "We are religious, we serve God, we see God in our suffering brothers and sisters." She did not ask for money, or help or donations of any kind, but pleaded for charity and understanding, first within the family, then toward those who are abandoned, lonely, needy. "We should love them as Christ loved us who gave his life for men," she said. Mother then ended by a fervent appeal to all present to pray regularly, stating her creed:

> Without prayer no faith
> without faith no love
> without love no devotion
> without devotion no service of those in need.

In various parts of the country, Mother was given similar rousing receptions. Crowds of people showed their enthusiastic support, their admiration for her work, their sympathy for this manifestation of divine love. Mother answered usually in the same way, spreading her message of peace and love: "First make your peace with God, then find strength to do your duty to yourself and to your neighbor from him."

"Prayer—faith—love—devotion," leading to service, selfless and persevering, continuous and generous, these are in her mind the successive links in the chain that binds people together, under God and his grace.

Prayer obtains faith, explicit faith, strong, effective faith. True, "you would not seek me if you had not found me." We cannot pray correctly to God without his grace. But that first prayer is a groping, an extending of one's hand in search, in supplication, in a desire to find. That prayer brings us the discovery of God, of his presence close to us, of his goodness, his power, his concern for us, his help, his action in the world.

To a young foreigner who acknowledged sadly that he did not believe in God, Mother answered, "Pray." She gave him my book of meditations, *Remain in My Love,* on the Gospel of John, and told him to use it daily. A fortnight later he came back and said, "Now I believe."

Prayer obtains faith; more prayer obtains a stronger faith, an active faith productive of good works, performed with the love the Spirit pours in those in whom he dwells. But it begins with faith. As Paul writes to the Romans, we are justified by faith in God, in God's promises, in God's Son who died and rose for our redemption.

Considering that God wants to save all human beings and gives to all the graces that are necessary to that end, we trust that people are justified by the faith in God that is according to the light they receive from God. If they accept God's word and do God's will as they know it with all their hearts, that includes implicitly the acceptance of Christ as the only one by whom we are saved.

When speaking to lay audiences, Mother likes to indicate the different links of the chain of causality, expressing them in the language of the New Testament genealogy of Christ: "Prayer begets faith, faith begets love, love begets devotion and service to the poor."

Thus we come closer and closer to God, as the generations came closer to the Son of God, Jesus Christ our Lord.

When speaking to her sisters or to religious, one more link is usually indicated, namely a preliminary condition for a successful life of prayer:

> without silence no prayer,
> without prayer no faith.

Mother explains it as interior and exterior silence, silence of the tongue, of the ears, of the eyes, of the imagination, silence, quietness of the soul, recollection leading to concentration, to intimacy with God.

Then and then only can prayer become in the words of Teresa of Avila "a loving communion, alone with the God by whom we know ourselves to be loved." Then is practiced the advice of Jesus "when you pray go into your inner room and close the door, and speak to your Father in secret" (Matt. 6:6), to your Father who knows what you need before you tell him, to your Father who loves you.

That silent, loving, intimate converse with God is the privilege of those who follow Christ in evangelical poverty and simplicity, in complete trust and self-surrender.

Mother also shows the connection between prayer and the apostolate, when she tells her sisters:

> The more we receive in silent prayer,
> the more we can give in our active life
> (*Advice*, July 1978).

This gem is one of the finest aphorisms of the spiritual literature. It expresses Mother's conviction that whatever good her sisters can effect results from the grace of God received especially in silent, intimate, receptive prayer, in openness to the Spirit of God.

PRIMACY OF PRAYER

The sisters devote three to four hours a day to prayer. They could give that time to the work. But they are told, "God comes first. You are the brides of Christ. Down on your knees to adore him, praise him, love him." Thus swings the pendulum in prayer: it starts with adoration; adoration leads to praise of the divine goodness; praise leads to love, surrender to the God for whom we live, from whom we come, to whom we go. Then back to praise and from praise to adoration of the divine majesty.

"Prayer is not work and work is not prayer," says Mother, establishing a real difference between the two main activities of a religious person. The primacy belongs to prayer, and so "we may not substitute our prayer by work," stipulate the Constitutions (No. 115). Once this is kept in mind and the required time and attention are given to prayer and the contemplation of God, then our work becomes prayer, a continuation, an extension, a realization of prayer. It actuates our contemplation in the world. As the Incarnation actuates the love of God for men, so our work actuates our love for him as we serve him in the neighbor.

Only people of prayer can bring God to the neighbor, can give to others what they have contemplated in prayer. Only the contemplative in silence can become a contemplative in action.

To her sisters Mother can say with pride and gratitude, "Jesus has drawn us to be souls of prayer." If this is true, and it must be, it constitutes one of the Lord's best gifts to his spouses.

"Jesus is our prayer, and he is also the answer to our prayer. He has chosen to be himself in us the living song of love, praise, adoration, thanksgiving, intercession, and reparation to the Father in the name of the whole creation" (Constitutions, No. 104).

This is an echo of Paul's "Christ lives in me" (Gal. 2:20). Christ prays in me, acts in, and through me, because I have become one with the incarnate Son of God, a child of adoption of the Father. The Holy Spirit through whom the adoption is effected, dwelling in the soul he entered at baptism and confirmation, guides the soul in prayer; he prays for the one who cannot pray or feels unequal to offer the prayer the Father deserves.

As a result we pray simply. "Our prayer is very simple," says Mother. Simple as the prayer of a child of God, trusting, accepting, surrendering to the will of the Father who loves his child. The simpler the better. God is perfect unity. But for the human being, who is a multiplicity, simplicity in prayer has to be acquired, or received as a special gift from heaven.

Mother did not explain what she understood by this simplicity, but those who have helped to train her sisters in the art of prayer know that it is no easy matter to reach peaceful, habitual, simple union with God.

The many vocal prayers the sisters usually recite daily will not help to acquire this simple, quiet union with God. Twice, at some years' interval, Mother asked, "Do you think we have too much vocal prayer?" And twice she was answered, "Yes, Mother, you have too much vocal prayer." As a result the amount of vocal prayer was curtailed to allow more time for mental, silent, mystical prayer.

THE ASIAN BISHOPS MEETING ON PRAYER

Mother was invited to address the Asian Bishops Conference at Barrackpore, near Calcutta in 1976. She then spoke to them of and explained what she understands by simple prayer.

The bishops had come from many countries of the East, from Japan, Indonesia, Taiwan, Australia, New Zealand, Hong Kong, the Philippines, Thailand, Malaysia, Pakistan, Bangladesh, Sri Lanka, and from various states of India. They met to study and discuss the possibilities of using non-Christian techniques and methods of prayer and contemplation, such as yoga, zen, and also charismatic prayer. Some exponents of these systems would expound their theories, give demonstrations, lead common exercises. As a result some light might be thrown on ways of prayer adapted to Asian cultures and thought.

"Mother, what did you tell the bishops when you spoke to them on prayer the other day?"

"I told the bishops: prayer is quite simple. We must not complicate matters. When Jesus was asked by his disciples, 'Master, teach us how to pray,' he answered, 'You will pray like this, Our Father . . .' He did not teach them any methods or techniques. He said simply that we should speak to God as to our Father, a loving father.

"I told the bishops that the disciples had seen their master pray often, pray even during whole nights; so the people should know you as men of prayer, they should see you pray, then they will also listen to you when you speak to them on prayer."

For Mother Teresa things were simple. God is perfect simplicity. To pray to him is a duty for all people; not for the learned or sophisticated only. Prayer requires faith, humility, a child's abandon and love. "After my talk," Mother added, "the bishops retired in small groups to discuss the matter and exchange their views. When they returned for the second talk, I told them, 'Let Jesus pray in you. Allow him to take over and express what you cannot say.' "

This was charming: Mother called on Jesus as an elder brother to express what his smaller brothers and sisters, still infants and unable to talk, would like to say. The idea is trinitarian, since Jesus in us, with us, for us, prays to the Father as the firstborn of the redeemed. This prayer will be essentially a prayer of praise and thanksgiving, as the one Jesus said, moved by the Spirit, "I thank you, Father, that you have revealed these things to the humble, to babes, and hidden them from the wise and proud" (Luke 10:21). It will be a prayer of surrender to the Father's will, "Father, your will be done, not mine" (Luke 22:42), a prayer of intercession also: "Father, that they all may be one like us" (John 17:11). Truly a prayer as rich, as broad, as deep and exalted as the feelings of the heart of Jesus.

"Let Jesus pray in you," as you are silently recollected, intent on his presence in the soul, all surrendered to the Lord.

Mother, obviously, spoke as one who has found, not as a seeker. When you live only for God and constantly remember him, when his glory is your only aim, your only purpose in life, when you have reached the stage of never thinking of yourself, prayer has become natural. Mother's advice of speaking to God in a simple, personal, intimate manner came straight from the gospel: "go into your inner room, close the door, and speak to your Father who is in heaven." Your Father who loves you will not only listen to you, but answer you.

St. Teresa of Avila also teaches that to speak to God is an excellent way of prayer, which leads the soul to union with the divine majesty. When one has been raised to mystical contemplation, the Spirit takes over. Then there is no problem, except that of obedience and faithfulness to God, and of continual detachment from the attractions of the world. But even in those not granted mystical prayer, the Spirit of God prays *"Abba,* that is *Father,"* as St. Paul teaches. In the same vein Mother says, "Let Jesus pray in you." Gradually the Spirit of Jesus will lift up the soul obedient to him and direct her prayer. But no technique or method will succeed in leading the soul to the mystical experience of God; only a gratuitous gift of the infinite, omnipotent, ever-gracious God can do that. Still by our faithfulness we can dispose ourselves for the reception of this grace and ask the divine majesty to grant it, if it be his will.

One day, when I was speaking with Mother of the promise Jesus made, "If anyone loves me, he will keep my commandments and my Father will love him and we shall come and dwell in him" (John 14:23), she made the terse comment, "Ah, the indwelling; yes, we have too long neglected it." Mother was bringing this truth to the minds of the bishops and also of the priests. This was one of the main preoccupations in Eastern countries, namely the discovery of God's presence and proximity. Many had traveled from Western countries to find the secret of this discovery. But the key was not in human hands, nor was it hidden in any cave, forest, or at the top of some high mountain. It lay in God's hands.

The prayer of the Name, the frequent repetition of the name of Jesus or of Father was a powerful means, and a true Eastern way, leading to union with God and perhaps bringing God's fatherly heart to bestow on his disciples the favor so much desired. By continuous prayer and attention to God, we can dispose ourselves for union with him. To this end, Mother wants her sisters to acquire the habit of simple and continual prayer. When on the road and during free moments, they finger their beads and pray the rosary; thus they remember God present in the world and in their soul.

INVITING ALL TO PRAY

Mother makes use of every opportunity to teach prayer and to lead others in prayer. She recommends prayer to those who come to her for advice, solace, spiritual help: whether they be poor or rich, simple people or influential.

Before going to Oslo for the Nobel Peace Prize ceremony, she was given a public reception in Delhi. She left in the morning from Calcutta; two hours by jet got her to Delhi, and the same evening she was back in Calcutta. On this occasion, she recalled, "I went to Rastrapati Bhavan to call on the president of India. When he met me, he pulled out of his coat pocket a card on which I had written the prayer of Newman, 'Jesus shine through me,' which we say daily. I had previously given it to him. The president took out the card from his pocket and told me, 'I say the prayer and it gives me consolation in times of stress and difficulty.' "

Mother added, "I had changed Jesus into Lord, because he is not a Christian."

"Of course, Mother, as long as people do not know Christ, do not believe in him as the Son of God, they should pray to the true God for light and strength to do his holy Will, according to the measure of grace granted them. We should help all to reach as high spiritually as the Holy Spirit invites them to go. It is marvelous to see how Indians are ready to pray. They respond more generally to the invitation to pray than people in the West do."

When Prince Charles came to India, he was given twenty-four hours in Calcutta. Of that limited time, one hour was earmarked for a visit to Sishu Bhavan, where Mother received him and took him round the children's home. A newborn infant had been brought in the previous day, picked up from the street, abandoned. He had the honor of being introduced to a royal highness.

"I took the prince to the chapel," said Mother. "We prayed for ten minutes together. He seemed impressed." To him also Mother gave a card with the prayer of St. Francis, "Lord make me an instrument of thy peace." Mother asked him to say it every day, as the Co-Workers do. It has become her accepted practice to pray with all visitors, whatever their rank.

In the parlor, on a fine day in February 1981, the usual scene takes place, whenever Mother is "in." Eleven U.S. professors and teachers from colleges in the deep South are conversing with Mother. They represent some organization that wishes to help her sisters. After handing over checks, asking Mother to sign pictures of herself, each one has a photo of herself taken with him. She submits to the ordeal with good grace, as usual. Then Mother takes over: "Before we part, let us pray together in the words Jesus taught us, 'Our Father. . . .' " All join in prayer. For Mother this is the apex of the meeting with these hardly known friends, the thing that rejoices her heart.

She has made prayer together the habitual practice at public functions, talks, speeches. When answering congratulations, when receiving honors or donations, at civic receptions, she either leads the assembly in prayer or formulates her own prayer, after having stressed the need of prayer. The least would be "Let us thank God for this wonderful opportunity and for all his good gifts."

SACRIFICE SHOULD ACCOMPANY PRAYER

A woman came to ask Mother Teresa's blessing and prayers for her son, three years old, who was unable to speak. She was a Hindu, her husband a Parsi. Mother asked the woman, "Is there anything to which you are very attached, something dear to you?"

The child's mother answered, "Yes, betel nut chewing. With me it has become a compulsory habit."

"Well," said Mother Teresa, "give it up. Offer it to God as a sacrifice and pray for your son's cure."

The woman gave up entirely chewing betel nut. Three months later the little boy started to talk. He continued to progress and became normal.

Some time later, the woman took instruction in the Catholic faith and became a Catholic with her son. A few years later, her husband reflected, "If that religion is good for my wife, it might be good for me also." He sought instruction, and when ready, was baptized.

Mother keeps a perfect balance between the cross and the resurrection, sacrifice and joy. She knows the sadness of seeing people suffer and live godless lives, but also the happiness of the glory of the Lord who reveals his love for people through his presence in the world and his giving himself to them.

She dares speak of sacrifice openly, without inhibition or constraint. Sacrifice for her and her sisters is their daily bread, something they take for granted. How otherwise could they prove their love and gratitude for the crucified Savior? Their day includes many sacrifices, from their rising up early morning at 4:40 A.M. to their retiring at 9:30 P.M. in crowded dormitories, without fans in tropical climates, without heating systems in cold countries. The long day includes prayer, hard work, rough food, coarse clothes, lack of any personal possessions, going out to seek and serve the poor.

Mother speaks of sacrifice wherever she goes, wherever they receive her as a modern prophetess speaking in the name of God. She extols the value of sacrifice before university students, who find it stimulating, and before rich businessmen, who usually shun the very idea. "I hope that what you give me comes not from your surplus, but is the fruit of a sacrifice you made for the love of God," she tells Rotarians or Lions or Knights, at a lunch during which they present to her a handsome check for the poor.

The gifts of children are especially appreciated, because they usually mean forgoing a picture, a sweet, an ice cream, and are the result of an act of love. Mother praised the generosity of the children of Scandinavian countries, where in many schools they gather funds resulting from sacrifices.

CONTEMPLATION

The constant remembrance of God through prayer, of his action in the world and presence in the soul, helps the sisters achieve Mother's claim, "We are contemplatives in action."

Contemplation in the strict sense is silent reception of God's action on the powers of the soul entirely directed to him. In prayer we seek God, in contemplation we find him, feed on him, are overcome by him, rest in him, in awe, admiration and gratitude. Contemplation in action must mean that we can find God in the work, in the events of life, find him present in ourselves as we go about our daily duties, find him in our brothers and sisters. For those who attain to this state, who receive this grace, it is a marvelous thing, strengthening, comforting, sustaining, a choice gift of the divine majesty who reveals himself to those entirely consecrated to his glory.

This same quality and grace Mother would like to find in her sisters and Co-Workers. She puts this state as the ideal they should tend to. "If we see Jesus in the poor and serve him in them, then we are contemplatives in the world," she says. "We serve God all the time." Mother sees God present in the world in an habitual manner. That Christ lives in the neighbor, that she serves him in the poor is for her a reality, a fact of life, not a concept or an abstract article of faith.

"I do not need to be at prayer to find God; I find him in the work, in the day's activity," she can say very simply. As a result of seeing God's guidance in the events of life, she does not have to plan ahead or worry about the future, since it is in God's hands. She awaits and looks for an indication from divine Providence, as a bishop's particularly pressing invitation, a property offered for a special work, a need forcibly brought out before her eyes.

True contemplatives in action are rare, for they require a special grace, a strong vision of faith, complete detachment from self-love, and an inner life centered on God: all conditions not easily fulfilled. This state may be presented as an ideal to generous people, intent on finding God at all costs. But to reach this state and live in it habitually requires a special grace and a strong determination. Few priests, few nuns, and few laypeople dispose themselves for this grace and receive it.

To be a contemplative while fully active in the world supposes that all the powers of the soul be focused on God alone and work only for his glory. The whole universe, people, and ourselves are then seen as proceeding from God, living in him and tending to him. When this view of the world as God's creation, guided by him, moving toward its assigned goal, enlightens the soul, when she becomes acutely aware that "in God we live and move and have our being" (Acts 17:28), she reaches a state of habitual surrender to divine Providence, complete trust in God's guidance, and consequent equanimity, joy, and serenity.

Contemplatives in action find themselves simply overwhelmed by the majesty of God's presence and the power of his action in the world. They marvel at God's presence in the human soul, and especially in their own miserable, sinful souls. They turn inwardly to their Lord to adore his sacred presence, praise him, surrender to his will. They discover God present and active in the world he creates, guides, and inspires; they see Christ present today in his faithful disciples and his suffering brothers and sisters.

Habitual contemplation in action may follow on the second conversion to God, when, goaded and sustained by a powerful grace, converts turn to God with continued determination. Henceforth they will prefer to suffer any torment rather than commit a deliberate sin. They will habitually choose the more perfect way of action, which usually proves the less attractive to nature. They will seek no human consolation but embrace joyfully the cross the Lord offers them. From such total surrender to God and desire to imitate Jesus at every moment of his life, flows a sense of freedom, as the soul now without fetters, can fly to her Lord, to whom she belongs entirely.

The soul then admires what Mother Teresa likes to call "God's humility," who in his utter graciousness deigns to make use of those rebellious, imperfect, and ill-adapted instruments we are, to carry out his divine purpose. The soul sees God at work in the world, finds him, discovers his hand in the events of her life.

CONTEMPLATION OF THE BLESSED TRINITY

The constitutions of the contemplative wing make an important contribution to the active sisters' spirituality by directing their sights on the fundamental mystery of the Blessed Trinity. While praying for the apostolate of the active sisters, the contemplatives also stimulate their spirit of contemplation, raising it above human contingencies and the consideration of the world, to bring it into the pure, ethereal light and life of the Godhead.

The contemplatives affirm,

"We are called in a very special way to remain immersed in the contemplation of the Father, Son and the Holy Spirit, in their love for one another as well as in their love for us manifested in creation, redemption and sanctification" (Constitutions No. 117).

And thus they profess: "We shall humbly and lovingly welcome the Triune God in the depths of our very being to continue in us their divine and eternal contemplation" (No. 118).

This is a beautiful, revealing, stimulating resolve to unite themselves to the primeval mystery of God's own life. Indeed, not only do we dwell in God, but he dwells in us. We are as the sponge in the ocean, resting in and full of its waters—of its power, its majesty, its mystery, its very essence, without exhausting it.

Pondering this truth should lead the soul to an acute awareness of God's infinite and eternal action by which he in Trinity takes place in herself, since he is present there. It should cause a deep-seated, overwhelming experience, climaxing in awe, admiration, gratitude, surrender in love to the God who *is*. There will remain habitually an immense respect for the divine Presence in silent wonderment, as we move about in the world God created for us and came to inhabit.

In this contemplation of the divine Presence of God in herself, the soul details,

"the beauty, majesty, and splendor of the Father,

"his tender and fatherly love"—first of all for his Son, Jesus, the Logos of the Father, preexistent in time, in the Father's bosom—

"become incarnate on earth in the history of salvation."

We ask him to send us his Holy Spirit,

to reveal to our feeble minds the sanctity and glory of our God; we request him to pray in us to our Father in union with Jesus, who sends us the Spirit, the Father, and the Son's substantial love. And Jesus prayed his Father "that the love with which you have loved me may be in them and I in them" (John 17:26).

This union to and contemplation of the three divine Persons forms an antechamber to mystical contemplation of the Godhead that the Lord may grant to the loving soul.

CHAPTER 10

Christic in the Poor

When you did it to the least of my brethren, you did it to me.
(MATT. 25:40)

Mother Teresa sees the poor and asks us to see them in a spiritual perspective, through eyes enlightened by faith.

Poverty is simply an accident that does not affect our essential dignity, value, and destiny. We are all children of God, irrespective of our intellectual and material possessions. "We must acknowledge the dignity of the poor, respect them, esteem them, love them, serve them," she says. And again, "We owe a debt of gratitude to the poor. The poor people are great people, most lovable people. Often I think they are the ones to whom we owe our greatest gratitude. They teach us by their faith, their resignation, their patience in suffering. They allow us to help them. And doing so we are serving Jesus."

The sisters, on returning from serving the refugees from Bangladesh, all said the same thing: "We have received from the poor much more than we have given them."

Many of the volunteers who come from various countries to help at Kalighat also confess, "We are struck by the faith and resignation of the people brought there in a dying condition. They taught us that it is so easy to die: just another action, the last one. They taught us how to die, without effort, trusting in God."

The poor show gratitude for small favors or services. Mother recalls with admiration that a dying woman I had helped at the Kalighat Home held my hand, and her last word was "Thank you." One is reminded of the Little Flower dying, saying, "My God, I love you." A last word, a summing up of a whole life, opening a door on an eternity of love and thanksgiving.

The question is often asked, "Are the poor as a class morally better than the rich?" According to Holy Scripture, the answer seems to be yes. Christ himself has said, "Happy are the poor in spirit" and "How difficult it is for the rich to enter the kingdom of God," when a young man whom he invited to follow him refused his offer and went away sad "because he was very rich." To the apostles who, not being very poor, expressed their fear asking, "Then who can be saved?" Jesus answered, "All things are possible to God" (Matt. 19:22-26).

In India also, it would seem, the answer to the question would be yes. The poor, as a group, are closer to God, more detached from human comforts, from material things. Having fewer obstacles on the way, they are generally God fearing, God worshipping, and accept what comes to them as the will of God.

"The poor show faith and patience in suffering," says Mother, "and we are privileged to serve God in them. We can console Christ in his distressing disguise in them, Christ suffering in his brethren." The poor are also challenging to those who wish to help them. "To serve well our poor, we must understand them; to understand their poverty, we must experience it. Working for them, we come to identify ourselves with them. Our sisters must feel as they feel, feel their poverty before God, know what it is to live without security, depending on God for the morrow."

Mother can turn a blind eye to the shortcomings of the poor, at least when she extols their qualities. When an American woman photographer saw her pushing back with extraordinary energy a whole column of destitute women invading the compound to profit by a free distribution, Mother requested, "Don't take this, please, don't show this." That was in 1981. The same scene had taken place several times in earlier years.

Love for the poor is rooted in the love of God. Mother says, "To serve the poor we must love them. In order to love the poor, we must first know them. And to know them means to know God. Then we must live with the poor: and to live with them means to live with God. Lastly, we must give our hearts in order to love them, and our hands to serve them, and this means to love God and serve him.

"But everything starts from prayer. Without asking God for love, we cannot possess love, and still less are we able to give it to others.

"We must have the conviction that in serving the poor we serve God. God is love. He loves you and me. If we love others as he loves us, it becomes evident that Christ is in the poor and lonely. The certainty of this reality is boundless for me.

"The poor people whom we gather each day are those whom society rejects and abandons. We try to give human dignity back to these people. As children of God they have a right to it.

"We take great care of the dying. I am convinced that even one moment is enough to ransom an entire miserable existence, an existence perhaps believed to be useless. All souls are precious to Jesus, who paid for them with his blood."

Sitting in front of an illuminated portrait of Christ, Mother Teresa, on the eve of the New Year (1977) said, "Let us know the poor. This knowledge will lead us to love them and love to serve them. The downtrodden and the unloved could be a productive part of society. They are our brothers and sisters. If they are given the opportunity they may do much better than anybody else.

" 'People are created for greater things—to love and be loved. Love and compassion alone can remove all divisions and hatred in the world.' 'We must thank God for the poor.' Indeed, by loving the poor we love God. God we cannot see, the poor are next to us; and by serving the poor we can serve Christ in them, who said, 'What you do to the least of mine, you do it unto me.' "

There is a double advantage in serving the poor, because as Mother says, (1) "We can give to the Lord, who needs nothing, yet accepts our gift gratefully because it is made to one in need who represents him." And (2) "When giving to the poor, we give to people who cannot reward us or return the gift to us, so we earn merit for heaven, as promised by Jesus."

"The poor also teach us: 'We can learn from them to accept a difficult situation and hardships, to be satisfied with few material goods, to make much of little.'

"The poor teach us humility: having little, they feel small, unimportant, dependent, ready to receive;

'they teach also to share what we have with others, as they often share with others poorer than themselves;
'they teach us solidarity, brotherly love, and compassion for those who suffer; they often show a deep attachment to their children, for whose good they deprive themselves of even the necessaries of life. Mother and her sisters have witnessed and reported some moving examples of parental love and compassion.' "

Mother loves to praise the poor. She has a special gift enabling her to discover and extol their qualities. Speaking to an audience of women, she tells her enraptured listeners, "You and I, being women, we have this tremendous thing in us, understanding love. I see that so beautifully in our people, in our poor women, who day after day, and every day, meet suffering, accept suffering for the sake of their children. I have seen parents, mothers going without so many things, so many things, even resorting to begging, so that the children may have what they need. I have seen a mother holding to her handicapped child because that child is her child. She had an understanding love for the suffering of her child. I remember a woman who had twelve children, and the first of them was terribly disabled, terribly handicapped. I cannot describe to you what the child looked like, mentally, physically, and I offered her to take that child into our home where we have so many like that, and she started crying and she said to me, 'Mother, don't say that, don't say that. She is the greatest gift of God to me and my family. All our love is centered on this child. Our life would be empty if you took her away from us.' "

Then Mother turned to her listeners and asked them to look into themselves, into their own family life, their relations with their neighbors, so that we may improve our society and become more perfect men and women. And she asked, "Do we have that kind of understanding love today? Do we recognize that in our homes, my child, my husband, my wife, my father, my mother, my sister, my brother, needs that understanding, that handshake?"

And so through Mother's and her sisters' instrumentality, we know better the poor, we penetrate into their minds and hearts, we are all led to be better in our own surroundings.

YAHWEH IS TENDER AND COMPASSIONATE (PSALM 103:8)

"We should experience toward the poor not pity," says Mother, "but compassion." Pity implies superiority; but we are fundamentally equal as God's creatures. Compassion arises between people on the same level, on the human level, all members of humanity knowing themselves as such.

St. Paul said of the Gentiles of his time that among their worst vices was their lack of compassion—they could see suffering without being moved by it; they could even—what is the acme of degradation—cause it and rejoice at witnessing it.

In this modern world, this vice taints and corrupts much of our society, when stories of violence and brutality are viewed by millions on the screen with gusto. The true Christian spirit revolts against this kind of entertainment.

But Mother asks her educated listeners if there are not around us glaring instances of self-centeredness, of ugly egotism, of sheer cussedness refusing to see the misery, the needs of others?

Christ Jesus had compassion on the multitudes of sufferers: he felt for the blind, the sick, the maimed, the hungry, the homeless, the captive, the lonely. He came to heal them, spoke to them in endearing terms, brought them hope, told them that they counted before God. Yes, they are important, for God who created them out of love keeps loving them. The compassion of Christ Mother shares. It is his gift to her; the sisters exemplify it—not only in words, but in constant action.

Mother knows the poor and their hardships. Like Christ, like Paul, she has experienced poverty, tiredness, hunger. After Paul, she can say, "I have worked and labored, often without sleep; I have been hungry and thirsty and often starving. I have been in the cold without proper clothes" (2 Cor. 11:27). Like Paul's compassion, hers shows an immediate concern for all her disciples: "Does one of you feel a scruple, I share it" (29).

The Prophet Ezekiel, when he came to visit the exiles beside the river Chebar, stayed first with them for a week, keeping silence. He would experience their sad plight as exiles before addressing to them God's message (Ez. 3:15). The missionaries similarly have plenty of opportunities to feel as the poor feel, to experience many of their hardships and to bear them confidently and cheerfully. With the apostle they may say, "I made myself all things to all men, in order to save some at any cost" (1 Cor. 9:22).

Even without having made the same experience, we can look and see the misery, listen and hear and ponder the tale of woe, and sympathize with the sufferer. My heart can go out to the needy.

The sisters' is a compassion that prompts to swift, efficient action. A calamity anywhere in the world invites them to offer help. Floods, earthquakes, the specter of famine raising its head, swarms of refugees fleeing their land due to political upheavals: Mother soon brings her sisters to render whatever help they can.

After the earthquake in Guatemala, even though she hardly knew where the country was located, Mother's immediate reaction was "people are suffering there, we must go to their help." Similarly with Ethiopia, where she had been several times and opened houses, "There is going to be a terrible famine there; we must do something about it." She feels for people she has never seen, because they are God's people.

The picture that made her world famous shows Mother holding in her arms a small child, looking sad and helpless, having lost his parents at the time of the exodus from Bangladesh. In her compassionate love, she seems to feel the pain of all humanity. Like all great pictures, it speaks for itself. Like the Christ on the cross by Velasquez, it requires no caption, no explanation, no comment. One just looks, gazes, understands, as the picture penetrates into the innermost of the soul—awakening in turn sadness, shame, compassion, and desire for such love.

On seeing a picture of herself on the cover of the Bengali translation of *We Do It for Jesus,* Mother commented, "They should have put the picture with the child." She was right. She wanted to focus the attention on devotion to the child, on compassion, on pure love.

The picture with the child in her arms depicts an essential aspect of the vocation of the Missionaries of Charity, namely to console, compassionate, feel with, as Jesus had compassion on the multitudes hungry for the word of God, for bread, for the love of God. But it reveals only one side of Mother's personality. There is another side, another picture, equally if not more human, the smiling face, engaging, befriending, conquering, trustful, optimistic, because God is good, God loves us. The joyful smile bespeaks trust, love, hope in the vision, the joy the Spirit pours into our souls—which Mother has abundantly, which she prays for daily and deserves.

THE POOR ARE HUNGRY FOR GOD

Especially when speaking to people entirely consecrated to the service of God and the neighbor, bishops, priests, seminarians, religious, Mother stresses that "the poor expect you will bring God to them."

To priests and seminarians, Mother likes to tell again and again the beautiful, the inspiring story she heard from one of her sisters after they had started their first house in Rome. "The sister found an old man in a small room in a suburb of Rome. She cleaned the room, put things in order, washed him, nursed him, until one day, the old man said, 'Sister, you have brought God into this house, now bring the priest also.' The sister did bring a priest, the old man made his confession for the first time after sixty years, and a few days later died in the peace and love of Jesus."

Good actions are the first link of a chain of goodness. "As I narrated this beautiful example at a meeting in the United States," said Mother, "after the meeting a priest came to me and said, 'Mother I had written to my bishop asking to be relieved of my sacerdotal functions and laicized. But now, after hearing what you told us, I have changed my mind. I shall write to the bishop to cancel my letter and state that I wish to continue in my ministry.'"

TO CARE FOR THE POOR IS A JOB FOR EVERYONE

To care for the poor is a duty, an honor, a favor, a blessing. Some hold nowadays that the responsibility of caring for the poor and the unfit, the handicapped and abandoned, the sick and suffering, devolves only on the state, that supposedly omnipresent, all-knowing, all-powerful providence. Mother Teresa does not think so. The care of the poor and needy belongs as a birthright to everyone.

"Recently," she recollected, "I was in Ethiopia, where they have a communist government since the revolution that deposed the emperor. I went to a minister to ask for land for a hospital that was badly needed, as there was none in the area. The minister told me, 'This is a communist government, and we believe that the care of the sick and the needy is the duty of the state, not of individuals or groups.'

" 'But you are not doing it,' I replied.

" 'No,' he said, 'that is true. So I shall help you to get some land.'

"So now we can look after the sick," concluded Mother.

Again, in Calcutta, at the civic reception given in her honor, after the Nobel Peace Prize, the chief minister, who presides over a leftist government in the state of West Bengal, mentioned in his very fine address, praising the work of the Missionaries of Charity, "Of course in a communist state the care of the poor and those in need should be the province of the state and not of the individual. But considering that we are not in a position to take up the full responsibility, Mother and her sisters are welcome to help in this work."

Mother Teresa, replying with great respect and affection for the chief minister, made her position quite clear: "I do not agree with the chief minister when he says that the care of the poor and needy is the sole responsibility of the state. It is the responsibility of everyone. Every person must be concerned with his brothers' and sisters' needs."

To the ancient question, "Am I my brother's keeper?" the answer today as every day will be "Yes, you are. If you have been favored with more goods, with better health and gifts than your weaker brothers and sisters, you owe it to them to share with them, to help them in their needs." In a family an elder brother or sister must help a younger, weaker or handicapped brother or sister, everyone recognizes it. But we are all members of the human race. And for believers in a personal God the reason is still much stronger, since we are all God's children, "the members of his household," as St. Paul tells us.

OBJECTIONS AGAINST MOTHER'S METHODS

Mother Teresa has been accused of not tackling the problem of poverty at its roots, of offering only temporary and superficial relief to sufferers without putting them back on their feet. On several occasions, those interviewing her have objected, "You merely distribute food to the hungry; what you should do is to give them means to support themselves. You should provide them with instruments, say with a fishing rod and tackle with which they might earn their living." Mother answered, "The people picked up on the street or brought to our houses are too weak to even hold a fishing rod; we try to give them back enough strength so that they can hold a fishing rod."

The accusation of temporary relief is baseless. It misses the point and does not make the necessary distinctions. In the homes for the dying sick in India, the sisters receive people who cannot even stand on their feet. The first concern must be to return to them a modicum of health and strength. Truly, they cannot be kept very long in those homes, as others need the beds. Once they are out of immediate danger, they are moved to some other institution where they may have a chance to recoup. In other houses the sisters receive people permanently disabled, cripples or sufferers from tuberculosis or terminal sicknesses.

There are also food distributions to the poor in soup kitchens; there simple rations are given to hundreds of poor women, widows, mothers of small babies, all living below the absolute poverty line.

Work for the children in the Sishu Bhavans or children's homes proves definitely constructive, as results already show. Those children have good prospects, if they can survive the first months, which are often critical for those who have been discarded by their parents, thrown away, or brought undernourished. They are given every help to recover, and most of them do. They will be provided with all they require, and receive as complete an education as they are able to assimilate.

The children are adopted by couples giving all guarantees that they are able to educate them well and will provide them with a friendly family atmosphere. The adoption system has been well organized: children are adopted by married couples either in India or in foreign countries.

Mother encourages childless couples to adopt a child, for their own and the child's good. She puts it strongly, "A married couple without a child is not a family—a house without a child is not a home." Without a child there is no occasion for sharing, for giving oneself, for concern for another, there is no living bond between the husband and the wife. Realizing this, many childless couples are happy to adopt a child and treat the child truly as their own.

Some married couples want to devote themselves more fully by adopting a crippled child, one that has little prospects of a happy life. They feel they can lavish more care, more attention, more love on a frail brother or sister of Jesus, weak, handicapped, dependent. There are wonderfully generous parents in the world God made and sustains by his love. Contact with their neighbors' sufferings, unhappiness, or limitations brings out the best in them. They thus develop their full spiritual stature, and become humble, unnoticed heroes.

In this spirit a married couple came to Calcutta and chose to adopt a blind child, whom they took back to North America. From the start they lavished their love on the child. Later a journalist succeeded in tracing the family and found that the blind child could swim, sing, play the guitar, and was happy in his new world. Then the question arose, which the reader may try to answer: Who had given more and who had received more, the adopted child or the adopting parents?

Those children who are not adopted are put through school. Mother has sent over a hundred boys in the Boy's Town established close to Calcutta, where they are trained for a job according to their abilities. They remain in the school until they can find a job and fend for themselves.

The girls are sent to various schools; they are not thrown on the employment market without skill and preparation. They are taught sewing, dressmaking, commercial subjects, typing, and shorthand.

When the chief minister came to inaugurate the new building of the children's home in Calcutta, the girls sang and danced for the guests. The chief minister remarked approvingly that the home had seen to cultural activities also. Even weddings are arranged, the expenses of the reception paid, and the girls given a small dowry to help the young couple get started in life.

POVERTY WESTERN STYLE

Mother says, "There are different kinds of poverty. In India some people live and die in hunger. There even a handful of rice is precious. In the countries of the West there is no material poverty in the sense in which we speak of poverty. There no one dies of hunger; no one even is hungry in the way we know it in India and some other countries.

"But in the West you have another kind of poverty, spiritual poverty. This is far worse. People do not believe in God, do not pray. People do not care for each other. You have the poverty of people who are dissatisfied with what they have, who do not know how to suffer, who give in to despair. This poverty of heart is often more difficult to relieve and to defeat. In the West you have many more broken homes, neglected children, and divorce on a huge scale."

Is it not shocking that in some countries, so-called advanced, a third of the marriages contracted end in divorce. They break up after five or ten years. What happens to the children, every kind heart will understand.

Many people do not accept any moral code beyond their own inclinations. Their spiritual poverty is far more difficult to cure than the material one. It affects our very being, our spirit, and our soul. It endangers the fiber of society, its stability and resilience. The disease runs through every class, threatening mostly the younger generation.

Still, even in rich societies and countries there are found many people in need, whether this be due to their own deeds or because they were powerless to change their own adverse circumstances. On reliable information, in 1981 in New York 36,000 people slept in the open, in railway stations, under bridges, in parks, in packing cases; and that night after night, under the rain or in the snow. They could not be or did not wish to be accommodated in night shelters for indigents.

In the West there are habitual delinquents in and out of prison; what happens to their wives and children? There are drunkards and dope addicts. During a visit to Tokyo, Mother's keen eye spotted a drunken man lying on the wayside. This sight gave her an opportunity to speak to her Japanese audiences of their own circumstances. "You are a rich nation," she said, "but on one of your streets I saw a man lying drunk, and no one picked him up, no one seemed to bother about him, no one tried to restore to him his human dignity, to bring back to his senses a brother, a child of God." Mother wanted people everywhere to become aware of the sufferers and the needy living close to them, in their own cities, towns, and villages.

In London, the sisters run a home to receive jobless workers not covered by social insurance for some reasons or other, and also handicapped and mentally afflicted people.

The sisters in Rome serve meals every evening to old men in a shelter close to the Statione dei Termini. They also go out at night to seek those who sleep in the open that they may give them a cup of warm milk and a blanket when they require one.

In a locality of East London, the sisters provide sandwiches to the hungry. They wished to open a soup kitchen to serve meals to the poor living in the area. "The local authorities refused to allow it," said the sister in charge, "on the ground that there were already several charitable organizations giving help and that if we opened another free soup kitchen, the locality would attract more poor people and would soon look utterly depressed."

In the richest towns, some poor people and many sufferers of painful terminal diseases will always be found, a challenge to sympathy and loving service. And the number of Christ's brothers and sisters who feel lonely is beyond all telling. So that we may hear the Lord Jesus saying, "When you visited them to cheer them up, to console them, to befriend them, to render them service, you visited me."

CHAPTER 11

Universality

Go out to the world, proclaim the Good News to all creation.
(MARK 16:16)

Mother Teresa is possessed by a burning desire for a universal presence and action. In this she mirrors St. Paul, who traveled from one place to another, establishing churches in as many lands as he could, craving to go to the extremities of the world to preach Christ.

A thousand of her sisters—nay, five or even twenty thousand sisters—could be fruitfully employed in the towns and villages of India. Many Indian bishops and officials entreat her to open more houses in their territories; yet she directs an increasing number of her personnel to other countries, where needs are great and the fields of the Lord ripe for the harvest.

From the start of her institute, Mother wished to go out, penetrate into distant lands, work among foreign peoples of whose languages, customs, ideas, ways of life the sisters had not the faintest idea. They searched dictionaries and pored over the pages of atlases to discover the where-abouts of countries called Fiji, Jordan, Papua, Yemen, Haiti. What language did their people speak, what were their staple foods, their customs, their religions? And how did you reach them? Next month or next week Mother would be sending five sisters to start work in some of those places.

Like Paul, Mother wishes to bring Christ to new lands, to make the message of God's love known by the poor everywhere, to establish islands of faith and hope, oases of love. At the foot of the crucifix standing in the staircase of the mother house, where all can read the appeal of the dying Savior, "I thirst," and the answer of his brides, "I quench," is spread a large map of the world with the inscription "Go and teach all nations." Mother means to drive the words into the minds of the young sisters, who, as they climb to the chapel or to their rooms several times a day, cannot escape seeing the command of the Savior to go to all nations. He seems to tell them, "Do not wait until the work of preaching the gospel is finished here in Calcutta, your Jerusalem, or even in India, your Judea; it will never be fully preached nor accepted; leave these shores and go throughout the world." And the sisters obey the divine command.

Mother craves universality; she wishes to enter and settle in many countries, thirty, fifty, a hundred different countries. The map of the whole earth, encircled by a rosary with its cross falling on India, forms the seal of the Missionaries of Charity, reproduced on their stationery and that of the Co-Workers. The sisters may have houses in a hundred different countries before their congregation is fifty years old.

Mother's desire to help the poor knows no limit. Has she not exclaimed, "If there are poor people in the moon, we will go there." These words are included in the text of the present constitutions; it must be the only religious document in which the members of a congregation are told they may have to go to the moon to fulfil their vocation.

The gospel tells us that "the crowds wanted to prevent Jesus from leaving them, but he answered, 'I must proclaim the Good News of the Kingdom of God to the other towns too, because that is what I was sent to do' " (Luke 4:43-44).

Several times foreign journalists asked, "When there is so much poverty in India, why must Mother Teresa send her sisters abroad to open houses in countries less in need?"

Mother replied to them, "The spiritual poverty of the West is worse than the material poverty of India. Why should we limit our work to one country when other countries call for us?"

Love knows no boundaries; it wants to spread, to embrace the whole world; it is an interior urge to give ourselves always more. The love of Christ urges us, drives us forward, to go out, to seek souls and spread the good news of the kingdom of God everywhere.

Christ sent his apostles to the whole world. Paul, Francis Xavier, many men and women following in their footsteps, felt the same desire to go always farther, to sow in new lands. Mother's aim is the spiritual good of those the sisters care for. What the sisters can do in that respect in some parts of India is limited. In other lands, the Americas, Central Africa, some countries of Europe, other Asian countries; the scope for spiritual action and influence is much vaster.

A pioneer sows, initiates, stimulates, organizes, energizes. Mother Teresa has moved the hearts of millions, caused them to share her concern for the needy and sufferers, by her journeys abroad, by her foundations and the publicity they received through the media.

It has been said, "Mother Teresa is the most influential woman in the world today." She would not be, had she limited herself to work in Calcutta, Bengal, or even the whole of India.

The symbol of the Missionaries of Charity and of the Co-Workers groups reminds all of the universal aim of the movement: the whole world held together by the rosary, a chain of prayer, and of links of love.

IMPORTANT CHANGES

Their desire for a universal action, and a more extended presence of Jesus in the world through their houses and their own persons, led the Missionaries of Charity to change at least two points of their original constitutions.

The foundations are to be decided by a deliberative vote of the general council. The superior general, at first, was to visit the place to ascertain conditions of living and work (No. 190). Now they have added "or her delegate," for the burden of work on the shoulders of the superior general has become enormous, and they are opening houses at the rate of one a fortnight, in various parts of the world.

In the first constitutions, Mother had specified that "no less than seven sisters shall dwell at every city or town foundation" (No. 189).

The number was gradually reduced to six, then five, and now the new edition of the constitutions stipulates, "no less than four sisters shall be sent to a new foundation." Mother always favored a larger number. But with so many applications from bishops for new houses, she relented, and the constitutions were amended on this point.

A second change took place. The first constitutions decreed, "There shall be no foundations in the villages" (No. 189). The sisters were to concentrate their apostolic efforts on the very poor living in slums, in bidonvilles, in the squalor of dirt and poverty of the biggest towns and their surroundings. There conditions of life prove more unhealthy than in the villages, poverty more nagging, and moral standards lower, as a rule, because the fabric of society has become looser.

But priests started urging Mother to start working in their rural parishes. At first she allowed the sisters to visit the villages and work in them for a few weeks, then return to their urban homes. But bishops and priests asked for a permanent commitment to their diocese or parish, even in rural areas.

Mother asked, "We are opening a house in such a village; it is not against our constitutions, Father, is it?" As I did not know, I kept quiet. But later the constitutions ratified the change in policy, by suppressing the sentence forbidding foundations in the villages. Another victory for the broad, universal outlook and concern for the good of the poor everywhere.

In the matter of language, English remains the language of the institute, now spread over the world. Other congregations have had Italian or French as their vehicular or link language. English offers today the broadest opportunities and is most generally understood. So the sisters with a working knowledge of English enjoy a definite advantage and can be shifted without much difficulty.

When the general chapter met in November 1979, the delegates represented the six continents. The institute was established in each one of them. The deliberations were conducted in English, the language of the congregation. At the end of the chapter, Mother asked me to address the members. I congratulated them on having become a truly worldwide organization to spread the love of God everywhere. Most of them were of Indian birth, but they had worked all over the world. A young team full of zeal and enthusiasm, they had blazed a wonderful trail. Sitting on the floor in their midst, Mother raised her voice to ask, "So, Father, I was right in making English the language of the society?"

"Mother, you were perfectly right; this was an inspiration from God; it has helped to make your congregation truly international."

Mother never asks for praise. But she deserved recognition and approval for her foresight, at a time when she had only a few Bengali-speaking girls as disciples, and some priests advised her to concentrate on an Indian language for their formation. Had she stuck to the local language, she would have limited her field of activity to Bengalis in India and Bangladesh. Now, the congregation was worldwide, had a far-reaching influence hardly anyone could have foreseen.

The sisters are also made to learn the language of the region where they work. In the process they all become bilingual, if not trilingual. Some speak five or six languages. The constitutions state that candidates must have an aptitude for languages. As this is required by their vocation to serve the needy anywhere in the world, we must expect that they receive the grace.

People have been struck by the facility with which the sisters learn languages and dialects, at least sufficiently to converse with simple people. It seems to be a charism rewarding their availability and obedience, their readiness to go wherever they are sent, at a moment's notice.

Mother also expects this promptitude from them. She writes reproachfully that she has heard that some sisters after six months in a locality were not able to prepare the children for first communion in their own language. "Therefore, Sisters, apply yourselves diligently to the study of languages."

In the matter of dress and lifestyle, the principle of adaptation has suffered a severe jolt, and even a setback. Mother's original idea had been to adopt the way of life of the people among whom she lived, as regards food, dress, living conditions, means of traveling. She decidedly broke away from the traditional religious habits introduced into India by foreign congregations. Long before Vatican II she seemed revolutionary in her white sari, she a European woman, moving about in a coarse cotton dress, as simple Indian women do.

In the institute's constitutions of 1950, it was said, "In India our dress will comprise a habit and a white sari with blue border" (No. 11). The society then existed only in India. By stating "in India" Mother left the door open for an adaptation of the dress in case the society spread to other countries with different cultures and habits. Adaptation to local conditions seems to have been in her mind more than a distant possibility. Did she then foresee or even hope that the Missionaries of Charity would expand to the point of reaching every continent?

But twenty-five years later, when the society has truly become worldwide and receives recruits from all continents, the revised constitutions state, "Our dress consists of a habit and a white sari with blue border." The qualification "in India" has been dropped; it has fallen by the roadside, a casualty of success. Now the sari has become an absolute rule; it must be worn everywhere, in every clime. And we see that in practice the habit remains the same in warm or cold climates, except for a cardigan or coat, which is worn, even by Mother, in countries where the temperature may go down to zero degree Celsius.

The point may interest the historian of religious movements. An original, daring idea has not been broadened, but narrowed down and dropped, and that for several reasons.

By wearing the same sari, of Indian origin, all over the world, the sisters have achieved a definite distinctiveness—they can be immediately recognized and identified in any airport of the world, in any photo wherever it be taken. They have gained in unity, cohesion, strength. They wear a uniform: already they have a tradition, a reputation to uphold, a common way of life to maintain. It would be unthinkable for them, for instance, to open a school for the children of the well-to-do.

The sisters have acquired a sense of belonging, of unity, an *espirit de corps*. And they can be sent as they are, from one pole to the other, without hesitation.

The desire of women religious to wear "the same habit as our foundress" is also satisfied. Uniformity of spirit, faithfulness to their constitutions and original way of life are strengthened by exterior signs, and the dress is an important one. But the question may be asked, "Will this uniformity always prove a help to the apostolate?"

The Indian sari is as foreign in Tanzania and Mexico, as was in India the Western-style religious habit. Mother Teresa changed into Indian dress the day she left the Loreto convent to immerse herself into Bengali life and start a new congregation. She then wished to live among the poor people of Calcutta, completely identified with them.

But the congregation has become worldwide; its numbers are no more expressed in two or three, but in four figures. So that the main problem has become to keep in unity the minds and hearts of religious coming from many different countries. And it is a well-known fact that many of the religious institutes that have given up exterior signs of unity and austerity discover that the change has great disadvantages.

Still, it will have to be considered whether in some areas the wearing of the Indian sari as religious habit does not affect the apostolic efficiency of the sisters, by making them unidentified with the local population.

CHAPTER 12

Foundations

I am the Vine, you the branches. If you remain in me and I in you,
you will bear much fruit. . . . It is to the glory of my Father that you
should bear much fruit.

(John 15:5,8)

"We have requests from bishops to open forty-one houses in India and
fifty-eight abroad," said Mother.

That makes ninety-nine; next month the total will reach one hundred,
and next year one hundred and ten, or one hundred and twenty. So the
problem is, where should they establish new foundations?

"And how do you decide, Mother, what applications to accept among
all these?"

"We go where needs are greater."

"The criterion seems sound enough; but how do you compare needs
in such varied circumstances?"

She says, "We use prayer and divine guidance."

Mother relies on the Holy Spirit to show where the sisters can produce
greater fruit for the glory of God and the good of souls. This guidance
will be obtained by continuous, fervent prayer, by openness to the action
of the Holy Spirit, who indicates by signs and events what we should do.
The guidance of the Spirit, so evident during the first years of the church,
as the Acts of the Apostles show, is still forthcoming today. The situation
of a young congregation, especially in mission countries, resembles that
of the early church. It is recalled that the Spirit inspired Paul not to go
and preach the Word in the Roman province of Asia. "They thought to
cross into Bythinia, but as the Spirit of Jesus would not allow them, they
went through Mysia and came down to Troas" (Acts 16:7).

St. Paul was constantly guided by the Holy Spirit. After long peregrina-
tions, he was finally led to Rome, having been told by Jesus, "As you have
been my witness in Jerusalem, so you must be also in Rome" (Acts 23:11).

Paul relied on the prayers of his converts, his friends, his co-workers.
He asks prayers "That God may show us opportunities of spreading the
Word." So does Mother Teresa: the prayers of her sisters, of the poor,
sick and dying in her homes, the prayers of orphans and crippled chil-

dren, the prayers of all her Co-Workers, especially of the Sick and Suffering, the prayers of the contemplatives, all added to her own prayer asking God's light, obtain for her and her counselors the light and guidance they need.

CONDITIONS TO BE FULFILLED

To a priest from Europe asking her if she would open a house in his country, Mother replied, "I have three conditions. First, the sisters must work among the poor. There are poor people everywhere, even in rich countries like Germany, Holland, Belgium. Second, they must be given sufficient time for prayer; work must not be so overwhelming as not to allow enough time for common and private prayer. Third, they must be given a priest of solid doctrine and virtue as spiritual advisor. Only when these three conditions are guaranteed, do I agree to open a new house."

Mother knows that her first responsibility is to ensure the spiritual good and the holiness of her nuns. The good of souls is her main aim. She wants to spread her network of love all over the world.

CHOICE OF FOUNDATIONS: CRITERIA

"We go," says Mother, "where there is greater spiritual need; in many countries, as in Latin America there is an acute shortage of priests and nuns to minister to the people, specially to the very poor. We go where there are greater spiritual opportunities, much spiritual work, people ready for religious instruction and the sacraments. We go where the people want us, which means that they will respond to and profit by our work. We go where the church should be present and is not or hardly at all; there we can bring the presence of Jesus. We go where there are good hopes of local vocations, girls ready to make sacrifices for God's glory, so that we can extend our work to other areas with little Christian presence. Also, we open houses out of gratitude for help received from some countries or regions."

"They write Mother from a town in South Korea where she would be welcome; but they say that the bishop is very poor and can hardly contribute anything to her foundation."

"That never stands in the way," she answers. "We shall get help from elsewhere. Lack of money is never an obstacle; we do not consider it. We went to Papua New Guinea because the bishop is poor and the people are poor. We have opened four houses there already. The work progresses very well."

Indeed, the criteria that prompt Mother to open new foundations are very similar to those St. Ignatius Loyola indicates for deciding the choice of ministries Jesuits should take up. They are to be guided always by their one aim in life: the greater glory of God and the spiritual good of humanity.

Mother ardently wishes her sisters to exercise a universal action. "We must be in every state of India," she said years ago. Now she can say happily, "We are in every state of India, in every territory, except Arunachal. We have not yet been allowed there. But we shall go there also, if the people want us."

Other causes that may influence the choice of new locations will be: sudden and unexpected calamities affecting large areas, as famines, floods, cyclones, earthquakes. The sisters first go in all haste to do relief work; then they establish a house to continue the work of rehabilitating the people, as happened in Guatemala after the earthquake, and in Andhra Pradesh after the cyclone.

The hope of finding good vocations in the area is a quite legitimate reason, since it will make possible a greater service of the poor in areas giving little hope of vocations.

Mother is especially attracted by countries or regions offering a challenge, by difficult situations where "something really beautiful for God" can be achieved. Such were the cases of

YEMEN

A country deprived of all Christian presence and of the Eucharistic Sacrifice for six centuries. "Now, with the sisters and a priest to minister to them, there will be Mass again in that country," Mother could report happily. This was to the glory of Jesus whose spiritual kingship is universal. Even if Christians are only a handful, "still perfect worship will be offered to the divine majesty, and Christ will be present among people there also."

ETHIOPIA

"Catholic priests and nuns risk being all expelled; the country is a prey to civil strife and war, but our sisters may be able to stay and exercise Christian charity."

GAZA

A disputed area, a sort of "no man's land" where the sisters will be angels of peace. Their mission will be to set an example, instil a new spirit among the people, as they pray daily, "where there is strife, let me bring peace."

AUSTRALIA

Work among the aboriginals. "I am told," said Mother, "that the aboriginals are very difficult to approach and do not easily give their confidence. Our Adivasi sisters of tribal origin and tradition should succeed in understanding them and gaining their confidence. This is a difficult work, therefore it must be taken up."

On 27 June 1978, Mother could say, "I am just back from Gauhati, the capital of Assam; we opened a house there. The chief minister and members of his cabinet were present. The archbishop could not come, but sent his vicar general. The house and garden have been donated by a Hindu doctor. At the ceremony I told them, 'Prayer is essential in life; it leads to faith, faith in God leads to love, love to devotion, devotion implies us to action. When you believe you love, when you love, you want to give your service, to give yourself. God gives us an example: he gives us everything freely; we must also give what we have, give ourselves.'

"They ask us in many places; so many that now I can put only four sisters to start a new house. We are going to open a new house at Agartala in Tripura.

"Then we open at Baroda; also at Hyderabad, where a Catholic man gives us a house. This is the capital of the big Andhra State and we must be there. Then we should go to Dibrugarh."

These towns are situated at distances of one, two, or three thousand kilometers from one another: east, west, north, south. The world shrinks in Mother's vision from celestial heights; and yet she remains practical about every detail.

Mother stopped speaking of India, and swiftly crossed the oceans:

"We have opened a house in Argentina; sisters are also leaving for Panama. Then there is Europe. We open in Liverpool. They ask us in Portugal—in Portugal," she repeated with some sign of astonishment. "In Spain, in France." It was the first time she had mentioned positive requests from those three countries.

Earlier, when speaking of France and Spain, she had said, with a touch of sadness, "Not yet, not yet." So something was moving in those parts of the world, perhaps a return to a more simple, evangelical spirituality and the care of Jesus for souls in the immediate present.

A few days later Mother said, "Tanzania is going well. Many vocations there. Then we have a request from the Sudan. The archbishop and the apostolic delegate want us. Khartoum, I think, and Wau."

"Yes; when foreign missionaries were asked to leave the Sudan, the Indian Jesuits were allowed in by the government. Your Indian sisters will have plenty of spiritual work and will certainly be welcome. This is a place where you should open houses."

With her head, Mother signified understanding and approval.

"What about the United States, will you open new foundations there?" I asked.

"We have several requests," Mother replied. "Detroit, New Orleans, Washington, D.C., and others."

"You should expand in that country. The people are so generous, they do so much for you."

"Yes, we also have good vocations from there."

"You should open a novitiate in the United States."

"No," she said, "we have aspirants and postulants there. For the novitiate they must all go to Rome. They must get out of their comfortable country, see something else."

I recommended at least one year of novitiate in their own country to strengthen spiritually her young recruits. After that she could send them out to different lands, surroundings, and ways of life. Probably Mother would adopt such a solution later; thus she would lose fewer vocations and incur less traveling expenses.

GUNTAKAL: A FOUNDATION BY MISTAKE

"In what houses have you been, Sister, before coming here?"

"I was at Guntakal, in Andhra Pradesh."

"Do you speak Telugu?"

"I learned it."

"What is the place like?"

"There are only a few Catholics. As they live mainly in the railway colony, they do not really belong to the place. They are apt to be shifted from one station to another. Our house there was really started by mistake."

"By mistake? What do you mean?"

"Well, Mother had left for Guntur with the idea of opening a house in the town. But she got down by mistake at Guntakal, an important railway junction, with a somewhat similar name. She asked, where was the Catholic church? She found the parish priest who was most happy to meet Mother. He said he could give us some land to build a convent: that this was truly God's gift. Then the bishop asked us to go there, and so we went to Guntakal. We built there a house of which I was the first superior. Mother told me I was the youngest superior at the moment. At least that is how I heard the story of the foundation."

"Our Lord has his ways, Sister. My parish church was built on account of a murder and a vow made by the mother of the murderer that she would build a church if her son who had killed his friend when returning home from the theater, was not hanged. Your convent was due to a mistake. Mother getting down at the wrong station. That is quite in the spirit and tradition of St. Francis. But what about Guntur? Have you opened a house in that town?

"No, not yet."

"You may go back to Andhra, since you have learned Telugu. The state offers great opportunities for the church and your institute."

Other sisters confirmed the story and laughed heartily at the idea of starting a house in the wrong place. Well, God has his ways—and sometimes his purpose comes to light later.

Ten days after this conversation, a terrible cyclone struck in Andhra. A tidal wave 19 feet high swept over a large area. An estimated twenty thousand people were killed and perhaps one hundred thousand cattle. One hundred and fifty villages were rendered homeless. Crops were destroyed, corpses floated in canals and tanks, lay on roads and farmlands.

"The killer cyclone of the century," the papers called it, as they published ghastly pictures of bloated corpses rotting by the waysides. The nation was alerted and help was quickly despatched. Catholic Relief Services volunteers were among the first to arrive on the spot. They were prepared for such eventualities.

To be of help, one needed to foresee everything to the smallest detail. If you brought rice, the people had no utensils to cook it; if you brought utensils, they had no fuel; if you brought them wood, they had no matches.

The Missionaries of Charity also heeded the call for help.

"We have been given eight free plane tickets, and I am going with seven sisters to some of the worst-affected areas," Mother said on a Tuesday.

Seven sisters were selected to go with Mother. Excitement was everywhere. The chosen ones were thrilled to go on this relief operation. This was their calling, their duty, and their privilege. They experienced again the stimulating feeling of being sent, going into battle, being of use. The unknown attracted them also; and for those still in training it would mean a break in the humdrum, regular life of the time of probation in the house. Their whole training led to this; and with Mother they would learn from a most experienced person how to deal with difficult situations.

On Wednesday they were off to Hyderabad, the capital of Andhra. Then from there by car to the affected areas.

From Thursday, Mother was touring the worst-affected area. Her first task was to take stock of the situation, assess requirements, meet people, find out the more pressing human needs, what could be done to safeguard the health of the people remaining in areas where water was contaminated, food not available, houses destroyed.

She would share the work with other groups, contribute whatever she and her sisters could give. "In this calamity, the help of everyone is needed," she told a newspaper reporter.

On Friday, along a canal she witnessed the mass cremation of hundreds of bloated bodies, extracted from water or mud, and ranged on funeral pyres—stretching over more than a mile, fouling the air.

Before this heartrending sight, a spontaneous cry surged from many wounded hearts, an agonizing appeal, "Lord, have mercy." Mother went down on her knees on the hard earth, the lashed, humiliated earth, and with her sisters, with volunteers and journalists, prayed. In this very religious land, it seemed the obvious thing to do, the only soothing balm for human wounded hearts. Mother asked the Lord to receive the souls of the dead in his love, to give them the peace and happiness that had eluded them on earth. She prayed also for the living left behind, who would have to fight and suffer—members of poor brother families.

Before such catastrophes, a believer requires strong faith. An agnostic neither finds nor provides any explanation beyond material causes. A fatalist subscribes to fate, "It is written," it had to happen.

When questioned by a journalist, Mother Teresa, a woman of strong faith in a loving, personal God, said, "He must have his purpose when he allows such things to happen." At the moment we see mostly the sorrow and sympathize with the sufferers; later we may see the painful happening in the perspective of God's plan for this sinful world.

Calamities spurred Mother to action, without dismaying her. "God must have a purpose when he allows these things to happen," she repeated pensively. She exterted herself to assuage the sufferings of those left behind: bereaved, shelterless, having lost their cattle, their crops destroyed, their houses razed to the ground.

The event served as a challenge to spread love—to share, to console, to deprive oneself, to give, give until it hurts, or perhaps in the joy of giving we would not feel the hurt, the deprivation.

When again questioned in Hyderabad, Mother said, "In all these tragedies, God is trying to teach us something. We are not able to understand him." No, not always, not immediately, while the burden of sorrow lies heavily on our brothers' and sisters' shoulders. But later, from the darkness a light emerges, piercing the darkness. People are quickened to generosity, to make sacrifices to help brothers and sisters they have never met, never known. In many parts of the world, collections were made, and we see that in order to help the sufferers, workers donate a day's wages, children forgo an ice cream, volunteers come to offer their services, goods are donated and shipped, and soon the work of rebuilding starts in earnest.

As a result of better planning people will enjoy more healthy villages, broader roads, stronger homes, more amenities. Wells are sunk, tanks are dug, the future looks brighter.

Evangelist Billy Graham, in India at the time, on returning from Andhra Pradesh, promised to raise the money needed to rebuild all the churches destroyed, irrespective of their denomination.

"How is the situation in Andhra, Mother?" we asked.

"The first stage of relief is over," she answered. "I brought back most of our sisters."

"What is your method or technique in such circumstances?"

"First, we must endeavor to prevent sickness and epidemics. To that effect, dispose of dead bodies, carcasses. Then give injections against outbreaks of cholera, purify water, make it fit for drinking by human beings. Then we try to bring families together, reunite the children lost with their parents, join again members separated. At present, people must rebuild their houses—that is not our job—and repair their roads so that supplies can reach them."

"But you sent supplies, did you not?"

"Yes, plenty. Now we are starting a house in Guntur. We have been given a place in a good location, near the railway station. It will be easy to receive supplies there and channel them from that place."

So the Missionaries of Charity who had come to Guntur just to help at a time of calamity, were now establishing themselves in that town.

A few days later, at Prem Dan, Sister Margaret Mary remarked, "If we had previously opened a house at Guntur, the region worse affected by the cyclone, it would probably have been destroyed. Now we can open one that will remain standing." Thus divine Providence guided Mother to start what had first looked like a foundation by mistake at Guntakal, to be followed by a solid foundation at Guntur.

FOUNDATIONS WITH A CHALLENGE

GAZA

The foundation at Gaza was started by Sister Damian. She studied at Loreto House, Calcutta, went to work for some time at the Kalighat Home for the dying, soon after it was opened, and decided to join Mother. She was No. 25 in the Upper Room. After one more candidate had arrived, they shifted the novitiate to the actual mother house.

During nineteen years, she was superior of different houses. A true pioneer, she started foundations in Tanzania, in Gaza, in Amman. Later she went to Bangladesh. Here is a universal outlook. "I wish I could go to China," she confided, "that would be thrilling."

"Do you know any Chinese language?"

"Well, at some time, I started learning Cantonese. Then I learned Hindi, Swahili, Hebrew, Arabic; now I am back to Bengali."

"You had trouble in Gaza, it seems?"

"The day we arrived there and went to the Catholic church, they told us, 'This morning the parish priest was killed in this house. See the stains of his blood on the wall. He was to give you this house to live in. Are you going to stay?' I answered the people, 'Yes, we shall stay here.' And we settled down in the house of the murdered priest. People would give no explanation for the murder, except that 'he had been here too long.'

"Well, I stayed there nine years. We had holy Mass only once a week. We worked among the poor. When finally I was changed and had to leave the place, the officials gave me a diplomatic exit permit to make things easier with the passport and customs authorities. They told me, 'You must be a Moslem?'

"I said, 'No, what makes you think that? We are Christian religious women.'

" 'Well, we have not seen Christians as friendly with our people as you are and as busy with the poor. Christians here are rich people, but you live poorly.' "

BEIRUT

Mother declared, "We must go to Beirut. People are killing one another." So she went with Sister Damian to look for a suitable place. "We came to a street in the no-man's land," said Sister Damian, "where they were shooting at one another from the two opposite sides of the street. I did not find the Arabic word, so I shouted in English at the top of my voice, 'Stop!' The firing stopped for a while as we walked in the middle of the empty road."

EAST BERLIN

Mother was clearly happy when she announced, "On 30 March 1981, we opened a house in East Berlin. This is our first house in an area controlled by the Russian-type Communists."

"How did you succeed in doing this, Mother? Did you apply, or did they ask you?"

"When I attended the meeting of the Catholic bishops at Fulda, during the *Katholiken Tagen* (Catholic days), I went with the bishops to East Berlin. There I told the archbishop that we would like to come and work in his archdiocese. He immediately agreed, and we obtained the permission of the civic authorities. They promised us visas for our sisters and a house. Now we have opened the house." The Lord was really blessing them. This permission partly resulted from their keeping out of politics and social systems and ideologies, and just caring for the poor.

Mother sent Indian sisters who had been in Essen and had learned some German. Soon the sisters could report that they were able to carry on with their work normally.

CHAPTER 13

Spiritual Affinities

Mother Teresa's religious training and formation as a Loreto nun was greatly influenced by the Spiritual Exercises of St. Ignatius of Loyola. She habitually had Jesuits as confessors, spiritual advisors, and preachers at the yearly retreat. When she started her congregation, her main helpers and advisors were two Jesuits.

Though influenced by Jesuit spirituality, she was neither overpowered nor cramped by it. She succeeded in developing a spirituality well her own. Its main lines have remained constant over the years. Starting with a God-given intuition, her doctrine gradually acquired personality and strength, and Mother succeeded in giving it a clear expression.

At present, it seems safer to speak of similarities rather than of direct influence or dependence, when considering the various facets or aspects of the spirituality of the Missionaries of Charity. The main elements it contains appear related to the spirit and doctrine of St. Ignatius, of St. Francis, and of St. Vincent.

The Ignatian aspects are as follows. For Mother as for Ignatius, the end of all activity, of all apostolate, is the glory of God and the good of souls. Perfection consists in doing in all things the will of God; the will of God is our sanctification.

The glory of God and the good of souls require of the religious, among other qualities and as part of their complete self-denial and surrender to God's guidance,

1. *Availability.* they must be ready to undertake any mission, any apostolic work, any task the church may entrust to them through their superiors.
2. *Mobility.* They should go wherever they are needed, travel to various places, be ready to leave at a moment's notice, go to another country, district, or town, according to the necessities of the moment.
3. *Adaptability.* In the Pauline sense, "to make oneself all to all men so as to win as many as possible to Christ"; this means to live with the people, among them, as one of them, to feel as they feel, learn new languages, adapt oneself to different cultures, out of love; thus the

incarnation is continued, Christ remains active in today's world, inspires it, and influences it through his human instruments.

4. *A universal outlook.* The whole world is the concern of the religious and their field of apostolate; the spiritual good and personal development of every human being forms part of their field of vision and their apostolic concern.

The fourth vow of the Missionaries of Charity guarantees this responsibility, just as the fourth vow of the Jesuit professed does. It makes the sisters fully available to those in greater spiritual and material need: the poorest spiritually, materially, socially, physically. Nothing must distract the religious from the essential aim of the institute.

The two key meditations of the Spiritual Exercises of St. Ignatius that have shaped the Jesuits and their followers are those of the *Kingdom of Christ* and of the *Two Standards.* They lead the exercitant to the desire and determination to follow Christ wherever he calls, in poverty, humility, obedience. The kingdom of Christ appears clearly as the end to which all human activity should be directed.

The Missionaries of Charity share Ignatius's seriousness and determination: theirs is a solid spirituality that brooks no weak sentimentality. It includes the desire to be eminent in the service of God, the will to excel spiritually. Mother says rightly, and her words appear in the constitutions. "I will give saints to the church." She will.

To that end the practice of the twice-daily examination of conscience, general and particular, guarantees seriousness in applying oneself to spiritual progress and the quest for excellence.

The Father's will is ultimately the glory of his beloved Son, a glory the Son returns to his Father.

Second, in common with Francis of Assisi, the Poverello, passionately in love with Jesus, who in his humility did not deem himself worthy of the priesthood and remained always a deacon, the stigmatized monk, bearing in his body the marks of the wounds of the crucified Lord, the Missionaries of Charity have the stigmatized monk, bearing in his body the marks of the really poor.

They share the humility of the Little Brothers, their simplicity and good humor, the evangelical type of life, bringing the good news of God's kingdom to all, and showing kindness toward all, especially the poor.

Mother, like Francis, favors a strict interpretation of the gospel teaching, taking our Lord at his word, in all trust, considering nothing impossible when it affects God's glory and the good of souls. Both founders are conspicuous by their spiritual joy, an all-pervading, ever-abiding cheerfulness. This joyful spirit lifts them above the contingencies of life, making them forget its small sides, its occasionally somewhat vulgar aspects, its painful disfigurements.

They see things in God's light, in the divine perspective, bearing the halo of immortality, the splendor of the things to come, the happiness promised to those who love God and keep his word.

The contemplative branch shares with St. Francis his love of nature, his admiration for the created world, as they sing the praises of the Good God. Like the Poor Clares, their life is one of penance and contemplation, centered on the eucharistic worship and presence.

The Missionaries of Charity, like St. Paul, like St. Francis, cultivate optimism and joy in the midst of the squalor, material and spiritual, found in the modern world. They discover goodness wherever it germinates, because God has thrown seeds of goodness in the world he loves, animates, and draws to himself.

Third, with St. Vincent de Paul, Mother shares the love of the poor and of children, care for the oppressed and downtrodden, freedom of movement and of action for her nuns, allowing them to go out and seek those in need; also the ability to enlist the collaboration of rich and influential people in the work of charity.

A rather pessimistic but realist prophet, Qoheleth, son of David, said, "What was will be again; what has been done will be done again; and there is nothing new under the sun. Take anything of which it may be said, 'Look now, this is new.' Already long before our time, it existed. Only no memory remains of earlier times" (Eccles. 1:9–11). In the church of Christ also, most works of charity have been practiced in previous centuries in a manner adapted to the times. The apostolic preoccupation of Mother Teresa's daughters, their style of life, love for the poor, total commitment to the service of the depressed and needy, spiritually and materially, may be seen as a replica, in original style and adapted to today's circumstances of the life of the Daughters of Charity, founded by St. Vincent de Paul and St. Louise de Marillac.

In his days, St. Vincent introduced a new type of religious life for women. Nuns were then usually confined to their monasteries, which they were allowed to leave only to start a new foundation. Vincent and Louise de Marillac put the Daughters of Charity on the street, much of the day, to seek the poor and needy in their houses. They were to clean, wash, cook, and look after the children of the sick poor.

St. Vincent de Paul, who had worked on the ships among the galley slaves as their chaplain, had personal experience of the hard and laborious life. He succeeded in obtaining the financial help and the personal contribution of many women belonging to the higher ranks of society. It is with one of these women, a widow, that he founded the Daughters of Charity, devoted entirely to the apostolate of the poor.

They soon spread to several countries besides France. They were generally respected, esteemed, and loved even by some anticlerics and atheists. The poor knew them as their friends. In the baskets they carried they brought bread to the hungry, medicines to the sick, warm clothes to those suffering from the cold.

The Missionaries of Charity of Mother Teresa may perhaps be seen as an updated, refreshed, rejuvenated group of Daughters of Charity, doing God's work in their own right, with their distinctive charism. They take perpetual vows, which the Daughters of St. Vincent could not do in their days, as church law then did not allow it.

The church has witnessed through the centuries beautiful examples of devotion to the sick and the poor. St. John of God founded a congregation of Hospitaller Brothers and is the patron saint of those serving the sick.

St. Camillus de Lellis, like St. John of God, was first a soldier. Later he felt that God called him to his service. He started a hospital to receive and care for the sick picked up from the streets and other poor patients. He served Christ in them. He was granted a powerful grace to see Jesus in his suffering brethren, whom he called his "Christs." He would even beg from them forgiveness of his sins—seeing the Savior living in them.

He showed great reverence toward the poor, considering himself before them as being truly in the presence of his Lord.

Christian charity of its very nature is all embracing; it moved Camillus, beside looking after the dying and the sick, to take care of other poor and needy people. He sought these everywhere. He was heard to say that if no more poor were found on the earth, "we would have to search them out and even pluck them from below the earth, going down into the underworld to find them," that we might serve the Lord Jesus in them.

For his time and his conception of the world, this exclamation parallels Mother's saying, "If there are poor people on the moon, we will go there." St. Camillus and Mother Teresa show the same passionate desire to serve and love the suffering Christ in his brethren, the same craving for universality in their charitable action.

With John of God and Camillus de Lellis, the Missionaries of Charity have an affinity of spirit and community of work. Mother faced a situation similar to the one they confronted in their own days. She was also called by Jesus to remedy such ills. She moved on lines parallel to theirs.

Fourth, a saint whom Mother gives as example to imitate to her sisters and of whom she loves to speak is the Little Flower, the charming St. Thérèse of Lisieux. Thérèse's autobiography portraits her as a wonderful instance of trust in God, humility, simplicity, love of poverty, surrender to divine Providence, acceptance of suffering, penitential life, zeal for souls, and burning love for Jesus.

Thérèse also practiced twinning, since she offered all her prayers and sufferings for the apostolate of a missionary priest, and later for two preachers of the gospel of Christ working in non-Christian lands.

Mother, when teaching her sisters the ways to holiness, to perfect love of God, can present St. Thérèse as a model all simple souls can try to imitate.

CHAPTER 14

The Fourth Vow

Christ emptied himself to assume the condition of a slave.
(PHIL. 2:7)

To the three essential vows of religion, a few institutes add a fourth vow, to stress their character or function.

The Benedictines take a vow of stability, of remaining in the convent or abbey they entered. There they exercise their particular charism in prayer and work, through the recitation of the Prayer of the Church and liturgical functions carried out with order, dignity, and beauty. The great monasteries have become eminent centers of learning, of contemplation, and schools of religious art.

St. Ignatius of Loyola introduced in the Society of Jesus he founded a fourth vow taken by the solemnly professed, of obedience to the Holy Father for the missions. This represented and actuated the leading idea of Ignatius and his first companions. Even before deciding to form a religious order, they had vowed to be at the disposal of the See of Peter for any mission or any work the pope might wish to entrust to them. They would leave home, country, security, everything, to go where the pope sent them and carry out the task entrusted to them. They were not to ask for traveling expenses, but be ready to go even where their lives would be in danger.

Mother knew that many religious founders started an institute with the poor in mind, especially for the education of poor children. Gradually others not needy were accepted, and, under social pressure, children from more favored families. As the standards rose, the poor were gradually replaced by the children of well-to-do parents who could pay, add social prestige to the school, obtain better results at the examinations, bring credit and distinction to the school.

With the Missionaries of Charity no such evolution, no social upgrading of their work is possible. Mother has made sure for all times that the society will continue to work for the very poor: otherwise it will cease to exist.

The fourth vow the Missionaries of Charity take, in addition to the three vows of poverty, chastity, and obedience prescribed by the Catholic church for all religious, binds them to wholehearted, free service of the poorest of the poor. This fourth vow determines their special character and activity. It limits their possibilities of action, in contrast with the fourth vow of the Jesuit professed, which may have inspired Mother to include this fourth vow. The Jesuits' fourth vow removes all limits to the scope of their apostolate. They must be ready to go to any part of the world to fulfill any task at the bidding of the Holy Father.

The Missionaries of Charity's fourth vow limits their activity to the service of a single class of people, but not to any geographical area. The aim is to force the sisters to do the hard thing. They may not take up more easy, perhaps more consoling apostolates. They must go to the very poor, the most abandoned, the most needy people, for the love of Jesus.

"Mother, when did you first think of introducing a fourth vow in your congregation?"

"From the very beginning, Father."

"Were you influenced by the fact that Jesuits have a fourth vow?"

"You Jesuits have a fourth vow of obedience to the Holy Father for the missions. We have a vow of wholehearted free service to the poorest of the poor. It is essential to our institute. A canonist told me. 'If a bishop wants you to take up any work that goes against your fourth vow, write to the Congregation of Religious; they will not allow it.' "

"Yes, of course. The fourth vow is an essential element of your congregation, a fundamental point of your constitutions. Even a general chapter could not change it without affecting the very existence and identity of your congregation; it would no more be the society your sisters have joined, and so they would be free to leave."

"Yes. Once a bishop wanted the sisters to make the people calling at our dispensary pay a small fee for their services. I refused to do so. We removed the sisters, and the dispensary was closed."

The bishop wanted the people to make a small contribution as part of his general policy of teaching them self-help, so that they might acquire a sense of respectability and dignity. But Mother could quote the gospel and the words of Jesus saying, "You have received freely, give freely." If the sisters started to accept payment for their services, where would they stop? Certainly no bishop could ask them to disobey their constitutions approved by Rome.

"Mother, what was your aim when you introduced the fourth vow?"

"Three things:

    to ensure faithfulness to our calling,
    to safeguard our poverty,
    to force us to trust fully in God.

Our calling is to be busy, only with the poor. Jesus called us to serve him in the very poor. There are enough of them in the world."

Mother knows that in the history of the church the decline in fervor of the religious orders usually started with a slackening of the spirit of poverty, with excessive possessions and personal spending by individual members. Thus the sisters are to accept no salary for any work, no material reward, enter into no contract, receive no pension or security. Not being paid, not earning, not possessing, forces them to rely on God alone, to show perfect trust. It also brings freedom of the spirit and joy in the Holy Spirit.

In some cases, the fourth vow may limit the availability of the sisters and prevent them from assuming tasks beneficial to souls. But the vow is necessary to safeguard their particular character and their aim, which finally serves the common good, since the sisters care for the more deprived, the more often neglected section of humanity.

"The prime minister of Yemen asked me," said Mother, "to start a sewing class for the daughters of the best families of the country. But I had to refuse. I did not know whether he would understand what our vows mean, so I said, 'We cannot accept because we gave our word to God to work only for the poor. When you give your word, you must keep it, mustn't you?' He said, 'Yes, of course.' 'Well, we gave our word to God to work only for the poor, because they are more in need. So we must keep it; we cannot work for the children of the upper class. But I am sure you will find some other sisters to do that very well.' "

The fourth vow brings them the freedom to devote themselves entirely to their aim, which is less glamorous, pleasurable, respected, socially esteemed, rewarding even in visible results. It forces the sisters to seek out the downtrodden, the forsaken, the abandoned, the needy, the sufferers. It has also the distinction of making them similar to Jesus in his "kenosis" or self-abasement. It can be compared to the second step of the self-abasement of the Son of God come into the flesh, of his kenosis as spelled by St. Paul, writing to the Phillippians:

"In your minds you must be the same as Christ Jesus:

His state was divine,
yet he did not cling
to his equality with God,
but emptied himself
to assume the condition of slave,
and became as men are;
and being as all men are,
he was humbler yet,
even to accepting death,
death on a cross" (Phil. 2:5–8).

Paul indicates two steps in the self-abasement of Christ: first he becomes man and does not allow the glory of his divinity to transpire through his humanity—he, so to say, keeps it down, hides it, to be in all things similar to human beings, humbling himself to the common level of humanity.

But then Christ goes a step further: he was humbler yet, accepting to die on a cross, as a malefactor, a criminal, a highway robber, a murderer, or a runaway slave. He accepts the cross. Truly he could not have shown greater humility; and that he did out of obedience to his Father and love for human beings.

Similarly with the Missionaries of Charity. By the three vows of religion —poverty, chastity, and obedience—they make a complete offering of themselves to God in all humility, detachment, self-denial, giving up all personal inclination and self-will. But they also wish to go a step further in self-denial and fall a degree lower in the esteem of the world, by limiting their work and activities to the care of the poorest of the poor. This they do for the glory of God the Father, to be more similar to their Lord Jesus Christ, and for the good of souls.

Thus, living in poverty and humility, they choose to work only among the humblest people, those of least condition, unrecognized by society. They will share the lot of Christ crucified, despised, abandoned by his own. This constitutes the second step of their self-abasement.

Therefore the disposition the Missionaries of Charity must endeavor to acquire is self-denial, utter self-denial, readiness to do what one is told, to go against one's natural readiness to do what one is told, to go against one's natural inclination to comfort and self-seeking. They must be prepared to put the neighbor in front and themselves behind, to serve always and everywhere, to accept whatever the good God sends, whether it be pleasant or unpleasant.

They will have to approach evil-smelling bodies without holding their noses, look at horrible sores and ulcers without batting an eyelid, go out when not feeling up to the mark, work long hours in heat or cold, return home tired, soaked in perspiration or drenched by rain, and do it all smiling, loving, praising God.

Self-denial is the emptying of self, of our human vessel of clay, of our mind and heart, imagination, sensibility, will and desire, so that God may fill this emptied vessel with his grace, his love, his strength, his charity, his zeal, his optimism, his cheerfulness. Jesus is the perfect example of this emptying of self, of accepting the hard things, of shouldering even the cross to obey his Father. By doing it he reconciled sinful people to the all-holy God, earning for them pardon and grace.

LOVE IS THE MOTIVE

The sisters' fourth vow, by which they bind themselves to wholehearted free service of the poorest of the poor, is motivated by love. This love must be in imitation of the divine love, without ulterior motive, expecting nothing in return. The giver gives because it is good to give, to make others happy, to share the good things we have with others unable to return the gift.

This is the love of benevolence, *agape* as the first Christians called it, in opposition to *eros,* the love of concupiscence, the eagerness to possess, to enjoy a thing desired. God himself is pure love, agape, pure self-gift. His love for us includes no ulterior motive, no craving for some good in return for what he bestows on us. God creates, saves, sanctifies us entirely freely. He takes the initiative at every stage, as we come from him in return to him, if we accept his gifts and turn to him freely, lovingly.

The fourth vow forces the sisters to do good to the poorest of the poor, those who cannot repay them. Even if the poor could contribute a tiny amount, a few crumbs or a few drops, the Missionaries of Charity may not accept any payment or compensation, nor any form of *quid pro quo.* Their service of the neighbor follows the pattern of God's love for us in its creative, salvific, and sanctifying aspects. God needs nothing; he possesses all perfection and complete bliss. We cannot add to his glory, to his happiness.

Still God loves us as people; in his goodness he gives us opportunities to offer him gifts that he welcomes. Similarly, the sisters' fourth vow neither destroys nor cancels the interpersonal relationship established between the giver and the receiver. The nun and the poor person face one another as people, with reverence and esteem. Both have an absolute value, a God-given personality; both are called to the bliss of heaven, as children of their heavenly Father. The receiver reacts; the reaction affects the giver, leads both to rejoice together.

The expression on Mother Teresa's face, when she holds in her arms a darling infant, proves it. A cuddled baby will take her proffered finger and press it with a spark of delight in his eyes. He holds it and will not let it go. The finger's owner rejoices, shares the baby's happiness, receives from him.

Mother confesses her happiness when a dying woman she had picked up from the street and brought to her home, took her hand and in her last breath said, "Thank you." She died as an angel, with delicate, refined feelings, overshadowing the miserable appearance of her emaciated body. When the personal relationship comes to life, our service elicits the best in people: friendship and gratitude.

CHARISM

"Each one of us has been given his own share of grace, given as Christ allotted it" (Eph. 4:7).

The Acts of the Apostles indicate that various people have received charisms or special graces given them for the good of the whole church, for the community, not for their individual benefit. Of course, these graces do affect the spirituality and activity of the one who receives them

(1 Cor. 12:1). St. Paul shows that at the beginning of the church the Holy Spirit gave signs, but mainly love. The first Christians shared everything they possessed in common. Their love for one another was so evident that people around them said, "See how they love one another." Thus was fulfilled the promise of Jesus, "At that sign they will know that you are my disciples, if you love one another" (John 13:35).

The Holy Spirit also grants charisms to members of religious institutes, according to their particular calling, aim, and mission, to help them achieve their function in the church and society. They receive the graces adapted to their vocation, guaranteed by their religious profession.

Thus the Friars Preachers, followers of St. Dominic, have as charism contemplation of the divine Essence, of God's wisdom and revelation that they may be able to preach the word of God and safeguard the true deposit of faith.

The Franciscan's charism will be more specially joy in evangelical poverty, preaching to the poor and sharing in the sufferings of the Lord Jesus. Francis of Assisi was the first person in recorded history to receive the stigmata, or the impression in his flesh of the wounds of Christ in his hands, feet, and side. Walking in the footsteps of Francis, Padre Pio in our own age bore the Lord's wounds in his body for a full half-century.

Ignatius and the members of the Society of Jesus he founded have as charism availability for the tasks the church entrusts to them, mobility, adaptability to different spiritual missions, devotion to the church and the Holy Father. Their charism is related to the fourth vow of the professed.

Similarly, the Missionaries of Charity's charism will be related to their fourth vow, their special characteristic. They have by now developed their character sufficiently to be differentiated from all other religious bodies. The sisters have found their identity, in a perfect unity of spirit, which is the spirit of the foundress. She has molded them according to her idea.

They are a congregation different from all others, in their aim, their methods, their approach. To keep them in this spirit, Mother did wish them all to come to Calcutta and stay for a time at the mother house, cradle of the institute, to imbibe its original spirit and live in its characteristic atmosphere.

The aim, clearly written in the first constitutions, repeated in the third edition, has been faithfully adhered to. Jesus is at the center of the sisters' life. His call for love, "I thirst," faces them daily morning and evening, in every one of their houses and chapels. Their one aim in life is to quench the thirst of Jesus for souls. The means to do this consists in working for the salvation and sanctification of the poorest of the poor. This spiritual aim will be achieved even by material means, showing forth the love of God for his children.

CHARISM—ORIGIN

God who calls gives the grace needed; when he calls a person or a group to a particular task, he gives the grace required to perform it. The divine call will determine the charism; it will affect the spirituality, the activity or apostolate, the style of life, the outlook, the life of prayer—with some variations among individuals, providing a fruitful diversity within an essential unity. The charism may develop and become richer, while always remaining in the line inspired to the founder by the Spirit of God.

Mother's charism, shared and inherited by her spiritual daughters, includes seeing the suffering Christ in the poor and serving him in them, "in his distressing disguise," as she says. This duty was imposed on her by the Lord, to whom she had been spiritually wedded for several years, whom she loved more than her own life.

It happened on that train journey, when she went through a mystical experience that overpowered her, whose memory never left her, of which she never doubted, that spurred her to a most difficult decision.

The Missionaries of Charity keep the feast of the Inspiration Day. It forms the cardinal intuition, the guiding force, the aim of Mother's life, of her religious institute, in a way even of her message of love to the world.

"We are contemplatives in action," says Mother. This requires a grace related to the call, a charism the Missionaries of Charity inherit in various degrees from their foundress. They may expect to receive it if they prepare themselves for this gift and open themselves to God's grace. Their following of Jesus in true evangelical poverty, in total abandon and trust in God, in cheerfulness, leads to it, prepares them for this gift.

"Contemplation of God is a gift of God to every Missionary of Charity" (Constitutions No. 116). This forms one of the boldest affirmations regarding the congregation contained in the constitutions. It can only have been made after mature, prayerful consideration. The reasons brought forth read: the sisters are

(1) "created in God's image and likeness with a natural power to know and love him"—this is common to all people.

(2) Drawn into the mystery of the life of the Blessed Trinity through baptism"—this is common to all the baptized.

(3) "Called to the intimacy of God's love as the spouses of Jesus crucified"—this is common to all religious.

We touch here the disputed question whether all people, or all the baptized, or all religious are called to contemplation of the divine majesty and to some kind of mystical prayer, and whether mystical graces are offered to all who seek God or are called by God to his service in the religious life.

No immediate assertion on these points is here made. The text is explained thus: "This life of contemplation is simply to realize God's constant presence and tender love shown in the smallest things of life," and our response, which prompts us "to be constantly available to him, loving him with our whole heart, whole mind, whole soul and strength, no matter in what form he may come to us" (No. 117).

It is further explained how they hope to be contemplatives in the heart of the world in which they dwell and work and serve God, namely "by seeking the face of God in everything, everyone, everywhere, all the time, and his hand in every happening." This exemplifies Mother's thoroughness: all for God, nothing for self, seeking God active in the world and finding his presence in the soul; and also "by seeing and adoring the Presence of Jesus in the Eucharist and in the poor" (No. 118).

True contemplation is not confined to seeking God's face, it implies finding him, knowing him intuitively. They have made their assertion simply but boldly. They consider it as part of their charism. Thus it should be the normal thing for them if they are faithful to their call, to their rule of life. In this rule nothing is left to self-gratification. It calls for complete detachment, echoing the exacting *"nada, nada"* (nothing, nothing) of St. John of the Cross. The nun is to empty her vessel of clay of all self-love, that it may be filled only with the love of Jesus. Everything is directed to Jesus. How far the religious will enjoy this contemplation of God will depend on the abundance of divine grace she receives, and on her response to it.

The Contemplative branch may probably hold as applying also to themselves what the great Teresa of Avila asserted of her nuns: "It is ordinary for us to receive graces of mystical prayer." The same applies to other strict contemplatives as the Poor Clares. Many of them receive mystical graces, but they pay for them, God knows.

To dispose herself for God's favors requires in the nun complete self-detachment, a passionate craving for God and willingness to share in the Passion of Jesus. It also supposes that one finds a spiritual guide, competent and experienced, able to lead on the paths to the summits of spiritual life.

CHAPTER 15

Interlude: With Mother in Rotterdam

"Mother Teresa is in Rotterdam to open a new house," says Jacqueline de Decker on the telephone from Antwerp, on 14 August 1977. "She would be happy to meet you. Try to go tomorrow; she will stay there till the 16th, evening. A diamond merchant from Antwerp is making all arrangements for her. He took me there to meet the sisters who will start the house. They are not yet in their own place; they are put up in a home for mental patients. Try to go to Rotterdam; Mother will be pleased to meet you."

By chance, the next day, feast of the Assumption of Our Lady, a priest tells me he would be happy to meet this famous Mother of whom everyone speaks. He will take me to Rotterdam in his car.

And so that evening we reached Rotterdam at 8 P.M. At 44 Vandersluis Street, we find a large five-story building, a most unexpected place for a house of the Missionaries of Charity, who look after the poorest of the poor. The sisters have found a temporary shelter in a Protestant home for mental patients. This is a beautiful place where each patient has a large, well-furnished room, provided with various amenities.

At the reception office, we ask a Dutch woman,

"Moeder Teresa, Mevrouw?"

The woman receptionist sends a call upstairs, then takes us to the lift, and up to the third floor. As we emerge from the lift, Mother Teresa is there smiling. She takes my hands in both hers, "Father, I am so happy to see you. How good of you to have come. We were waiting for you."

She looks well and rested. Sister Frederick follows her. Four young sisters come smiling, and ask, "Do you recognize me?"

There are three Indian sisters and a Dutch sister.

The sisters occupy the rooms of a small wing of the house. The first room has been transformed into a very devotional chapel. The Blessed Sacrament is reserved in a fine tabernacle, while close to it a crystal vase holds a wick burning in oil. Three vases with lovely flowers adorn the altar. The Netherlands are famous for their flowers, waterways, cheese, and bicycles.

On the wall, by the side of the crucifix, letters cut from black paper have been pinned to form the words, "I thirst," the reminder of the inspiration, aim, and spirit of the Missionaries of Charity.

After a prayer, we join the sisters in their parlor next to the chapel. They bring us a light supper of eggs, tomatoes, and bread. What strikes most is the quiet, joyful mood of the young sisters recently arrived in this foreign land, unaccustomed to its cold climate, its strange tongue, different habits, other ways of life. They take it all in their stride, with confidence in the Lord who sends them to do his work. Truly, they have been well trained, they exude confidence and joy in the Lord.

We talk about the work. "How was Cambridge, Mother?"

"You know, I have become a Protestant," she laughed. "I received a doctor of divinity degree from the university."

"Yes, and you preached in the university church to a lot of professors and students, and you spoke to them in a very Catholic way."

"How do you know?"

"I have a copy of your sermon."

"How did you get it?"

"It has been printed and circulated. And how was the function?"

"Oh, it was all in Latin and very formal. I did not understand a single word. Nor was anyone allowed to speak except the officials."

"Of course, you would have liked to deliver your message at the convocation itself. When did you preach, in the afternoon?"

"Yes, at 5 P.M. The church was full, absolutely crowded. They had issued tickets, and still there were people standing or sitting everywhere, in front, at the back." She made a sweeping gesture with her hands: "thousands of people."

This was not the usual British understatement; but with all those who would read her excellent sermon, there must have been many thousands in spirit, if not in flesh.

"There are no more Sisters of the Word," said Mother, "they are now all included in the Missionaries of Charity. There will be only one congregation with two branches, one active and one contemplative."

"The contemplatives are only in the United States. Do you intend to start them also in other countries, say in India?"

"Yes, we may later have houses in some countries. At present there are five novices and five postulants in the Bronx house. Sister Nirmala is the superior."

"Does she train the novices to contemplation herself?"

"Yes, she is very good. They have eight hours of prayer a day. They go out two or three hours every day to speak of Jesus to those who wish to hear. Not to groups; to individuals, to people sitting on benches, in hospitals, to the sick."

"Hospitals will offer good opportunities for spiritual talks. The sick have time to pray and often yearn to hear someone talk to them of God."

"Yes, I met a sick young man who told me he had difficulties in believing about Jesus. He did not pray. I gave him a book. When I met him again, he said he had read it and had no more difficulties. He was convinced."

"Yes, prayer does help; it obtains grace and peace of soul."

"When the sisters find no one who wishes to listen about God, they return home for the day. So now we have the contemplative branch in our society. Not two congregations, but one. I shall settle that matter with Rome."

This was a way out. The contemplative wing had been slow to start. After more than a year, only five novices and some postulants. Yet the time was most propitious: Mother Teresa's name had been in all the American papers; she had spoken publicly at the Philadelphia Eucharistic Congress, been mobbed by the crowds, acclaimed by Bishop Helder Camara, had received doctorate on doctorate from famous universities, and been awarded several international prizes. She was an acknowledged beacon of light for all charitable works, especially Christian works of mercy.

"In the Philippines," Mother went on, "we have opened a house. Madame Marcos, the president's wife, invited us. She saw to everything herself, had three houses built, one for a children's home, one for the dying, one for the sisters. She said it had to be done quickly: they employed two hundred workers, and in fifteen days all was ready."

"You will have plenty of spiritual work there, Mother. People have a deep devotion to Jesus and to his mother. You should also find many vocations."

"Already nine girls want to join us. Yes, the government helps us. Some priests and nuns are in jail for opposing the government. Those in power do not want the government to be criticized. So, no politics."

"That will not present any difficulty for your sisters; you always keep out of politics. A letter came from Sister Rose-Mary of Mexico, thanking you for the spiritual books and asking that we send some more. She says they are short of good books for prayer."

"They have changed their house," said Mother. "Sister Frederick, do give Father the new address. And also the sisters' address in Guatemala, and also that of Port-au-Prince, Haiti."

Within a few minutes, Sister Frederick came back with the addresses, neatly written on a slip of paper. If the books were not sent to these houses, it would not be Mother's fault. She was remarkably efficient, quick and interested in every detail of the sisters' lives. She did everything on the spot, never procrastinated, took even small matters seriously. Her efficiency was contagious. In her wake, even those of a procrastinating type rose to action, were goaded by the love of God to bestir themselves for the poor and the suffering members of Christ.

"Yes, Haiti, I was there," she mused. "The people are very poor, live in miserable huts, all huddled together with their cattle and goats and chickens, all in the same place, one room to a family. But the people are so good. The archbishop called us. We opened a house there recently. There is plenty of work for us."

Success had not spoiled Mother. Among the poor she wished to live. In this rich Rotterdam, in a five-storyed building with all the comfort it offered, in this place where a rich diamond merchant from Antwerp offered to pay all their expenses, see to all their needs, Mother's mind went back with yearning to the poor of Haiti, Guatemala, Papua. Those names came back repeatedly in her conversation. Contact with the wealthy and the powerful had not affected her. She loved the poor for whom she had started her Missionaries of Charity. She yearned to serve Jesus in his suffering brothers and sisters, as he had himself directed her to do.

"I passed through Africa," she went on, "When I was in Ethiopia, that man with a beard from Cuba was there also."

"Fidel Castro?"

"Yes. Things are changing in Ethiopia. They will send away all the missionaries, they told me. But they said they would not send away our sisters because we work for the poor."

"Will the Communists allow you to remain? And you need a priest to minister to your sisters, at least from time to time."

She made an evasive gesture. She never worried about the future—it rested in God's hands. The present was her field of action, always looking bright and challenging.

"In Tanzania, things are going well," she continued. "The novitiate has been opened at Tabora."

She was a general reviewing her troops, considering how to train them in an efficient manner, how to strengthen her positions.

"There are now tertian sisters preparing for their final vows in Rome," she said. "But I want them to come to Calcutta. Six months in Rome, then six months in Calcutta for their year of tertianship. And from Calcutta I shall send tertians six months to Rome. We exchange personnel. But they must come to Calcutta." Like a mother hen, she wanted all her brood to be around her. Calcutta remained the mother house; nowhere else could the original spirit be imbibed. All the young members had to breathe the vivifying atmosphere in which the society was born and had been nurtured. They would not as yet go on pilgrimage to the Upper Room to marvel at the power of God's grace, no, not yet. The mother house recalled the heroic years, the first fervor, the total detachment and perfect trust in God of the beginnings, the joy of singing the praises of the divine majesty, that could now be heard in the chapel nearly uninterruptedly.

"Yes, Mother, the numbers of the sisters increase fast. Where will you stop?"

She smiled peacefully, gratefully, serenely.

Around nine o'clock, mindful that they have their evening prayer and a usual strict routine and must rise early next morning, I proposed to retire. But the young superior objected: "No, Father, not yet. For once Mother is with us, do not hurry."

"But I thought you had your rules and regulations?"

"Oh, we are not like the others. Other nuns when their superior general is present are on their best behavior. With us, the contrary happens: when Mother is there, we are at our worst; everything is allowed."

So we talked for another hour, recalling spiritual experiences, all centered on God's love.

The next morning as we enter the chapel, the sandals of the sisters are at the door. Inside they are barefooted; but there is wall-to-wall carpeting to keep them warm. A sister arranges flowers before the Blessed Sacrament.

The bishop arrives alone. A tall, commanding figure, with strong Dutch features, he radiates power, interior strength, dammed and canalized. He invites us to concelebrate Mass with him in English, my fellow Jesuit priest and myself. During the Mass, the bishop reads a fine homily on the basis of Christian love. Christ said, "Love your neighbor as I have loved you." This was no easy matter even for the Missionaries of Charity. Mother and the sisters were deeply touched by the thoughtfulness of the bishop, who had taken the trouble to write out fully his exhortation.

At the time of communion, the bishop said, "I shall give you the Sacred Host, and Father will present you the chalice." And so we did. Mother came first. I looked at her as she approached the cup of the Blood of Christ with intense devotion and put her lips to it. Then I gave the cup of love of Christ to the five sisters, who drank from it with similar devotion and self-surrender.

After communion, the bishop said, "Now let us pray silently for a while." But Mother, according to their custom, started a prayer they all recited together, then a second one of Francis of Assisi, then a third, then Anima Christi. Then Sister Frederick launched into a song expressing the joy of the Christian united to Jesus. Lustily they sang. Perhaps it was too much and not conducive to the intimacy to which the communion to the Body and Blood of Jesus invites.

After the mass, we left the chapel and removed our liturgical vestments in the next room. As he finished doing so, the bishop said,

"I want them to be a presence, a spiritual presence here."

Mother had mentioned that this was his purpose, but now he said it openly, as to unburden his heart.

"They will do that well, my Lord." I replied.

"Spiritual life here is very weak," he said.

We returned to the chapel for quiet prayer after the Eucharistic Sacrifice. When a sister came to call us, we moved to the small room serving as parlor.

Three chairs had been disposed on three sides of the table, and on the table three cups. I pushed a fourth chair for Mother. The bishop sat between the two priests; thus Mother faced him.

During the half-hour conversation, the bishop seemed in admiration before the small nun, known all over the world, looking so simple, yet having succeeded to an extraordinary extent. Mother showed to the bishop her habitual respect for the representative of the Lord Jesus. While he was taking notes in his diary, her eyes were fixed on him, as if she hoped to seize some of his spiritual power or strength of character. There was no small talk; they immediately dealt with the apostolate.

"Mother, you still know them all?" asked the bishop.

"Yes," she replied.

"How many novices do you have?"

"Three hundred and twenty-six."

Each time the question was put to her, the number increased. It was the simple truth.

"Do many leave? Do many drop out?"

"No. Very few leave after their vows. We keep 97 percent of the sisters."

"What do you require of the candidates?"

"They should apply for the right reason; to serve Jesus in the poor. They should know something of our kind of life. They should possess sufficient health, a sound judgment, a good moral character."

After a pause, Mother added, "Those who are too intelligent are not for us; they may not have the humility to accept our simple work."

Mother knew that girls coming to her with a craving for intellectual pursuit, or with problems, would not find the atmosphere congenial, the spirituality satisfactory, the works that had to be performed suited to their personality. There was perhaps an exception for those with a medical degree; but they also would have to limit themselves to living in a simple community and working in hard conditions.

"Is it true that you sleep only three hours a day?" asked the bishop. Mother made a sign yes with her head.

"She has been doing so for many years," I added.

"Why do you do that, or how do you do that?" asked his Lordship.

"I have to," she answered. "Night is the only time when I can work, think of the sisters, write, arrange the work."

She did not explain that she worked and wrote and prayed till one in the morning, then lay down to sleep. At half past four, she was again in the chapel making the stations of the cross. She had to accompany her Lord to Calvary, quench his thirst for the love of human beings. How did she do it? Well, she had the grace. Christ who lived in her, sustained her; there was no other answer.

"And after Mother Teresa, what will happen to the Missionaries of Charity? Who will run the society?" asked the bishop.

"That will be no trouble," answered Mother. "God will find a more humble person, more obedient to him, more faithful, someone smaller, with a deeper faith, and he will do still greater things through her."

This was her standard answer to the oft-repeated question "After Mother Teresa what or who?" She did not consider herself indispensable. God was all powerful. Whether he would find among the sisters one more humble, more faithful, more obedient to his guidance than she had been, we do not know. That he would find excellent nuns to run the society was certain. They would not have the charism the foundress had received, nor would they require it, since the society was a going concern, with constitutions approved by Rome and already put into application with great success.

It is interesting to note that Mother considered humility to be the first quality God requires in an instrument he uses for his glory.

"What do you think of women becoming priests?" asked the Bishop.

"Jesus did not make his Mother a priest," answered Mother. "No one would have been more worthy of the favor of the priesthood than our Lady, who had given to Jesus his body; none was purer, none knew better the heart of Jesus. Yet she was happy to remain the handmaid of the Lord, to serve him in all humility. And Jesus did not appoint her a priest at the Last Supper. If he did not make women priests, why should we change?"

The bishop then looked at Mother inquiringly, "I have a worry; I must write an article for a paper on the topic 'What will be the church of the future?' Mother, what do you say?"

Several magazines and reviews had carried articles on this very topic. People tried to uncover the future, to predict the course of things in the church. Would there be women priests? Married clergy? Changes in the structure of parishes? What of the youth? Would the church move to the right or to the left?

For Mother these questions had little interest.

"The future is not in our hands," she answered. "We have no power over it. We can act only today. We have a sentence in our constitutions that says. . . ." She was trying to find the right words, but failed. "Sister Frederick, do get the constitutions," she requested. Sister went out to fetch them and soon returned with the book.

"You must know the constitutions by heart," remarked the bishop. Mother shook her head no.

"Here is the passage," said Mother. "We will allow the good God to make plans for the future—for yesterday has gone, tomorrow has not yet come and we have only today to make him known, loved, and served" (No. 22). Our Lord told us not to fret about tomorrow, which is in God's hands. So we do not worry about it. Then Jesus is the same yesterday, today, and tomorrow. Jesus is the same. He is the same today and tomorrow, and only he matters," she concluded.

Her philosophy of life was clear, pragmatic, built on faith and trust in God: do today what you can, what you ought to do, what is expected from you, and God will take care of tomorrow.

The bishop was writing. Mother kept silent. Again she looked at him, her lips tightly pursed, staring at his face with his downcast eyes. Was she trying to assimilate his seriousness of purpose, his strength, to peep into the secret of his power? Or was it just out of gratitude for the man who had received her so well in his diocese, and under whom her sisters were going to work for the glory of God?

No doubt, she thought of herself as much smaller than him; while he thought of her as much greater, more spiritual than himself. That was very beautiful and inspiring. Each one respected and admired the special character and grace God had bestowed on the other.

"You have removed a burden from my back," said the bishop, as he stopped writing and closed his diary. "I have my article; four points ready, and no need to worry any more. Thank you very much, Mother."

The bishop then explained how the sisters could draw money from the bank account opened in their favor. "They should contact Mr. X., who speaks English." Everything was being foreseen to make their apostolate smooth and their presence comfortable: it was the Dutch character at its best.

Then, after expressing his gratitude and his good wishes for the sisters' apostolate, the bishop took leave.

What struck one most during those two days was the cheerfulness of the young sisters. This new pioneering enterprise in a foreign country— except for one of them—was different from what they had previously known. The language, culture, climate, eating habits, living conditions, everything was unfamiliar to them, and they were alone to face this new world. Yet the sisters showed a remarkable composure, a complete lack of fear and anxiety regarding the future. Theirs was the joy, the happiness of God's children; they felt safe in their trust, their confidence that God was with them and they were doing his work. They lived in the spirit of their constitutions, enjoining on them complete trust, total surrender, and cheerfulness day and night, whatever might happen to them.

Was this not the answer, the living answer to the bishop's last question: "Mother, what after you? What will the congregation become?" The sisters answered in fact, "The Missionaries of Charity have been well trained, they have imbibed the spirit of their foundress, they go forward cheerfully with no fear of the morrow."

When the bishop has left, we speak again of the apostolate. "Here," explains Mother, "we won't have any children's home, no children in the house. The sisters will go out. All the work will be outside."

"What, visiting people?"

"Yes, helping them at home, visiting the sick, comforting the dying, helping all those in need."

This had been Mother's first idea, at the time she did not want any institutions, no work in the sisters' houses, to force them to go out, looking for souls, seeking the needy. They must be the Good Samaritans searching for the travelers fallen by the wayside, unable to proceed alone. They must comb the lanes and by-lanes of the world, look inside hovels, seek the abandoned, the lonely, the downhearted, those unable to help themselves.

They will be in the town a presence, comforting, solacing, soothing. But also an example to the eyes of the modern world, so that people may say, "See how those disciples of Christ love one another."

Rotterdam provided an instance of the already well-established manner of starting a new foundation. At the invitation of the bishop or a top government official, Mother or her representative went to see the place and discuss matters. She then reported to the counselors, who discussed and approved the plan. Then four sisters went ahead as scouts, either to the house allotted to the society or in a makeshift place, from where they would look for a suitable definitive location. After a few days, when Mother arrived, the first group had looked around to assess the needs of the place and its possibilities. They appraised Mother of the situation. She guided, directed, corrected. There was a first inauguration, with the bishop celebrating the Eucharistic Sacrifice for the sisters and blessing the house. Mother would leave the sisters strengthened, to pursue the foundation of the convent.

With local help, things then got moving in a big way, so that when Mother came back after some months they could have the official opening of the new house, already well at work. In the presence of the bishop or his representative, of some political or civic officials, of friends and benefactors, the blessing of the house and its dependencies would take place, accompanied by prayers, speeches, good wishes, and notices in the local papers. Much work had already been done. Candidates to the congregation had often been recruited. God's work was progressing smoothly.

Here in Rotterdam help was forthcoming from many sides. The bishop's enthusiasm would prove contagious. Many people were ready to help with their labor and resources. Protestants had welcomed and sheltered the sisters from the very start. "The people help us generously," said Mother. "Our Co-Workers have provided all that is needed. Everything has been donated. And already we have an aspirant to the society from this country." This would prove a great help to the sisters hampered by the language problem. One young sister, recently out of the novitiate, was a Dutch girl. God had prepared the way for a successful foundation.

Money would be no problem. The town swam in wealth. People rejoiced at having a good cause to spend it on. "All this has been given," said the sister who prepared the food. "Mr. M. gave us bicycles," said another sister. "Here everybody cycles, so we shall do it also."

The mention of the bicycles that rejoiced the hearts of the young sisters showed that they were adapting themselves well to local conditions.

There was some little trouble about the social security arrangements, fully developed in the Netherlands. The sisters were asked to pay the usual contribution for social insurance; but Mother did not want them to. This went against her idea of poverty for the sisters, who were not to receive any state payment or compensation for their services, nor any pension of any kind.

The church authorities were also worried that in case of an accident or any mishap due to them involving third parties, they might be called on to pay extensive damages, which would be a terrible blow if they were not insured. The question was solved through some person quietly paying the needed contribution for the sisters.

CHAPTER 16

Conscientization

To improve significantly the lot of the poor and underprivileged, we must first reform the social order, and to that end make people aware of the injustices, inequalities, and iniquities so common in the world. Both the rich and the poor, the "haves and have-nots" must be conscientized or made aware of what is wrong in our politico-socio-economic organization and our human relations.

The question has been often asked, "What have Mother Teresa and her congregation done in this respect?" The answer, which may not satisfy everyone, is "They have done much to conscientize the rich, those in power and those with influence. They have done something also to bring the poor to reflect and to act."

THE WELL-TO-DO

Mother Teresa has conscientized large sections of society in scores of countries to their duty toward the less affluent and the needy members of society. She taught people to respect, care for, and serve one another. She made many aware of the existence of the poor, of their sufferings, and of the extent of hunger and sickness, disease and misery existing in the world.

She brought home to many the dignity of the poor, their qualities and merits. She made known the material, moral, and spiritual needs of many members of the human family. Yes, she made us feel that we are truly members of one great family, being coresponsible for one another.

By her influence and her action, by her words and her smile carried into millions of homes through the media, not just once but repeatedly, she has proclaimed the greatness of the poor. Without bitterness, eschewing controversy, without lending support to any "ideology," without connection or link with a political party, she did her work as a religious.

Mother showed that in every human person there is a child of God, loved by the Father; that in every suffering brother or sister we should see the suffering Jesus, who said, "What you did to the least of mine, you did it unto Me." Each time an honor was conferred on Mother, she said, "I receive it in the name of the poor."

When addressing a meeting of doctors, she exhorts them, "Do not forget the poor; they are your brothers and sisters; they need your attention. Hospitals do not want the dying destitute, even when free beds have been endowed, because they say they are meant to bring people back to life; deaths spoil their statistics. So the dying are pushed back, from one hospital to another, and then back to the road where they were picked up."

To teachers she says, "Do not neglect the weaker children. Consider the problems of the slow-witted, the dropouts, what will they become in society, if you do not look after them?"

To nurses, as to the hundred Spanish nurses who brought her three white flowers, Mother says, "Your vocation is beautiful, a call to service; take equally good care of the less fortunate."

When addressing a meeting of Rotarians, or Lions, or Knights, she tells them, "You are men with influence; you have power, you have money; use them well for the good of society, especially for the benefit of the poor."

Thus she has advised officials, ministers, heads of states, always insisting on charity, on love for all, especially for those more in need.

In her talks to bishops, priests, seminarians, Mother says, "Your charism is to preach the Word of God and to minister the sacraments. That is your work, the work you alone can do, for which God has chosen you and set you apart. The poor are hungry for the Word of God, for the bread of life. It is for you to break to them the bread of Christ."

Mother not only advises, but leads to action and shows how things can be done. She approaches company directors, moves officials, leads volunteers. They go out to clean the drains in which mosquitoes breed, that would later bite children and spread malaria and infectious diseases. She makes people remove garbage to clean up slums, provide drinking water, bring electricity. She helps to train for jobs. She was at the head of a procession collecting funds for a students' welfare home.

HELPERS AND VOLUNTEERS

Mother brought many helpers and volunteers to awareness of the situation of the very poor, through direct contact with them. She advises, "Discover the other through direct contact, while you serve him." This is no classroom exercise, but field training.

Mother wants love and service in practice. She tells us, "To anyone who comes here to join us, I first say, 'Go to Kalighat. Go tomorrow. Fall on your knees and serve the dying poor.' Yes, go to the home for the dying and learn your lesson, not out of a book, but in the rough and tumble of life, among real people, in a setting you will never forget.

There are no beds at the Kalighat Nirmal Hriday Home for the Dying. The patients are close to the earth to which many of them will soon return. Thus, to attend on them one must bend low, kneel, shed all superiority complex, all care for nice hands and polished nails.

"The smell there was at times abominable," confided a volunteer. "Some of the sick had wounds with maggots in them. Scabies had to be scraped, bandages sticking to the flesh removed. When a patient screamed out of pain, I saw even the sister in charge disappear into the next room. I think she could not bear the shouts of agony that still hurt her, even after years of service in this place. When the wounds had all been dressed, the noise and cries subsided. The silence was broken by an occasional gasp. Then all were back to feeding, like infants hungry for food."

The day's work had begun with prayer, quiet prayer and a hymn; it ends with prayer, bringing all closer to the Lord of life and death, the good God who alone offers some hope of happiness to this suffering section of humanity.

Of this suffering humanity, the reader can alleviate the pains. A French nurse, working as a volunteer, is busy giving injections. Several of her patients express their feeling of pain. "See," she says, "the needle has become blunt. Twenty, twenty-five, thirty times the same needle must be used. Of course it hurts the patients. Then there is the danger of transferring germs. The needle is passed through alcohol—but this precaution may not be sufficient. In our hospital, one needle, one injection. One needle for every patient, then it is thrown away. But here needles are in short supply. Who will send all the needles required? Tell your readers to send needles and instruments, rather than complicated medicines we cannot use in these circumstances."

"I was given no powder to put on the wounds," reports an American sister who has come to help for a few months. "If the bandages stick to the wounds, it is certain that the patient will feel pain when the bandages are removed. I did buy some talcum powder at my own cost; but the other sisters had no powder. So please ask for powder for the sick."

When these volunteers return to their well-provided hospitals in the West, they will be more careful, more sparing in the use of cotton wool, bandages, instruments, medicines. They will save for poorer patients somewhere in the world. They will do so out of love for a poorer brother or sister, out of consideration for a child of God whom they have come to love without knowing.

THE PUBLIC

Mother's words reached millions, not once only, but repeated times, thus strengthening the impact made on the consciences of her listeners, who were mostly open-minded and large-hearted. To all, Mother taught,

(1) respect for the poor;

(2) respect for all human life, including the unborn, the newly born, the weak, the handicapped, the mentally retarded; and

(3) the primacy of love in social relations: the gospel can be reduced to one sentence: love one another as God loves you; this is the basis for the solution to all human problems.

How well inspired were the Japanese producers who planned and executed a twenty-four-hour nonstop show on the theme "Love saves the world"; they allotted a half-hour to Mother Teresa and her Missionaries of Charity to show how they exemplified love and actuated it. Their aim was to make the whole nation aware that

love, not hatred;
concern, not indifference;
self-gift, not egoism

would save the world rocked and shocked by the Hiroshima bomb, and today threatened by an arsenal of ten thousand devices, each one of them a hundred times more destructive than the Hiroshima bomb. The existing nuclear weapons could destroy every human being, every animal, fish and bird, and poison every tree and plant, if ever there were an all-out nuclear war.

Love, not hatred, could alone solve both our giant problems and our day-to-day difficulties. Always human life should be protected, every God-given life.

The spiritual capsule Mother addressed to her sisters all over the world as her message for September 1980 was

"Thank God for the gift of life,
    for the poor,
    for the society of the Missionaries of Charity."

To solve problems, Mother Teresa uses a direct method:

(1) she outlines the principles governing the moral issue;

(2) she describes facts, striking instances that depict the needs or the injustice of the situation; and

(3) she advises: what we ought to do, what we can do, what we shall do. Her argumentation shows

no bitterness, but strength and sweetness;
no fanaticism, but common sense;
no class prejudice, but universal charity.

She knows that God sees in our hearts what hides there. She considers no one as of low estate, since everyone possesses the exalted dignity of being a child of God.

Mother does not indulge in long discussions, but follows the example of Churchill during the war, who had on his desk a tray marked "Action Today." Mother has no "in" and "out" trays—all is in her head: what she must do and what she will do, for her God's service and human needs brook no delay. She says, "We see a need, we go to meet it; we fill it; at least we do something about it."

Speed is essential; especially in emergencies, when people cannot wait, when delay means loss of lives, as lives may hang on a thread, especially the lives of small children.

Love is active; love does not ask questions, love solves problems.

THE POOR

To improve the conditions of the weaker sections of society, it is essential that the poor be conscientized. The poor must be made aware of their dignity, their worth, their abilities, their potentialities, their higher needs, their rights. The gospel tells them, "Blessed are you the poor in spirit," the humble, the obedient to God's law, the often neglected and over-looked, if not even oppressed.

The children of the poor must be educated, to try and pull them out of their shabby or ugly surroundings, and prepare them for a better life. Informal education for the illiterate grownups may help to make them reflect and move them to constructive action.

To teach the poor to keep things clean, their children tidy, was Mother's very first work, when she was still alone. Later, with a few helpers, she taught the poor children to wash, to comb their hair, wash their clothes, sing, pray, play. "As reward for regularity I give them a cake of soap," Mother would say. This soon developed into work for a better environment, improved health, prenatal care, clinics for sick children, feeding programs, training for jobs.

But to get the people of the slums to work together for the improve-ment of their living conditions proves very difficult. To get the children living on the street away from it and into a properly run school may be an uphill task.

The Missionary Brothers living in Howrah report that they go every Sunday to the railway station to gather the boys aged between six and twelve years and bring them to their home to give them a good meal. "They come, a hundred or one hundred and twenty of them, the same boys Sunday after Sunday."

"How do they live on weekdays?"

"By pilfering, stealing, carrying parcels or luggage—jobs reserved to the licensed porters—or making the rounds of the market stalls to pick up whatever has been thrown away. They either ran away from home or were told by their parents unable to feed them, 'Go and fend for yourself.' They sleep in empty wagons, under bridges, on benches. They have no future, except stealing, vice, drugs, and jail.

"On Sundays we bring them to our home, to have a bath, we bandage their sores, sing with them, gave them a good meal and they go back to their avocation."

"Do you not try to get them admitted into some boarding school, some institution, to get them off the road?"

"Yes, we try, but they will not go. They prefer their freedom, playing cards, smoking and drinking and stealing. Only one boy agreed to go to our Boys' Town to receive a good education and training for a job."

This shows that some compulsion is necessary to eradicate bad habits and train children to a useful and respectable life. No progress is possible without a moral basis, a moral foundation, and the desire for a higher kind of life.

Mother may attribute their misery and bad habits to lack of love, of a home, of loving parents. But the problem of their future remains.

CHAPTER 17

No Partisanship, No Politics

Render to Caesar what is Caesar's and to God what is God's.
(LUKE 20:25)

The Missionaries of Charity endeavor to be acceptable to all and accepted by people and groups of different shades of political and social ideologies, in order to win all people for Christ. Founded on love, they build on love.

Love unites, never divides, never sows seeds of dissension; love does not suspect, does not distort, does not incriminate; love never judges, never condemns, but finds excuses—not for the sin, which is always ugly and harmful, but for the sinner, who remains God's child. Those who love shun evil, but receive back the evildoer. They do not condone injustice, but try to correct it or get it corrected by its perpetrator.

So the Missionaries of Charity try to change the hearts of people, as did John the Baptist; the hearts of those in power and of the rich, by their example, their pleadings, their prayers.

The political systems, the social structures are not their concern. They leave these matters to those able to speak with wisdom and competence on the matter of government. But they remind those in power of the dignity and the rights of the poor.

The Missionaries of Charity are not called to man the barricades for this or that cause. They do not stand on the picket lines with strikers, do not shout political slogans, nor carry banners. They keep away from all that causes strains among people, all that activates a contentious spirit. Like Christ their master, they bring peace, love, and compassion into people's lives, not strife, enmity, and rivalry.

On several occasions, reporters and interviewers tried to enlist Mother Teresa's support for their own or their papers' ideologies, their own programs, their political or social goals. She always refused to be led their way, to back left or extreme left, right or extreme right. It was not always easy.

After speaking of her work to alleviate the lot of the very poor and try to put them back on their feet, several times she was met by reporters who objected, "Yes, Mother, but don't you think that in the present circumstances, the most pressing task is to change the political and social order? And if this cannot be done otherwise, by strong, even violent action? You are busy helping a few individuals, whereas we should first concentrate all our energies on changing the system and removing the abuses."

Mother did not fall into the trap, nor did she lend support to any political or economic system. When people try to blame the system or the structures, she lays the blame at their own door. The fault lies with their selfishness, their egotism, their greed, their pride, their lack of justice, their sinfulness.

Mother answers, "We must start by changing people, changing ourselves. Yes, we are wrong, sin is wrong, we lack love for one another that is the cause of the misery of so many. The suffering of some can be blamed on the greed of others." The remedy for us today, as in the days of John the Baptist, lies in sharing what we have. Those who love one another share their goods with others.

In France, in Italy, in Latin America, interviewers at times tried to get Mother's support for Marxist theory, for revolution, for the violent changes they considered necessary. "First let us work to change the structures," they said, "then uplift of the masses will follow naturally; poverty will be eradicated or even outlawed."

Mother always refused to give any party or ideology her support. Even a well-known bishop wished to have a public disputation with her on the effectiveness of her method. But she rejected the idea and proposal. "I will not dispute with him," she said. Her stand was clear. It need not be argued for or against. Others might follow another path. She did not deny that in some countries structural changes might be necessary or desirable. But the matter was not within their calling. They were the Good Samaritans picking up the sick and dying on the road of life, bandaging their wounds and helping to put them back on their feet; they did not run after the robber barons to arrest them and imprison them.

No doubt in several countries the situation had become explosive. The masses would no more take their oppression lying down. They stood up for their rights. The Catholic church had to take a stand on many burning questions of the day, and she took it. Naturally among church leaders some inclined toward strong means, others toward an irenean policy. But everywhere the church spoke for the oppressed and the sufferers of injustice.

The church is committed to justice for all. At the historic meetings of Medellin and Puebla in Latin America, the bishops and church leaders stood squarely for the principles of Christian justice, the rights of the poor, equitable distribution of land and property, social legislation guaranteeing to all the possibility of working to support their families decently.

Pope John Paul II spoke most powerfully for justice, warning those in power of what might happen to their countries if they did not heed the cries of the poor for a just order. But at the same time he condemned antireligious Marxist philosophy, materialism, and violence. "We say no to violence, yes to peace" was his clarion call.

Mother echoed it in one of her letters to her sisters: "We say no to violence, yes to peace."

The policy would give to the church some martyrs of justice and charity. Not a few priests, religious, and laypeople were put to death for their advocacy of the rights of the poor. Archbishop Romero of San Salvador was murdered in his cathedral, shot dead while standing at the altar offering the Eucharistic Sacrifice. He had promised the Holy Father some time earlier, "Holy Father, no violence, never." His opponents chose violence and killed this heroic shepherd of God's people, messenger of the peace Christ brought into the world, that we might receive it and share it with all people.

For Mother Teresa it is evident that the man and the woman consecrated to God must struggle to bring peace, understanding, love among individuals, classes, nations.

Keeping out of politics as a firm policy served Mother and her sisters well. It helped to make smooth and swift their progress throughout the world. Nowhere have they been accused or suspected of siding with any party or group. They are at home with everyone, appreciated by rulers and politicians of various tendencies.

In Ethiopia, the Missionaries of Charity were first admitted by the emperor on the recommendation of one of the princesses. The communist government that toppled the empire did not send them away; it allowed them to stay, since they worked only for the good of the poor. Mother said, "They ask us to open another house in Ethiopia. When first I went there, a priest from the country criticized us: "Your sisters are untrained, unqualified; they lack this and that. . . . " I said nothing. I never answer when they criticize us. We do our best. Our work will speak for us. Now the same priest tells us, "You are saving the church in this country. All priests and religious are being sent away. Only your sisters are welcome." They even ask us to open more houses."

"Yes, you are not suspected. You keep out of politics. You do the work of the Lord."

"No politics," said Mother, "just the work of Christ. There is a terrible famine in Ethiopia," she added pensively, "worse than last time. I shall have to get them some supplies. People are starving, we must act."

At least twice in India, Mother Teresa did take a stand on issues that were considered political, but which she judged to be mainly of a moral character. Though matters of government policies, they were moral issues affecting the free decisions people had to make in conscience.

The first time this happened was during Indira Gandhi's first term of office as prime minister. There had been a move to encourage sterilization in order to check the tremendous increase in population taking place in the country, due to a high birthrate and a lowering of the death rate resulting from better health conditions.

Indira Gandhi's protection and also affection for Mother had always been evident. She met her repeatedly without any ceremony. Mother could see Indira Gandhi whenever she went to Delhi, if there was any need to call on her. Indira Gandhi gave Mother a free pass on the Indian airlines, after the railway minister had given her a pass on the Indian railways. In 1976 Indira Gandhi decided to confer on Mother an honorary degree at the convocation of the Santiniketan University founded by Tagor, of which the prime minister is traditionally the chancellor.

At that time the government had sponsored a policy of sterilization of both men and women in the reproductive ages. Inducements were offered in the form of material benefits. But some officials, in order to show good returns, used their influence to get people sterilized, especially in some rural areas.

As she arrived at Santiniketan to receive the honorary degree, Mother was the ambassador of the church in a special manner. The controversy over sterilization was now at its height; the church authorities considered this to be a matter affecting the people's consciences. Mother carried with her a letter from the president of the Catholic Bishops Conference of India, stating the position of the Catholic church, opposed to any compulsory sterilization of men and women. Mother quietly delivered the letter to the prime minister and made her own plea.

Later, when Mother met Mrs. Indira Gandhi in Delhi, she spoke again of that burning topic, which caused much anxiety to Catholics and put many officials, doctors, and nurses in a difficult position. "I told her," said Mother, "you will not be blessed for doing this."

Mother proved to be a good prophetess. Opposition grew to what was popularly considered compulsory sterilization. In every Hindu family, there must be a son to perform the last rites for his departed father, who otherwise cannot be well reborn nor ascend to heaven. So when the prime minister called for reelection to Parliament, she was defeated at the polls. This was not many weeks after Mother's prediction.

Mother wrote to the aggrieved prime minister, who had tasted the bitter food of defeat, a most kind letter, thanking her for her never-failing help and sympathy. Indeed, a sister in charge of the abandoned children's home in Delhi recalled, "Mrs. Gandhi, while being prime minister, several times telephoned us to say, 'We had a dinner yesterday; there are some vegetables and other eatables left over; send your van to collect them for the children.' So great was her concern for our children, even in the midst of her very busy life."

Soon after Mr. Morarji Desai had taken over as prime minister to head the new cabinet, the president and the secretary of the Catholic Bishop Conference of India and the archbishop of Delhi one afternoon called on the prime minister to offer him the congratulations and good wishes of the Catholic community and also their services for the welfare for the nation. Mr. Morarji Desai, who received them well, chuckled, "You are not the first to come; Mother Teresa was here before you, she came this morning."

Mother certainly never allows the grass to grow under her feet; she moves fast in the service of her Lord. She remained on good terms with the leaders of the country, until she made what they considered to be another incursion into the political field.

AN OPEN LETTER TO PARLIAMENT

A private member's bill introduced in Parliament had received the support of the government majority, so that it was certain to be passed and become law. Its name was Freedom of Religion Bill but it aimed at making conversion to Christianity especially very difficult, if not altogether impossible.

Mother Teresa took up the cudgels for true religious freedom, the freedom to choose and practice, without any hindrance from political quarters, the religion dictated by one's conscience. Since the matter was serious and urgent, Mother took her pen and on 25 March 1979 sent "An open letter of Mother Teresa of Calcutta to Mr. Morarji Desai, Prime Minister of India, and the Members of the Indian Parliament, regarding the Freedom of Religion Bill, 1978."

The letter began with a plea that everyone may be allowed to follow the religion of his choice. It read,

Dear Mr. Desai and Members of our Parliament,

After much prayer and sacrifices, I write to you asking you to face God in prayer, before you take the step which will destroy the joy and freedom of our people.

Our people—as you know better than I—are God-fearing people. In whatever way you approach them—that presence of God—the fear of God is there. Today all over the country everybody feels insecure because the very life of freedom of conscience is being touched.

Religion is not something that you and I can touch. Religion is the worship of God—therefore a matter of conscience. I alone must decide for myself and you for yourself, what we choose. For me the religion I live and use to worship God is the Catholic religion. For me this is my very life, my joy and the greatest gift of God in His love for me. He could have given me no greater gift.

I love my people very much, more than myself, and so naturally I wish to give them the joy of possessing this treasure, but it is not mine to give, nor can I force it on any one. So also no man, no law, no government has the right to prevent me or force me, nor anyone, if I choose to embrace the religion that gives me peace, joy, love.

Having developed the first point, Mother introduced a second plea, regarding another subject dear to her heart, though not directly connected with the Freedom of Religion Bill. She now speaks of the right to life and of abortion that frustrates it. She continues, addressing the prime minister:

You took over your sacred duty in the name of God—acknowledging God's supreme right over our country and her people. It was so beautiful. But now I am afraid for you. I am afraid for our people. Abortion being allowed has brought so much hatred—for if a mother can murder her own child, what is left but for others to kill each other. You do not know what abortion has done and is doing to our people. There is so much immorality, so many broken homes, so much mental disturbance because of the murder of the innocent unborn child, in the conscience of the mother. You don't know how much evil is spreading everywhere.

Mother then made a direct appeal to the prime minister, already in his eighties, asking him to consider these two issues in the light of God, the light of eternity.

Mr. Desai, you are so close to meeting God face to face. I wonder what answer you will give for allowing the destruction of the life of the innocent unborn child and destroying the freedom to serve God according to one's choice and belief. At the hour of death, I believe we will be judged according to the words of Jesus, who has said,

I was hungry, you gave me food
I was thirsty, you gave me to drink
I was homeless, you took me in
I was sick, you took care of me
I was in prison, you visited me

Truly I say to you, for as long as you did it to these the least of my brothers, you did it to Me."

Gandhiji has also said, "He who serves the poor serves God."

Mother then speaks of her own personal experience, of her aim and ideal.

I spend hours and hours in serving the sick and the dying, the unwanted, the unloved, the lepers, the mentally retarded, because I love God and believe in his word: "You did it to me." This is the only reason and the joy of my life: to love and serve him in the distressing disguise of the poor, the unwanted, the hungry, the thirsty, the naked, the homeless, and naturally, in doing so, I proclaim his love and compassion for each one of my suffering brothers and sisters.

Mr. Desai and Members of Parliament, in the name of God, do not destroy the freedom our country and our people have had to serve and love God according to their conscience and belief. Do not belittle our Hindu religion saying that our Hindu poor people give up their religion for "a plate of rice." To my knowledge, I have not seen this done, though we feed thousands of poor of all castes and creeds, though thousands have died in our hands beautifully in peace with God."

Mother ended this open letter in her customary way by an appeal to prayer, to call people to prayer, to pray together and do penance:

I pray, and beg you that you order a day of prayer throughout the country. The Catholics of our country have called an all-India day of fast, prayer, and sacrifice on Friday, 6th April, to maintain peace and communal harmony and ensure that India lives up to its noble tradition of religious freedom. I request you to propose a similar day of intercession for all communities of our country—that we may obtain peace, unity and love; that we become one heart, full of love and so become the sunshine of God's love, the hope of eternal happiness and the burning flame of God's love and compassion, in our families, our country, and in the world.

God bless you
(Sd/) M. Teresa M.C.

The letter was publicized; but it did not have the desired effect on the prime minister. He answered Mother. He was not convinced by her arguments. Mother had written as the woman of strong convictions she is. Mr. Morarji Desai, a deeply religious man, always ready to defend his ideas and actions, did not seem pleased nor to relish the sermon and the appeal to his conscience, presented in no uncertain words. As was his right, he wrote back to Mother.

Some time later, at the end of a spiritual conference to the sisters preparing for their perpetual vows, Mother suddenly asked, "Father, what would you answer Mr. Desai?"

Taken aback, for I had not noticed her among the sisters seated on mats on the floor, I blurted, "So, Mother, you were there? I had not seen you."

"Yes. And what must I answer?"

In a conciliatory spirit, I replied, "I would not answer."

"But he wants an answer," she countered.

"Then, you might write gently, respectfully, without giving in on the principles of religious freedom for all, the innate right to adopt and follow the religion of one's choice. I would avoid any controversy and not try to have the last word. He may not like that. He is the country's prime minister, a gentleman eighty-two years of age, and a strong character. Do not antagonize him; appeal to his sense of fair play."

Mother did answer thus. She also went to Delhi to see him personally. But this time he did not receive her. He was busy.

"So," Mother confided later, "I went across to the president's palace. I sent in my name and was immediately invited to come in and ushered into his office. I gave the president the card on which I had written the prayer of Newman. I explained the prayer to him and the president put the card into his coat pocket."

Mother had warned the prime minister: "You will not be blessed for this." A few days later he lost a vote of confidence in Parliament. The country went to the polls, and at the elections the ruling coalition was defeated and Indira Gandhi came back to power with a thumping majority.

Twice a prophetic voice had spoken. Twice a moral issue had been at the start of the downfall of a prime minister and of the popularly elected government. Twice the people had voted to support the moral rights of the individual.

The second brush with a prime minister had been widely publicized, whereas the first had remained unknown to the public at large. This prompted some magazines to accuse Mother Teresa of partiality in favor of a political party, by pointing out the moral flaw of one party leader and not of his rival. This was not correct. But only a select few were aware that Mother had objected to the policy of Indira Gandhi regarding sterilization.

Writing to the papers about this matter to clarify the position and whitewash Mother's reputation for impartiality might have started a new controversy. It remained that Mother had twice interfered in what many considered to be a matter of politics.

CHAPTER 18

Proclaiming the Word of God

A voice cries in the wilderness: Prepare a way for the Lord, make his path straight.

(MATT. 3:3)

Mother Teresa has another job: she has become public relations officer of the church. She attends important meetings in various countries and explains the position of the church on the disputed questions of the day, as the family, birth control, family planning, contraception, euthanasia, sterilization, divorce, and other controversial subjects.

Pope Paul VI himself asked her to speak at important meetings to explain the teaching of the church on burning topics; at Milan, she was one of the speakers addressing a crowd of seventy thousand people in a football stadium.

Mother could fulfil her wish to be a messenger of God's love and speak of the greatest proof of God's love who sent us his beloved Son Jesus. To speak of Jesus to multitudes had been the dream of her youth at Skoplje, the reason why she had left a happy life with her family and gone East as a missionary. Like Paul, like Xavier, she felt the urge to speak of Jesus. For many years she had felt somewhat constrained, explaining, "We cannot preach Jesus as we would like because we receive help from governments, agencies, the public." But now she was given full liberty and first-rate opportunities to speak of Jesus before the learned and multitudes. But her chance was her cross. She is no extrovert enjoying facing the crowds, as some critics who do not know her, surmised. Naturally shy, she has to overcome herself to face a crowd. Perhaps it has become easier as she gets accustomed. Still, she says, "that is the worst of all, this publicity, being in the limelight, having to appear in public, when I would prefer to be washing the sick and dying."

To make her Lord known, she was prepared to do what hurt her nature. That the Lord had asked much from her, she at times confessed, as she did opportunely at Cambridge, when she said, "I remember some time ago a very big group of professors came from the United States and they asked, 'Tell us something that will help us.' And I said, 'Smile at each other.' I must have said it in a very serious way, I suppose, and so one of them asked me, 'Are you married?' and I said, 'Yes, and I sometimes find it very difficult to smile at Jesus, because he can be very demanding.' "

Yes, saints have known how demanding the Lord can be, and others —not quite saints—also. They experienced the reality of the words "My Father will prune them, that they may produce better fruit still" (John 15:2). God prunes, purifies, tests, and exacts much from those he loves, those who take seriously the invitation, "Be perfect just as your Father in heaven is perfect" (Matt. 5:48). Jesus has asked much from his chosen spouse, because he wanted her to be beautiful in his eyes.

But then there is the happiness of being his witness and of announcing him to the world, thus working for his glory. "I agree to go to various functions," says Mother, "because it gives me an opportunity to speak of Jesus, to people who otherwise never hear about him." St. Paul asked his converts to pray that God might give him opportunities to announce the gospel of Jesus. Mother has had such opportunities more abundantly perhaps than any other person of her time. She made full use of them, as she proclaimed with authority and with deep feeling the gospel of God's love for us.

Mother Teresa has been an ambassador of Christ and of the Catholic church before kings and presidents, prime ministers and ministers of many states, whether believers or nonbelievers in God and in Christ.

She met the French president Valéry Giscard d'Estaing. During his visit to India, he had wished to call on Mother in Calcutta, but his schedule did not allow him to do so. At his request, Mother went later to see him at the Elysée Palace in Paris. She met President Julius Nyerere of Tanzania, and opened a house and a flourishing novitiate in his country. She met President and Mrs. Marcos of the Philippines several times; in this country also she opened several houses and a novitiate.

Mother called on King Baudouin and Queen Fabiola several times. She met Prince Philip and Prince Charles, the king of Norway, the emperor of Ethiopia, Prime Minister Fraser of Australia, President Pertini of Italy, President Reagan of the United States. She spoke to the heads of government of Mexico, Haiti, Egypt, Bangladesh, Cuba, and many others. Nor is the list closed; it is added to several times a year.

On most occasions, the conversations or the gist of them was diffused through the press, the radio, and television. Thus Mother's views, her creed, her gospel have been made known to hundreds of millions of people.

What has been the effect of her talks to political leaders, writers, scientists, journalists, thinkers, artists, communicators? No computer could estimate their influence. But pointers emerge that strike the eye. Several heads of state asked Mother to establish foundations in their country and even took personal interest in their establishment.

After he had received Mother at the White House, and he and the First

Lady had remained with her one hour, reporters asked President Reagan what he had said to Mother. The president answered them, "When you are with Mother Teresa, you listen." He had listened because Mother had something to say, something good, elevating, stimulating, that goes deep down into the inner recesses of your soul. In the same spirit, people all over the world have listened to her, students and professors, members of civic bodies, professional men and women, children, large multitudes.

A MESSAGE FOR OUR TIME

At various times God has made use of saints, prophets, sages, and other chosen instruments to bring a message and give an example to their contemporaries and to succeeding generations.

God our Father used Francis, the Poverello of Assisi, to preach detachment from riches and love for all. He used Dominic the Preacher to propagate the true faith and combat heresy. He used Ignatius Loyola and the Society of Jesus to strengthen church unity and the authority of the Vicar of Christ. St. John Bosco and the Salesians he entrusted with the care of town youths at the time of the Industrial Revolution.

God inspired the Little Flower, St. Thérèse of Lisieux to encourage humility and childlike confidence in his Providence at a time when intellectual pride claimed, "science will explain everything; we do not need God to explain the world; man will become able to control the forces of nature and decide his own fate." The young maiden, though secluded in her convent, cut off from contact with the world, through her autobiography, read by millions, preached intellectual sanity and humility, trust in God, whom we should approach as a child comes to his loving father.

Today, we find in many countries a consumerist society, bent on spending mainly for material comfort. Occasional overproduction has resulted in wastage on a colossal scale. Coffee has been burnt in railway engines, wheat destroyed, food dumped into the sea, fruits allowed to rot on the ground rather than be brought to market, to keep up the prices.

Standards of life in different countries are staggeringly unequal. Millions die of malnutrition and disease, while some injure their health through excessive eating and drinking.

In the realm of ideas and theories, writers have evoked and fostered a split society, class hatred, a godless humanism. Men, previously over-confident in their own power, now fear a nuclear conflict that might destroy them all.

Scientific discoveries and technical progress made possible mass production at very low cost. But as a result, capital displaces labor, making it more productive. This tends to depersonalize work, thus taking away the pride and joy of a task well done, the sense of personal achievement.

We witness today, in the international field, power blocks, strife, strained relations between countries; in the national context, pressure groups, lobbies, rivalries, fight for power, corruption on a huge scale, oppression of the poor. And in the social field, the family breaks up, divorces have reached unprecedented high levels, abortion and euthanasia have been generally legalized and even financed by the state.

One may well consider that again in our age, to help us correct our defects and make us turn to him, God uses Mother Teresa as a messenger, as a prophetess, as an energizer. Her teaching and example, her disciples and followers help to bring the good news of the gospel in a new setting and circumstances.

Mother Teresa's message is simple: She tells today's world, "God loves you—love one another." "We are carriers of God's love," she can boldly claim of herself and her daughters. And she can add, "whoever you are, you can become one also."

Through her words and actions, she brings a message from God that unfolds itself into the following main points:

1. The dignity of the human person created in God's image and resemblance, coming from him and returning to him; thus the duty to respect life, all God-given life: the unborn child, the weak child, the handicapped, the oppressed, the destitute, the sick, the suffering, the dying
2. Trust in God, based on faith, relying on prayer
3. Love, including understanding, sympathy, compassion, devotion, service
4. Sharing all the good things of God, the spiritual and material goods we hold in trust—which means action and action without delay
5. Joy, the happiness of the children of God, optimism, serenity, gratitude.

By her life, her action, her example, Mother refutes the popular materialistic humanism. She has built her house on rock, not on sand, and the rock is Jesus.

A WOMAN OF TODAY

Mother Teresa belongs to her age; she possesses to a high degree its main qualities: single-mindedness, efficiency, speed. For her the work of God brooks no delay, no forgetfulness. It is the King's command.

She thinks of the work all the time, she prays it, acts it. She solves problems quickly. While we are talking in the parlor, three men enter. They explain their case: they are high-caste people; unfortunately a daughter has conceived a child from a low-caste servant. The girl cannot have the child at home, cannot keep him without being socially ostracized and unable to marry a decent man. Mother asks,

"Is there any love for the child?"

"What do you mean?"

"Does the mother wish to keep the child, to take him back after a few years? Or does she want to abandon him altogether? Has she any love for her offspring? If she has love, we shall keep the child until she comes back to take him. If there is no love for him, then we shall have the child adopted by a good, reliable family."

"The mother does not want to keep the child," answers one of the men. Mother then quickly writes a note on a slip of paper requesting the sister in charge of Sishu Bhavan to receive the expecting mother, keep her until after the time of her delivery, and keep the child. Mother gives the note to the men and instructs them to take the girl to the home for children.

This standard procedure takes less than ten minutes. A case is settled, a child's life is saved, a woman's honor is safeguarded. Of course, such quick decisions leave plenty of time for careful consideration of important issues. People who are habitually united to God and live "under the protection of his wings" may call on him in time of need; he will guide their steps.

Mother insists on the necessity of prayer for those engaged in the apostolate. She opposes and refutes the modern tendency to activism. Speaking of the sisters and herself, she states before nearly every audience, "We are not social workers, we are religious. We are women dedicated to God, of our own free will, consecrated to his service. In our lives God comes first.

"We live in poverty; we leave the world. We are not of the world, though we remain in the world." She adds that to show their intent they dress differently from the people of the world. Also to that end they pray the rosary on the road. Thus, living away from the preoccupations of the world, they show to all that they belong to God.

Moved by a deep Christian sense, Mother asserts the value of every person, the value of life itself. "We must thank God for the gift of life," she tells us. And she campaigns for the right of the unborn child to live, a right so often denied nowadays by laws permitting, even facilitating abortion. For her, abortion is murder, to call it bluntly by its name; it is an act that offends against the law of nature, against the law of God.

On many occasions and at such diverse places as at a meeting in a football stadium in Milan, walking at the head of a procession in Rome, before the king and state dignitaries in Oslo, on the television screen in Japan, in Melbourne, in Glasgow, indeed in scores of places, Mother has unequivocally condemned abortion, the killing of the unborn child, and condemned the modern practice of euthanasia, by which a crippled, old, or sick person is made to die.

Then, in an age that sees in many countries the state being worshipped as a deity, truly a Moloch, all powerful, all knowing, to whom the individual is sacrificed, there is need of leaders who stand up for the rights of the human person. Countering this tendency to depersonalize people and make them subservient to the state, Mother extols by word and example the respect, esteem, understanding, love due to every human person.

In an egoistic world, Mother underlines the beauty, the joy, the glory of sharing, of caring for others. She asks her audiences, "Do we care for the members of our own family? of our own institution? Do we know our neighbors? talk to them? Are we interested in the welfare of our community?" She stresses the point that we should show personal concern for our neighbor, knowing others as God knows them and loves them personally.

Then there is the material aspect of life: the consumers' society we witness in some Western countries is characterized by excessive spending and by a considerable wastage of resources. Reflecting that millions of people go hungry every day, Mother advises thrift, the readiness to do with less, to save, to economize. There should be self-restraint and even a dose of penance in our lives. We should look not to earth, but to God, crave for spiritual riches rather than for the perishable things of this world.

EXTENSION OF THIS INFLUENCE

Mother Teresa's influence has probably proved greater outside India than in the country in which she started her work, devoted most of her time and opened the majority of her foundations. The reason for this is that Indian society is strongly organized and deeply traditional. Christianity has made only a limited impression on the intelligentsia, and still less on the masses. There exists a general respect for life, kindness and sympathy for those who suffer, but the poverty of the majority allows them little scope for sharing or giving.

The impact of Mother's speeches was felt mostly in the richer countries of Europe and America. There many find themselves disappointed with the material comfort they enjoy, and wish to return to a more simple life, to sharing with other members of the human community.

Some pointers help to gauge the extension of this influence on individuals and groups:

1. The number of Co-Workers and volunteers devoting part of their time and resources to help the poor and needy has increased steadily to reach about three hundred thousand.
2. Donations of money, food, clothes, medicines are on a colossal scale, while many people write, "I want to help."
3. Film shows in schools, parish, and community halls, organized spontaneously by admirers and sympathizers are numbered in thousands. They bring Mother's gospel and action before the eyes and hearts of a multitude of children and adults in many countries. Their effectiveness is proved by the great number of sacrifices made by

schoolchildren who wish to share their good things with others less fortunate. This augurs well for the next generation.

4. The many articles published in the press and magazines of various countries must move very many to holy desires and actions. Unless the readers were truly interested, reporters and journalists, photographers and television crews would not travel from faraway places to India to record what is being done for the poor and suffering members of humanity by Mother Teresa and her sisters.

All this proves that a deep impression has been caused, moving people to action. When John the Baptist was preparing the way for the Savior of humanity, people asked him, "What must we do to improve ourselves and our society?" To the same question asked today, Mother Teresa's answer rings in our ears: "God loves you. Love one another as he loves you. Love is sharing. Love is giving the best we have, as God the Father loved us and gave us his Son, Jesus."

CHAPTER 19

The Awards

His master said to him, "Well done, good and faithful servant; you
have shown you can be faithful in small things, I will trust you with
greater; come and join in your master's happiness."

(MATT. 25:21)

To help Mother Teresa in her work, God sent her the awards. The many
distinctions and awards Mother received proved to be a tremendous
power for good, a great help to the development of her institute and
foundations. They brought her not only financial assistance but also
publicity and recognition. Officials and especially the media took notice
of this person and made known her activity in an ever-widening circle.

World-famous awards are news. Their recipients are mentioned in
dispatches and in the press; the public becomes aware of their existence
and achievements.

International awards often come at the last stage of a life of service,
work, or research. But for Mother each award proved to be a stepping-
stone to further progress, or a higher rung on the ladder to greater
achievements. They provided her with first-class opportunities to proclaim her faith, publicize her ideal, enroll more helpers, start new ventures. They also brought her in contact with leaders of nations, while
millions of people heard her speak, saw her, admired her, worshipped
her, learned about her through the media.

Perhaps no living person has received as many world-famous awards
as Mother has. It started with the Magsaysay Award bestowed on Mother
in the Phillippines. Her action and reputation were still mostly local. The
award brought her national recognition and at least a mention in the free
world press. The Indian government was naturally proud to see one of
their citizens singled out for an honor bestowed on an Asian charitable
worker. It brought credit to the nation.

It also made Mother welcome to open houses in the Philippines, the
only Christian and Catholic country of Asia. Mother would always be
received with honor by the president, his wife, and the high officials of
the country. Indeed, she later started several houses with the help of the
First Lady, Mrs. Marcos.

On 6 January 1971, the John XXIII Award for Peace was given to Mother by Pope Paul VI. It was hailed in the Catholic countries of Europe, where it brought her work to the conciousness of the people.

The Kennedy Award was naturally publicized in the United States. The money went for the building of the Nirmala Kennedy Center in Dum Dum on the outskirts of Calcutta. Senator Edward Kennedy came to visit it.

In December 1972, Mother was honored by India, when the Jawaharlal Nehru Award for International Understanding was conferred on her by President V. V. Girl in the presence of Indira Gandhi, the prime minister.

On 25 April 1973, she received the Templeton Award from Prince Philip. The event made Mother still more famous in England, since all the media carried the news.

The Balzan Prize, perhaps the largest award in terms of money, if not the most famous, was given to Mother by President Pertini of Italy in Rome; it proclaimed her work in that country and in the neighboring lands.

THE NOBEL PEACE PRIZE

Then came the most glamorous award, the most publicized, the Nobel Peace Prize, the one no newspaper anywhere in the world can ignore. Given in the presence of the king of Norway during a ceremony televised and shown to hundreds of millions of viewers, it brings the acme of celebrity. This time the audience was the world, and the echoes of the proceedings were heard for several months.

In 1979, one afternoon Mother appeared with Sister Camillus at our presbytery and immediately broke the news, "This morning I got a phone call from the government in Delhi to tell me, 'Congratulations, you have been awarded the Nobel Peace Prize.' It is for God's glory," she commented and started speaking about the work.

For her, during several months, there would be no peace. Journalists, reporters, photographers, television crews, friends, well-wishers, officials came to congratulate her, interview her, take photos, ask for autographs, inquire about her plans. Enthusiasm was all around at a high pitch.

A few days after the announcement, Mother, astonished herself, could say, "I received a heap of telegrams as high as that," and she raised her right hand 40 centimeters from the table. "It is incredible. Heads of states, ministers, even one from President Tito and one from the Chinese communist government."

A telegram from an American publisher said, "I congratulate you for having remained faithful to your first call and inspiration." This showed perfect understanding of her life and main merit: a woman of faith, love, and devotion. She had never vacillated, never departed from her calling and ideal. The Nobel Prize would only make her more devoted and efficient for the cause of the suffering Christ in his brethren.

IN OSLO

The Oslo ceremony proved to be the big show all expected. It turned out to be even more striking than usual.

Accompanied by Sister Agnes and Sister Gertrude, Mother arrived at the airport in a freezing atmosphere; only hearts were warm. Mother wore only a cardigan over her sari. A kind gentleman put his coat over her shoulders to protect her against the bitter cold. The Indian ambassador took her to his home, where she was garlanded by his daughter in true Indian fashion, and introduced her to a number of personalities.

Ann Blaikie, Jacqueline de Decker, friends and collaborators from the early days had come, ready to help and make the event also a family reunion and an apostolic occasion.

Mother chose to stay in a convent, as she usually does. The nuns saw to it that she was not besieged by callers and interviewers. She could pray peacefully. She needed her Lord's support, for the splendor, the glamor, the praises were an ordeal for her. But Mother also knew that the ceremony would provide her with the best opportunity she had ever had to preach the word of God. She would proclaim his love for the poor and suffering, for all his children, and stand for Christian principles and for the right of the unborn child to live.

She would preach before the king, ministers, ambassadors, members of parliament, university professors, and beyond them to tens of million people listening to the radio broadcasts, watching the proceedings on television—this time her audience was the world. The gold medal of the Peace Prize bears the inscription *"Pro Pace et Fraternitate Gentium."* For peace, friendship, and love between men and women of all nations, this nun had spoken eloquently, fought courageously, worked indefatigably. The world acknowledged her determination, her initiative, her self-sacrifice. Some knew already, as she had made it clear in her acceptance speech, that her motivation and her strength came from the one to whom she had vowed her life, Jesus the Son of God, the perfect lover.

At the award ceremony, Professor Sannes explained that the committee of the Nobel Peace Prize had decided to honor Mother because she had fulfilled its ideal of peace and brotherhood among all people.

For the first time in its long history, the Peace Prize had been awarded to a nun. Another Catholic religious, Fr. Dominic Pire, a Belgian Dominican priest had received it some years earlier for his charitable work in the other part of Bengal that is now Bangladesh.

The following day Mother was to deliver her speech, and as usual she took charge of the proceedings. The podium became her pulpit, the university hall assumed for a while the dignity of a house of prayer, a house of God, reverberating with his praise and his oracle.

Speaking without notes, after making with her right thumb a small cross on her lips, Mother invited the learned, the august audience to pray. She led them in prayer to the one true God. Then she developed her usual themes centered on love and life, bejeweling her speech with some of the best instances culled from her life's experience. She spoke movingly of God's love for us, of the joy of serving Jesus in the poor, of the dignity of every person as a child of God, of the right of every one, even the unborn child to live, respected and loved.

AFTER OSLO

On her return from Oslo via Rome, Mother had fever for several days. She did not come down to meet the crowd of daily visitors, but worked in her room. A group of sisters who had taken their first or their final vows a few days earlier, had to be given their assignments. There were important changes of personnel to be made. Mother was fully busy.

On the twenty-seventh of December at 5 P.M., I went to see her, gave a message to a sister, and insisted that Mother should not come down. The sister soon returned, asked me to go to the chapel on the first floor. There at the back, Mother was praying. I prayed next to her for a while. Then she invited me, "Come to the sacristy." There we could talk without fear of being disturbed by outsiders.

Immediately, Mother expressed her intimate reaction. "It was wonderful," she broke out as greeting, "they all prayed in a place where they had never prayed before. We were all gathered in the hall for the award and when I was given a chance to speak, I said, 'This is a prize for peace, let us pray together for peace in the world, let us ask God to give us peace, to make us the instruments of his peace.' They had all been given the prayer of St. Francis of Assisi, and we started, 'Lord, make me an instrument of your peace.' It was wonderful, they all prayed. And you know there are but very few Catholics in Norway.

"Then I spoke against abortion. I told them, 'This is the International Year of the Child. I speak in the name of the unborn child. Abortion means killing a child, a human person. You do not want your child to live —you destroy him.'

"Later there was an ecumenical prayer service in the Protestant cathedral. We all prayed together for peace and unity and love among all people. I spoke to them on this topic. I am sure you must all have been praying for me here; that is why it went so well."

"Yes, Mother, we all prayed for you here, while you were giving your witness to Jesus in Norway. It came out on television and the radio. Millions of people must have watched it, heard it, and prayed with you as you prayed for peace in the world. The Indian radio broadcast your speech, and we could hear you saying the words to God who loves us!"

Mother added, "When I passed through Rome on my way back, the Holy Father told me, 'Go and speak like that everywhere.' "

As could be expected, as she knew very well herself, Mother's speech had been received with mixed feelings. But she was happy that she had witnessed before the world to her faith in God, her faith in God-given life, her respect for the human person, and had spoken for those yet unborn who cannot speak.

The glamor, the enthusiastic reception receded into the background. What truly rejoiced her heart was the fact that hundreds of people, gathered in the university hall to witness the yearly ceremony presided over by the king of Norway, had for the first time prayed together.

Mother's Co-Workers distributed sheets with the prayer, to people seated on both sides of the hall. Unfortunately, the center was overlooked, and the king, who sat there, was not given a sheet. After the prayer, Mother went on speaking and strongly condemned abortion. There was a shudder in the hall when she stressed her point, saying, "I repeat it, Your Majesty, abortion is murder. . . ."

"The next day," recalled an eyewitness, "it was a furore in the press." In Scandinavian countries with numerous abortions, with legalized abortion, this view of strict Catholic morality could not please everyone, far from it. But the speech in its outspokenness did please the Holy Father, who encouraged Mother to spread the message of respect for life, even of the unborn.

AN UNSUCCESSFUL EFFORT

Some time after Mother's return from Oslo, I asked her, "Did you go to Teheran?" She looked at the questioner, as if to say, "Who told you about the plan?' Then she answered somewhat sadly, "They did not invite me to go there."

In fact, she had been approached with a request to go to Teheran, meet Ayatollah Khomeini and try to obtain the release of the American hostages. Not a word had transpired about this in the press. No one had mentioned it. Mother had waited several days in Rome, either at the request of the Holy Father who had himself tried to secure the release of the hostages, or of another party.

Mother had asked the Indian government whether they had any objection to her attempting this mission of mercy. As an Indian citizen she understood that the move had political undertones and implications, even if for her this was purely a work of mercy and compassion for suffering people.

She waited in Rome with Sister Gertrude for an answer from Teheran. Meanwhile, she sent Sister Agnes back to India alone. Sister Gertrude had pioneered the work of the Missionaries of Charity in North Yemen; she knew Arabic and could understand the Islamic mind; one of the society's six qualified doctors, she had done excellent work among the lepers in Yemen.

Unfortunately, no positive answer was received from Teheran, inviting Mother to go there. So Mother and Sister Gertrude flew back to Calcutta on the twenty-first of December, a day the bishops of India had recommended be kept as a fast day to obtain peace in the country and good elections. On the plane they asked if Mother wanted any special food. Sister Gertrude answered that they were fasting. Thus ended with prayer and penance the first lap of the Nobel Peace Prize Award.

ENTHUSIASTIC WELCOME HOME

The second lap proved to be, as expected, the time of the media, of reporters and photographers besieging the motherhouse, of friends come to congratulate, garland, present checks, of civic receptions and public meetings.

This was a trying period, when Mother made efforts to get back to her work: she had to deal with the problems of expansion, opening new houses, and of training and posting her personnel. She understood the claims of the world, wanting to know about her life, her work, her ideal, her mission. She would give some three months to these duties, a consequence of her celebrity and success. It was part of her apostolate: people could thus learn, reflect, and join the movement of spreading love—they could at least make an act of love for God and the neighbor.

Many felt moved to generosity. There were ripples following in the wake of the Nobel. In Norway the people made a generous contribution, which was truly a people's prize. In Calcutta, some friends would have liked to equal the gift from Norway. They had stamps printed bearing Mother's picture and the words "A token of love," and sold them through volunteers for a rupee each. The chief minister himself had patronized the scheme and given twenty thousand rupees to cover the printing expenses. Volunteers, especially students, sold the stamps.

In India and many other countries, the press published stories and reproduced photographs of Mother and her sisters attending to the dying, nursing the sick, serving lepers, looking after children. Magazines exalted Mother's work and dedication. A newspaper said, "If you ask people in Calcutta who is the most loved person in West Bengal, nine out of ten will answer, 'Mother Teresa.' "

Indians were generally proud of Mother, whom they considered rightly one of their own. Indeed, when at Oslo, a reporter had asked her, "Do you now not consider yourself a citizen of the world?" she answered simply, "I am an Indian citizen." By choice, no doubt; she had asked for it. She had also been accepted by the nation as one of their own, "Ma Teresa" as all called her.

Third lap. The highest authorities of the country were going to recognize once again Mother's merit, devotion, and faithfulness. It came, it would seem, as a consequence of the Nobel. The prime minister of India decided that Mother Teresa would be awarded the highest dignity and honor of the country: the Bharat Ratna—Jewel of India.

THE BHARAT RATNA

On 22 March 1980, the president of India conferred on Mother the highest honor of the nation. In a solemn, impressive ceremony, Sanjeeva Reddy, the president, in the presence of Mr. Hidayatullah, the vice-president, and of Mrs. Indira Gandhi, the prime minister, by granting this honor, expressed to Mother the gratitude and admiration of the country and of its leaders.

One of the first acts of Indira Gandhi, after taking office as Prime Minister for the second time, had been to put Mother Teresa's name on the honor list, right at the top, as high as she possibly could. The Bharat Ratna had been previously given only to very few eminent and highly placed Indians, such as presidents and prime ministers.

The ceremony spelt pomp and splendor from the moment one entered the presidential palace, amid extensive grounds, close to the Moghul Gardens. Guards in colorful uniforms saluted the authorities and distinguished guests as they arrived to witness the ceremony. Mother passed through all this pomp in her white sari, sandaled feet, the cross of Jesus on her shoulder, fingering her rosary whenever no one had to be greeted.

Mother brought with her Sister Dorothy, the fourth to join her, after Agnes, Gertrude, and another, so that when she arrived at the Upper Room of the Gomes house, Mother could write gratefully, "Thank God, now we are five. . . ." At present she could say, "Thank God, now we are fifteen hundred in thirty countries."

Dorothy, always smiling quietly, looking a picture of health, had taken the congregation to Latin America, learned Spanish, gone to Australia, then back to Calcutta, then to Delhi as regional superior.

As the ceremony unfolded itself according to the rules and to protocol, Mother was gently, quietly praying as usual. This time she was given no opportunity to speak and to lead the audience in prayer. She was at the receiving end, to be congratulated without objection. She could preach only by her recollected attitude, a person living in God, for God.

But after the ceremony, she told the reporters besieging her that she accepted the honor in the name of all the poor and also received it in the name of all those of all religions who devoted themselves to the service of the poor.

The next twenty-four hours, the media would proclaim all over India in sixteen major languages, in two hundred lesser ones, through the sayings and instances taken from this nun's life, that Christians had something to give, something good, universally beneficial, something needed by our society in these days. Truly it was for this she had come to India;

and now, without having to utter a word, Mother preached the gospel of Jesus.

But at this hour of glory and fulfillment, as she received the adulation of the crowds, as the highest authorities of the country voiced their approval, could Mother be really, truly happy? She had just been sorely tried. Her heart was deeply wounded and stood bleeding, due to a terrible accident that had happened to one of her houses in London.

On March the eighteenth, a fire had broken out in the North London home where twenty-five poor women were living. When the flames had been quelled and silenced, it was discovered that eleven people had been burned to death. The B.B.C. first announced that four sisters working in the home must have perished in the fire. This was later disproved. In fact, five sisters used to work there during the day; two of them stayed for the night, while the others returned to their community house not far away. But a volunteer helper, a girl of eighteen years had been killed, and this was a cruel blow for her parents and her family.

The home and its inmates had been shown on television and highly praised at the time of the Nobel Prize Award. Now it again entered the news, in sad circumstances, gutted, shrouded in mourning, cause of sorrow for the families of the defuncts.

At the time of the accident, Mother was opening a new house at Allahabad. From there she came to Delhi for the reception of the Bharat Ratna at the president's palace. Over the phone she was told some details of the sad happenings. What could she do, except pray and encourage her sisters to surrender to God's will in the hour of distress. "Is my presence necessary?" she inquired. She received the answer, "No, not at this stage." Cardinal Hume had come to console the sisters and the surviving inmates. Now they had to look for another suitable shelter.

Struck by this mixture of joy and pain, some among the friends of Mother Teresa asked themselves, "Is the timing of this accident not the good Lord's way of telling us: enough of success, of glamor, of praises, of being in the news. Go back to the cross, on which I thirst—that is your calling—and work silently, humbly, unrecognized, in toil and sweat, just for me, you my brides, dear to my heart."

On the evening of the twenty-second, Mother took the plane to return to Calcutta. Due to land at 10 P.M., it arrived only at 2 A.M. the next day, a Sunday. She was driven to the motherhouse. At 4:30 A.M. she was in the chapel as usual. Soon she was leaving for Baruipur to attend a civic reception in her honor and another reception given by the bishop and the Catholic community. The next day, she was off to Hubli, on the west coast, more than a thousand miles away. There she was to open a new house. "She looked fresh," commented one of her counselors. "She can do it; she has grace."

A few days later, she was off to Benares to receive an honorary doctorate from the Benares Hindu University. "How many doctorates do you have, Mother?" someone asked. "I don't know," she replied. "Some months ago it was fifteen; now, perhaps twenty."

From several countries they were writing, phoning, sending cables to request her to accept an honor, a doctorate, some distinction. From across the ocean a request came, "Could you convince Mother to attend our convocation? That would offer her a wonderful opportunity to spread her message of love for all people. We guarantee her an excellent reception. Our students will be thrilled to meet her. Please use your influence." Mother was most willing to oblige; but where was the time? "In June I must go to Europe, then Africa, then America, Japan has asked me. . . ."

Among all her awards, there is one that must have moved Mother in a special manner, as it reawakened happy memories of her youth. On 28 June 1980, Mother Teresa was proclaimed at her home town of Skoplje, a "Meritorious Citizen." She had left her native town in 1928, and this was only her third visit home.

In June 1981, in Washington, D.C., President Reagan and the First Lady received Mother at the White House to confer on her a high honor.

A distinction that was especially appreciated by all her friends and admirers—and by philatelists all over the world—was the postal stamp the postal department of the government of India issued in her honor, on 27 August 1980. At the public ceremony at which the first sheet of stamps was handed over to her, the director pointed out that this was the only time they had issued a stamp in honor of a living person. The policy of the department was to commemorate and honor only dead people. But for once they had made an exception to their rule.

The stamp bears Mother's picture and the side of the Nobel Peace Prize medal carrying the words *Pro pace et fraternitate gentium.* The First Day cover carried four pictures of Mother, showing her in different moods, and also a reproduction of her autographed words "God loves you, love others as He loves you. God bless you. M. Teresa, M.C." Thus Mother's creed would penetrate into many houses and into stamp collectors' albums.

The stamp was of the value of thirty paise—the rate for an ordinary inland letter. It was expected to be widely used; but a few weeks later, the postal rate was enhanced to thirty-five paise, thus curtailing the stamp's usefulness.

THE AWARDS AND THE APOSTOLATE

The awards helped to bring Mother the favor, protection, and collaboration of important people.

After the Nobel Peace Prize, Jaipur, the old princely capital of the Jaipur state, the lovely pink city—so called for the color of its palaces— offered Mother a wonderful welcome, in a place with very little Christian presence. The chief minister presided, the dowager Rajmata sat on the dais, crowds of people came as devotees to honor Mother Teresa and receive what they rightly called her blessing. Schoolchildren brought their offering, the chief minister of Rajasthan presented a check for 100,-000 rupees, the Rajmata donated an acre of land in the city for a house for the dying and destitute.

The scene was repeated several times with minor variations in different parts of the country. And this went on for months.

On her return from a journey to Kashmir, Mother was happy to report, in April 1981, "Sheikh Abdullah gave me a more beautiful instruction than all the fathers ever did. I was at Jammu to open a new house. We wished to register a property in our name, but there is an article of the constitution of Kashmir and Jammu that says no foreigner may own land in the state. So I told Sheikh Abdullah that we have only one sister from his state and we cannot register land in her name. On the spot he spoke to the prime minister, and they decided to amend this article so that our society might own the property we intended to work in. Within a few days the assembly approved of the change, and we could have the land registered in the name of our society.

"The sheikh spoke with eloquence of the love of God and the service of the neighbor. He said that this love in action was a proof of the existence of God and of his power, of his action through people. It was wonderful to hear him speak."

In 1981, the sisters in Bangladesh got into trouble with the authorities regarding passports, visas, or customs. The sisters working there had perhaps not followed all the rules and regulations, and in a world of restrictions, permits, and licenses, they had gotten into hot water. Of the gospel injunction given by Jesus to his followers, "be simple as doves and prudent as serpents," they had obeyed mostly the first half. It was not found sufficient, and some of them were ordered to leave, within a short time.

On her return to Calcutta, Mother was informed of the matter. She lost no time and took the first plane for the capital of Bangladesh. She was met at the airport by the Indian high commissioner—or ambassador—and the archbishop. The high commissioner would normally show such a mark of respect only to presidents and ministers. But Mother belonged to the small number of people having received India's highest honor.

Mother called on President Zia, who received her cordially. "I told him," she confided after her return, "your customs give plenty of trouble, they give plenty of trouble." Anyway, the president settled the matter to Mother's satisfaction, and the threatened sisters remained to do their work of charity as they are called to do.

Soon after that Mother left for Kathmandu, the capital of Nepal, to settle some other difficulty. The king of Nepal, when a small boy, had been a student of that same Loreto School, at Darjeeling, where Mother had been a novice, had taken her first religious vows, and later made the famous retreat after her call and inspiration.

The sisters were working at Kathmandu, as were the Jesuits. But Christians and also many others resented that conversion to Christianity was forbidden by law. Any adult who after sufficient instruction decided to follow the gospel of Christ and was baptized, could be jailed for this so-called offense. Some courageous converts had actually been arrested and thrown into jail, at a time when the world ratified conventions to ensure freedom of thought, opinion, and religion.

Mother Teresa apparently was not going to Kathmandu on that account nor to discuss that matter, but in connection with the place where her sisters were to work. In this case also, she succeeded in settling matters satisfactorily.

POSTSCRIPT

The great award, the only prize that really matters, the undying honor and cause of perfect happiness, God himself, we trust, will give in his own time. Indeed, Jesus foretold it: "What you did to the least of my brethren, you did it unto Me; come and join in your Master's happiness" (Matt. 25:23).

CHAPTER 20

The Media and the Apostolate

Let your light shine before men, that seeing your good works, they
may praise your Father in Heaven.

(MATT. 5:16)

"Mother Teresa is truly a 'media person,' " concluded Ann Petrie after
the ceremony of the awarding of the Bharat Ratna in the presidential
palace in New Delhi. She had come to India to make a one-hour television
film on Mother and had come to talk about it, seeking information and
advice from those who knew her heroine.

We had strongly advised her to incorporate as much as possible the
work done by the sisters, even though she had been told to film Mother.
But Mother without her sisters would be not "Hamlet out of the play,"
but rather Hamlet alone, without any play. And the play was worthwhile,
the play would go on long after Hamlet had died.

"Do you think it will be possible to get a shot of Mrs. Gandhi talking
to Mother Teresa?" asked the producer." It would be wonderful to catch
the world's two most famous women conversing together and to be able
to show them to the world on the same small screen."

"Of course," we said, "they are bound to come together, they will be
attracted to each other and you will have no difficulty in getting an
excellent picture of them, if you find yourself in a good position. They
are both camera conscious, allowing themselves to be filmed, smiling to
all, speaking unhurriedly, while the photographers are at work. But
mainly they have the sense of the media and their importance, and they
find themselves where the action is important."

And so it happened. The president, Sanjeeva Reddy, gave away the
awards. When the official ceremony was over, Indira Gandhi came to chat
with the recipients and congratulate them. Of course, the first one was
Mother Teresa, who had received the highest distinction. The two
women knew each other well, respected and esteemed each other. And
they were together for the television cameras. The Indian television was
there, some others, and many reporters and photographers, having a
field day. Mother Teresa would soon be seen on the screen of all cinemas
that give the news and on television all over the country. Her fame would
still soar higher than previously.

"A media person." Mother could be grateful to the media—they had made her, made her work possible, helped her congregation to develop fast, and spread in many countries. The media had served her from the time of the arduous beginnings. Without them she would have remained a humble worker, helped by a few nuns in Calcutta and its surroundings. But God sent her the press, the radio, the camera, the television, and hers became a different story, a world success. The media were rewarded, as Mother served them well also. It was both, give and take, giving and receiving.

"If I go to heaven," Mother says, "it will be on account of all that publicity; I hate it. Why all this fuss about us. Others do the same work as we do. Do it perhaps better. Then why single us out?"

On receiving the Bharat Ratna had she not said, "I accept this award in the name of all those of all religions who devote themselves to the service of the poor." That was a kind thought: all those who work for the poor, not only Christians, but workers of other denominations also.

Others may have been doing the same good work, but for the media there is only one Mother Teresa. They made her, they cling to her, they are faithful to her. Unless perhaps something happens and then. . . . *La donna e mobile*—no, *la fama e mobile.* Not woman but the crowd changes quickly, and then suddenly oblivion and complete neglect.

For the present, Mother profits by the personality cult characteristic of her age—our age—so well served and intensified by the needs of the television screen. On television one must be immediately identified. And Mother happens to be not just another religious—but the nun in a white, blue-bordered sari. The television screen is not for groups but for a person, not for long speeches but for pictures.

The camera gets hold of her, does not let her go, turns around her, shows her wrinkled face when at rest, her charming smile when she looks at someone, the sandaled feet, the cross on her shoulder, the labored hands of a strong woman from the hills of Yugoslavia. "God made me a great gift," she says, "He gave me a strong health." Then the camera lingers on the rosary she holds and usually fingers; to end returning to her face, with her brow covered by her habit.

When standing, she tries to make herself as small, as inconspicuous as possible; yet she remains the center of attraction.

The press also, that Fourth Estate, that modern power able to build up, to praise and magnify, to distort out of all porportions, to kill or cripple, played its part from the start. The press made of Mother a heroine. It proclaimed her deeds all the more enthusiastically because she did not try to push herself, but rather tried to remain always in the background. The press found in her a worthy subject of praise: a person selfless, just trying to do good to everyone, especially to the downtrodden. And the press rose to the occasion as one. But they went about it in their own way, the modern way, also serving the personality cult.

Repeatedly journalists have questioned those who know the heroine, entreating them, "Please tell us all you know about her, especially what relates to her person: What does she eat? How long does she sleep? What does she read? Is she very intelligent? What are her defects? Why does she succeed? Is she a good traveler?" and then the big question: "And after her what is going to happen? Will all that beautiful movement come to a halt?"

Yes, beautiful is the word. Mother's two favorite words, after the Holy Name, are "wonderful and beautiful," always with a spiritual connotation, a relation to God and to his work in the world. "Something beautiful for God" has come to sum up Mother and her sisters' aim, activity, and function in today's world.

Malcolm Muggeridge has the merit of having launched Mother's fame abroad, and of spreading it in a big way. A master of the media, able to control them and give them a direction, he interviewed Mother for the B.B.C. This was at the time she hardly knew about television, which she never watched anyway. In the studio, fingering her rosary, without any makeup, unaware that she was to be projected before half of the English people, she proved an unusual subject in more ways than one.

A Catholic nun, coming from India, working in the slums of Calcutta among the most depressed people, interviewed by a famous commentator, writer, producer. "He had a sheet of paper with a series of questions ready," she recalled. "He put me two questions, which I answered; then I took over and he put his paper away." "I took over"—that was unusual for a first interview. And taking the lead role when one faced a famous interviewer on his home ground was the sign of a strong personality, or better of a prophetic person, led by the Spirit of God. This Muggeridge understood, and he came to Calcutta with a BBC crew to take a film depicting the work of this prophetic nun.

At the mother house where he stayed five days to film the sisters, as they were about to start, Mother exclaimed, "Let us do something beautiful for God." The words took root, bore immediate fruit, were a tremendous success. The film, shown all over the English-speaking world, made Mother Teresa and her Missionaries of Charity famous. "Something beautiful for God" proved to be a joy forever.

Later, Mother explained who her God was, to whom she belonged, to whom she was wedded, for whom she worked, the Face and sacred Presence she saw and found in the poor she served, when she specified, "Father, tell them: we do it for Jesus."

Tell them? Tell whom?—Those who ask and those who listen, those who know us and those who misunderstand us; tell them what is our motive force, our aim, our strength; "Jesus, whatever we do is for Jesus."

No religious personality, with the exception of John Paul II, has attracted the same number of viewers, has been listened to by as many eager ears, has had such an influence on the general public.

Bishop Fulton Sheen had up to twenty million viewers for his half-hour broadcasts on "Life Is Worth Living." He could spread widely the message "God loves you."

Billy Graham's revivalist meetings have been widely televised, especially in English-speaking countries. He did much to spread the gospel message.

Mother Teresa has been repeatedly shown on Eurovision, on U.S. nationwide networks, relayed by satellite to various other countries. She has become familiar to television audiences, to radio listeners, in the whole noncommunist world. Her short speeches made and continue to make a tremendous impact on people's consciences. The effect is compounded, deepened by the films and slides shown in schools, in parish halls, in community centers of many countries.

Unbelievers, atheists, have been affected as well as believers in God and religious people. No religious personality has a better, a more constant opportunity to preach his message than Mother. It was said that by her appearing repeatedly on television she had done more to make the Christian faith known in Japan than all the missionaries together living there for the last twenty years.

A JAPANESE FILM

One day, Mother said, "A Japanese team has come to take a film of our work. I told them to start with the ceremony of the vows and explained to them what it means. So the mass will be shown on the television screen in numberless Japanese homes." This was truly a God-sent opportunity. The sisters would take their final vows, make their lifelong commitment to God during the Eucharistic Celebration.

The Japanese team had come to take a full-length feature film of Mother Teresa and her sisters' works prepared by a Japanese nun who had worked for it in India during a year.

On the appointed day, the team was there filming the ceremony. It did disturb somewhat the recollection and prayerful atmosphere, but the purpose made it worthwhile. The lights were on and off, as the filming of the main parts of the ceremony proceeded.

After the church service, the crew came to film the reception of the new, finally professed sisters by the other sisters at the mother house. This is a colorful and moving ceremony. As we were leaving the church, "Come to the mother house, Father," said Mother, "we now have the final reception of the sisters in the congregation. We receive them as Indian brides are received by the womenfolk of their new family."

Together we drove there. The Japanese team was soon ready for work. The newly finally professed sisters arrived. Their parents were present, a few guests, priests, and nuns. But the ceremony would be witnessed by millions as the television recorded the lovely scene.

As they arrived, the brides of Christ were given a sign on their forehead, in the Indian fashion. They were garlanded and led in procession with songs and dance, while from the verandas of the upper floors flower petals were showered on them.

The song was a Hindi *bhajan,* a multistanza religious hymn woven around the Name of Jesus. Rhythmical, mystical, it fitted the occasion perfectly. As in the Song of Songs, the bride sings the praises of the divine Bridegroom, so the newlyweds thought of him to whom they now belonged for life. "I am my Beloved's, and he is mine." For all those present this was a moment of intense beauty, of deep emotion, and a foretaste of heaven's happiness. All who shared in this bliss wished that time might stop to allow them to remain longer under the spell. The dancers swayed in the breeze around the brides walking slowly two by two, while the singers sang and the petals fell gently on heads and shoulders.

When the brides had reached the grotto of our Lady at the end of the courtyard. Mother said, "Now I am going to receive them." She read to them a formula she had typed on a sheet of paper, telling them that from then on they were full members of the congregation of the Missionaries of Charity. She added some advice regarding the love they were to bestow on Jesus and on the poor in whom they were to find their Lord. Mother's voice was throbbing with emotion. The Japanese crew members were on their toes, directing their portable lights on the main actor—the main human actor, that is. They came as close to Mother as they could, to get a close-up of her face and expression. But she continually moved around the sisters, trying to escape from the limelight; but nothing could prevent the crew from following her wherever she went.

"Will Mother tell them this night where they go?" one of the counselors was asked. "No," she answered, "this evening it is too late to distribute the tasks to so many. They will be told tomorrow their destinations."

Thanks to the media, what had been witnessed and enjoyed by only a few friends would now become an edifying and stimulating spectacle projected before millions of people in faraway lands.

CALCUTTA: A CITY OF CONTRASTS

Reporters and cineasts coming to Calcutta to cover Mother Teresa's work usually have a field day and follow a similar course. Calcutta being a city of contrasts, if one takes a quick look at its ugly side, its three thousand slums, its numerous people lying on the street pavements—it is often difficult to discern whether they are sick and dying or simply sleeping unconcerned, unaware of what goes on around them—one can be painfully horrified. There is here plenty of matter that will strike readers in the Western papers and picture magazines.

Calcutta can be depicted as an ogre, a monstrous Ugolin, condemned to perpetually devour his own children. The city's name comes from the Goddess Kali, its patroness, worshipped daily by thousands in a famous shrine. The Goddess Kali sports a necklace of forty skulls, those of the people she has killed, including the skull of her husband, whom she destroyed by mistake. What can anyone expect from a city established under such patronage, considering that destiny cannot be controlled by human power?

Against this grisly background of Calcutta and its crowds, its noise, its dirt, its beggars, it is easy to introduce Mother Teresa as the rescuer, in the manner of a heroine of classical Greek tragedy, fighting single-handed the forces of evil surrounding her—or even as destiny herself. Then, in Calcutta's abode of misery, dread, and despair, Mother Teresa stands up, wielding broom and pail, to start cleaning up the dirt in the slums, to pick up the dying from the footpaths, and bring a basket of food to the orphaned children.

Some journalists and photographers understood that this method of reporting and presenting Calcutta—if not the whole of India—to the eyes of the world might not be quite fair. "Don't educated Indians resent the publicity made about Mother?" asked several reporters.

"Of course, they do. It shows only one side of the picture. Calcutta is a city with many facets, a kaleidoscope of life. Most visitors see only a tiny part of its squalor and riches. They stay in a five-star hotel, while not far away a leper sits on the footpath, asking for alms. They hardly get a glimpse of the culture, the politeness, the generosity, the tolerance, the friendliness of its inhabitants.

A proof of the virtues of the general public of Calcutta can be found in the very respect, the admiration, the devotion even, shown to Mother for her admirable work, and in the help and collaboration she has received from every class of society, every official, and most organizations, whatever their political affiliation. Calcutta is justly proud of the Missionaries of Charity; Mother Teresa is truly the city's most beloved citizen.

CLEARING UP MISUNDERSTANDINGS

Of course, there have been misgivings and misunderstandings, which the media several times helped to clear up or dispel.

After Oslo and the Nobel Peace Prize ceremony, Mother remarked, "It was not all approval; there were some dissenting voices, in India, in the press." Some, yes; not many nor very powerful voices. That must be expected, if we are to enact the gospel fully, live according to its teachings and warnings and be similar to Jesus who suffered criticism for the good he had done.

Again at Benares, the media were called on to make the aim of the Missionaries of Charity clear. At the request of Bishop Patrick D'Souza, Mother took ten of her sisters who were to make their final profession to that city. These Hindi-speaking brides of Christ, in an open-air ceremony attended by a large crowd, with journalists and photographers present, made their final profession during the celebration of the Eucharistic Sacrifice. Meanwhile a commentator explained to the largely non-Christian audience the meaning of the vows.

There had been opposition to the work and even the presence of the sisters in the holy city of the Hindus, the chosen place for a pious death. To have one's corpse or ashes thrown into the holy Ganges for many pious Hindus means purification from the accumulated sins of previous existences and release of the soul from bondage.

Thus crowds of old, sickly people, including beggars, come from distant places to die in the holy city. This caused trouble to the sisters, who had started a home for the sick and dying destitute. Reports and complaints reached the police that a considerable number of people died in the home. Were the sisters killing them? How did they look after their wards? What treatment did they give to the sick or old people? The police came to inquire, to check numbers and conditions in the home. They were soon convinced that the sisters were not responsible for the high mortality rate. It remained that the sisters' reputation had to be established on a strong basis. Hence the public ceremony of the vows; the press proved very helpful as it publicized the sisters' ideals, dedication, and work.

IN THE WAKE OF THE NOBEL PRIZE

After Oslo, Mother was besieged with invitations to civic receptions in various parts of the country. Reporters and photographers requested interviews to be published in papers and magazines of many countries. Television crews came to film her and her activities. All this took so much of her time that she had to fix a limit to such engagements. "In March," she said, "it must end; I must go back to my work, see my sisters, visit houses, plan new foundations." This was easier said than done.

In March, another Japanese television crew appeared on the scene. They were sent to take a half-hour film depicting Mother and her sisters' work of love. Mother said, "No, sorry; this is all over. It has lasted long enough. No more glamor and publicity. We go back to our humble and simple life of service." But the Japanese friends appealed to Fr. C. Van Exem, who saw the tremendous good that could result from this film being shown all over Japan. He prevailed on Mother to collaborate with them and push back her deadline once more.

As they started work, they first directed their lenses on the heroine, that little woman of indomitable energy. Then they turned to her work, to the pictures of slum children, of lepers, of dying people stretching out their emaciated hands, trying to grasp something solid, their protruding eyes throwing a last, pathetic flicker of life.

The aim, the doctrine, the teaching, the rationale of the pictures interested much less. Only those people accustomed to reflect on the meaning of life, of death, of God, of religion, would inquire about them and listen to the lesson.

But, especially after the Nobel Peace Prize, the news and picture magazines proved very useful in making Mother's ideas and ideals known. Reporters from many countries arrived, descending on Calcutta in droves. Television crews, radio and magazine reporters came to cover the story. Some time later, in Paris, in other world capitals, Mother Teresa's picture was on the cover of the big sales magazines. This meant a readership of many millions.

A French journalist in Calcutta, gathering material for his report, on being asked, "How many people in France and Belgium know Mother Teresa and her work?" answered, "I would say that one person in three have heard about her."

In July 1980, *Life* published a sensitive, moving article inspired by the diary of Mary Ellen Mark, illustrated with beautiful pictures. It would be read by a couple of million educated persons.

Cassettes have been produced, giving Mother's addresses at congresses, university convocations, public meetings. They convey her enthusiasm, her vision of faith, her belief in God's love and in the essential goodness of humanity. They echo and spread her clarion call for self-denial, charity, sharing, and brotherly love, especially toward the most needy among us. She comes out more forcefully when heard than when read, when seen than when imagined. The picture accompanied by the voice strikes harder. Hence the success of the film, and of the film strip accompanied by a commentary in her own voice.

Television and the press have made Mother Teresa a world figure and announcer of the good news that God loves the world more than we can imagine. Our thanks go to them.

CHAPTER 21

The Energizer

You will be the crown of which we are proudest in the presence of
our Lord Jesus when he comes: you are our pride and our joy.
(1 THESS. 2:19–20)

It seems paradoxical that Mother Teresa, who was called and set out to
work among the poorest of the poor to bring them Christ, has had
probably a greater, and certainly a more widespread influence on the
educated and on people of independent means than on the very poor.
She came into direct contact with a small number of the very poor, but
spoke to and influenced a very large number of well-to-do people.

Mother never addressed large groups of poor slum dwellers, of down-
and-outs, of unemployed without social security, of people living from
hand to mouth, not knowing where their next meal would come from, or
whether it would come at all, though she did move among these people
and comfort them.

But she spoke to large audiences during the international Eucharistic
Congresses, at meetings, civic receptions organized in her honor, and on
the occasion of the opening of new houses. The media have helped to
spread her influence far and wide, mostly among the educated, the middle and upper classes.

The very poor do not read magazines and reviews; but tens of millions
of educated people read Mother's appeals in favor of the poor and were
impressed by her action, while many wished they could also do something
to help those in need.

The very poor do not listen at night to the radio news, do not watch
the television programs, since they possess neither radio nor television
sets. But hundreds of millions saw Mother on television shows, listened
to her speeches, admired her example and reflected on her mission of
bringing God's love to the world of today. As a result many were moved
to make a contribution to the well-being of the underprivileged.

At Cambridge, Mother spoke to fifteen hundred of the nation's best
professors and students, future leaders of their country. At various convocations in the United States, she spoke to tens of thousands of college
students. In Tokyo, she addressed priests and nuns, teachers, thousands

of students, and schoolchildren massed in the Catholic cathedral, and appeared several times on television. Again her influence affected mainly the better-educated section of the country's people. She brought home to them the sorrowful plight of the alcoholics, the drug addicts, of children saddened by the breaking up of their parents marriage, and of the unborn child.

The Nobel Peace Prize sparked off a series of scintillating articles in magazines in most of the world's capital cities, meaning millions of copies and still more readers. Some forty books have been written dealing with Mother's work and person, translated into scores of languages. Who reads all this material? Who listens to the cassettes diffusing her speeches? Who watches the pictures shown in schools and parish clubs? Mostly people of comfortable means in the rich countries.

ORGANIZING THE POOR

Common action organized among the poor has been on a limited scale. In India and the developing countries of Asia and Africa, most of the beneficiaries of the sisters' direct work are below the stage of self-help. They are the utterly poor, often on the verge of starvation, the permanently undernourished, unable to rise, to organize themselves, even to cooperate with any plan of uplift. For them, the main problem is to exist, to ward off hunger, sickness, and death, to continue to live; in this struggle many succeed fairly well, doggedly pulling on somehow, somewhere.

In the Latin American countries, there is better hope for corporate action, because the poverty is not so intense, so deadly, so crushing, so exhausting. There poor people may be seen wearing shoes, shoes of sorts, and have a change of clothes. There the sisters do try to and at times succeed in achieving that the poor contribute to their uplift, as a group. In places where the poor are not starving, but may lack a practical ideal and stimulation to improve, the sisters report, as they do from Panama, some comforting news, and that not very long after their opening a new house in the place.

The archbishop of Panama had come to Calcutta to plead his case before Mother. He wanted the sisters for his people, who numbered a million, of whom 700,000 were Catholics. They were not in any great, desperate poverty. Many were poorer spiritually than materially, for lack of an adequate number of priests and nuns to care for them and move among the poorer section.

Mother sent her sisters. Soon they could write, "We have organized the people to build two churches." This is wonderful. The people themselves have been energized, brought to action, made to work for their uplift. They feel respectable, useful, united. And Mother may be happy: thanks to the initiative of the sisters there are two more tabernacles, two more centers from where Jesus will radiate, console, inspire, bring love to the poor of the city.

The sisters reach a good number of the very poor, especially through their homes for the dying, their dispensaries and their work for the lepers. Mother influences them indirectly and through the people she has trained and organized. Her time has to be increasingly devoted to directing her society, training her nuns for their work, starting new foundations and providing for their needs.

Mother never loses sight of her main duty, but does much for the poor by influencing public opinion, meeting leaders of countries, the people who have knowledge, means, and consequently power.

THE MISSIONARIES OF CHARITY

Mother's best and most powerful means to spread her ideal, fulfil her God-given mission, and realize her personal aim, is to be found in her congregation of the Missionaries of Charity. They number about two thousand sisters—including the novices—and increase by some two hundred members yearly. They work in some two hundred fifty houses spread in the six continents, and the foundations increase by twenty-five a year in the 1980s.

What the foundress obtains from her nuns is hardly believable and totally unrelated to their human gifts, talents, and powers. But then they are supported by an army of Sick and Suffering people who offer for their apostolate their prayers and pains, and helped by a large contingent of Co-Workers and friends devoted to the same ideal. Thus the sisters can act as powerful multipliers, stimulating by their example, inciting and inviting to generosity those people they approach.

THE SISTERS AS ENERGIZERS

Every house of the Missionaries of Charity stands as an invitation to give, to contribute to the work of charity, to share with our less fortunate brethren.

The sisters serve as a catalytic agent affecting the moral life of many around them. They provide opportunities for good deeds by the affluent and well-to-do, who often look for an outlet for their generosity or await to be prompted, goaded, encouraged to act in favor of the needy, or who simply require to be organized in a practical way. "What can we do?" many ask today, as they did in the days of John the Baptist. His answer still rings in our ears: "If you have two coats, give one to the man without any."

The sisters insert themselves into a community without difficulty, because they move about daily, are seen on the roads, taking street cars, buses, with a bag in their hand, carrying food or medicines, ready to give.

They enter houses, inquire about people and their needs. Then the poor are seen knocking or ringing bells at their doors; often queues are formed of hungry folk waiting for rations or other help.

Since they possess nothing, all they give must first be a gift to them. Those who possess generously come forward, happy to help, to be useful, to raise themselves above the small cares and contingencies of their daily life.

With each new house, the sisters are inserted into a part of the world they come to serve. They are inserted by God, since they are sent by him, to be, under his authority, an extension of the incarnation. Christ, through them, becomes present in new localities, making his presence felt and acting through his instruments. Thus the supernatural process of the Incarnation continues.

But to serve a community well the sisters must also integrate themselves into it. They must learn at first hand the material and spiritual needs of the people to whose salvation and sanctification they are to contribute, working with and under the divine impulse. They seek to discover how God's grace works in these concrete circumstances, what human response to it is, and what they themselves can do to contribute to the work of grace. They repeat Mother's words, "What are the needs? The more pressing needs? The essential things to be provided first of all? What are the remedies we can offer?"

The sisters also become part of the larger local community. They help to bring together its constituent elements, persons, families, social groups. They are to be a link of love, bringing the more comfortable into contact with the poor and needy. They form a chain of links of love, links as those forming the rosary they carry and pray, links of prayer and good works.

The result for the community should be a small degree of sharing of material resources through sacrifices and gifts. But mainly there will be respect and understanding for one another, sympathy and openness of heart. These virtues will influence also family relations, since good of its very nature tends to spread.

The good action by being repeated becomes a habit; the habit affects the character, improves it, brightens it. The more affluent will spend less on themselves, as conscience reminds them that close by some men and women lack the bare essentials of life.

Every house of the Missionaries of Charity is called to be, and generally is an oasis of love, irradiating the light of Christ shining through it.

THE BROTHERS AS ENERGIZERS

The Missionary Brothers of Charity are another result of Mother's zeal and initiative for the glory of God. Since they have their own identity as a religious congregation, the sisters' constitutions merely record the fact that "The male branch known as the Missionary Brothers of Charity was also founded by Mother Teresa in March 1963" (Introduction, page 4).

From the start Mother aimed high: to direct and train the first candidates to the brotherhood, she thought of the Jesuit provincial of Calcutta, Father Robert Antoine. She talked over the idea with him and won him over to the project. "We both wrote independently to father general of the society in Rome, to ask his permission," recalled Father Antoine. "But the general refused, saying that I had been prepared for another work."

Father Antoine, a scholarly person, became head of the department of comparative literature at Jadavpur University, Calcutta. He translated the tragedies of Sophocles and Aeschylus into Bengali, thereby manifesting another aspect of the church's activity, her contribution to human culture and understanding. He did come to help Mother Teresa as chaplain of the home for the dying at Kalighat.

The good God came to Mother's help, as usual, and soon after sent her another Jesuit priest, Fr. Andrew Travers-Ball. An Australian missionary, he volunteered to transfer his allegiance; he was immediately allowed to help Mother establish the brothers' wing. Under his direction, the brothers were established as a separate congregation, and their constitutions were approved. Young men joined the new institute in large numbers.

The brothers soon spread to other countries; first they went to Vietnam and Campuchea, which was still Cambodia. From both countries they were forced to withdraw with the advent of communist governments.

Then Brother Andrew took some brothers to Los Angeles and opened another novitiate there. Later the brothers went to Hong Kong, Korea, Japan, Macao, Taiwan, Guatemala, Mexico, France, Madagascar—and the list of new foundations is far from ended.

As the numbers of the sisters and the brothers went on increasing, one day they reached the parting of the ways. Like Abraham the patriarch and his nephew Lot, Mother Teresa and Brother Andrew agreed to separate in a friendly spirit and go on developing according to their own inspiration (see Gen. 13:12). Of course, some connection between them remained, especially in India, where Mother's name and fame, credit and influence are an asset the brothers may well use. As one of them declared, "when we go to work at the Howarth Station, if we are challenged by the railway police, asking us, 'what are you doing here?' we answer, 'We are Mother Teresa's brothers.' Immediately all opposition melts like butter in the sun."

The brothers may expect to become a congregation of pontifical right as soon as they have a sufficient number of finally professed members and fulfil the other required conditions. They deserve a study of their own, embracing their character, spirit, methods, activities, prospects. It remains that the credit for their existence belongs to Mother Teresa, who, under God's guidance and protection, planted and nurtured this sapling, which now transplanted, can be considered as an offshoot of the parent tree. May it continue to grow and prosper to God's glory.

The brothers have taken over some works started by Mother and her sisters, for which men are better equipped. They now manage the large leprosy center for men started by Mother Teresa, one of the works she has most at heart. Situated at Titaghar, in the industrial belt of Calcutta, the center has a 115-bed hospital for bad cases of leprosy. It is looked after by ten brothers and some lay helpers. Attached to this center is a rehabilitation and employment organization benefiting about a thousand people, thus helping the lepers support themselves through productive work. About seventeen thousand people afflicted with the disease, but living at home, come once a week to receive their medicines and a checkup at different mobile centers situated in the region. Thus, fifteen brothers organize and activate a movement benefiting eighteen thousand sufferers. At the same time, the center helps to prevent the extension of the disease among many families having one or several members affected by leprosy.

The multiplier factor is seen at work: Mother Teresa started a good work with a small team of religious; a few dozen people devote themselves heart and soul to it; hundreds of friends contribute the needed resources in medicines and money; and twenty thousand sick people are helped. Again we see how love shows initiative, love unites, love spreads, love overcomes, love purifies, love dignifies, love saves, love brings happiness.

If such a system and organization can spread over those areas where leprosy is rife, it might be possible to eradicate the disease within one or two generations. Yet, sad to say, the incidence of the disease in the country has not yet declined. The director of health services of the government of India, in his report for 1981, stated that in spite of an extensive use of antileprosy drugs and a good infrastructure of distribution centers, statistics of new cases showed that the incidence of the disease was not on the wane.

This seems to prove that drugs alone and their administration do not suffice. General living conditions need to be improved, especially as regards cleanliness and eating habits.

Mother Teresa remains deeply interested in the Titaghar work she started with her sisters; she bears most of the burden of the heavy monthly expenses incurred, with alms she receives. She also goes to visit the center to meet the patients and encourage the brothers in their noble work, performed entirely for Jesus.

CHAPTER 22

The God-Seekers

Taste and see how good the Lord is, Happy the one who takes shelter in him.

(PS. 34:8)

Mother dreamed of developing still another dimension of love, pure love of God, a life dedicated to the contemplation of of the divine Majesty. Those entering it would consecrate themselves to attend only on God, seek his face, center all their activities on him, harbor only his thought.

She knew that God wants some men and women to be all intent on his service, completely detached from the cares and distractions of the world: people who shoot arrows straight at the sun of justice, and never see them return to earth, for God attracts them to himself. She knew also the power of intercession of those consecrated to the contemplative life, a power the world may not always recognize and esteem at its true value.

On one occasion during her first years in the new institute, she had gone to a municipal office to obtain exemption from some taxes. She applied for her own institute and also for the Discalced Carmelite nuns, who being cloistered, could not go out and needed to be represented.

The official answered, "Of course for the Missionaries of Charity there is no difficulty, since you work entirely for the poor. As for the Carmelites, I do not see what they do for society."

"What," exclaimed Mother, "but I can do nothing without them; they are essential to my work; it is they who obtain for me the help I need for heaven. They devote their whole life to prayer for the needs of men." What she said, she meant.

Then one day Mother thought of starting her own powerhouse, to support and strengthen her sisters working in the slums, among the lepers, the destitute, the dying, the abandoned. She would establish a contemplative congregation with a modern bent, having a window open on the world. They would be linked to the poorest of the poor by their style of life, and would go out two or three hours a day to speak to them of the God who loves them. They would bring them hope, give them a purpose in life, and kindle the fire of faith in their souls.

"On the sixteenth of June, I must be in New York to open our new house for the new institute; that will be a great day," said Mother. "We are launching the contemplative wing: the Sisters of the Word. I wish I could join them. I have always wanted to be a contemplative. Be with Jesus the whole day, think only of him, speak only of him. The sisters are to go out to speak of Jesus to whomever is ready to hear."

On 25 June 1976, in the Bronx, New York, Mother inaugurated the Sisters of the Word, a sister congregation to her Missionaries of Charity. Mother had chosen a name inspiring and also intriguing: the Sisters of the Word.

The Word: did the name indicate their function? or their nature? Were they to be the hearlds, the carriers, the transmitters, the sharers of the Word God spoke in time to people to enlighten them, guide them, sustain them, console them during their pilgrimage, often arduous, towards their heavenly home, to the bliss their Father had prepared for them? Or did it remind them of their nature, their dignity and happiness as the sisters of the infinite Word the Father speaks from all eternity, his perfect image, his most beloved Son? Then, they were the Father's daughters, in his Son, with him and through him the Incarnate Word's sisters—reserved to his service, chosen and consecrated to his Son by the Father himself. Their contemplation then found its inspiration and inception in their very title, which plunged them straight into the primeval mystery of God's secret being.

This was the revelation of the New Testament, the priceless knowledge Christ brought us; he made known the richness and splendor of God's being, the trinity of persons sharing perfectly the divine Essence in an act of boundless love, image of the love we ought to have for one another. That love the sisters would derive from their contemplation of the God-head, beginning from the prologue of St. John's Gospel, that flash of light thrown on God's mysterious life: "In the beginning the Word was and the Word was with God—" Yes, the Father had the Word abiding with him, substance of his substance, light of his light, true God of true God, with him perfect happiness.

The Sisters of the Word were launched into the contemplation of the divine mystery. They had taken off as they pronounced their name, with closed eyes, in deep silence, all centered on the Father's beloved Son, to whom they belonged, who lived in them. The Sisters of the Word had only to follow this source of their contemplation, and allow the Spirit to raise them as high as he wished.

This new branch Mother Teresa had started in the New Continent and not in India, the country of her adoption, of her sufferings and glory, her Jerusalem. What motivated her choice? One day, she was asked, "Mother, why did you start that new institute in the United States and not in India, where most of your sisters dwell and work, where you are well known and have a much stronger basis than in the United States?"

"Because," she answered, "in the United States they are ready for it. In India they are not. In the United States the time is ripe."

Mother is perceptive for God's action in the world. She senses the movements of grace, the way the Holy Spirit leads souls. "In the United States," she explains, "you have a very rich society, becoming increasingly materialistic and permissive. But there is also a strong religious current, a desire for realizing God; thousands of young people come to the East in search of some sort of illumination and religious experience. They join neo-Hindu and Buddhist groups. In the United States, Eastern religious establish flourishing centers of prayer and meditation. The genuine Catholic spirit of contemplation, a quiet, humble, silent search for God, in poverty and self-denial, should attract many led by the Spirit."

Then Mother thinks that in the modern world, anxious to share, to give, to spread the good news, those who have found Jesus and discovered the love of the Lord, may wish to have an outlet for their pent-up zeal. Let them bring the message to others who may share their fellowship and happiness.

"I always wanted to be a contemplative," Mother added, "just to be with Jesus, to think of God only."

"Yes, that would be wonderful, Mother. But yours is an active temperament, calling you to action; it is clear the God wants you here."

"I may one day retire there to pray," said Mother, with insistence.

St. Paul had expressed the tearing asunder of all souls passionately in love with their Lord, when he exclaimed, "I wish I could die and be with Christ. But then for your good I must live, and so my soul is torn apart" (Phil. 1:23–24). The soul craves to be busy only with her Lord, to entertain him, attend to him, sit at his feet with Mary of Bethany, shedding all cares and worries. But then the Lord's glory may require that the lover remain at work in a distracting world.

"Sister Nirmala is in charge of the contemplative," said Mother. "She will train them well."

To start this new wing of her congregation, Mother needed a gifted leader and teacher, pioneer and organizer. She herself would hardly be able to visit the new foundation two or three times a year, for a few days. Her charism and personality could operate only from afar; the spirit had to be carried through an intermediary whom she had herself formed.

Sister Nirmala's family tree was rooted in Nepal, in the Himalayas, a region where live many Hindu and Buddhist ascetics and seekers for God. Her father, an army officer, had sent his two daughters to study at the Patna women's college, run by the Apostolic Carmel nuns. There, Sister Nirmala heard of Mother Teresa and her work and decided to join her. Both she and her sister became Catholics. She joined the Missionaries of Charity, while her sister entered the Apostolic Carmel convent. Sister Nirmala was first trained for the active apostolate: seeking and discovering the poor and needy, looking after aching bodies and souls, the sick, the dying, the abandoned.

In the contemplative life, she now had to devote her energies to the pursuit of God, not in the slums, in the bustle and noise of cities, in overcrowded lanes or on pavements, but in silence and solitude. She would pass hours on her knees, the senses subdued, the attention fixed, quiet, receptive, on the infinite God.

She was to train young recruits leaving the world for the hard life of contemplation. Would they accept her, see in her an expert? Would the teacher not be like a hen hatching duck's eggs: would the ducklings emerging from the shell recognize her as their spiritual mother and guide?

Though mainly given to contemplation, the sisters would go out in search of souls in need and pour out the burning lava of their pent-up love for God. They would be a beam of light seeking souls in darkness, seeking those who did not dare expect them, helping those who felt the need of them. They would be like a touring service car on call, to help people stranded or fallen by the roadside to rise up and start life again.

After her return from the United States in 1977, Mother one day dropped, in a matter-of-fact way, a bombshell. "There are no more Sisters of the Word. There are only Missionaries of Charity comprising two wings: one active, one contemplative. We are one religious institute, with the possibility of moving from one branch to the other. A sister of the active wing may go over to the contemplatives and vice versa. The revised constitutions will settle this matter."

Now the name had perished. The contemplatives were no more a separate entity, struggling to develop on their own. They were back in the fold of the Missionaries of Charity to whom they owed their inception, their characteristic mini-apostolate, their dress and way of life. They would profit by the strength and success of the whole congregation.

Why had Mother decided to incorporate them into the parent body so swiftly? Did she feel impatient at the slow beginnings? Had she expected a flood of applications rather than this repetition of the first arduous steps in the Upper Room, when after several months of struggles, she could write—proudly in those days—"now we are three" then "now we are five," and several months later "now we are seven and we expect one more." Perhaps a founder can go through those slow pangs of giving birth to a congregation only once. At sixty-five you must go faster than at forty: the end approaches too fast, there is no time to lose.

Or perhaps the foundress saw the difficulties in the way of being the superior general of two difficult religious congregations. What would Rome say? And was it practical? Yet the contemplatives were her off-spring. Only her authority, name, and prestige gave them a chance to succeed, at a time when vocations to contemplative institutes had become scarce.

Whatever the determining factor, the result was clear: the contempla-tives were back into the fold. Optimism generally prevailed. The two branches, lending support to each other, would be a mutual source of strength, inspiration, and spiritual enrichment.

Sister Nirmala issued in New York the single sheet of information serving as prospectus for candidates. Mother's ideals and thoughts formed the framework of this announcement, which made the essential features of the new branch clear as it said,

Missionaries of Charity Contemplatives adopt a contemplative religious life based purely on the gospel and in keeping with the best traditions of the church, with deep personal and liturgical prayer, eucharistic adoration, silence, solitude, penance and a closely knit community of love, a life marked by the simplicity, joy, and freedom of the gospel, fully open to all that is beautiful and sacred in the social, cultural, and spiritual heritage of the people among whom they are.

Their aim is to quench the infinite thirst of Jesus Christ for love by the profession of the evangelical counsels and the wholehearted free service to the poorest of the poor, according to the teaching and the life of our Lord in the gospel, revealing in a unique way the kingdom of God.

Their special mission is to labor at the salvation and sanctification of the poorest of the poor by living the love of God in eucharistic adoration, contemplation, silence, solitude, and penance in a life marked by the simplicity and humility of the gospel, bringing the love of God to the spiritually poorest of the poor, by going out to them for at most two to three hours a day and proclaiming the good news by our presence and spiritual works of mercy.

The contemplatives run no institutions for the proclamation of the love of God. They avail themselves of every opportunity they can have to proclaim God's love anywhere and everywhere wherever they can find the poorest of the poor.

They do not deal with crowds but with individuals, person to person, or family to family, or when necessary, very small groups of three or four where close personal contact is not possible.

Thus the sisters were called upon to share the light, the strength, the joy they derived from their contemplation of the divine mysteries. It reminded one of the ideals of St. Dominic, who wanted his monks to *"contemplata aliis tradere,"* namely bring to others the fruit of their contemplation. The sisters were to go out and share with the poor the incomparable riches they had gathered in their prayer and attention to God.

They would actuate today the words of Peter and John to the lame beggar, waiting hopefully for alms, "Gold and silver we do not possess, but what we have we give you, 'look at us—in the name of Jesus of Nazareth, get up and walk' (Acts 3:4–6) that you may believe in him who came from heaven that we may receive eternal life." They would give not what the man was asking for, not what he expected, but a better gift, imperishable spiritual life.

The sisters were to be like bees, toiling the whole morning, gathering the sweet drops of divine knowledge, and then distilling spiritual honey to the poor without money to buy it.

Like Moses, they would stand before God, listening to his instruction. They would also beseech him, "Show me your face; let me have a glimpse of your glory." Like the prophet, they would ascend on mount Sinai, and at times come down with a glow of light on their forehead, for God manifests himself to those who crave him, who crave only him.

With Peter, James, and John they would be present on Mount Tabor, and see their Lord in his glory, so that later they might convey the message as eyewitnesses: "What we have seen, heard, touched with our inner senses of the Word of life, that we make known to you, so that you may share our joy and your joy may be complete" (see John 1: 1–4).

With whom did Mother wish them to share their spiritual treasures? Mother's main preoccupation, her first intuition, remained ever present as a guideline: they would seek the poorest of the poor.

The latter's solitude, dereliction, sadness, they also knew, for like all contemplatives they had passed hours with their Lord crushed by the sins of humanity by sadness, fear, and disgust, as he anticipated the way the world would treat him. They could tell the poor the only effective word of consolation, "Our Lord went through it, he suffered as you do. Unite your troubles to his sufferings; accept and offer with him for the salvation of humanity."

Having shared with their Lord his agony, his sadness when he was abandoned by all his disciples, the opposition of the wicked, the pains of body and soul he suffered, they could pour balm on the souls of their suffering brothers and sisters.

Not only would the sisters go out to meet the poor, they would also invite them to come where they live. "The poorest of the poor of all castes and creeds are welcome to our place, to come and make reparation and renew their lives, by deepening their knowledge and love of God, of themselves and of their neighbor in the light of the Word of God, in deep silence, prayer and penance."

The three characteristics of the Missionaries of Charity are to be reproduced in the contemplative branch: "The spirit of this society is one of total surrender, loving trust and cheerfulness as lived by Jesus and his mother in the gospel."

Aspirants should possess an absolute desire of giving themselves totally to God and living for him alone and for his kingdom, no matter what it may cost them. Also a strong desire and capacity for contemplation, silence, solitude, and a life of penance.

"They should desire to live, pray, and serve the poor according to the constitutions of the Missionaries of Charity; be healthy in body and mind, able to bear the hardships of this special vocation, be able to acquire knowledge, enjoy a cheerful disposition, and have plenty of common sense.

"They should have completed high school and possess some natural or acquired talents or training, and be not less than twenty-one years of age."

It devolves on the superior to find out if the candidate possesses at first view the qualities required to make a contemplative. She knows that the person who knocks at the door of a monastery and says, "I want to find God" has the first sign of a contemplative. And if told, "It will be a long, hard, exacting process," answers, "I shall labor and pay whatever price he wants to find him," that person has the second sign of a contemplative in the making.

No vocation proves more demanding than that of a contemplative. But here, as also happens in other callings, some are truly "naturals," who find themselves at home in their search for God from the first day.

Their longing for God as an habitual attitude finds its perfect expression in the inspired words of David, king and prophet, when he was staying in the wilderness of Judah:

> God, you are my God, I am seeking you;
> my soul is thirsting for you,
> my flesh is longing for you,
> a land parched, weary and waterless.
> I long to gaze on you in the sanctuary,
> and to see your power and glory.
> Your love is better than life itself;
> my lips will recite your praise,
> all my life I will bless you.
>
> (Ps. 63: 1–4)

Sister Nirmala writes, "Missionaries of Charity (contemplative) has naturally grown in our society as a need and as a fruit of the union of the Missionaries of Charity with the Lord. It ultimately came into being on the feast of the Sacred Heart of Jesus, 25 June 1976, in New York, as God's special gift to the people of the United States and the world, as a love memorial of the forty-first Eucharistic Congress in Philadelphia in the bicentennial year of America."

Sister Nirmala then describes their day:

"Our day begins at 4:30 A.M. and ends at 10 P.M. Besides the divine office we spend two hours in meditation and two hours in eucharistic adoration daily. Once a week we have eucharistic adoration from 11 P.M. to 12. Two hours a day we go out to the poorest of the poor proclaiming God's love. We have strict silence throughout the day, excepting at lunch, supper and half an hour after supper. We have extra recreation on Sundays, Thursdays, and feast days. One hour of our eucharistic adoration is done in the parish church daily, to enable anyone whoever wishes to take part in it.

"People are welcome in our chapel also."

The old Desert Fathers would probably have judged this way of life sufficiently austere—and the monks of Mount Athos also.

For their life of contemplation and penance, the sisters would find an example to imitate in the West Asian monk Charbel Makluf, recently canonized by the pope.

Sister Nirmala writes, "*We Do It for Jesus: Mother Teresa and her Missionaries of Charity* is the book I like best among all the books written about our Mother, as it is the closest to the reality and is also so human. Another thing that makes me and my community here like it specially is that we are going through the same experience of the hard beginnings. It is so wonderful to see how history repeats itself. The book has been a real inspiration to each one of us and strengthened the sisters here in the spirit of our Mother."

Of course they are going through the same labor pangs as the active branch went through, thirty years earlier. As contemplatives, they must expect to undergo more trials, pass through a deeper and longer experience of the dark night, and be less consoled and stimulated by visible success and rapid expansion. Those are the realities of the life of contemplation, all centered on God, in union with the Passion of Christ. But the pure light of glory will also shine brightly at times, as the Spirit fills them with the knowledge and love of God.

On her return to Calcutta in September 1981, Mother was happy to announce, "We started many houses—already twenty-three this year; only two more are needed for a Golden Jubilee of Jesus. Among the new houses, there are two in Washington, D.C., one active, one contemplative." So now they were two. When would they be ten?

THE CONTEMPLATIVE BROTHERS

Not satisfied with the care and direction of her two branches for women religious, Mother still found time to exert herself to organize a congregation of contemplative brothers.

At Lippstadt she had mentioned the possibility of their coming into existence in hopeful words. Later she reported that the scheme was progressing. There were candidates for the congregation-to-be. "In Rome," said Mother, "Sister Frederick is organizing them."

Keen as she was on getting the contemplative branch of the brothers started, Mother could not devote very much time to this project. This congregation, like every serious religious work, proved difficult to start. It had the support of Mother's prayers, of her name and prestige, of her influence in higher religious circles. But she also required an able religious to help her in this task. As the Lord had sent her Father Travers-Ball, with his training, experience, and zeal, to launch the active branch of the brothers, so now she needed a similar person to pilot the contemplative branch of the brothers.

They also needed a house, a superior, an experienced master of novices to train them in the difficult art of contemplation, rules, a regular prayer life, a clear aim and order of the day. They had also to be recognized and approved by the Roman Congregation for Religious.

On 14 June 1978, Mother broke the news that Brother Sebastian, a priest from South India who had joined the Missionary Brothers of Charity, had been master of novices in Calcutta and in Los Angeles, had now come to Rome to train the novices of the Brothers of the Word. "The contemplative Brothers will be called 'Brothers of the Word,' " said Mother. "They are seven candidates. They are very keen." And so, the beautiful name, so inspiring, had been salvaged and given to the contemplative brothers.

Later Mother declared that for technical reasons, the new group had not been accepted by Rome as a religious congregation; they had obtained the status of a "pious institute."

In 1978, a decree from Rome erected the contemplative brothers pious union under the name: The Missionaries of the Word.

Its aim: to quench the infinite thirst of Jesus Christ on the cross for the love of souls by the profession of the evangelical counsels and by wholehearted and free service of the poorest of the poor.

Its special mission: to labor at the salvation and sanctification of the poorest of the poor of the whole world.

Both the aim and the mission are exactly what Mother Teresa wrote in the constitutions of her sisters.

The means to accomplish the aim will be

—To live the Word of God in a life marked by poverty, humility, joy and the freedom of the gospel—To love and adore Jesus in the Blessed Eucharist—To love and serve Jesus in the distressing disguise of the poorest of the poor.

The brothers will have daily eucharistic adoration during two hours, contemplation, sacramental and liturgical life.

They will also go out to seek the spiritually poorest of the poor daily during two or three hours, to proclaim to them the Word of God.

The spirit of the members will be one of total surrender, loving trust and cheerfulness as lived by Jesus and Mary in the gospel.

The prospectus advertising the new pious union states "Our founder is Mother Teresa of Calcutta. With gratitude and appreciation we look up to her for guidance and inspiration."

The Missionaries of the word can report that their apostolic ministry bears good fruit as they go to visit and comfort people spiritually in distress and bring them back to God and to the sacraments. They go to pray and have weekly adoration of the Blessed Eucharist with the inmates of a night shelter close to the Statione del Termini, and also with the prisoners of a Roman jail. Truly their life of prayer and sacrifice brings them grace, courage, and initiative for their work among the spiritually poorest of the poor, to the glory of the Lord Jesus.

CHAPTER 23

Joy in Suffering

It makes me happy to suffer for you, as I am suffering now, and in
my own body to do what I can to make up what is still lacking from
the sufferings of Christ for the sake of his body, the Church. (COL.
1:24)

"I was consoling a little girl who was sick and had much pain," said
Mother. "I told her, "You should be happy that God sends you suffering,
because your sufferings are a proof that God loves you much. Your
sufferings are kisses from Jesus." 'Then, Mother,' answered the little girl,
'please ask Jesus not to kiss me so much.'"

This was very beautiful that the child did not say, "Please ask Jesus to
stop kissing me" but merely "Ask him not to kiss me so much." Even very
courageous adults are heard to say at times, "Lord, please do not afflict
me too much; this is about all I can bear."

Mother is truly entitled to give advice on suffering and speak of its
usefulness in spiritual life. She has come close to human suffering all over
the world. She has bent over afflicted people compassionately for more
than thirty years, consoling, encouraging, helping to offer up pains, trials,
and death.

She meditates daily on the sufferings of her master. Daily she accompa-
nies Jesus to Calvary as she makes the stations of the cross, the first thing
in the morning at 4:30 A.M., when the rest of the world still sleeps com-
fortably.

Suffering for the Christian is all at once a gift of God, an occasion of
merit, a means of sanctification, a source of grace, and mainly a link of
love with Jesus.

Its dignity and value is not given to all to understand and appreciate.
It remains always for us a mystery, as do many other elements in God's
plan.

Suffering is a great gift of God:
those who accept it willingly,
those who love deeply,
those who offer themselves
know its value.

Suffering purifies, detaches, elevates, merits, obtains, dignifies, and unites to Jesus. It makes us share in his Passion and therefore in his glory. "With Christian suffering, with Christ in glory," so says St. Ignatius, inviting the chosen person to walk in the Lord's footsteps. And as Christ deserved our forgiveness by his Passion and death, so his disciples and co-workers united to him earn graces for the world.

Suffering is a school of holiness. Suffering makes us overcome our pettiness, our limitations, and provides us with an opportunity to rise to heroism.

Even for the unbeliever, suffering brings gifts, if it be accepted. Albert Camus, the French writer, himself a sufferer from tuberculosis, said, "Illness is a convent, which has its rule, its austerity, its silences, and its inspirations." Yes, it is also a door opening on a passage leading to the spiritual realm.

From the very beginning of her new apostolate to the world's poorest and worst sufferers, Mother wished to enlist the spiritual help of sick and suffering people who would lend the support of their prayers and sacrifices to her sisters. She writes in 1953, "Everyone and anyone who wishes to become a Missionary of Charity—a carrier of God's love—is welcome. But I want especially the paralyzed, the crippled, the incurables to join—for I know they will bring to the feet of Jesus many souls. In our turn—the sisters will each one have a sister who prays, suffers, thinks, writes to her, and so on—a second self. We shall be able to do great things for love of him, because of you."

The sick, the suffering, and handicapped will be welcome to enter into the spirit of the Missionaries of Charity and share their aim, which is purely spiritual, as Mother explains it, relating it to the sacrifice of Christ offered at the mass.

"You see, the aim of our society is to satiate the thirst of Jesus on the cross for love of souls—by working for the salvation and sanctification of the poor in the slums. Who could do this better than you and the others who suffer like you? Your sufferings and prayers will be the chalice in which we the working members all pour in the love of souls we gather round. Therefore you are just as important and necessary for the fulfillment of our aim. To satiate his thirst we must have a chalice—and you and the others, men, women, children, old and young, poor and rich, are all welcome to make the chalice. In reality you can do much more while on your bed of pain, than I running on my feet. But you and I together can do all things in him who strengthens us."

Thus working, praying, and offering together, those in the fields and those in their sickbed or their home, help one another, support and encourage one another. This causes great joy to Mother; in a letter to the sick and suffering she says, "How happy I am to have you all. Often when the work is very hard I think of each one of you, and tell God, 'Look at my suffering children and for their love bless this work,' and it works immediately. So you see you are our treasure house—the power house of the Missionaries of Charity.

"Personally I feel very happy and a new strength has come in my soul, at the thought of you and others joining the society spiritually. Now, with you and others doing the work with us, what would we not do, what can we not do for him? As for you, your life is like a burning light, which is being consumed for souls."

"The Sick and Suffering," remarked Mother one day, "at times write such beautiful letters that they should really be published." In deference to this wish, here are a few choice letters that show the high feelings animating those who offer their trials and pains for the apostolate of the Missionaries of Charity, and also how they themselves benefit by this linking with an apostle working in the field.

Miss G. writes,

To me, sickness did not come as a thief in the night, nor force itself on me as a companion of my youth. Its nature, long unknown, suddenly revealed its ugly face: cancer. The very word makes one shiver.

Scripture tells us that Jacob fought with God during a whole night. I did the same: rebellion surged within me—at times, it still does. Going through hospitals is a harsh schooling. We come last: Number 24. The special cases receive the attention of the professor, the lecture hall, the amphitheater, and everything is explained to them. We, poor mortals, know nothing of what goes on. The day I learned what my disease was, I had to put all things at their right places.

Well, the missionary life has always attracted me. Since I could not marry, my children are Peter, Roger, John—missionary priests. Then I have a daughter of Mother Teresa, Sister J., and a Carmelite convent in Madagascar. All these make me forget the dreadful sickness and make me find joy.

At night, when suffering keeps me awake, I take off to visit my children and my sister, and with them I offer and I pray. I accompany them and remain with them in their classrooms, with their poor people and with their sick. Then, I go to visit my silent Jesus in the quiet Malagasay Carmel chapel. Suffering and prayer go well together.

Am I unhappy? No. I have found joy. I receive my Lord in communion every morning; and at night, I go forward to meet my "children." And so, every day I must smile, always smile to God.

Josette V. writes,

I have just read the book on Mother Teresa of Calcutta, describing how she started her work and her congregation, and my whole being vibrated. I am forty-three years old and suffering since the age of twenty-eight. I underwent ten operations and also some very painful treatments. Hence I had plenty of joy and wealth to share in the love of my beloved Jesus.

I had a very fine situation in Paris, a pleasant life with my family; then with a single stroke the beloved Lord took away everything I had: health, situation, home, wealth. And yet, I was dazzled by love, by material and intellectual poverty.

I discovered a love without limits, craving to share, which fights and weeps over all the distresses of the world.

Now, I act with the means God gives me in favor of those more deprived than myself. Is it not marvelous that I with nothing left to me can offer them hope, my unshakable faith and a boundless love in the simple casket of a generous and warm smile?

But since it is possible to adopt a missionary, it would enrich me to do so, since without being able to move I can fly over there to share his work and hardships, by my love and prayers.

We all suffer, terribly at times, and loneliness weighs heavy if no friendly hand comes to our aid. But what Mother Teresa and her sisters do is a jewel of love, a gift constantly renewed. What abnegation, what fortitude they require to perform a hundred times the same humble services.

We are soldiers of Christ in our way; we bear him with love and gratitude, for our Well-Beloved has offered us the best part: his cross. He helps us to carry it, and mystery of grace and love, his cross carries us. We must remain very small, trustful, in a total surrender to the Father, who loves us so much, while we may delight in tasting the greatness of his love.

The Lord is present in the midst of all our trials. I offer him everything and he gives me a hundredfold in return. He wishes to rest in us and sanctify us beyond expectation.

Marie writes,

To be able to collaborate by my sufferings and prayers with Mother Teresa and all her beloved daughters is a choice blessing for me. And so I say my prayers faithfully; and now to have known my sister through her photo has intensified my prayer life and the offering of all my physical sufferings. All this is for our beloved Lord Jesus. I suffer much physically and often find myself in a spiritual desert. At the same time, I am appalled by my unbearable misery. But God loves me as I am, and I tell him my gratitude for being so completely dependent on him. What matters is to love always and to surrender to God unconditionally.

To be twinned with a missionary in the active apostolate gives the suffering person an aim, a concrete purpose of life, so difficult to find for people habitually bedridden, or unable to move much. Thus Mrs. B. writes to Sister L.:

I am Mrs. B., who has adopted you spiritually. I am sixty-two years old, married, and the mother of two big sons, both married. Since eleven years I suffer from asthenia and must take medicines without interruption. I am unable to do any work. The first years my sickness proved very hard to bear.

I have prayed much and offered everything to God for the conversion of sinners. One day God put into my hands the review *Love Without Boundaries,* in which I read of Mother Teresa's work for the poorest of the poor, and of what all of you do, who follow in her footsteps with such great love and such self-denial for the love of Christ.

I wished to be a soul linked to you—you nursing the very poor while I help you with my mental and physical sufferings. On the seventeenth of May, I underwent an operation and offered everything for the love of God.

Pray that I may be worthy of being your co-worker and that together we may share the same heart and present all our sufferings to Jesus for the salvation of souls.

Dear Sister, since I have adopted you not a day goes by without my praying for you, offering my sufferings for you, not a day when I do not love my own family and my neighbor more, and offer it all for you. How happy you are, living for love in the midst of this materialistic world, that seems to care only for money, pleasure and comfort. Now I do not envy those to whom everything smiles, but feel quite satisfied with what the Lord sends me. I am with you in the love of Jesus.

Yvonne writes,

I was so glad to receive your long letter and to learn about your life of charity. I was interested by all the details of your daily life. It is so beautiful to work for poor people.

I offered my prayers and sufferings for you and your family and hope that heaven has given them peace and love between them.

I have not yet recovered the health that Jesus promised me. I suffer that I cannot do my housework. My old friend is eighty-seven years old, and it is not easy for her to look after the household. Each night I say to God, "I must accept suffering for the poor people of Sister M. and for herself."

Whenever I am better, I go to the woods of Vincennes, near a lovely lake with wonderful vegetation, and I forget all that I cannot do any more, like teaching, going to meetings, attending prayer groups, walking, swimming . . . and I say to myself, "God's will for me is suffering, while it is a life of charity and devotion for Sister M." I pray much, as I very often feel without courage. At times I am tired of suffering—so you must pray for me also, sometimes. With my sincere affection.

By being linked with a worker active in the apostolate and corresponding with him, the sick or suffering person may be helped to overcome the feeling of loneliness or even of uselessness that may assail him. Thus Miss J. D. writes how happy she feels now that she is linked with a missionary sister, active in God's field:

The joy I felt on recieving your letter must have made the good God smile. I am one with all of you, the Co-Workers of Mother Teresa, and discover the great happiness of being united to the apostolate of Sister M. I rejoice at this exchange of loving kindness shuttling between heaven and earth.

Though I suffer, I dare say that this week God gave me his peace, for I know that from my bed I shall be able to quench the thirst of Jesus for souls.

Even the relatives of the sick and suffering come to appreciate the benefits derived from this linking of a sick person with an active worker in the field of the Lord. The husband of a sick person writes to the organizer of the movement,

I owe you a big thank you for having put my wife in contact with Sister S. Through the mail.

My wife who suffers from nervous depressions since 1968, was forced to undergo last April an operation for which she did not feel prepared.

She wrote about it to Sister S. and offered all her sufferings for this sister. At present they correspond regularly, and my wife begins to understand that there is a deep reason for her moral suffering, her loneliness, her anxiety. She accepts better her state. She used to repeat often that she was useless and that it was better for her to die, and thus to deliver her son and her husband from this encumbrance.

Believe me, a complete change has taken place in her. Though she still suffers, and perhaps more than previously, she now knows that she suffers for a person in need of her sufferings and her prayers.

Miss G. writes,

I am a spinster, aged forty-two years, afflicted by several ailments and completely deaf, which is very painful, as it isolates you from others.

I am ready to accept all the inconveniences caused by this deafness, to give up music, lectures, friendships, meetings, spiritual retreats, and sermons so that other souls may not remain deaf to the call of God's grace. I accept this intellectual poverty, and there remains to me to feed my spiritual life only reading. The Lord does manifest himself, but only seldom.

By offering all my trials for a Missionary of Charity, I try not to close myself to the world around me.

From Haiti comes a charming letter:

Dear Brother, your short letter gave me much pleasure. I am seventy-six years old and this is the first time in my life that I receive a letter, for I can neither read nor write. I never attended any school; neither did my parents. But I had very good parents, and I try to walk in their footsteps till the end. I became blind three years ago. I had the good fortune of being admitted in the asylum of Cape Haiti, where we are one hundred and forty-four men and women, nearly all advanced in age.

We live here as in a passage leading to Paradise, all brothers and sisters together. We help one another and encourage each other. We chat, we laugh, we sing many canticles and psalms. We pray much together. The more sturdy among us pray visits to the sick and dying.

Life is still good because there is love and hope and peace. We pray for the Missionaries of Charity and for Mother Teresa, while we admire your devoted service and we are proud to be your brothers. We also thank you for your kind prayers, and assure you of our sincere affection.

Charles F., who had offered the rest of his life for our dear Mother Teresa, has returned to our Motherland. Now we pray to him, for he was already very saintly down here, and Mother Teresa may also pray to him. He was seventy-six years old, crippled and suffering much since the day a heavy wheelbarrow had gone over his back. His life story would read like a novel, in which the trials of all kinds would outnumber the sweet hours. But in this man, toughened and chiseled by suffering, there beat a heart without bitterness. He was an example to all his brothers; with what fervor did he pray for Mother Teresa of Calcutta!

Horatius, ninety years old and blind, is the pride of our choir. With great feeling, he leads us in singing, "On the road of life, be my Light, O Lord." With all his heart he also prays for the brother with whom he is twinned.

Thus the Sick and Suffering in many parts of the world go on offering, loving, earning an attractive bank balance for heaven. Over the years their numbers have increased, keeping pace with the numbers of the Missionaries of Charity, sisters and brothers. In 1982 they were some two thousand seven hundred members, each of them twinned with a Missionary of Charity. The beneficiaries of this twinning may not always suspect the generosity of a sick friend who deserves grace from God for the apostolate of those working in the field.

Mother Teresa's dream during her first months in the Upper Room when she had only a few companions, has been realized. Then she wished that a chain made of links of love should encircle the world as the beads of a rosary. Also the offering by her collaborators of their sufferings would be like the drops of water falling into the chalice at mass, to become part of the wine offered to God, the wine the Holy Spirit changes into the Blood of Christ during the Eucharistic Sacrifice.

Jesus does ask some of his chosen disciples, "Will you agree to suffer so that another can do the work of the apostolate, the work of bringing souls to me?" The answer then comes without hesitation, "Yes, Lord, I will."

CHAPTER 24

The Co-Workers

We, though many, are one body and members of one another, as
Scripture says, for Christ has linked us together with the chains of
love.

(ST. CYRIL OF ALEXANDRIA, *On the Letter to the Romans*)

The U.K. Central Committee meeting of the Co-Workers was taking
place at the Brompton Oratory Parish Hall. Some thirty delegates representing different branches of the United Kingdom were present.

After the prayer, at the very start of the proceedings, the honorary
treasurer, Mr. Davis, put everyone in the right atmosphere of gratitude,
admiration, and generosity, as he said, "I must start by relating an instance that happened to me a few minutes ago. I do not live in London,
so as I reached Waterloo Station, I took a taxi and told the driver, 'Please
rush me to Brompton Oratory, I must be there by ten!'

" 'Well,' said the driver, 'Sir, I am accustomed to rush people to church
on Sundays, but this is the very first time I have ever been asked to rush
someone to church on a Wednesday. Pardon me for saying so.'

"As I did not want to look too holy, I said, 'I am not really going to
church, but to a meeting of a charity.'

" 'May I ask what charity you are attending, Sir?'

" 'Certainly, it is the charity of Mother Teresa and her sisters.'

" 'Well, Sir, if you are going to a meeting of the charity of Mother
Teresa, your fare is on me. Please put it in the collection.'

" 'Thank you very much, I certainly will do so,' I replied. And the fare
amounted to £1.30. I am putting it in the collection.' "

All the audience clapped. Many eyes were moist. This was perfect
charity: an humble man, of limited means, giving to a person he had never
met, to help the poor, without even asking his name to be recorded.

The meeting proceeded in that same spirit. Act after act of generosity
were recorded, acts of love for God and the neighbor, performed by
children and grown-ups, by the poor and the well-to-do, by individuals
and groups. As the delegates representing various geographical units
from all over the United Kingdom rose to speak, with flashes of light and
dashes of humor, the sacrifices of the year were spelled out and summed

up in eloquent figures. Some pearls shone with special brilliance, things that remain in the mind, never to be forgotten.

An Anglican priest narrated how, on an ecumenical pilgrimage to Lourdes, he had offered a big candle to our Lady. Later, an unknown person came to him and said, "You work for Mother Teresa, don't you? Well, here is a check for her charities." The check was for £3,500. When he presented the check to the honorary treasurer, he was told, "Well, we just needed £3,500 to pay the bill for a shipment of food to Mother Teresa. And here you bring me the exact sum."

"Next year," concluded the Anglican priest, "When I go to Lourdes, I shall offer to our Lady a still bigger candle."

A woman reported, in a gentle, matter-of-fact way, the work done by her section. "We went to show a film on Mother Teresa to a Recognized School—one where the judge sends delinquent children," she said. "What kind of offenses have the children committed?" asked someone. "Well, pilferage, and T.A.D., as they call it, that is, *take and drive* a car not belonging to you or your parents. Youngsters of fourteen, even twelve, take a car and drive it away. When caught they are sent to a special or Recognized School. To show and explain the film to those kids proved no easy matter. I thought I was wasting my time: the youngsters just grunted and grinned.

"They did not seem very interested in poor people in India and all that. But some weeks later, I stood speechless for a while, on finding in my mail a letter from the sixty boys of the Recognized School and a check for £75, which they said were the proceeds of a sponsored swim they had organized for Mother Teresa's charities."

A representative of each district of the United Kingdom read the report of their activities. Such meetings were taking place in scores of countries, proving that the Co-Workers of Mother Teresa were a wonderful organization to promote love and generosity.

Most great religious founders started first an order for men, then one for women. Such was the case with Benedict, Francis of Assisi, Dominic, Vincent de Paul, Alphonsus Marie de Liguori, John Bosco, and James Alberione. The notable exception was Ignatius of Loyola, who adamantly refused, as did his successors, to pilot an order of women working with the same aim and spirit as his Society of Jesus. Teresa of Avila and John of the Cross had worked hand in hand to reform the Carmelites. Mother Teresa, in reverse order, started first a congregation for women, then one for men, both working for a similar purpose.

Later, several of these great religious founders, prompted by their zeal for God's kingdom, endeavored to use the huge potential offered by the Christian laity, and organized third orders or similar groups to enlist laypeople in their movement. The third orders of St. Francis, of St. Dominic, of Carmel, spread among the laity the ideals of their founders. They encouraged them to share their spirit of renunciation and holiness, while remaining in the world, in their family and avocation. These associations of laypeople, with or without vows, all aimed at holiness of life.

Mother Teresa's Co-Workers can be seen following the same idea and tradition. Linked with the Missionaries of Charity, they share their aim of serving the poor for the love of God. The members, encouraged to pray for the society and its works, follow its spirit and adopt its aim.

Mother innovates in the sense that she does not limit her Co-Workers to Catholics, but accepts all Christians, other believers in God, and eventually nonbelievers of good faith, who share her love for the poor and for all people.

Jesus said to the large crowd of his followers, and through them to all future generations, "Be holy as your Father in heaven is holy." He did not reserve holiness to a few chosen persons, he invited all to live a holy life. The Co-Workers try in their own way, according to the grace given them, to fulfill this ideal.

The Co-Workers' movement started in an unplanned manner, as a small group of women wishing to help Mother in her work. "First we had patrons, as the organization developed and became known in a small circle. Later we dropped all glamor, all titles," says Ann Blaikie, the first chairperson and organizer of the work in Calcutta. Mother gradually gave them directions as the movement grew according to circumstances, first in India, then among people who had known Mother in India and returned to their countries of origin, where they enrolled their friends.

As the years passed, the Co-Workers numbered ten thousand, then twenty, forty, eighty, one hundred thousand, two, three hundred thousand. The numbers go on increasing daily. Large numbers alone are not the aim. What matters is the spirit the movement introduces, the change it brings in outlook, the interest it helps to acquire in one's immediate neighbors, and in the less fortunate members of society.

The Co-Workers organization has some loose ends, so as to exclude no one of those wishing to be part of it. The Eskimos, the Christmas Islanders, the isolated members of Poland, Hungary, cannot easily attend meetings due to the large distances separating them from other members or groups, or to political factors. Still, they can all live in the Co-Worker spirit.

The movement did evolve, as was to be expected of an organization developing according to the inspiration of the Spirit of God. At first, the members came together with the aim of helping materially the sisters. Prayer was introduced at the meeting and in the house; Mother advises all to build on a spiritual foundation. The Co-Workers say daily the prayer "Lord makes me an instrument of your peace." Hours of adoration, days of prayer are organized wherever possible, though without any compulsion. Members of various denominations and religions have their own different practices.

The aim of the Co-Workers movement has also been more and more to spread love at home, to share with the neighbors, to attend to the needs of members of the community.

Love begins at home. Universal love urges us to share with the people close to us, surrounding us, as also with those we have never met. A truly universal charity will prompt us to make sacrifices in order to help brothers or sisters in a faraway land of whom we know little, beyond the fact that they are needy brothers and sisters of Christ, whom we love and serve in them.

A WAY OF LIFE

An American Co-Worker writes, "It is beautiful to see how the way of life has caught the heart and the spirit of our people. What a grace to see how Mother Teresa has affected people to want to know and love Jesus, to want to serve him in the needy people around them. More and more people are longing for Jesus to become the center of their lives. Through their life as a Co-Worker this is opened to them.

"In our town, we have eight communities of Co-Workers, typical of the communities scattered across our country and across the world. We meet once a month for a time of prayer and sharing . . . a time to be with Jesus in silent prayer for an hour or so, and then a happy time almost like a monthly family reunion. For there is, indeed, a feeling of 'family' among Mother's Co-Workers.

"Many of our meetings are followed by a community service to the poor. We go to the needy together. We spend the day in prayer and in real love for those who are alone and without anyone to care for them. More and more groups of Co-Workers are now doing this, combining their day of prayer with a common work of mercy. It is beautiful."

LIPPSTADT: WORLD MEETING OF CO-WORKERS

"We had a wonderful meeting at Lippstadt in Germany," said Mother, reminiscing happily. "A large number of Co-Workers from many countries attended. The Germans did things very well. They put up the delegates in their own houses. No one had to stay in a hotel. I had asked the members to put aside the money needed for their travel during the year, so that no family should be put to any hardship on account of the meeting. We surveyed the work of the different links, the Co-Workers, the Sick and Suffering with Jacqueline de Decker, the Contemplatives with Father Gorrée. And you know, there is a new movement, a fourth link, that of the children. The meeting lasted two full days, the fifteenth and sixteenth of August 1976."

The reports showed the meeting to be a landmark in the history of those who help the Missionaries of Charity, and try to live according to the ideals of Mother Teresa. Already in 1973, the first international meeting in London had established guidelines for the Co-Workers' spirit and activities. Three years later, Mother could say, "There are about eighty thousand Co-Workers around the world; some are known, some are unknown."

Arriving at Lippstadt, Mother was met by representatives from fourteen countries, eagerly waiting to be be briefed by her. They had come to listen and to learn, to refresh and strengthen their enthusiasm for the cause of serving Christ in the poor. They would return to their countries taking back with them the message they had heard from the foundress herself. Mother could thank God for this marvelous flowering, encircling the earth in its links of love.

True to God's call, she delivered in a keynote address, her always striking and welcome message. "I thank God for this wonderful opportunity to visit you. . . . In this meeting we will really grow to love one another as Jesus loves you and loves me. We are here to deepen your prayer life, for our mission is a mission of love, a mission of compassion, especially today when so many people are hungry for God. My concern is for one thing only, that we really become the Co-Workers of Jesus.

"A Missionary of Charity is a carrier of God's love. At the Annunciation as soon as our Lady had received Jesus she went in haste to give him to others. We must have Jesus in our hearts if we want to become true Co-Workers of Christ. We have to receive Jesus, we have to receive his love, his compassion, and we have to be in haste to give him to others. If that is not our concern, then we are wasting time. Just doing work is no reason at all, but our reason is to bring peace, love, and compassion to the world today. We need that deep love, that deep union with Christ, to be able to give him to others."

From the start Mother insisted that their whole outlook must be essentially spiritual; that the foundation of their movement, which leads to action, is faith in God and in Jesus Christ, devotion and love for Jesus, and hence service for these in whom he suffers today. And by doing so, "the Co-Workers will proclaim that Christ is alive." She recalled her words at the Eucharistic Congress of Philadelphia: "Jesus made himself into the bread of life to be able to satisfy our hunger for God, our love for God. And then to satisfy his own hunger for our love, he made himself the hungry one, the naked one, the homeless one, and he said, "When you did this to the least of my brethren, you did it to me."

Mother makes the point that if we can discover this truth and live it, we become, as she says, "contemplatives right in the middle of the world, because we are touching Christ twenty-four hours a day." We have first to discover this truth through faith, prayer, and meditation; then we can endeavor to live it in a practical, constant manner. This constitutes an aim not easy to achieve, a program of life leading to holiness.

Mother adds, "One thing I would like very much to stress. We must all try to keep the work for the poor a work of love, and to be able to keep it like that, it must remain on a sacrifice basis. We do not accept salaries for the work we do; neither do we become a fund-raising organization.''

Mother wants every penny, every cent donated, to go to the poor and also that the donor's intention, if expressed, be respected. What matters most is the spiritual quality of whatever we do for God and for the neighbor, the meaningful sacrifice, the service of love.

She says, "I would prefer you not to ask people to give a regular amount of money each week, each month. I do not allow it in India. We depend on divine Providence, and I would not like people to think that we are after their money. The Co-Workers also must depend on divine Providence. If the people give it, thank God; but please do not have regular things that will lead you to spend time in raising money, in making money. And no advertising, no writing letters to beg for money, no making things for selling. Let us bring the spirit of sacrifice into the lives of our people. I think Jesus wants us to be like this, and I will repeat it again and again if necessary. Let us offer all this work now for the glory of God, and also that we may become instruments of peace, of love, of compassion."

Mother described the spiritual picture of the living organization that is her dream: the chain of love encircling the world, made of links connected between themselves and all depending on Jesus, source of their love, their union, their life and activity. That love is called to spread all over the world, in ever-increasing manner and with greater strength, through the active presence of the Missionaries of Charity and of their Co-Workers.

"In every country we have a chairman or president, but I would like to use a very simple word instead. I would like to use the word *link* like a branch, a link, a joining. I would like the fifteenth chapter of St. John to enter into our life. Jesus said, 'I am the Vine, you are the branches.' So let us all be like the branch. The Society of the Missionaries of Charity is the branch, and all the Co-Workers are the small branches joined to that one branch, and we are all joined to Jesus. I think that is the best picture of what we are supposed to be in the world. All the different links in different countries are joined to that one branch, the Society of the Missionaries of Charity, and the Missionaries of Charity are joined to the one Jesus. And all the fruit is in the branches in each of the countries.

"It is a very beautiful picture of what we are. The Missionaries of Charity and the Co-Workers should be joined together and to Jesus; and let us not forget that the fruit is on the branch. All of you must be joined; you must know each other and you must be linked like that, and I feel this will really bring a tremendous presence in the world."

Mother sums up beautifully her advice thus: "My dear Co-Workers, look at the cross and you will see Jesus' head bent to kiss you, his arms extended to embrace you, his heart opened to receive you, to enclose you within his love. Knowing that the cross was his greater love for you and for me, let us accept his cross in whatever he wants to give, let us give with joy whatever he wants to take, for in doing so they will know that we are his disciples, that we belong to Jesus, that the work you and I and all the brothers and sisters do is but our love in action. This love for each other is the great means to be holy—and to be holy is a simple duty for you and for me. I pray for each one of you that you become in your family first the joy of Jesus as the sign of his Father's love, as the hope of eternal happiness, as the flame of burning love, and so spread his fragrance of joy everywhere you go. God bless you."

ROME

At the next general chapter of the Co-workers, held in Rome six years later, the same aim of holiness and concern for the family remained paramount in Mother's mind. "We shall hold a meeting of the national links of the Co-Workers in Rome from the thirteenth to the sixteenth of May," she said, "and we shall insist mainly on the family."

Mother was full of this subject. She had been speaking on it in several places, as in Australia, then during two trips to Japan. Everywhere she pleaded for the strengthening of family bonds and for union and happiness in the family, for love and attention between its members. She knew well that the family tended to break up in many countries.

And so six years after Lippstadt, the leaders and organizers of the Co-Workers were to meet in Rome. They would review the situation of the movement, solve problems of organization, choose the new national links where that was needed, and stimulate all to a better service of the poor.

For a while in March, Mother did have second thoughts regarding the desirability and usefulness of bringing together members from faraway countries. "So many people are hungry in India and other countries, and we are going to spend so much money traveling," she remarked once in a wistful mood. But friends pointed out that the poor would lose nothing, since the members would pay for their expenses from their own pockets. Rather, the meeting would make the work of helping the poor more efficient and better organized.

On 13 May 1982, Mother was in Rome to greet Co-Worker representatives from thirty-two countries at least. The meeting soon appeared as a family reunion. The organized Co-Workers in the world numbered about three hundred thousand. Many more tried to live in the same spirit, imbued by the same ideal. Prayer and meditation alternated with business sessions. Some participants later confessed that they had profited as much spiritually as they did from their yearly retreat. On the closing day, 17 May, the Co-Workers were received in private audience by the Holy Father.

Pope John Paul II expressed his appreciation for the spirit of the

Missionaries of Charity and those who share in their work, and encouraged them to continue to labor for the Lord and for the sufferers of humanity. "The love of Christ," he said, "is evident in the apostolate of the Missionaries of Charity, because they work for the poor, the marginalized, the homeless, the orphans, the dying." Then the pontiff asked, "How can you nourish that love?" and he answered, "You can find such a love by daily contact with the Eucharist, the great sacrament of Christ's love."

Then, addressing himself directly to the Co-Workers, the Holy Father said, "You, my dear ones, have found the way to help the Missionaries of Charity in their effort of love through your prayers, your suffering, your material help. Your quiet, invisible support is an important contribution to spread the love that comes undivided in the name of Christ. May God bless your generous work of help and may the blessing of the Virgin Mary stimulate you to faithful service."

CHAPTER 25

Volunteers in Calcutta

Jesus turned round, saw them following and said, "What do you want?" They answered, "Rabbi, where do you live?" "Come and see," he replied.

(JOHN 1:38–39)

Attracted by this story of love in action, hundreds of people have come to offer their service for a few weeks, a few months, a year or two. They came from France, Belgium, England, the United States, Canada, Germany, the Netherlands, Italy, Malta, the Scandinavian countries, among others. Most of them were young, open-minded, generous. Many were seeking God, seeking Jesus. Many had found God but wished to deepen their spiritual life. A few had lost faith in the world, in life, in goodness, in God himself.

They usually returned home purified, enlightened, strengthened, enriched with a new purpose and energy. They had been edified by what they had seen and heard.

The first days or weeks of their stay in Calcutta, helping the sisters in their work among the very poor, the dying or the babies struggling for life, could cause a shock. Several new arrivals had cried at night on recalling the galling experiences of the day. Later their sadness turned into joy—as Jesus had promised his apostles—the joy of finding God, the joy of sharing, of giving and receiving. For all of them this was a spiritual experience, as a few testimonies will show.

Miss D. recalls,

"At Howrah station on Christmas Day, we were several volunteers from different countries helping five or six sisters to distribute blankets, clothes, rice, sweets, milk powder to the poor. There were lines and lines of them. I had never seen so many poor people. They had been given cards in advance, so that only the genuinely poor were to be helped, not the professional beggars or work shirkers.

"They had come early, not to be disappointed, lined up, waited for hours. They came up in order, received their parcel, and went away. There were mothers with infants in their arms, with a child sitting on their hip; also old people leaning on a stick or supported by a grandchild.

"We worked the whole day, even forgetting to eat, unaware that we were getting tired, standing on our feet so long. We bent over these people's miseries, sharing their pain, their lack of comfort. Still we could bring into their lives a flicker of peace, of joy, of hope, gifts of the divine Spirit, kindling some happiness in their hearts. It was good to share with them, and we could learn much from their patience and their surrender to the divine Will.

"But then a most painful moment arrived: there were still many people standing, waiting to be served—perhaps some without cards had infiltrated the lines—anyway, they still stood before us, when we had nothing more to give. Nothing, not a biscuit, not a grain of rice, not a blanket to cover the old, emaciated bodies during the cold nights, nothing to cheer up the children, nothing. . . . It was dreadful. For these last people life must have been a series of disappointments; they went away sadly. As for us, we had experienced another aspect of poverty: not to be able to give to those in need.

"At night, remembering the long hours of work, we had the happiness of having given ourselves, the joy of helping people we did not know, had never seen before, would never meet again, people of another race, another culture, whose language we did not understand. We had served them in pure faith, seeing them as God's children, our brothers and sisters.

"The only communication with them had been a flicker of acknowledgment in their eyes, a sign of gratitude.

"At morning prayers in the chapel, we could hear the words of Jesus, 'What you did to the least of mine, you did it unto me.' 'To you, Lord, to you, dear Jesus? Is it possible?' 'Yes, to me.' "

A young lady confessed, "I wanted to find God. I felt I was slipping spiritually in the rich and materialistic society in which I moved. I wanted a break; and so I came here among the poor. I prayed and I revived my ailing faith."

Another said, "I wished to do something useful for my fellow humans, after finishing my studies and before entering a profession."

"What subjects did you study?"

"I am a trained nurse."

Another confessed, "For many years I had no religious practice; I had no faith left. But now it is coming back. This contact with the poor and the fact of devoting myself completely in the service of people who cannot give me anything in return, are bringing me back to God."

"Yes, by doing good we come to believe. We do God's work and in return we receive the grace of faith."

"When I arrived here," she continued, "and started work in this terrible poverty of Tiljala, I wept as I saw the ill-fed children. Every evening I wept alone in my room before going to sleep. I just could not bear the sight of this misery. Then slowly I noticed how the poor accepted their condition. Their spiritual outlook, their peace crept over me, so to say, and overcame me. I also noticed how the sisters go about their work, with confidence and joy. I became more spiritual and less preoccupied with the material conditions of life. I turned to God in prayer and surrender. My stay here has been a retreat for me, a purifying and strengthening experience."

Several benevolent helpers stated that their stay in one of the houses, and their sharing the work of love and devotion of the Missionaries of Charity, had truly been for them a retreat, a spiritual purification, leading to the discovery of God's proximity.

Some start by questioning; but then with morning and evening prayers, with time for meditation, adoration, and spiritual reading, away from the noise of the world, from television commercials, glossy magazines, they turn gradually to simple faith in God. They do not carry cameras, but vitamin tablets. They do not use their fingers to click pictures, but to bandage wounds and wash children. When they return home, they find themselves enriched beyond their expectations.

Many helpers come to India with the definite aim of finding God or discovering his will for them. A young woman stated, "I arrived a fortnight ago. I intend to work in India for six months and shall go wherever they send me. I want to find out if I have really a vocation to the religious life."

"How many children are you in your family?"

"We are nine children. I am the oldest, being twenty-three; I am a trained nurse. For ten years I have been thinking of giving myself to God. Here with prayer and the work of charity, I hope to discover whether I am called to the religious life or not. First I must find out if I am made to be a nun—that is, to give myself to God for life, in a total and definite commitment—not as an experiment for a year or two, but as a complete donation of my whole self. Then, if I am called, what religious institute should I join; not necessarily Mother Theresa's."

"Of course, not. There are various possibilities, adapted to different temperaments, gifts, inclinations. You must find out where God wants you. But you are right, the more important question is to discover if God calls you to live for himself only, and devote your life to his service."

A young woman sat on a cement bench in the courtyard of the mother house. She showed a touch of the elegance typical of the French woman.

"Are you French?"

"*Mais oui,*" she replied.

"Then let us speak French. Tell me, how did you happen to land here?"

"I came to India with a group of French youths in search of God. We thought the East was the right place to find him. We had heard much of Indian spiritual men detached from everything, who had gained personal experience of the only true reality. And so we joined a month-long course in transcendental meditation under the guidance of an Indian guru."

So she was one of the hundreds of American, German, British, French, and other young people who came to seek the wisdom of the East. Some of them knew nothing of Christianity; others, both Protestant and Catholic, out of ignorance, disappointment, or frustration came to the East to seek fulfillment.

"In the West," some of them complained, "religious men and women speak to us mostly of the community and the brethren, of the needs of the third and the fourth worlds, of sharing, giving money, food, clothes, and medicines. But not about God." So, in search of a John the Baptist, his index finger pointing to heaven, they traveled to the East, the ancient land of culture and philosophy, and especially of the God-seeking holy men.

But the approach and the method, and also the end of the search were completely new to these seekers. The young woman had been told that the divinity resides within man. There was no need for her to seek him outside: God was within her. He was there naturally, not only by grace as Christians teach and believe. Humanity was to realize the divine power residing within, through concentration, through detachment from earthly cravings, through one's own willpower.

Four or five hours a day, the group were taught to meditate. They endeavored to rise to a higher level of consciousness through their own powers with the help of a special technique that brought them peace and quiet. The natural setting, selected for its magnificent landscape, its beautiful surroundings in the hills, its pleasant climate, proved a great help. Of course, the session was expensive, since it included excellent living conditions.

At the end of the course, three among the forty participants decided to perform some service that would benefit the weaker members of humanity, to which they still felt bound. Having heard of Mother Teresa, they offered her their services, which were immediately accepted. The day after their arrival they were at work. This time, to seek God meant to sleep on a mat, bear the heat of the sun, eat unappetizing food, wear themselves out carrying buckets of water, cleaning hospital wards, nursing destitute sick people.

"And how does this compare with your days of meditation?"

"Well," she answered, "This is the spiritual retreat inside out."

"Will you remain long at this search and this work?"

"Perhaps; why not?"

"This is not what you had come for, but you may find God more truly now. Let your days be work and prayer, prayer and work, inspired by faith, love and devotion."

Two young men came in and said, "We want to meet you. We read your book on Mother Teresa."

They introduced themselves: one was a Norwegian, fluent in English, preparing a doctorate, visiting India for a few days. "I cannot stay long, because I am doing my military service and have still five months to go through. I put together all my leaves and managed to come here for a few weeks. We have no organized group of Co-Workers I know of, in Norway."

"There may be individual helpers of Mother Teresa," I replied. "Anyway you have a chance to start a group of Co-Workers, now that you have come into contact with the Missionaries of Charity, and can speak of their spirit and works when you return home."

He wore a cross on his coat, to show he was a committed Christian. The other was a Swede, a doctor of medicine, dressed in very simple pants and shirt and a shawl. He also spoke English.

"I am more useful than my friend here in this country," he chuckled. "There is plenty of work for a medical practitioner. Dispensaries here have long lines of patients waiting to be attended to. Most people have only small ailments, though. The situation is not as bad as I had expected, after going through Desmond Doig's book, *Mother Teresa: Her Work and Her People,* and seeing its terrible pictures. I thought it was worse than it really is."

"Yes, the picture painted by reporters and journalists can be misleading, when they depict Calcutta as a city of filth, sickness, and misery, and in the midst of that horror, Mother Teresa's kindness, encouragement, and smile, helping the destitute to die peacefully. They build her up as a heroine and a saint, against a background of squalor and carelessness. The technique of the Greek classical tragedy. Or, if you prefer, Christ and anti-Christ. But in fact, Calcutta is the cultural capital of India, a city boasting more private theater groups than Paris or New York, with an astonishing number of poetry circles, music and dance groups, and literary magazines.

"True, there are officially close to three thousand slums. Two hundred thousand people are reported to be living on pavements, with no dwelling of their own. Professional beggars are not forbidden to ply their trade as in some other cities. Several thousand of them prefer to do so, rather than to find a shelter in a vagrancy home or an institution. A large number of these professionals hail from outside Bengal. That goes to prove that they know Calcutta people are generous and one can make a living here.

"But real, genuine poverty there is, due to lack of education to sickness and unemployment. These poor people deserve all the help we can give them.

"But you will discover that among the poor one finds acceptance, sharing, and gratitude, because most of the poor are religious. They resemble the 'anawim,' the poor in spirit Jesus referred to in his Sermon on the Mount. He called them happy, blessed indeed, because the Word of God finds a ready welcome in their hearts they are prepared to listen to it and enter God's kingdom.

"Do you intend joining the brothers or working permanently with Mother Teresa, Doctor?"

"I am thinking of joining 'the Ark' of Jean Vanier, if he starts a permanent group in Sweden," he answered. "You mention him in your book."

"Yes, Mother's aim and Vanier's are similar; but their organizations and methods are poles apart. Vanier, I am told, relies mainly on volunteers who are free to come and go when they like. Most of them seem to have no definite commitment. When they are tired of that life of service, they may return home and take up another vocation. With Mother, the young religious are expected to commit themselves for life, to sign up and not look back, once they have put their hand to the plow of service to the poorest of the poor. She knows how many helpers she has and can count on them to go wherever they are sent.

"The aim of serving Christ in the poor is the same; the philosophy and the methods quite different, the approach to the problems also. It is said that Vanier reflected for a long time before deciding on a loose organization, allowing his co-workers to stay as long as they wish and no longer. While some leave, others come; a few may feel called to remain permanently. Wheras Mother follows the traditional practice of the church. She trains her young religious and asks them to make a definite, permanent, final commitment through perpetual vows."

"Mother seems not to trust her own religious, though," he objected, "since you quote her as saying, 'If they are not to be faithful, God may as well destroy this congregation.' "

"Yes, she said this more than once. But it does not imply any lack of trust in her present sisters. See how much she dares ask from them, what responsibilities she entrusts to her young superiors and pioneers. Repeatedly she praises them, 'They are good, they are generous.' She knows she can send them to a foreign country, to a faraway land of which they know next to nothing, and that at a moment's notice. Immediately they are ready to go, to start a new house, as superiors or members of a community with no income, no provision for livelihood, simply depending on divine Providence.

"But the future is in no one's hands; it rests with God. Mother prays God that it will never happen, and it may never happen. But if it did happen that one day the congregation fell away from its calling and spirit of humility, poverty, obedience, and faithfulness, then it would be better that God let the congregation die. Other religious founders are known to have spoken in the same way. No single religious institute is necessary for the existence and holiness of the chruch. If any one of them no more fulfills the aim for which it was established, God may allow it to wane and disappear. But Mother Teresa and her sisters pray that God may keep them faithful to their commitment to live and work only for his greater glory."

CHAPTER 26

Finale: A Symphony to God's Glory

Jesus said, "Eternal life, Father, is knowing you, the only true God, and Jesus Christ whom you have sent."

(JOHN 17:3)

People ask, "Has Mother Teresa fulfilled her aim, her ideal, her dream?"

The constitutions of the Missionaries of Charity clearly express her aim, which is "to quench the thirst of Jesus Christ for souls and for the love of men." The sisters promise it every day; "Jesus, I shall quench your thirst for souls."

Mother's ideal and purpose is to make the love of God known by as many as possible, especially by the less favored persons, the dying, the destitute, the children, the handicapped, those whose life seems to have been a failure. She brings them the love of God and stimulates their love for him in return.

Her dream? Yes, it did look like a dream, hardly realizable; yet it has come true. The dream of the Upper Room of the house of Michael Gomes, where she occupied first one room, then two, then three, then the whole upper story; the dream she made at her night prayers, when the first sisters who had believed in her call and leadership were blissfully asleep; the dream she shared with them in her dynamic spiritual instructions: "We shall weave a chain of love around the world—yes, a chain of love." And she drew it on paper, had it printed on their stationery: a chain of prayer, of grace, as the rosary beads encircled the whole world, with their cross falling on Calcutta, from where the movement had started. A chain of love for God and for the neighbor, embracing the whole world.

The dream has come true. "It is all God's work," says Mother. And so it has been, it is, and it will be.

An objection has been raised: "But all that Mother has achieved is only a drop of water in the ocean—human misery and suffering remain."

Yes, Mother has spoken herself in those words, at least during the earlier years. But things have moved and progressed at a very fast pace.

What the congregation now effects can no more be compared to a single drop of water accruing to the ocean. The sisters' work should be likened to a rivulet, a stream, continually increasing in volume and in power.

First they reached a few individuals. But going out to the crowds, moving among them, they now contact and affect millions of people, for whom they work, with whom they work on whom they work.

their impact has become enormous in magnitude, in quality, in depth, in extension. It has marked not only the hundreds of thousands of the very poor they have helped, but perhaps still more the millions of men and women and children who like us have felt the desire to be better, less self-centered and egoistic. Millions of people have contributed their time, their sacrifices, their wealth, to Mother's work and also to the work of other charities.

We have all felt stimulated to greater generosity. Someone suggested, "Why not write a book showing the influence of Mother Teresa on our society and suggesting what we lay people can do to make the world a better place to live in." This may be such a book.

The media people have risen to the challenge. As a result, hundreds of millions of people have watched this epic story on television with admiration and often with throbbing hearts. Some bit their lips as they tried to prevent their tears from running down their cheeks, while others wept unashamedly, praying, "Lord, how beautiful this love and self-sacrifice are; give me to know them also, even if in a small way, at my measure."

LOOKING TO THE FUTURE

At the end of a talk describing the wonderful work of the Missionaries of Charity, the same question is always asked, with a note of apprehension: "Will this beautiful movement not come to an end with Mother Teresa? Her personality looms so high, her influence is so overpowering, she seems to do everything, to be everywhere, as the indispensable leader. She is like the magnet attracting and holding together around herself many particles of iron. The magnet removed, the particles fall apart. What will remain after her?

"Or, if you like, the symphony has been played, directed by a genial maestro, a dynamic, charismatic conductor. The conductor dies, the members of the orchestra return home, individual players, no more an orchestra. Only the echo of the symphony lingers in the ear and mind."

Yes, Mother is a magnet who has attracted countless particles of iron and has welded them into a vessel that floats—it will not sink. She is a charismatic conductor whose orchestra played to our enchanted ears "something beautiful for God" as she likes to call it. But if an accident should happen to their conductor, the musicians will not be disorganized, the orchestra not disbanded. They are seasoned artists who will choose another conductor from among themselves, one who knows the scores by heart, and is able to direct the orchestra, one who has been trained in the same tradition.

Whenever Mother is asked, "What will happen after you?" she answers with complete trust in God, "God will find another person, more humble, more faithful, more devoted, more obedient to him, and the society will go on."

The second part of her saying is certain. As for the first part, we do not know. The successor will neither have nor need the personal charism of the foundress; that is, her own charism and virtue, her faith and trust in God when nothing as yet existed and she did not know how she was to carry out her calling and mission. The successor will not need these gifts, since the society is erected, approved by Rome, organized, prosperous, and respected. It attracts candidates and helpers all over the world.

That Mother has obtained such prominence is due not only to herself, but to the media fond of strong personalities, inclined toward hero worship and personality cult. The priests working with her organization try to correct this imbalance, by stressing that the sisters do the work, that Mother would be nothing without her two thousand, soon three thousand devoted sisters.

God looks after his own. The charism of a religious founder passes on to the members of his order as long as they are faithful to their vocation. The missionaries of Charity inherit the charism of their foundress, which is expressed in their vows and constitutions.

The dynamic movement started by Mother under the guidance of the Spirit of God should last. The acid test will come when Mother hands over the reins of government, when her own personal charism, her spiritual influence, her galvanizing and energizing, stimulating and entrancing presence will have given place to a shadow of herself.

It will be for her nuns a purifying moment, ushering in a new era of faith and humility. Having lost their charismatic foundress, the prophetess listened to by many in the world, they will gradually drop out of the news and the limelight. Less conspicuous, less noticed, they will continue to do their work faithfully, zealously, as usual only for Jesus.

When Jesus, having finished the work for which he had been sent, returned to the Father, the apostles had to take over. They were conscious of their unworthiness. They knew their lapses and shortcomings. They had quarreled on the road. They had shirked the occasion of suffering with their master. Now they find themselves without him. But then, the Holy Spirit comes to strengthen them; he unites them as a team under a God-appointed captain. Glamor and reliance on their master for every decision are over. The apostles must now direct the church themselves.

Something similar should happen to the Missionaries of Charity. The foundress has seen to it that the congregation is established and approved. The election of a superior general will take place according to the rules set down in the constitutions. Mother Teresa, who fired her sisters with faith and zeal for the cause of Jesus, has certainly succeeded in uniting them at all levels by a strong bond of charity. The election of her successor should therefore prove smooth, and the new superior general be accepted by all, in a spirit of faith and obedience.

The spirit of Mother Teresa will live on through her recorded speeches and utterances, through her religious congregation she founded, through the laypeople she galvanized to join in her work of charity and be in the world, according to her proud claim, "messengers of God's love."